£399

36

THE CAPETIANS

The Capetians
Kings of France, 987–1328

Jim Bradbury

hambledon
continuum

Hambledon Continuum is an imprint of Continuum Books
Continuum UK, The Tower Building, 11 York Road, London SE1 7NX
Continuum US, 80 Maiden Lane, Suite 704, New York, NY 10038

www.continuumbooks.com

First published 2007

British Library Cataloguing-in-Publication Data
A catalogue record for this book is available from the British Library.

ISBN 978 1 85285 528 4

Typeset by Egan Reid Ltd, Auckland, New Zealand
Printed and bound by MPG Books Ltd, Cornwall, Great Britain

Contents

To those who have taught me

Illustrations

Plates

Between Pages 178 and 179

Maps and Text Illustrations

Preface

I guess it is obvious that anyone who spends much of their life reading, teaching and writing history, has needed education and training to do it. As is common, I have in earlier prefaces mentioned some of my university tutors, but have not thanked other teachers. As one gets older one tends to realize how much is owed to others. I wish to dedicate this book to all those who have taught me, in whatever capacity.

During World War Two I was evacuated to Wycombe Marsh near High Wycombe in Buckinghamshire. I was lucky because with my mother and siblings I went to live with my paternal grandparents. I reached school age during the war and attended the Marsh Primary School. I do not remember the teachers – only one little girl whose name I recall after all these years, though I shall not embarrass her or myself further by revealing it. I do recall going into brick-built shelters against German air raids. I can only say that I believe the teachers there set me on the right road so that I always enjoyed my schooling.

At the end of the war we returned to Hackney, where I went to London Fields Primary School. I made friends there who were my companions for the next decade or so. I remember something of the teaching, particularly by my class teacher, Miss Attwood, who gave me much encouragement. I was entered as a candidate for the Bluecoats School, Christ's Hospital, but failed to impress sufficiently. I am actually rather glad about that because I do not now think I should have enjoyed boarding school education – though I am sure it is an excellent school.

I am also thankful because otherwise I should not have gone to Dame Alice Owen's Grammar School in Islington – 11+, selection, and all that. The school, though dating back to the 17th century, has now moved from Islington to Hertfordshire. I have visited the former site on occasions, sadly seeing the old buildings flattened and replaced. Anyway, I enjoyed my secondary education. One reads so many accounts of unhappy schooldays that I feel I must have got something wrong, but the fact is I could not have had a better schooling. Of course some things were difficult. I caught scarlet fever from bathing in an open lake the summer before I was due to start at Owen's, and missed the first half term. I am grateful to my first form teacher, Mr J. E. Smith, who helped me over the problem of a late start. He was also one of my A-level English teachers and produced some of the school plays, in several of which I took small parts. The pleasure was not least because Owen's was a boys' school, but the girls' school was only over the road, and the plays were a rare opportunity for the sexes to mix.

History teaching at Owen's was consistently good but at first I planned to study English. I did not much enjoy Latin at school but in those days you needed Latin to take up an arts degree. My Latin teacher was Mr G.A. Hutchings (Hutch), who managed to get me through A-level. I enjoyed his Roman History lessons more than those on language – and wanted to study ancient history – but I had never learned Greek (then necessary). Among the History teachers were Mr R.W.N. Vellacott, and in the sixth form, Mr S.G. Strong and Mr R.A. Dare. Mr Dare taught medieval history, and gave me my first serious taste for that period. At the time I equally enjoyed Mr Strong's course on modern US history. I had an odd reason for going into the sixth form. The rule on age for taking O-levels was changed, and I was too young to sit at the end of my fifth year. My father wanted me to leave and start work, but was persuaded by my mother and teachers to let me stay on and take O-levels at the end of the first year sixth. After that it seemed wasteful not to spend another year and take A-levels. My father was conned into this and had to support an unemployed son for some years – though I did do holiday jobs to earn a bit. My first encounter with the Capetians came in Mr Dare's lessons. I failed to obtain my next objective, to get into Oxford, an ambition from reading Thomas Hardy for A-levels (specifically *Jude the Obscure*) – demonstrating my thoroughly rational approach. At some expense to my parents I took two entrance exams and failed both. At one I received an exam paper on a period of history I had never studied, but did not have the courage to complain.

I also applied to King's College in London and fortunately was accepted there, making the decision to concentrate on medieval history. I am grateful that things worked out as they did, as I also enjoyed this part of my education. I attended lectures on various other periods and learned a good deal by listening to such as Brian Manning, Gareth Bennett and Michael Howard. For medieval history I had two very different mentors: the first Gerald Hodgett, whose lectures were amusing, and whose style I admired; the second Charles Duggan, who was my tutor, a dedicated Roman Catholic with a main interest in the Church. I had been brought up a Baptist and was turning to atheism at the time. This in no way prevented him being always polite and fair but I think he was a bit concerned about my views. One also received help from fellow students. I have recently made contact with two who were a year ahead of me but became friends and gave encouragement, the medievalist Brian Collins, and the modernist Malcolm Thomis, one now in New Zealand, the other in Australia.

I went from King's to the Institute of Education in London to study for a PGCE. I then became a schoolteacher, appointed first to Shoreditch School. Politics had inclined me towards the new comprehensives, though the experience of teaching there was tough for a novice. My second appointment, chosen for family reasons, was in a quieter rural area – I thought – as History master at the Manhood School in Selsey, West Sussex. After eight years there I moved to what was then Borough Road College where I taught trainee teachers and various certificate and degree courses. I was encouraged to initiate courses on British and European medieval history by the then head of History, George Bartle, and also at various times taught on Roman Britain, the reign of Elizabeth I, the Tudors and Stuarts, and 20th-century British history! I may have forgotten others. I was much helped by colleagues, among whom I still number several friends. I stayed there as the college became part of West London Institute of Education, and left before it became part of Brunel University. I will conclude by saying that, like all teachers, I owe a debt to those I taught. I do not regret my schooling or my career in education, quite the reverse – I am grateful for it all.

I also continued my education during my career, attending a taught MA at King's London in 1975–76. My tutors all contributed something of importance to my education. The first was Julian Brown, who departed during the course of that year but who taught how to approach manuscripts. The second was Christopher Holdsworth, whom I still count as a friend, and who held the general seminars. The third was Allen Brown, who later supervised my (uncompleted) D.Phil. He gave me an interest in castles and medieval warfare that has never gone away. The work for a doctorate was undertaken part-time for eight years. Towards the end of that period Allen became seriously ill and rather than complete the work under another supervisor I abandoned it in favour of writing books – the first being *The Medieval Archer*. The research work was used in my later book, *Stephen and Matilda*.

Education of course never stops. From the time I took the MA I attended the early medieval seminar at the Institute of Historical Research in London, pretty regularly for over 20 years. It was conducted by among others Christopher Holdsworth, Allen Brown, John Gillingham, Michael Clanchy and Jinty Nelson. I also occasionally went to the crusades seminar under Jonathan Riley-Smith. Over those years I heard so many papers by research students and established academics, that there is no way to credit their contribution except in general terms. Reading remains a vital part of self-education but there is nothing to compare with hearing historians speak about their own work. I prefer the informality of seminars, but the same comments are true of organized lectures and conferences. I should particularly like to note my gratitude to all those who have given papers that I have heard over the years, for example, to the Historical Association, the Medieval Society and conferences at the IHR, the Anglo-Norman conferences at Battle, the knighthood conferences at Strawberry Hill, the King John conference at East Anglia, and the medieval conferences at Harlaxton.

To conclude this self-indulgent preface, I feel bound to recall my links with France. Several of my earlier books had a French connection – including the warfare books and *Philip Augustus*. I have spent more holidays in France than anywhere else on the continent. My first trip was as a student with my brother David. We hitchhiked through France and stayed at youth hostels, reaching the Mediterranean coast and returning via Paris. That visit gave a great feeling for the country and some idea of its extent. I met my wife Ann in 1957 and we married the following year. We have spent many holidays in France, including camping trips when our children were growing up. On one holiday with my sister-in-law, Marian, and her family, we went to Spain and back via the Mediterranean coast of France. Once we journeyed with my friend and colleague at the Manhood School John Savill and his family in their Dormobile to Brittany. On other occasions I recall camping in the grounds of a château and a family holiday with our son and daughter at a gîte in Normandy. More recently we have sought the comfort of hotels – on the Loire, by Lake Annecy and in Paris. Many of these 'holidays' in latter years were partly concerned with work on a book and visits to churches, castles and battle sites. Most recently this has been true of trips to Paris and Bordeaux for this volume. I shall never forget our recent visit to the castle remains under the Louvre. Every year when possible I have watched the Tour de France on TV. I quite enjoy the cycling but to be honest the real attraction is the tour through the French countryside. France and its history have given me an enormous amount of pleasure and this book is more a labour of love than a result of any hard work.

I should also like to thank all those concerned at Hambledon, particularly Tony Morris who first broached the idea of this book to me as part of the series on dynasties. In addition my thanks go to Ben Hayes, to Joanna Kramer and staff at Continuum, to Eva Osborne for her assistance with the images, and to Jonathan Styles, who between them have seen this work through to publication.

Jim Bradbury
Selsey, 2006.

Abbreviations

ANS	*Anglo-Norman Studies*
ASC	*Anglo-Saxon Chronicle*
CMH	(New) *Cambridge Medieval History*
Lavisse	E. Lavisse, ed., *Histoire de France depuis les Origines jusqu'à la Révolution*, vols ii & iii, Paris, 1901, 1903
MGH	*Monumenta Germaniae Historica*
RHF	*Recueil des Historiens des Gaules et de la France*, ed. M. Bouquet & L. Delisle, 24 vols, Paris, 1869–1904
RS	*Rolls Series*
SHF	*Société de l'Histoire de France*
SRG	*Scriptores Rerum Germanicarum*
TRHS	*Transactions of the Royal Historical Society*

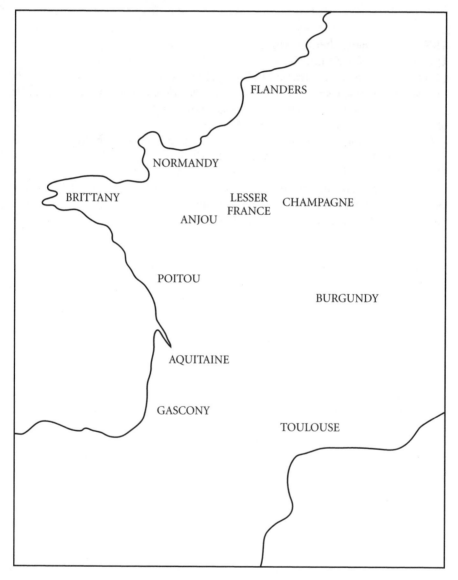

FLANDERS

NORMANDY

BRITTANY

LESSER
FRANCE   CHAMPAGNE

ANJOU

POITOU

BURGUNDY

AQUITAINE

GASCONY

TOULOUSE

The Principalities of Early France

Carolingian Francia

In 987 Hugh Capet became king of West Francia. His direct successors ruled France until 1328, and subsequent kings of France for the following centuries came from a branch of the same family. One hardly needs to argue about the importance of the accession of Hugh Capet. Our first task is to investigate the nature of its significance, which requires some understanding of the preceding period.

In our first chapter we shall seek to trace the progress of the region we call 'France', from being part of Roman Gaul to becoming part of the realm of the Franks under the Merovingian kings and then the Carolingians. During the period 'France' became an important part of Europe within the empire established by Charlemagne. Following that, the Carolingian Empire broke into smaller units, as kingdoms and principalities. Through this period we see the rise of the Robertian family, to which the Capetian kings belonged. They became rulers of part of West Francia under the Carolingians, and then kings of West Francia.

Historians and others have sometimes underestimated the achievement of the early Middle Ages. Inevitably we shall concentrate on the politics around one particular family, but we must keep an eye on the wider changes in society and Europe. As an initial reminder that men in 1000 were not all brutal barbarians of limited understanding, let us note a remark of the Burgundian monk Ralph Glaber who spent most of his life in West Frankish monasteries. He wrote of an earth 'which is reputed to be shaped like a globe'.[1] We do not have to wait for Columbus and the Renaissance for knowledge and achievement that have some significance for the modern world. Nor should we underestimate the contribution to learning and culture of women in this early period – as several modern historians have made clear.[2] On the other hand education did not spread very far down through society, even in the church. A Merovingian prelate described a priest whose Latin was not up to the job, who had baptized someone 'in the name of the fatherland and the daughter'.[3]

The tenth century saw a major change in the history of West Francia as it is best called at this period, when the Carolingian Empire broke up. The family of the Robertians now competed with the Carolingians in West Francia. They eventually displaced the Carolingians as others had done in a now separate East Francia. In West Francia the Capetians are sometimes referred to as the third 'race' of kings after the Merovingians and Carolingians.[4] The 'profound transformation' that saw the end of Carolingian rule applied to all parts of that empire.[5] It divided, and descendants of Charlemagne continued for a time to rule its parts. Carolingian domination remained powerful into the ninth century, but then waned to disappear by the end of the tenth century. Historians have concentrated on the emergence of 'France' and 'Germany', but this is to view developments with the benefit of hindsight. The most obvious change initially was the disintegration of the empire into parts – 'a mosaic of territorial principalities' – though it was probably more gradual than Dhondt believed.[6]

In East Francia, the future Germany, Carolingian rule was overthrown earlier than in the West. It lost something of its Frankish nature, becoming more Saxon. The Saxon dynasty seemed assured of success. Henry I the Fowler, and his successors the three Ottos – I, II and III – ruled for a century, to 1002. Yet before long the Ottonian dynasty lost sway and East Francia became an elective monarchy. No dynasty gained the same hold in the East that was to occur in West Francia. The rise of the Robertians was less rapid and less obvious than that of the Ottonians, but in the end more lasting. The Robertians, the family of Robert the Strong, gained a hold over much of the west, becoming counts, dukes or marquises in and around Paris. Their direct descendants, 32 of them, known now as the Capetians and their successors (the Valois and the Bourbons), would reign in France for eight centuries. It is worth noting that by the end of Capetian rule (in 1328) the geographical boundaries of modern France had still not been finally established. What we witness is the beginning of the development of France, but not its conclusion.

Carolingian rule came to an end after some two centuries. The late Carolingian rulers of West Francia were by no means nonentities or incapable – quite the reverse. Most modern historians see them as good and competent rulers, though Dhondt sees the period as 'a long agony'.[7] The Ottonians took over in East Francia, the Robertians in West Francia. The latter emerged from the nobility of Carolingian Francia. In the tenth century the family became dukes of the Franks, ruling the region around Paris for the kings. The family produced three kings before establishing uninterrupted dynastic rule. The change was not sudden or unexpected, though we can date its inception to a precise moment in time – Senlis in the summer of 987, when Hugh Capet was crowned king of the West Franks.

THE MEROVINGIANS

We need to look at earlier events in Francia in order to understand 987 fully. There is a parallel between the decline of the Merovingians, who were replaced by the Carolingians, and the fall of the Carolingians who were replaced by the Capetians. The Franks as a people had entered Western Europe during the barbarian migrations at the time of the Roman Empire. The Romans had given some unity to the region they conquered and called Gaul. There was not overall unity, since Roman Gaul comprised three separate provinces – Belgic Gaul, Celtic Gaul, and Aquitaine.

The Merovingians

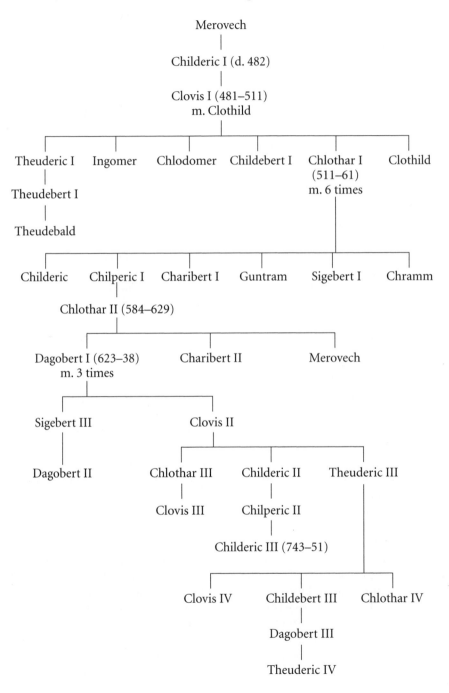

Merovech

Childeric I (d. 482)

Clovis I (481–511)
m. Clothild

Theuderic I   Ingomer   Chlodomer   Childebert I   Chlothar I   Clothild
                                                    (511–61)
                                                    m. 6 times

Theudebert I

Theudebald

Childeric   Chilperic I   Charibert I   Guntram   Sigebert I   Chramm

Chlothar II (584–629)

Dagobert I (623–38)   Charibert II   Merovech
m. 3 times

Sigebert III   Clovis II

Dagobert II   Chlothar III   Childeric II   Theuderic III

Clovis III   Chilperic II

Childeric III (743–51)

Clovis IV   Childebert III   Chlothar IV

Dagobert III

Theuderic IV

The Romans named two of the Germanic groups who entered Gaul in the third century as Franks: the Salians who settled in the region of the Low Countries, and the Ripuarians who crossed the Rhine and settled around Köln. Many Franks were employed as federate troops. They were described as fair and clean-shaven, their kings as long-haired. They established their own power as the Roman Empire declined and collapsed. Southern Gaul remained more influenced by its Roman past than did the north, and retained a separate language – the *langue d'oc*, the tongue in which yes was 'oc' (Languedoc) as opposed to the northern *langue d'oïl* where 'oïl' was yes. The Catalan and Provençal languages derived from the *langue d'oc*.

The differences between north and south were not only in language but also in social structure and outlook. Roman law survived in the south. Gaul contained various ethnic groups, including Bretons, Flemings, Burgundians, Goths, and Basques as well as Franks. The greatest historian of the age was Gregory of Tours, a Frank who lived in the later sixth century. He was born into a Gallo-Roman family and was taught rustic Latin by his mother so that he would be understood. The Roman world was about to disappear, yet much of it remained – in organization, in manners, in language. The Roman pattern was the basis for the new political structure that appeared under the Franks and their contemporaries.

The first great dynasty to rule the Franks was the Merovingian family, descended from Merovech – who never himself became king. Merovech's son was Childeric I, the first great Frankish ruler. As chieftain of the Salians he allied with the Romans against the Visigoths and Saxons. The grave of Childeric I was found at Tournai in 1653 and contained a ring engraved *Childerici Regis*, confirming that he had taken the royal title. Childeric I's son Clovis I, king of the Salians (481–511), established the Frankish kingdom in Gaul under the Merovingian dynasty. In 486 he defeated Syagrius at Soissons, thus ending independent Roman states in Gaul, and confirming Frankish domination. Clovis' base was around Paris and Soissons. He also won control of the Upper Rhine. Later he captured Bordeaux and united the Frankish tribes under his rule. In 496 he converted to Roman Catholic Christianity, though most barbarians became heretical Arian Christians. This gave the Franks a connection to the papacy that other barbarian tribes lacked and also won support from the Gallo-Roman population. Bishop Remigius of Reims, who baptized Clovis, told him: 'adore what thou hast burned and burn what thou hast adored'.[8] Clovis took this to heart and defeated the Visigoths at Voulon in 507. Merovingian power thus moved to the Pyrenees. By Clovis' death in 511 the Frankish kingdom, the nucleus of later France, had been established.

In reading Gregory of Tours one is struck by the constant disorder of the time – brother against brother, son against father, murder and mayhem. The bane of the Merovingian dynasty was its system of inheritance, division between sons and warfare between them. Family murders, assassinations and wars were commonplace; children were thrown down wells, relatives' throats were slit. There were hangings, poisonings, burnings, drownings and decapitations. Clovis I had four sons who shared his inheritance and fought against each other. It was not until 558, when Chlothar I (511–61) was 70, that he finally reunited the territories. Then his son Chramm rebelled, was captured, shut in a hut with his wife and children, and all burned alive. Chlothar I finally ruled his lands in peace, but died of a fever a year later.

There were enough sons left for a four-fold division and a repeat of the internecine warfare. Chilperic I (561–84) murdered his wife in bed. Sigebert was murdered by two slaves with poisoned daggers. A nephew seized Sigebert's wife Brunhild and committed incest with her. Chilperic I married Brunhild's sister, Galswintha, but tired of her and she was found strangled in bed. There is a story that one day Chilperic, 'the Nero and Herod of our time', found his new wife Fredegund washing over a basin and smacked her bottom. She thought it was her lover and cried out 'what do you think you are you doing, Landeric?' She saved herself by having her husband killed.[9] Eventually, as the brothers finished each other off, Chilperic I's son Chlothar II (584–629) inherited the kingdom. In 613 he defeated Brunhild, who had continued to oppose her husband's enemies. He had her tortured for three days, then tied by her hair, arm and leg to the tails of wild horses and ripped apart when they were whipped away at a gallop. The Frankish kingdom again had one ruler.

In the meantime that eastern part of Francia, Austrasia, had become almost independent territory under Pepin I of Landen, a royal official appointed as mayor of the palace. Much the same happened in Burgundy. Chlothar II quashed the independence of Burgundy but could not overcome Pepin. On Chlothar II's death his son Dagobert I (629–38) took over the Frankish realm. Merovingian control declined as mayors of the palace increased their hold on separate parts of the kingdom. Dagobert was a stronger king than once supposed. He restored some authority and established power over the Bavarians. He opposed the pagans but was defeated by the Wends. His main achievement was to bring relative stability for a quarter of a century. Dagobert was a patron of the abbey of St-Denis in Paris where he was buried.

There was a period of transition between Merovingians and Carolingian rule, which saw a gradual decline in monarchical power. A number of mayors established control over regions within the realm. Two areas became dominant, the forerunners of later France and Germany – Neustria in the west, and Austrasia in the east. Pepin of Landen, the ancestor of the Carolingian family, was mayor of Austrasia. He died in 640. The mayors hardly found life easier than the kings and seem to have re-enacted the struggles between royal sons. There were wars between the mayors. Ebroin, mayor of the palace of Neustria, was murdered in 687 by one of his officials who fled to Pepin II of Heristal for refuge. Gradually Austrasia came out on top under Pepin II who became mayor of the palace of Austrasia and united it with Neustria. He also won control of Burgundy. The king still presided over annual Frankish assemblies, but Pepin of Heristal governed. His legitimate sons took over Neustria and Burgundy, but in the end it was his illegitimate son Charles Martel who came to dominate.

THE EARLY CAROLINGIANS

The first mention of the Pepinids, the family that we now know as the Carolingians, was in the seventh century. They established themselves in Austrasia, that 'most germanized' of the Frankish kingdoms, with centres at Trier, Mainz, Köln, Reims and especially Metz.[10] The founder of the family, Pepin I, gained large estates in Austrasia and was made mayor of the palace. Fellow founder of the dynasty was Arnulf, bishop of Metz, whose son Ansegisel married Pepin of Landen's daughter Begga. Their son was Pepin of Heristal, mayor of Austrasia. In the male line the family descended from Arnulf rather than Pepin, but those descendants inherited Pepin's office.

CHARLES MARTEL

Charles Martel was an illegitimate son of Pepin of Heristal. On Pepin's death his widow Plectrude sought to aid her own sons by imprisoning Charles, but he escaped to become mayor of Austrasia, sending Plectrude to a convent. The Muslims had advanced through Iberia and posed a major threat to southern Gaul. They sacked Autun in 725 and the duke of Aquitaine sought aid from Charles Martel. The latter's military successes included victory at Tours in 732, halting the advance of Islam into Gaul.[11]

Charles' nickname of 'Martel' (the Hammer) dates from the ninth century. He is seen as the founder of the Carolingian dynasty. Power seemed to rest now with the mayors and the kings were seen as puppets left to 'enjoy their mistresses, their meat and their wine'. Charles Martel ruled Neustria and Austrasia, with Neustria as his base. He opposed threats from Bavarians, Saxons, Alemanni and Frisians. He campaigned against the Aquitainians, Burgundians and Thuringians. Martel's conquests provided a landed base for the Carolingians. He was seen as the protector of Christendom though he distributed church lands to supporters in return for troops. From 737 Charles ruled without a Merovingian king. The pope called him '*vice regulus*' (vice-king). Charles Martel died at Quierzy on 22 October 741. Though he never used the title himself, the abbey of Echternach recorded the death of 'King Charles'.[12] Like his father, he was buried at St-Denis.

The curse of Merovingian rule continued in the tradition of dividing the inheritance. Martel's sons followed the same practice, Carloman the Elder taking Austrasia while the illegitimate Pepin the Short received Neustria. For a time there was joint rule. The Merovingian Childeric III was restored to the throne in 743 but the breaking point had been reached, and Pepin the Short now replaced one dynasty by another. Pepin's brother Carloman was probably forced to enter the monastery of Monte Cassino in 746, which conveniently removed him from the scene. In 751 the last Merovingian king, Childeric III, was deposed and entered the abbey of St-Bertin, where he died in 755. Pepin the Short took the royal title in his own right.

The Carolingians

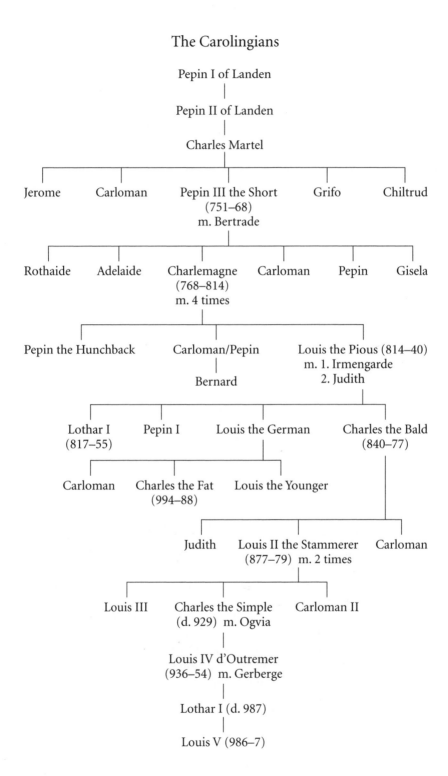

Pepin I of Landen

Pepin II of Landen

Charles Martel

Jerome — Carloman — Pepin III the Short
(751–68)
m. Bertrade
— Grifo — Chiltrud

Rothaide — Adelaide — Charlemagne
(768–814)
m. 4 times
— Carloman — Pepin — Gisela

Pepin the Hunchback — Carloman/Pepin — Louis the Pious (814–40)
m. 1. Irmengarde
2. Judith

Bernard

Lothar I
(817–55)
— Pepin I — Louis the German — Charles the Bald
(840–77)

Carloman — Charles the Fat
(994–88)
— Louis the Younger

Judith — Louis II the Stammerer
(877–79) m. 2 times
— Carloman

Louis III — Charles the Simple
(d. 929) m. Ogvia
— Carloman II

Louis IV d'Outremer
(936–54) m. Gerberge

Lothar I (d. 987)

Louis V (986–7)

PEPIN THE SHORT (751–68)

Pope Zacharias was pressured into accepting the new king and declared: 'it is better to give the name of king to one who has the wisdom and the power rather than to one who has only the name of king without the authority'.[13] Pepin the Short was crowned by Boniface in 751 and by Pope Stephen III in 754.[14] The anointment was a 'novel act' which enhanced the idea that the king had sacred power.[15] The rule of the Carolingians had begun. Pepin the Short's reign has been seen as merely a 'prelude' to Charlemagne's, but he introduced significant changes to Merovingian policies over the papacy and Italy.[16] In return for papal support Pepin twice aided the pope in Italy, defeating the Lombards. In 756 the Lombard king, Aistulf, was killed when his horse threw him against a tree. Pepin confirmed Italian estates to the papacy. He possessed a large demesne in Austrasia and Neustria. He won Septimania from the Muslims and, in eight annual campaigns, conquered Aquitaine. The Basques submitted and Waiofar, who had earlier sheltered Pepin's rebel half-brother Grifo, was killed. Pepin the Short died in Paris on 24 September 768.

CHARLEMAGNE (768–814)

Charlemagne, or Charles the Great (*Carolus Magnus*), was born in 747, the oldest son of Pepin the Short.[17] He was an Austrasian Frank with a short thick neck, a nose 'slightly longer than normal', a stomach 'a trifle too heavy' probably from his love of roast meat, large lively eyes, and a thin voice. He liked swimming but grew stout. He was moderate in his drinking but not in his eating. We learn much from Einhard, from a rich and landed family, who knew Charlemagne and wrote his biography.[18] Charles was probably illegitimate, his mother being the concubine Bertrade – though she did marry Pepin after Charles' birth.

Pepin sent his sons Charles and Carloman on an expedition to Aquitaine. Carloman turned back and Charles alone defeated the rebel Duke Hunald. The conquest of Aquitaine dominated the first part of Charlemagne's reign. On his father's death in 768 Charlemagne shared rule with his brother Carloman until the latter's death in 771. Charles' initial share was western Aquitaine, Neustria, Austrasia and Bavaria. Charles ignored his nephews' claims and took over most of his brother's territories. In 781 he established the kingdom of Aquitaine for his son Louis (the Pious). A key moment in European history occurred on Christmas Day 800 when Charles was crowned with a gold crown by Pope Leo III in Rome as 'emperor of the Romans'. The old Roman imperial title had continued in the hands of the Eastern Roman emperors at Constantinople but Byzantine rule was in disarray under the female Irene who had blinded her own son. Some believed this left an imperial vacancy and Charles could present himself as *the* Roman emperor, though Charles also saw his empire as a new entity, with Aachen not Rome as its capital.

Charlemagne's vast conquests deserve the title of empire. He was certainly more than an ordinary king. He had also accepted the role of defender of

Christendom. The imperial title gave prestige and suggested a new Europe-wide power. It was the beginning of the Holy Roman Empire. If Charles complained about the coronation, it was over its presentation as if in the gift of the pope. Charles believed that he already possessed the imperial crown before the coronation. He had taken it two days before. The papal act, to him, was merely confirmation – it was an argument that would run. Charles earned his title of 'the Great' through his military successes and dominance in Europe.[19] No medieval ruler after him would emulate the breadth of his power but the imperial title would cause problems in the future: over who had the right to grant the title, over power in Italy, and not least over how it should be inherited – leading to dissension on almost every imperial death.

Charlemagne's greatest conflict was with the Saxons, a frontier war and a clash with paganism. Saxony was roughly equivalent to later Lower Saxony. The war extended over 33 years from 772, with 18 campaigns, a savage war of conquest though presented as a conversion of pagans accused of such barbarisms as cannibalism. The *Annals* claimed the Franks would fight 'until they [the Saxons] were conquered and converted or totally annihilated'.[20] The Saxons had no overall ruler but found a wily war-leader in Widukind, who gave Charles severe problems after rebelling in 778. In 782 a Frankish army, led by officials, was beaten in the Süntel Mountains. Charles took his revenge by assembling Saxons at Verden and carrying out a mass execution of some 4,500 persons which, like all such acts, aroused more opposition than it destroyed. Frankish domination led to ruthless control. In 785 the death sentence was imposed on Saxons who attacked churches, ate meat in Lent, killed bishops or priests, refused baptism, or followed pagan burial rites.

North of the Elbe trouble continued. The *Annals* claimed that 'like a dog that returns to its vomit they [the Nordalbingians] returned to the paganism they had once thrown up'.[21] Widukind surrendered in 785 and agreed to baptism, but rebellions continued. In 804 Charles ordered the deportation of 10,000 Saxons from both sides of the Elbe, including wives and children. Their lands were handed to Slavs and Franks. Charles did moderate his laws in 797, when fines replaced some of the death sentences.

Charlemagne had to contend with the Vikings. He constructed a fleet against their raids and built fortresses beside rivers flowing into the North Sea. His establishment of the Dane March was the beginning of Denmark. He fought pagans to the east, including an eight-year war against the Avars. Charles' son Carloman defeated the Avars in 791, and the religious site at the Ring was destroyed in 796; the Franks carted away 15 wagon-loads of treasure. Charles conquered Carinthia and established the Avar March, basically modern Austria.

Charlemagne continued his father's efforts on behalf of the papacy, making several expeditions to Italy and invading Lombardy. King Desiderius surrendered and Charles seized the Iron Crown of Lombardy for himself. He confirmed his father's territorial grants to the papacy with additions. Charles' son Pepin was later made king of Italy.

Bavaria was ruled as a duchy by Charlemagne's cousin, Tassilo III, who renewed his oath of fealty to Charles without enthusiasm. Charles' conquests encircled Bavaria. Tassilo sought independence and married a daughter of Desiderius. Charles believed Bavaria was vital for defence against the Avars, and sought control. When Tassilo refused Charles' summons in 787, the latter invaded the duchy. Tassilo submitted but then rebelled again. He was captured and sentenced to death, but threw himself on Charles' mercy, and was sent into the abbey of Jumièges. Charles replaced Tassilo by his own brother-in-law Gerold, who ruled Bavaria until killed during a rebellion in 799.

One of Charlemagne's few defeats came from his incursion into Iberia. The Franks under Charles Martel had halted the Islamic advance into Gaul but the boundary between the faiths remained dangerous. In 777 Charles answered an appeal for aid from the Muslim emir of Zaragoza against a rival. Charles led an expedition in 778, but failed to capture the stronghold. On hearing of the approach of an Ummayad army, he withdrew. During the retreat his rearguard was ambushed by Basques at Roncesvalles – the scenario for the *Song of Roland*. A new effort in Iberia was made by Charles' son Louis, who captured Barcelona in 801 and Tortosa in 811, resulting in the establishment of the Spanish March. Charlemagne built an enormous empire but its power and unity were not as great as might be supposed – to be noted when considering the degree of 'decline' of Carolingian power. Charles spent most of his time in Austrasia and his grasp on the more distant regions was never very tight. Much of Charlemagne's expansion was spurred by opposition to pagans and Muslims as much as by desire for territory.

Charles operated a fairly efficient central government, using the kind of officials employed by the Merovingians – chancellors, chamberlains, constables, cellarers, cupbearers, seneschals, chaplains and so on. Financial and written records were kept. Capitularies containing royal decisions were issued, divided into chapters or articles (capitula) – the first at Heristal in 779. Instructions in writing were sent to officials.

The multiplicity of nations within the empire, and its size, made control of the regions a major problem. Counts were appointed to act for the king, some 300 in all.[22] The counts enforced the capitularies, so far as they could, kept order, collected taxes, dealt with justice, and commanded troops. Charles developed a system of representatives begun by the Merovingians, appointing *missi dominici* to check agents in the localities. The *missi* covered broad regions, perhaps the whole of Aquitaine, or up to half a dozen counties. They were men of standing with power to investigate the counts. They worked in pairs, one layman and one ecclesiastic.

Charlemagne's marital state was as ambiguous as that of most early Frankish kings. It is sometimes difficult to know whether a partner should be designated as wife, concubine, or mistress. It is generally said that Charles had five wives – Himiltrude, 'Desiderata', Hildegard, Fastrada, and Liutgard, as well as numerous concubines. Many of these ladies produced children for him. Whether Himiltrude was truly Charles' wife has been questioned. She was a noble Frankish lady who bore Charles' oldest son, Pepin the Hunchback, but was abandoned after two years. The marriage to the daughter of Desiderius, king of the Lombards, was arranged by Charles' mother and did not last long. She is called 'Desiderata' but her name is not mentioned in the sources. Pope Stephen III disapproved of this match, exploding: 'what folly, what madness, for a Frank to marry a woman of the stinking Lombard race'.[23] It was a political alliance and Einhard, the chronicler and friend of Charles and his children, said 'nobody knows why' Desiderata was sent back home.[24] It was the only occasion of bad words between Charles and his mother. Charles preferred to risk the Lombard alliance rather than stay married. Notker thought the explanation was her failure to bear a child. Charles' main marital partner was Hildegard, a noblewoman from Swabia, whom he married when she was 13. She was praised for her mildness and beauty and bore him four sons and five daughters. The sons included Carloman (later renamed Pepin), Louis, and Charles. Her children were the offspring Charles favoured. She died in childbirth. Fastrada was the daughter of an East Frankish count, a rather domineering lady for whom Einhard had a healthy respect. She died in 794. Liutgard was from the Alemanni, and may not have been a wife, though Einhard says she was. Other partners included Maltegard, Gerswinda, Adelaide and Regina. Einhard makes the situation fairly clear when he mentions one daughter 'by a concubine whose name I cannot remember'.[25]

Charles' oldest son, the probably illegitimate Pepin the Hunchback, resented his father's favour to the other offspring, and planned rebellion. On one occasion Pepin feigned illness in order to attend a meeting with conspirators. The court poet Fardulf overheard the plotting and went to Charles, knocking on his door. Charles ordered the women with him to open up. They slammed the door in Fardulf's face, 'bursting with laughter and stuffing their dresses into their mouths'. When Fardulf forced open the door, they hid in the corners of the room. Charles listened to his story and acted. Pepin was put into a monastery. Fardulf was made an abbot! Carloman became Charles' designated heir, taking the name of Pepin. The court poet Angilbert, who, against Charles' wishes, 'followed the urge of his love' with Charles' daughter Bertha and produced several illegitimate children, was also given an abbacy. What did one have to do at Charlemagne's court *not* to end in an abbey?[26]

Charlemagne encouraged learning and his court was a centre for European culture. Leading intellectuals gathered there, including Alcuin, Peter of Pisa, Paulinus, Paul the Deacon, and Odo of Mainz. Charles showed a personal interest in learning. He possessed many books and writing tablets, and kept notebooks under his pillow to practise writing when he had time. He spoke Latin and knew some Greek, and his studies included mathematics and astronomy. Charlemagne may have set up a court school for his sons and for the sons of nobles. Charles berated young nobles who preferred sport, luxury, or idleness, urging them to study. Literature appeared in the vernacular as well as in Latin, while the neater Caroline minuscule script developed in the eighth century. Classical works were copied and interest in them revived. The palaces, including Aachen and Salzburg, were models for architectural design but because much building was in wood, few examples survive.

LOUIS THE PIOUS (814–40)

Charlemagne developed a pain in the side after hunting, and then fever. He died at Aachen on 28 January 814 and was buried in the chapel. He was succeeded by his son Louis the Pious, who was seen as a poor successor to a great father, responsible for the start of the decline of the Carolingian empire. Dhondt saw this as 'a feeble reign' by 'an incapable sovereign' who 'ruined his house'. The view depends on Louis' 'excessive liberality' in granting away royal demesne to obtain support.[27] Bordonove considers Louis as 'only a caricature' of his father who 'lacked moderation and judgement'.[28] But other historians have shown the importance of his reign.[29] It was a period of reform, with Frankish integration, and the birth of a new European civilization.[30] Louis saw himself as Theodosius to Charlemagne's Constantine, and some have agreed.[31] Under Louis the empire became more truly Frankish than under Charlemagne.[32]

It has been thought that Charlemagne bit off more than any of his successors could chew. The large empire was unlikely to survive in the state that Charlemagne left it, but the changes that followed were not necessarily for the worse. Louis had been given Aquitaine as a subkingdom. Charles had planned to divide the empire between his sons, as he did in the 806 Division. The deaths of Charles the Younger in 810 and Pepin in 811 meant that Louis succeeded to the whole. In other words, unity was preserved through the accident of deaths rather than by design. Charlemagne in 813 crowned Louis as co-emperor at Aachen.

Louis and his twin brother Lothar were born in 778. Louis' father made sure that he was associated with Aquitaine, where he had been born and baptized, from an early age.[33] Louis saw the empire as a whole and made efforts to integrate it. Charlemagne had conquered Saxony but Louis made it a part of the Carolingian world. Louis' was a more peaceful empire with emphasis on culture and the economy. Above all he emphasized the Christian nature of the empire: peace, justice, and protection of the church. The major thrust of Charlemagne's reign had been the expansion of Francia. Louis' policy was defensive rather than aggressive, in Reuter's view 'a conscious decision'.[34]

Louis' name recalled the greatness of the Merovingian Frankish realm, being a form of 'Clovis'.[35] Louis' nickname of 'the Pious' reflected the Christian nature of his empire and his reputation for piety. He has also been called 'the Debonair' (le Débonnaire) in more modern times, to mean that he was easy-going or good natured.[36] In some respects he was a model Christian ruler with close advisers who were religious leaders, not least Benedict of Aniane, the 'second founder of Benedictine monasticism', who supervised a programme of monastic reform.[37] Louis' leading administrators were clerics, especially bishops – some of whom were also landed magnates. One reason for his pious reputation was a readiness to listen to and even heed ecclesiastical advice.

Carolingian rulers possessed great influence over the church, decided major ecclesiastical appointments, and at their peak controlled 200 abbeys. The empire was divided into 21 ecclesiastical provinces in 814. The prelates, largely chosen by the emperor, proved to be an important prop. Louis demonstrated strict religious opinions, driving prostitutes from Aachen (a little hypocritical considering the lax marital habits of the Carolingians). Louis acknowledged his sins, calling an assembly at Attigny to perform public penance, confessing his part in the death of Bernard of Italy. Louis ruled Aquitaine for his father from 781 and led campaigns into Spain. He married Ermengarde who died in 818 and then, after viewing available nubile maidens at Aachen, chose Judith the daughter of Count Welf of Bavaria – a match that 'opened up a Pandora's box of possibilities'.[38] Louis was crowned by Pope Stephen IV as western emperor at Reims in October 816.

Louis the Pious faced new Viking raids. Between 834–37 the Northmen sacked Dorestad four times. The attacks from Slavs, Bulgars, Moravians and Obodrites – as well as Saracens and Vikings – were considerable. Louis also faced rebellion by his nephew, Bernard of Italy – the illegitimate son of Pepin of Italy. Bernard was defeated and condemned to death. The sentence was commuted to blinding, but in any case the unfortunate Bernard died soon afterwards.

Louis is now seen as governing his lands more as an integrated empire than Charlemagne had. In Barraclough's view Charlemagne's administration had been 'rudimentary', little more than imposed rulers.[39] There was a 'lack of central control'.[40] The *missi* were not permanent officials, and administration depended on Frankish counts who were military rulers rather than officials, paid in lands rather than money, soon tied to their counties and founding local dynasties. The main attempt at central control was through assemblies called twice a year, attended by counts and bishops. Louis gathered a more effective bureaucracy, using men 'from the ranks of the lesser sort who are faithful'.[41]

Louis' second wife, Judith, was chosen for political as well as personal reasons.[42] Her family was powerful and she became a focus for opposition after the birth of her second child, Charles, on 13 June 823.[43] She favoured him over the sons from Louis' first marriage. Favour to Charles provoked hostility from the other sons and their supporters, including the minister Wala, count-abbot of Corbie. The opponents accused Judith of adultery with the chamberlain Bernard of Septimania. In 830 there was rebellion against her, and Bernard was forced to flee. She was put in a convent. Louis the Pious and Charles were confined at St-Denis, but Louis was soon restored. A new partition was made in 831 between the sons – Pepin, Louis the German and Charles the Bald. Lothar, though a disgraced rebel, was to have Italy.

Louis the Pious' main threat came from the discontent of the sons by his first marriage. Pepin rebelled in 833 and was beaten, his lands given to Charles. Louis the German took to arms but was in turn defeated. Lothar joined forces with his full brothers to produce the most powerful opposition coalition to date and Louis the Pious was defeated at the Field of Lies near Colmar in Alsace in 833. He was deposed and imprisoned in the abbey of St-Médard at Soissons. Judith's son, Charles the Bald, was shut in the abbey of Prüm, while his mother was sent to Italy.

The fall of Louis the Pious was short lived. The sons could not stay united against him and lost popular support. Louis was restored in 834 and crowned again at Metz in 835, a 'new beginning'. It is now argued that Louis' final years were not wasted and the crisis 'proved surmountable'.[44] A new kingdom was established for the young Charles the Bald in the west. There was further trouble and a final division under Louis the Pious was made in 840.

Louis' reign certainly produced 'little glory', yet he had made efforts to protect his inheritance and is no longer considered an utter failure.[45] Some historians have pointed out continuing imperial power and cultural achievements, fulfilling work begun by Charlemagne. Louis dealt firmly with problems in his later years. Lothar was packed off to Italy in 834, and only returned on invitation in 839, his resistance 'broken'.[46] Louis the Pious died at Ingelheim in 840 and was buried at Metz.

THE TREATY OF VERDUN

Louis the Pious had three sons by his first wife, Ermengarde: Lothar, Pepin, and Louis the German. By his second wife Judith he had the son Charles the Bald. Pepin predeceased his father in 837 and Louis the Pious died on a Rhine island in 840. A majority of nobles opted to support the eldest son Lothar, who attempted to 'take the empire' but lacked the strength to ignore his brothers' claims.[47] Louis the German and Charles the Bald formed an alliance that Lothar could never altogether overcome.

The German lands, eastern Francia, became attached to their king, Louis the German. His sons married into the southern German nobility. Louis was seen as a ruthless and sinful character. On his deathbed Louis the Pious said of this son, 'he has brought his father's grey hairs with sorrow to the grave'.[48] Louis the German's son, in a vision, saw him punished in the afterlife by being dipped into a vat of boiling water every other day. Louis the German's hold on East Francia if anything became firmer through time, though he had to subdivide his lands between his sons.

Lothar had to face Louis the German and Charles the Bald in 'the violent battle' at Fontenoy-en-Puisaye near Auxerre in 841.[49] Lothar was defeated in a conflict that affected the face of Europe. The empire could not be kept intact. Lothar fled to Aachen. Charles and Louis, their support more firmly established, held an assembly with celebrations and games including mock battles, and each promised not to make a separate deal with Lothar. Prolonged negotiations led to a new division, confirmed by the treaty of Verdun in 843, a treaty that 'changed the face of Europe'; a 'pivotal date in European history' by which 'the unity of the empire was broken'; 'the first great European accord whose consequences proved durable'.[50] There had been divisions before and there would be changes later – the division was not written in concrete, but it stands as a key moment in the movement from Europe-wide empires towards the national divisions that dominated Europe thereafter. It marked the collapse of Charlemagne's attempt to keep Francia united. The remark of Florus of Lyon may not have been strictly true, but its sense is valid. He wrote 'there is no longer anyone recognized as emperor'.[51]

According to one source the division was based on convenience, lands added that were 'adjacent and fitted into the territory already held by each brother'.[52] Louis the German took the eastern lands – east of the Rhine and north of the Alps. Lothar I received a central territory, the middle kingdom that included Lorraine, Burgundy and Italy, running from Italy to the North Sea. Charles the Bald was to have the western lands, including what became the Netherlands, Belgium and Switzerland, from the Meuse and the Scheldt, along the Channel coast to northern Spain. Lothar was the least satisfied; he had more to lose, and part of the settlement depended on some of his supporters going over to his brothers, and taking their lands with them. The territories of Charles the Bald were particularly well grouped to survive as a unit. The agreement at Verdun marked the change from a period of few alienations of royal land to a situation where the three rulers were forced to give lands in return for support. Decline of royal power from that time seemed inevitable, though it was gradual rather than sudden.

There is a noticeable change in the temper of Carolingian politics during the later years of Louis the Pious and those following his death, marked by tension between his sons. The explanation lies largely in the fact that Louis had legitimate children by two wives and the two families became rivals. His second wife, Judith, and her son Charles the Bald, created the problem. Judith was strong-willed and combative. Her Welf background gave her expectations of a significant political role. She was provoked by the sons of the first marriage, who had forced her into exile. She was recalled, proving more rather than less difficult thereafter. She had considerable influence over her husband, which she used in favour of her own son at the expense of his half-brothers. This was the fundamental cause of the tensions, fights and troubles between them.

LOTHAR I (843–55)

The eldest son by the first marriage, Lothar I, already associated in rule with his father, took the imperial title on the death of Louis the Pious. However he had to compromise with his brothers. No one of them had sufficient power to ignore the other two. Thus the three had a conference at Yütz near Thionville in 844, and further meetings at Meersen near Maastrict in 847 and 851. The archbishop of Reims, Hincmar, at first helped Charles to protect his kingdom from the ambitions of Louis the German. As a result Lothar and Charles moved closer together and had annual meetings without Louis.

Lothar I died at the abbey of Prüm in 855. For the first time the Carolingians had 'no imperial paterfamilias'.[53] Lothar I's territories were further divided in three between his sons. Louis II took Italy (of which he had been king since 844), much of the south, and the imperial title. He was anointed twice and crowned three times by the pope. Lothar II received the northern area with Francia and Frisia. Charles of Provence was given Provence and Burgundy, though he was only young in 855. His uncle Charles the Bald coveted those lands too. All three of Lothar I's sons died without legitimate heirs, 'the real turning-point' of the Carolingian empire.[54]

LOTHAR II (D.869)

Lothar II faced a serious threat from the Vikings, now attacking major cities including Paris, Orléans, Tours, and Blois. His uncles, Louis the German and Charles the Bald did not improve the situation by fighting each other – the most critical moment for Charles the Bald during his reign. The uncles and nephews also opposed each other: Charles and Lothar against Louis the German and Louis II. Louis the German invaded the west in 858, but made terms with Charles the Bald in 860. Lothar II had troubles with the church after separating from his wife Theutberga to enter a liaison with Waldrada, whom he finally married in 862. Theutberga was accused of having anal sex with her brother and, even more amazingly, of producing a child thereby!

Charles of Provence died in 863. Louis and Charles the Bald then joined forces against Lothar II. Lothar died suddenly of a fever, possibly malaria, in 869. Further divisions of the empire occurred in 870 and 880; on the latter occasion the middle kingdom was joined with East Francia. During the following century the authority of the Carolingian rulers gradually declined and was increasingly restricted in extent. There is no simple explanation but it partly resulted from divisions of the empire – of land, power and wealth. Then there were the conflicts between the divisions plus attacks from outside, notably from the Vikings and from the east. Mostly the invasions were beaten off, but they absorbed much imperial effort and expense.

The most telling explanation is the gradual change in the structure of the empire. Charlemagne had governed through representatives in the regions. He appointed *missi dominici* to check local government, and counts to command border areas. Gradually local counts and other appointed commanders (dukes and marquises) took power to themselves, depriving the kings of resources and wealth. The *missi* also developed local rather than central interests. As the kings lost wealth so their control declined and local rulers became more independent. The period saw the gradual rise of larger, powerful territorial units, or principalities, in which the kings had less and less ability to intervene.

Another factor was the hardening of territorial divisions, at first fluid and reversible, dictated by how many sons the emperor had, but becoming more or less separate kingdoms. The imperial title was associated with East Francia, basically Austrasia. The western division, basically Neustria, became a separate kingdom. The central division, named Lotharingia after its original holder

Lothar, survived for a time but was too diverse geographically and ethnically to remain a unit. The kingdom of Italy split off. The northern part, retaining the name of Lotharingia or Lorraine, became the target of East and West Franks.

What we see gradually emerging are the kingdoms of Germany (in its medieval form as the Holy Roman Empire), and France – though the initial 'France' was a much smaller unit than its modern counterpart. The historian Dhondt refers to the early smaller 'France' as *'France Mineure'* and we shall follow him by calling it Lesser France.[55] By Lesser France we mean the area around Paris and Orléans, including the Île-de-France, the base of the early Capetians. Lesser France became a principality alongside and roughly equivalent to (for example) Normandy or Brittany. Thus Lesser France became a unit within West Francia – which makes more sense than saying that France was a part of France with inverted commas around one term or the other.

CHARLES THE BALD (840–77)

The rules of Lothar I, Lothar II, and Charles the Bald overlap, but it seems useful to pursue each separately. Lothar I had sought to remain emperor but never had power over the whole. This was even truer of his son, Lothar II. In the meantime Lothar I's brother and half-brother, Louis the German and Charles the Bald, established more permanent realms in East and West Francia. This is not to say that ideas of uniting the empire were dead or that the new rulers were weak – but it does stress the gradual reshaping of Europe.

Charles the Bald was the youngest son of Louis the Pious by his second wife, the 'most beautiful Judith', that 'lovely Rachel', noted for her learning and always active on behalf of her only son, to her death in 843.[56] He had been well educated, called the 'learned king' and the 'most cultivated of the Carolingians', taught by Walafrid Strabo amongst others.[57] A contemporary poem called Charles a 'lovely boy', perhaps more complimentary then than now.[58] Charles' actual (later) baldness is uncertain; the name may be a physical description but some historians think it might have been a joke at the expense of a hairy individual – and perhaps as opposed to the hairy Bernards.[59] On the whole, though, we are inclined to think that Charles lost his hair early. Coins and illustrations show him crowned, hiding the evidence, but demonstrating a large moustache.

Charles seems to have possessed a sense of humour, if we can take at face value the tales about him. In one story he conversed with the Irishman, John the Scot, after an evening spent consuming alcohol. Charles asked the difference between a drunkard and an Irishman; the Irishman replied 'only this table, my lord'.[60] He also kept a court jester. Charles gained favour with his father through the rebellions of his half-brothers. By the time of Louis the Pious' death Charles was a major political player, having received West Francia in 837 and Neustria in 838. He was crowned king of West Francia in 840 by Hincmar archbishop of Reims. Charles has, anachronistically, been called the 'first king of France' though he was born in Germany and taught by an Austrasian monk, and his kingdom was West Francia. Nor was West Francia yet a unity; it comprised five subkingdoms.

Charles first married Ermentrude, daughter of the late Odo count of Orléans in 842, with whom he had 11 children. After her death he married his concubine Richildis in 870. She was sister of Boso the Lotharingian. Charles the Bald survived his half-brothers, and eventually succeeded his father as Holy Roman Emperor, crowned by John VIII on Christmas Day 875. He has been called 'the last Carolingian emperor' as well as 'one of the greatest Carolingian kings'.[61] As we have seen, he had a long struggle with his half-brothers. He had contested rule in the west with his half-brother, Lothar I. Charles and his younger half-brother, Louis the German, had won the battle of Fontenoy in 841. Lothar was beaten again in 842 at Moselle, a victory that confirmed Charles' control in the west, recognized by the treaty of Verdun. Charles then held off an attempt to take his lands by Louis the German. In the end the deaths of all his half-brothers brought relief though he still faced rebellion by his son, Carloman, whom he defeated and blinded.

The other great threat to Charles came from the Vikings, who attacked Rouen and Paris in 845 and again in 848. In 856 they established a base at Jeufosse, only 60 kilometres from Paris. In 857 the Vikings attacked Paris and the abbey at St-Denis, whose abbot Louis was captured – he was later ransomed by Charles. Charles' enemies, including Pepin of Aquitaine, Robert the Strong, and the Bretons, allied with the Vikings against him. Charles also hired Viking troops, and in 860 allied with the Viking Weland. Somewhat inconsistently he ordained punishments for selling weapons, armour, or horses to 'foreigners' – including Vikings.[62] He made efforts to improve coastal and river defences, including fortified bridges.

Charles appointed trusted men to command threatened frontier regions, as marquises over marches, such as the Breton March, the Spanish March, and the March of Burgundy. Counts over counties performed a similar function, but the marches were larger, incorporating groups of counties, and often falling under families that developed hereditary succession. This was to prove a significant development as the empire gradually disintegrated into smaller units.

Not least important was the emergence under Charles the Bald of Robert the Strong over the Breton March which included the counties of Anjou, Blois, Tours, Autun, Auxerre and Nevers. Recent historians have re-examined Charles the Bald's policy, and have questioned Dhondt's view of Charles as the villain of the piece and 'arch-squanderer of the fisc'. Charles' role was probably less dramatic; we need to take a more moderate view. He re-organized defence in a sensible manner under a few important military commanders. This did not weaken the empire at the time; the steep decline of royal power came later.

Charles appointed either trusted followers or close relatives to the key positions. In 856 he gave his son Louis command as king over Neustria. He created a kingdom of Aquitaine for his son Young Charles in 855. He meant to keep central control and chose men not previously associated with the areas of their commands. The intended family role is obvious and only family members were given kingdoms rather than marches. Under Charles the Bald central power did however continue to wane, despite his best efforts. Dhondt enumerated the alienations of land which diminished royal wealth and brought 'the material ruin of the Carolingian royalty'.[63] This is to state the case too severely; the loss was less ruinous under Charles, and less sudden. Charles also retained a considerable demesne, and was not notably less powerful at the end of his reign than at the beginning. Dhondt's 'material ruin' was not yet apparent or inevitable.

Rebellion was common despite Charles' harsh treatment of rebels. Most of the favoured magnates remained loyal, including Boso, Hugh the Abbot, and Baldwin of Flanders. Charles took over Aquitaine in 848, consigning the sons of Pepin II of Aquitaine to a monastery. Though Robert the Strong's career hinted at future possibilities, he was successfully employed as a commander by Charles. Charles kept control and Robert's sons were not allowed to inherit their father's territories and position. Charles also had the strength to move Robert himself to Burgundy in 865. This led to Robertian interest there as well as in Neustria. It was not an additional acquisition, though, rather a strong king moving a major officer from one region to another – seeking to avoid rather than promote a family hold. The Seine Valley became the base of Charles the Bald's power rather than Robert the Strong's.

This was, however, a vital period towards the development of principalities in West Francia. Charles recognized the power of certain magnates in parts of his realm, though he did not endure opposition easily. Control of Aquitaine and the south was a recurring problem for the Carolingians. Charles besieged Toulouse in 844 but had to abandon it. Bernard of Septimania was captured and beheaded in 844, his son William in 850. Their county of Autun was passed by Charles to Robert the Strong, leading to rebellion by Bernard's son, Bernard Hairypaws or Hairyfeet – apparently a comment on his foxy nature rather than his appearance.[64] Charles the Bald was anointed as king of Aquitaine in 848 and handed Toulouse by Count Fredelon. Aquitaine was in a state of disorder, politically and economically. It was said there were wolves roaming the land in packs of 300, killing and eating humans.[65] Pepin II of Aquitaine was captured and placed in the monastery of St-Médard at Soissons in 852. He escaped and remained at large until his death in 864.

Charles the Bald retained the kingdom of Aquitaine and in 855 passed it to his son Young Charles. The latter proved less than grateful. He married without his father's consent and rebelled. Charles the Bald suppressed the rebellion. In 864 Young Charles apparently intended to play a joke on one Albuin after a hunt, by ambushing him and stealing his horse. Albuin believed the assault was genuine and hit Charles on the head with his sword. Charles was brain damaged, never fully recovered, and died two years later. Aquitaine then passed to Charles the Bald's next son, Louis the Stammerer.

Other major regional rulers to emerge under Charles the Bald included Boso, Hugh the Abbot, and Baldwin of Flanders. Provided they acknowledged him,

Charles was prepared to accept their powerful position. Charles agreed to fulfil various obligations – to church, magnates and people – and to keep the law and give justice. His oath was the basis for similar agreements pressed upon succeeding kings. This has been seen as the development of an 'unwritten constitution' that monarchs had from now on to accept.[66] Together with the emergence of elective monarchy it would place greater restraints upon kingship.

Louis II died near Brescia in 875 when Charles took over Italy and most of Provence. Charles had been offered the imperial crown, vacated on Louis II's death. Louis the German opposed Charles' coronation, and some of Charles' subjects agreed, believing the king should concentrate on defence against the Vikings. Nevertheless Charles set out and was crowned emperor, and king of Italy. Louis the German died on 28 August 876. Charles attempted to seize his half-brother's lands but was frustrated by Louis' son, Louis the Younger of Saxony, who defeated him at Andernach in 876. Charles escaped but it was a blow to any broader ambitions.

Pope John VIII appealed for Charles' aid and the new emperor returned to Italy. One should not underestimate his personal belief and wish to live by Christian principles. He respected the church and the papacy. He once wrote, in the only letter definitely attributed to him, that war could only be defended if fought 'to gain peace', describing himself as 'a man who walks in the image of God'.[67] His desire to aid the papacy may not have been merely for political motives – he already held the empire.

However, Charles the Bald now became ill. He died in a hut at Avrieux near Maurienne on 6 October 877 at the age of 54. His corpse produced such a stench that it was hastily transported to Nantua near Lyon for burial. The bones were later moved to St-Denis, which Charles as its lay abbot had made the family mausoleum. The Capetians were to follow the late Carolingians in this. Charles the Bald was the last West Frankish king to become emperor. Though he did not see himself in such terms, he was 'one of the makers of France'.[68] It is important to note how the direction taken by late Carolingian monarchs pointed the way for the Capetian monarchy.

DEVELOPMENTS IN CAROLINGIAN FRANCIA

Let us sum up the developments in Carolingian Francia. It had been part of Roman Gaul. The southern region was more enduringly Romanized than the north, but Roman influence remained important into the barbarian Frankish period. The region was invaded and taken over by the Franks, and a Frankish realm established under Merovingian kings. The later members of that dynasty lost power and gradually became dominated by their major officials, the mayors of the palace, who ruled parts of the realm as in Neustria and Austrasia. One such family, the descendants of Charles Martel, provided a new line of kings, seen as 'upstarts' in their royal beginnings.[69] Their outstanding figure was Charlemagne who was recognized by the pope as a new western emperor. His successors retained the imperial title along with considerable power in the western world, notably under Louis the Pious and Charles the Bald.

Under pressure the Carolingian empire tended to break into parts, the key moment being the treaty of Verdun in 843, 'the burial of the idea of … a united empire'. Florus of Lyons thought that now there were only 'kinglets'.[70] That is how we see it in retrospect, but at the time there was no certainty about what would follow. There were other similar divisions which gradually hardened into the establishment of separate kingdoms, notably East and West Francia, or what we can begin to call Germany and France. By the death of Charles the Bald much of the political geography of the west was still fluid and uncertain. At this point the Robertian family was simply one family that had done well under the Carolingian kings and emperors.

2

The rise of the Robertians

There are three major themes to this chapter. The first is the decline and collapse of the reigning Carolingian dynasty. Our contention is that the late Carolingians were not consistently weak and ineffective. In consequence we must suggest that the Capetians took over a position that was stronger than generally thought. The second theme is that of the external threats to Francia during the late Carolingian period. In particular we suggest that the Viking raids and invasions were seen as a more potent threat by contemporaries than by historians. The third theme is the rise of the Robertian family to become rulers of a principality, and then kings of West Francia. We would stress here the strength of that family before becoming kings, and their continued strength after 987. These points add up to a revision of the view of dynasty change that has usually been presented.

ROBERT THE STRONG

Charles the Bald's most significant appointment of commander and official was that of Robert the Strong. Robert was the founder of the Robertian family and hence of the Capetian dynasty. We need now to examine the later Carolingian period, during which the Robertian family appeared, became powerful, provided kings, and in 987 finally replaced the Carolingians. The ninth century has been seen as a 'welter of civil wars, dynastic conflicts and intrigues … a pointless confusion of mediocre names' – but we need to examine the period and perhaps come to a more positive conclusion.[1]

The previous history of Robert's family is obscure. It is almost certain that he came from East Frankish Austrasian nobility. His descent is disputed because of lack of contemporary information. Various medieval sources give some information on the origins of the family, but they differ and later became distorted.[2] It is thought that Robert's ancestors were counts in Oberheingau and Wormsgau, probably related to the Carolingians. It is impossible to trace his origins exactly, but one can discount the later medieval myth of descent from a butcher. Richer, the son of a warrior and likely to have accurate information, wrote that Robert's father was a German noble called Witikind. Another early source, Aimoin a monk of Fleury, said Robert came from the Saxon race.[3] There is no conflict between these two pieces of information, which can be accepted. Robert probably came west because of a difference with the East Frankish ruler Louis the German.

Robert's father was probably a count in the Rhineland, and in the west Robert was made count of Anjou in c.861.[4] He was given command of north-western Francia, or Neustria. Robert was a favoured commander but not yet a territorial prince. He commanded troops in Neustria and defended it for the king – he did not rule it. Robert was also appointed by Charles the Bald as a *missus dominici* in Maine, Anjou and Tours. He was therefore a royal military commander and administrative official. Being favoured by Charles the Bald fits the pattern of that king's trust in Austrasian nobles.

Robert's further rise came from his military ability and successful defence of Neustria against the Vikings, though we should discount the idea that he was a spotless hero while the rest were traitors making terms with the enemy. Robert too, when it suited, was prepared to ally with and employ Vikings. It was a time of imminent danger for West Francia. Northmen sailed up the Garonne to Toulouse; they attacked Flanders, Aquitaine, Rouen, Bordeaux, Paris and Chartres. Dudo of St-Quentin thought their attacks had turned Francia into 'an almost empty desert'.[5] Robert became the Christian champion defending Francia for the king. From 863 he won three victories in as many years.

When Charles the Bald made his son Louis the Stammerer king of Neustria, Robert the Strong was compensated with the counties of Autun and Nevers. In 865 Robert was recognized as a magnate in Burgundy. Charles had reason to revise his decision, and restored Robert as leading commander against the Vikings, since no one else could do the job so well. After a brief rebellion in 856, Robert was reconciled to Charles and made count of Angers and ruler of the Breton March in 861. Robert went on to aid Charles against Pepin II of Aquitaine. He was also made lay abbot or count-abbot of the important abbey of St-Martin at Tours. At the time the church desperately needed lay protection and this was a common way of obtaining it. Lay warriors and magnates were given authority over certain monasteries. They were called abbots but their function was protection rather than religious leadership. It gave power to appoint abbots and deal with matters relating to the house. Holding one or more lay abbacies gave the lord concerned considerable political power. The rise of the Robertians depended a good deal on the collection of such lay abbacies.

Robert the Strong was killed, appropriately enough, defending Francia against the Vikings at Brissarthe north of Angers in 866. It was an heroic death in what proved to be a Frankish victory. Robert had trapped the Viking leader Hasting inside a church where he had taken refuge. Robert had removed his armour when the Vikings made a surprise sortie, during which he was killed. Robert had been married to Adelaide, daughter of Hugh of Tours and widow of Conrad I, a further East Frankish connection. He left two sons – Odo who became count of Paris, and Robert. The sons were young in 866 and Robert the Strong's position as leading commander in the west passed not to his sons but to Hugh the Abbot, lay-abbot of St-Germain at Auxerre, who acted honourably as guardian to Robert's sons.

Hugh the Abbot came to West Francia in c.853, like Robert switching allegiance from Louis the German to his cousin Charles the Bald, and being rewarded as a result. Hugh was a Welf, son of Conrad count of Argengau and nephew of Louis the Pious' wife Judith. He was thus related to Louis the German and Lothar, as well as to Charles the Bald. He was employed by Charles as a *missus dominici* but lost royal favour in 861 and took refuge in Lotharingia. Hugh and Charles were reconciled in 865 and, on the death of Robert the Strong, Hugh took over some of Robert's abbeys and control of many of his territories. In particular Hugh succeeded as leading commander against the Vikings in the west.

LOUIS II THE STAMMERER AND THE ESTABLISHMENT OF THE ROBERTIAN FAMILY

Louis II the Stammerer (le Bègue) (877–79) was Charles the Bald's son and successor in West Francia, crowned in 877. He was the first to call himself 'king of the West Franks'.[6] Louis' brother, Young Charles, had died in 866; the other brother, Carloman, had rebelled and been blinded by his father and put in the abbey of Corbie. He was later released but posed no further threat to his brother.

Louis the Stammerer's health was not good and he has been seen as an 'undistinguished' ruler.[7] He apparently did stammer, never a mannerism to assist a king. In 862 he married his concubine Ansgard without his father's consent. Later, under pressure, he repudiated her in favour of Adelaide daughter of Count Adelhard, a Burgundian magnate. Hugh the Abbot remained the mainstay of royal government, referred to as *ducatus regni* (director of the realm).

A persistent factor in the history of the late Carolingians was their progressive loss of wealth and power. Partly this came from the need for each new king to build support – support that had once been expected but was now difficult to exact. The main method was to make grants of land in return for allegiance. Louis was particularly generous with counties, abbeys and demesne and thereby reduced his direct income considerably. This was necessitated by Louis' rejection of most of those close to his father and his promotion of new men. Louis' gifts caused resentment from those who did not receive them.

Louis the Stammerer faced increased Viking activity requiring greater reliance on magnates who could defend West Francia. In the south, Bernard of Gothia refused to recognize Louis, acting virtually as king in his own realm. Louis built an alliance and defeated Bernard, but his lands passed to other nobles rather than the king. Louis also faced rebellion by Boso, brother-in-law of Charles the Bald who had become count of Vienne and of Bourges. He later acquired Autun and controlled most of Burgundy and Provence. Charles the Bald made Boso duke in Italy, who married the daughter of the emperor Louis II. The division of the empire became firmer in 878 when Louis the Stammerer met his cousin Louis the Younger (son of Louis the German) at Fouron, and agreed another division of Frankish lands between east and west.

Robert the Strong emerged under Charles the Bald, and Charles had been forced to recognize that he could not ignore the claims of the successful commander against the Vikings. Hugh the Great succeeded to the position of

Robert and posed a similar threat to the monarchy. The disbursement of lands and wealth by the ruler to win support paid off less than usual, since Louis the Stammerer only survived until 879, and the process had to begin again from an even lower starting point of royal resources. Louis died on 10 April 879 leaving three sons, Louis III (879–82) and Carloman II (879–84) from his marriage to Ansgard, and Charles the Simple born posthumously to his second wife Adelaide. In 879 Charles the Simple was too young to receive a share. Louis III succeeded through the support of Hugh the Abbot but the stronger kingdom of the East Franks could not be ignored, and its ruler Louis the Younger intervened to get an agreed division. At Vienne in 880 the surviving Carolingians met and agreed that Louis the Younger should keep Austrasia, Louis III should have Neustria and Lesser France (in effect West Francia), while Carloman II received the south with Burgundy and Aquitaine.

Both sons of Louis the Stammerer were crowned at Ferrières. Carloman II immediately faced problems from Boso who declared himself king of Provence and sought to control Burgundy. Hugh the Abbot supported Louis III and was his chief commander as marquis of the Breton March. Louis won an important victory over the Vikings at Saucourt in Picardy in 881 but he reaped few benefits since he died at St-Denis in 882 when chasing a young woman into a house while on horseback, and banging his head on a low lintel beam.

Hugh the Abbot's support then switched to Louis III's brother Carloman who took over in the west. He defeated the Vikings at Avaux north of Reims in 882 but he only reigned until 884 when he in turn died young (aged 17 or 18) after being wounded in the leg when hunting in the forest of Lyons. His successor in the west was the only surviving descendant of Charles the Bald, Charles the Simple, son of Louis the Stammerer. He was only five in 884.

With the death of the older brothers came the end of a central Carolingian administration. There was a decline in the use of *missi dominici*. No royal capitularies survive after 888, perhaps none were issued. Coinage declined in quality and quantity. By the time of the last Carolingian only Reims continued to mint royal coins. Kings rarely travelled outside their restricted power base. Reims, parts of Lotharingia, and Laon 'the final bastion of the Carolingians', were the only remaining territorial possessions.[8] Local magnates, beyond the royal demesne, went their own way, acknowledging royal authority only when it suited them. The number of magnates swearing fidelity to the king declined through the late ninth and tenth centuries. Only half of the magnates gave fidelity to Charles the Simple, only a quarter to Lothar.

CHARLES THE FAT (881–88)

Charles the Fat, the great-grandson of Charlemagne, was large as the result of illness. He may also have been epileptic. Recent work suggests that he was not permanently or chronically ill, and suffered from malaria rather than epilepsy.[9] Older historians found little to praise in Charles, though few were as vituperative as Stubbs who found him 'dangerous and unmanageable, a diseased, idiotic, raving madman'.[10] Recent historians have been a little more moderate and in MacLean, Charles finally found a modern defender. One of MacLean's major arguments is that Charles the Fat's poor reputation depends on the biased and hostile account in the continuation of *The Annals of Fulda* by Liutbert of Mainz. A consideration of other accounts, notably the Bavarian continuation of *Fulda*, presents a different view of him.[11]

Charles the Fat was the younger son of Louis the German. During his father's lifetime he gained lands in a division with his brothers. On his father's death in 876 he received the kingdom of Alemannia with Rhaetia (Swabia). Charles the Fat was the last Carolingian to rule East Francia, and the last to rule East and West Francia together when his fellow Carolingian rulers died off in turn. The pope recognized him as king of Italy in 879, and as emperor in 881. The Pope hoped for aid against the Muslims in return, but did not receive it.

Charles the Fat's position was improved by the death of his main rivals. His brother Louis the Younger died in 882, when Charles took over Bavaria, Franconia and Saxony.[12] Charles then reunited the Carolingian Empire after the 'dynastic catastrophe' of the premature deaths in the west of Louis III in 882 (chasing a young woman on horseback), and Carloman II in 884 (wounded in the thigh hunting) – though Hugh the Abbot retained his position of strength.[13] The West Frankish nobles invited Charles to take over in 884, which he did in 885.

The unity of east and west was vulnerable. The fisc in Aquitaine and Burgundy had practically disappeared, and with it real imperial power, even over the church. The last Carolingian capitulary was issued in 884 by Charles the Bald's grandson Carloman. The decline was sudden, since most of the fisc had been retained by Charles the Bald. Dhondt thought there were no more capitularies and no more *missi*. However, the decline may have been less steep than Dhondt believed. Jane Martindale examined the fisc in Aquitaine, using material ignored by Dhondt, and queried the latter's conclusions, in particular the condemnation of Louis the Pious for loss of wealth.[14] It was only after Louis' death that the size of the grants increased. She stressed the significance of the *villae regiae* and palaces, retained and visited by the kings. Some grants were to restore ruined lands, and some merely confirmed earlier grants. The loss of territory, fisc, and hence wealth, has been exaggerated.[15] Simon MacLean has suggested that under Charles the Fat there was a change in government through the use of charters rather than capitularies, and that *missi* were still used – Ruodbert is referred to as a *missus* in one of Charles' charters.[16] Charles used charters to dispense patronage, retaining the Carolingian hold over the provincial magnates. He travelled around the empire more than most of his predecessors.

Charles the Fat was more concerned with the east of his empire and only visited West Francia twice, though he retained an interest in the region. Nearly half of his surviving charters were to West Francia. He also used major magnates to represent him: Odo in Neustria, Rudolf in the kingdom of Burgundy, Bernard Hairyfeet in Aquitaine, Berengar of Friuli in northern Italy – and the magnates appeared at his court. The main change was from the old imperial centre to a new one in Charles' base region of Alemannia (Swabia and part of Switzerland), previously a 'Carolingian backwater', where he established a new capital.[17]

To the east there was a constant threat from Magyars, Slavs and others. While these peoples remained pagan the threat seemed even more necessary to combat. Hugh the Abbot led the military defence in the west but in 885 he became seriously ill, and Robert's son Odo was made count of Paris and took over command. The Vikings pushed up the Seine and besieged Paris in 885 for a year. It was defended by Bishop Gozlin and Count Odo who worked closely together.[18] The Vikings failed to take the city or to break through the bridges to the right and left banks. Gozlin died during the siege, leaving Odo in command. It has been said that Charles the Fat 'had the power to combat the pirates; he had not the heart'.[19] He did intervene and remained overlord of those who bore the brunt – including Count Odo who operated on his behalf. However, Odo's efforts should be credited partly to Charles the Fat. If there was delay in Charles coming to Paris it was because he was active elsewhere, including in Italy. According to MacLean, Charles the Fat's efforts against the Vikings were no worse than those of other kings – unless you believe the Mainz continuator.[20] Charles sent Henry duke of Saxony to relieve Paris though he was killed in the attempt. Then Charles raised a force that he led to the city. He made terms with the Vikings – a normal ploy – whereby they were not allowed into Paris or through the bridges but were promised a tribute on condition they moved on – Burgundy was their choice. Odo later went to court to collect the tribute to be paid – there is no evidence he opposed the settlement. Count Odo received from Charles the lands previously held by his father Robert the Strong in Neustria and on the Lower Loire – including the county of Orléans and the lay abbacy of St-Martin of Tours. Odo's rise was largely *through* Charles the Fat, not from hostility to him. Odo sought Charles' confirmation of his grants and spent time at court. Charles welcomed a loyal magnate of proven family and military ability.

Boso of Provence remained a threat but Charles the Fat forced him to give up his lands by 881. The only other thing we know of Boso is his death in 887. Charles took up Boso's son, Louis (the Blind), and supported his promotion in Italy. Louis' fall was not due to Charles. Carloman's illegitimate son, Arnulf of Carinthia proclaimed himself king of East Francia at Frankfurt, and was elected in 885. Charles at first worked with Arnulf but then they clashed and Arnulf brought about Charles' downfall. In 887 he was forced to abdicate and died in 888. Carolingian control in East Francia was lost. The unity of the empire was over. The Carolingian Empire broke up internally. No Carolingian could regain overall control. Imperial authority was retained in theory, but imperial presence and resources declined in the regions.[21]

On the death of Charles the Fat, Charles the Simple was only nine. Odo, son of Robert the Strong, was count of Paris and chief defender of the west – as his father had been. As the empire disintegrated, Paris rose to greater prominence. It had never been the main base of Carolingian rule. The rise of the Robertians occurred in parallel with the rise of the city. When Paris was besieged by the Vikings from 885–86, it had been Odo who led the heroic defence. Charles had to recognize Odo as his major commander against the Northmen, following in the footsteps of his father Robert the Strong. The siege was an important moment in the history of Paris and the Robertians. Hugh the Abbot, the previous commander, had been ill and taken no part in the defence, dying in May 886. Odo inherited his position.

In East Francia, the 'last emperor' (Charles the Fat) was deposed in 887 by supporters of his illegitimate nephew, Arnulf of Carinthia, partly because he was no longer physically capable of ruling.[22] In 887 Charles probably underwent a trepanning operation to cure his unbearable headaches. If so, the operation ended the headaches, and his life, on 13 January 888. Less dramatically (by another account), the 'operation' may have been a blood-letting, in which case the cause of death is less clear – possibly a stroke.[23]

The break up of the Carolingian Empire was not so much due to the rise of the aristocracy or the decline of the monarchy, as to another succession dispute.[24] Charles the Fat had no legitimate sons. His 20-year-old marriage to Richgard failed to produce children, not helped by Charles vowing to remain celibate. Richgard was accused of both virginity and adultery (with Charles' leading adviser Liutward)! It may be that husband and wife agreed on a strategy to allow a separation so that Charles could produce a legitimate son to inherit the empire.

Attempts to promote Charles' illegitimate son Bernard and to legitimize him failed. Charles planned divorce, probably in order to marry his mistress, Bernard's mother to assist legitimization. His efforts came too late. The divorce was pushed through on dubious grounds – that Richgard had committed adultery with Liutward bishop of Vercelli. He was dismissed from office and she confusingly claimed to be a virgin. She was sent to the convent she had founded at Andlau, where she died and was buried in 900 (and sanctified in 1049, when presumably the virginity claim carried more weight than the accusation of adultery!).

Arnulf arrived with a force at an assembly of magnates at Tribur in November 887. The magnates declared Charles the Fat too ill to rule. Arnulf of Carinthia, the illegitimate son of Carloman of Bavaria and grandson of Louis the German, was elected king of East Francia. He also took Lorraine. The Robertian, Odo count of Paris, was elected king of West Francia and crowned at Compiègne by the archbishop of Sens in 888. Charles returned to Alemannia. His illness was no invention; he deteriorated and died on 13 January 888. There were still Carolingian rulers to come, but Dhondt sees the death of Charles the Fat as 'the end of the reign of the Carolingians', and MacLean as 'the end of an era'.[25] Regino of Prüm noted that 'after Charles' death the kingdoms which had obeyed his authority, as if lacking a lawful heir, dissolved into separate parts'. The Bavarian continuator of *The Annals of Fulda* concurred: 'many kinglets (*reguli*) sprang up'.[26]

There were still Carolingians, and some would rule parts of the empire in the following century, but none would have the same wide authority. In 888 there was no adult Carolingian available, only the minor Charles the Simple. Descent in the male line of Carolingians was no longer seen as the only claim to a Frankish throne – bastards and those descended through a female could hope for success. New dynasties were established as a result of there being no adult Carolingian in 888.[27] The magnates now decided who would rule West Francia – until the Capetian dynasty established itself.

ODO, KING OF WEST FRANCIA (888–98)

Odo was the first non-Carolingian ruler of West Francia and the first Robertian king, but he ruled in the Carolingian manner seeking continuity rather than change.[28] Regino of Prüm saw Odo as 'an energetic man (*vir strenuus*) who excelled through his beauty, great stature, strength and abundant wisdom'.[29] He was crowned twice, at Compiègne by Walter archbishop of Sens on 29 February 888, and then in November at Reims – by which time his position was more secure. Before the second coronation Fulk archbishop of Reims had tried to find a Carolingian for the West Frankish throne – first Guy of Spoleto (who was crowned at Langres but returned to Italy), then Arnulf of East Francia (who preferred to recognize Odo), and finally Louis of Provence (whom Fulk finally abandoned in favour of Odo). Odo introduced 'a new era', of transition between Carolingian and Capetian power.[30] For a century power in West Francia alternated between the two families.

Odo was powerful in the west before his election but he seemed less powerful as a king. He stopped the Carolingian practice of granting away fisc. He was not a wealthy monarch, but at least he realized the fact. Parsimony in grants became royal policy. Odo's election was the beginning of Robertian and therefore Capetian rule but, at the time, it seemed more a triumph for the nobility than for the Robertians. Dhondt thought this was when the principalities emerged, but it now seems too abrupt an idea of the development.[31] By 890 there were six kings ruling separate parts of the former empire, all except Odo with Carolingian ancestry. The others were in most cases enthroned as the result of deaths – William for Bernard Hairyfeet in Aquitaine, Ramnulf II for Ramnulf I who died in Poitou in 866, Baldwin II for Baldwin I Ironarm in Flanders in 879, Richard of Autun (the Justiciar) for his brother Boso in Burgundy, Herbert II of Vermandois for Herbert I. At least Odo had the advantage of facing inexperienced princes not yet entrenched in their regions.

This period is seen as the era of principalities, of princes controlling the regions, while the king of West Francia was only able to intervene through the prince. Richard the Justiciar called himself 'duke of the Burgundians'.[32] The other counts looked like kings in their principalities – Aquitaine, Flanders, and so on. When Odo tried to pass lands to the count of Berry at the expense of William the Pious of Aquitaine, he failed. One of Odo's grants was made 'so far as the count himself consents'.[33] Odo rarely moved outside Lesser France.

Arnulf of Carinthia, the illegitimate son of Carloman of Bavaria, replaced his uncle Charles the Fat in East Francia. He was recognized as emperor by the pope in 896. However, Arnulf became ill, was partially paralysed, and never ruled the whole empire. He died in 899 and was succeeded in East Francia by his young son, Louis the Child – a succession seen as 'a catastrophe' with disputes and instability.[34] One effect was to encourage Magyar encroachment with accompanying devastation and massacre. The need for urgent defence fell to the dukes of Bavaria and Saxony, and hastened the development of principalities in East Francia. Louis the Child was the last East Frankish Carolingian ruler, ruling until 911. By that time East Francia consisted of five duchies – Saxony, Bavaria, Franconia, Swabia and the disputed Lorraine. East and West Francia hardened into separate and self-contained kingdoms.

The imperial crown became tied to Italy and disputed between East Frankish and Italian contenders. Guy II duke of Spoleto was elected western emperor in 891. His son, Lambert, succeeded in 897, but died without heir the following year in a hunting accident. Arnulf of Carinthia eventually imposed himself in Italy and was crowned emperor but suffered a stroke and returned to Germany where he died in 899, the last Carolingian emperor. Louis, son of Boso, received the imperial crown in 901. He was later captured by Berengar and blinded, thereafter known as Louis the Blind. Louis gave up his wider ambitions but returned to Provence, which he held for 20 years. Berengar was assassinated in 924 and Rudolf II returned. He was in turn opposed by Hugh of Arles, who was crowned king of Italy in 926 and kept the title until 947. His son Lothar succeeded but died in 950.

Louis the Child died without heir. The only surviving Carolingian was Charles the Simple in the west. In East Francia the magnates met at Forchheim and elected Conrad the Young, duke of Franconia and son of a Carolingian mother. Conrad I had to establish himself and also faced renewed Magyar attacks and civil war against his own princes. Conrad I died in 918. In short, imperial disputes and troubles in East Francia gave a welcome breather to West Francia, which kept out of the broader disputes.

There was a genuine Carolingian claimant to the West Frankish throne in Charles the Simple, though he was only seven when Odo was elected. Odo had support from his brother Robert, whom he made count of Paris. Robert acquired several lay abbacies, including St-Martin at Tours, as well as the counties of Tours, Blois and Angers; he was also appointed as marquis with the traditional Robertian task of defence against the Vikings. There were renewed threats also from Magyars and Saracens. The Magyars overran much of eastern and central Europe. King Odo had some success against the Vikings with victory at Montfaucon-en-Argonne in 888, during his first year as king. In the battle Odo was struck on the head, but survived. He won a further victory at Clermont. In a third battle, on the River Allier, the royal standard bearer was killed, but Odo was again successful. His victories led to recognition of him as king by Baldwin of Flanders and Arnulf of Carinthia.

Odo was the last king of the West Franks for three centuries to have a major interest in Aquitaine. The count of Gothia was William the Pious, son of Bernard Hairyfeet, who had been count, duke and marquis for Charles the Bald and ruler of Toulouse and Septimania. The count of Barcelona was Wilfrid the Hairy. (The southern rulers were a hirsute bunch). With Aquitaine in mind, Odo called an assembly at Orléans in 889. Richard the Justiciar, count of Autun, made himself duke of Burgundy but was prepared to recognize Odo as king.

Odo was diverted by troubles closer to home, including a rebellion by Baldwin II of Flanders in 892, angered by Odo's failure to support his interests over the church. Baldwin seized St-Vaast and was excommunicated. Baldwin's ally, Walter count of Laon, held that city for him. Odo captured Laon and beheaded Walter. Archbishop Fulk had helped in the upbringing of the young Charles the Simple, having 'reared him from the cradle', so his move to support the Carolingian was hardly surprising.[35] A coalition of prelates and magnates favoured Charles, who (with Odo still living) was crowned king of the West Franks at Reims.

There was now conflict between the Robertian king and his Carolingian rival, each with magnate support. The nobles of Austrasia supported Charles and those of Neustria were for Odo – another pointer to the Germany/France division that was emerging. Odo captured Reims and Charles fled to Worms to take refuge with Arnulf. He later moved to Burgundy under Richard the Justiciar. Flodoard a canon from Reims wrote that Charles turned to the Vikings in his search for allies against Odo – though as we have seen this was not an unusual move, even if much condemned by Christian chroniclers.[36] In 895 an agreement was reached between Arnulf and Odo at Worms, leaving Charles with Laon, and a promise that he should hold part of the West Frankish kingdom. Arnulf was keen to pursue his interests in Italy.

King Odo became ill at La Fère-sur-Oise, fell into a coma, and died on 1 January 898 at the age of 40. The first Robertian king was buried at St-Denis, to become 'the mausoleum of the Capetians'.[37] Odo had fulfilled his main task of opposing the Viking invaders. He had won seven battles in five years and caused the Vikings to flee on nine other occasions. He had also improved Frankish defences. Odo had no surviving son. Charles the Simple had been recognized by Odo as his successor, and the throne returned to the Carolingian claimant.

CHARLES III THE SIMPLE (898–923)

Some historians have seen the tenth century as a period of disaster for Francia; Lot thought it would have been 'better had it never existed'.[38] Charles the Simple had been crowned at Laon in 893 but was only able to gain control of West Francia after the death of Odo. The end of Carolingian rule was not inevitable – in fact Carolingians ruled for most of the next 100 years in West Francia, and in 898 most magnates preferred Carolingian rule. Ironically, in 911, Carolingian rule did come to its end in East Francia. At first sight, Charles the Simple seemed in a stronger position than Odo had been, accepted more widely through the old empire – but appearances were deceptive, 'an illusion' perhaps.[39] Most magnates recognized Charles however reluctantly. An important exception was Baldwin of Flanders.

Charles the Simple faced the same problems as Odo. In addition, from 917, there was a Magyar threat to the west. In the last 23 years of his reign he made only one effective intervention in Aquitaine, and that through the church. Charles retained authority in Lesser France, but he had to allow Odo's brother Robert to keep Neustria, and to grant the area around Rouen to the Viking Rollo. West Francia was becoming a conglomeration of almost independent principalities: Flanders, Burgundy, the divisions of Aquitaine, Normandy, Vermandois, Brittany and the territory held by the Robertians.

Odo's brother, Robert, had been a potential successor but showed little enthusiasm for the throne, and supported Charles the Simple. He was rewarded by being recognized as marquis between the Seine and the Loire as of Neustria. Robert resumed the traditional Robertian position as defender of the west. Charles also recognized a marquis over Burgundy in Richard the Justiciar, and of Aquitaine in William.

Charles the Simple was the youngest son of Louis the Stammerer, too young to make his presence felt earlier when his older brothers had divided the kingdom, too young to prevent support going to Charles the Fat in 881. Richer suggests that he was debauched, neglected judicial work, and was 'not sufficiently practised in military ways'.[40] Charles' nickname of 'Simple', by which he is commonly known, may be misleading. He was neither stupid nor incapable; the nickname (Latin *simplex*) meant rather Charles the Straightforward (*sans détour*) or the loyal/the honest/without guile – however, the name of 'the Simple' is too well used now to abandon.[41] One might note though that a slightly later chronicler at St-Maixent called him 'Charles the Stupid' for abandoning his men in 919.[42]

The Viking troubles continued through the early tenth century. One of Charles' most important decisions was to recognize a Viking leader as holding the western part of his realm from him. In 911 by the treaty of St-Clair-sur-Epte Charles accepted Rollo as ruler of the region around Rouen, the basis of the principality of Normandy. Vikings had attacked Vimeu and Burgundy, burning down the abbey of St-Martin at Tours. Rollo besieged Chartres but was defeated by Odo's brother Robert, so that Charles made the 911 treaty from a position of strength.

The intention was to attach Rollo and his men to the king, with a promise to defend the coast from further Viking inroads – thus setting up a buffer region. Rollo agreed to receive baptism, which occurred in 912. The Viking leader was to marry Charles the Simple's fourth daughter, Gisela. There is a problem over this claim of Dudo's since she may not have been born until after 911 – but possibly there was a marriage clause in the agreement. Rollo's dynasty ruled Normandy over a long period, and William the Conqueror was a direct descendant. Charles the Simple has been much criticized for his grant to Rollo, but it worked, and Riché sees it as a daring move.[43] Rollo proved loyal and turned against

Charles' enemies when the latter was imprisoned, seeking and helping to obtain his release.

Charles the Simple had some success in Lotharingia, where Riché believes he showed courage. Lotharingia, traditional Carolingian territory, was a concern for Charles throughout his reign. From 910 to the end of the reign, of 58 surviving diplomas, 21 dealt with Lotharingia. Charles' chief advisers were from Lotharingia. He took advantage of the weakness of Conrad the new king of the East Franks to regain power in Lotharingia. The end of Carolingian rule in East Francia meant that its population was more willing to accept the western Carolingian as king. Lotharingia gave some hope of recovery to the old dynasty. To strengthen his claims, Charles married the Lotharingian Frederuna in 907.

Unfortunately for Charles his hopes in Lotharingia led him to antagonize his former supporters. The East Franks were hostile to his attempts and Conrad of East Francia tried to recover Lotharingia, though he failed. Charles favoured a Lotharingian adviser in Hagano, who was made a count in 918, and became a kind of leading minister. Though probably a noble, Hagano's origins are obscure, and he was seen by West Frankish nobles as an upstart and resented. In an assembly at Soissons the Robertian, Robert of Neustria, was placed on the king's right and Hagano, as if his equal, on the left. This was too much for Robert who went home and left Charles to face the other nobles without his support.

Eventually Robert joined a rebellion with Ralph of Burgundy and Gilbert of Lorraine. Charles defeated Gilbert who fled to Germany and sought the protection of Henry I, his father-in-law. Gilbert wanted to recover Lorraine but when he failed to persuade Henry to help him, turned instead to Robert who joined him in a new magnate rebellion from 922. Their united power was too great for Charles the Simple, who fled, was deposed, and imprisoned until his death in 929. According to Flodoard Charles was unsuitable to continue as king, he had not acted as a Christian king, he had favoured Hagano, he had neglected to keep truces, he had made military attacks on a Sunday, he had fought during Lent, and he had allied with pagan Vikings.[44]

ROBERT I (922–23)

Robert of Neustria, brother of King Odo, inherited the former Robertian position in Lesser France, 'virtual lord of West Francia from the Seine to the Loire', holding a host of major lay abbacies including St-Germain-des-Prés, St-Martin of Tours, St-Denis, St-Armand, St-Aignan and Marmoutier.[45] In 920 Robert turned against Charles the Simple, for which the chronicler Richer called him a tyrant and a usurper.[46] According to Richer, Louis IV later accused Robert of being 'envious of my father's kingdom' before depriving him of it.[47] Twice, in 920 and 922, Robert defeated Charles and was elected king by a magnate assembly on 29 June 922. Next day he was crowned at St-Remy in Reims by Walter archbishop of Sens.

Robert I thus became the second non-Carolingian ruler of West Francia and the second Robertian king – but his predecessor was still alive. Charles the Simple, at liberty again, raised a force in Lotharingia and came against Robert at Soissons in 923. Charles watched the initial stages from a nearby hill. Robert was killed in the fighting but Charles the Simple was defeated. The chronicler saw it as 'a victory for each side'.[48] Herbert of Vermandois and Robert's son Hugh recovered the situation, and Charles had to retreat.

Herbert tricked Charles into a meeting at St-Quentin, where he seized and then imprisoned him at Château-Thierry. Some expressed their horror at the deed, but none was prepared to act. Charles the Simple was deposed again. Charles' son, the young Louis (IV), escaped, rolled in a bundle of fodder. Charles' wife Eadgifu, daughter of Edward the Elder of England, took Louis to exile in England. Henceforth he was known as Louis d'Outremer (from Overseas). Charles the Simple remained in prison at Péronne until his death in 929.

RALPH I (923–36)

Ralph, son and successor of Richard the Justiciar in Burgundy, gained the throne of West Francia in 923. Ralph was neither a Carolingian nor a Robertian – though he was related to the Robertians through marriage. He marked the transitional period between the two dynasties, being the third non-Carolingian ruler, and the third ruler of a principality, to have ascended the throne. Ralph was a compromise candidate since the stronger lords, Hugh the Great and Herbert of Vermandois, were prepared to accept him rather than each other. Hugh the Great was the son of Robert I but made no move to claim the kingdom, preferring to restrict himself to the Robertian principality. Rodulfus Glaber (the Bald), a Burgundian monk, wrote that Hugh asked his sister Emma who should be king. She replied she would rather embrace her husband's (Ralph's) knees than her brother's (Hugh the Great's).[49] Dhondt believed that Ralph's election 'sounded the death knell' for the Carolingians, but it was only a step along the way.[50]

Ralph was elected at Soissons on 13 July 923 and crowned by Archbishop Walter of Sens at St-Médard. Support was limited, mainly from Hugh the Great – but that alone suggests Robertian power. Lotharingia remained Carolingian in its sympathy. One advantage for the new king was his marriage to the 'beautiful and intelligent' Emma, daughter of Robert I and sister of Hugh the Great – thus attaching him to the Robertians.[51] Otherwise Ralph was in a weak position, not recognized in Normandy, Brittany, Aquitaine or Lotharingia. He lost authority north of the Seine and did not retain the two major supports of the late Carolingians, Reims and Laon.

Ralph faced threats from the Vikings and the Magyars. Hungarian hordes moved west against the Lombards, Saxons and Franks, into Lotharingia and Burgundy. They reached Champagne but then halted to Ralph's good fortune rather than through any effort on his part. A new period of Viking pressure began in 924. Ralph had to pay tribute in 924. He won a victory over the Loire Vikings in 925, but they were allowed to settle around Nantes, and it seemed that a second Normandy might emerge. This led to Ralph ceding the Avranchin and the Cotentin to William I Longsword of Normandy, thus extending the boundaries of that duchy, increasing its ruler's power, and buying his loyalty and recognition in 933.

There was a further threat from the German king, Henry I the Fowler. Henry duke of Saxony had succeeded to Conrad I in East Francia in 919. The succession in Germany seemed heading for an elective system from candidates among the dukes. Henry came close to establishing a permanent Saxon dynasty, winning victories over the Magyars, Slavs and Bohemians. He recovered Lotharingia in 925 and was a natural ally for Ralph's opponent, Herbert of Vermandois. Herbert imprisoned Charles the Simple, which in one way strengthened Ralph's position, but posed the potential threat of his release to support Charles whenever Herbert chose.

Herbert II count of Vermandois was descended from Bernard of Italy and hence from Charlemagne, and saw himself as a Carolingian. His father, Herbert I, had become count of Vermandois in 896 and accumulated wide possessions. Herbert I was assassinated in 902 when his son succeeded. After treacherously imprisoning Charles the Simple, Herbert II extended the family territories, taking Péronne and Reims. To prevent the release of Charles the Simple, Ralph granted Herbert Péronne. It was claimed that Herbert's men poisoned Seulf, archbishop of Reims, to replace him by his son Hugh at the age of four.[52] The child Hugh was elected and accepted by King Ralph. He was sent off to Auxerre to study. The event shows the power of Herbert, and the degree of fear he generated, as well as the weakness of the church and the papacy. It did, however, initiate a long dispute over the see. Ralph attempted to recover Reims in 931, besieging the city in support of a new archbishop, Artaud, formerly a monk at St-Remy. After three weeks the citizens opened the gates and Ralph took over. Archbishop Hugh, now eleven, was deposed – but it was not the end of the dispute.

On the death of Roger count of Laon in 926, Herbert of Vermandois took the town and made his son Odo its count. This led to a clash with the king, who appointed the previous count's son to succeed. Herbert attacked Laon in 927 and declared Charles the Simple restored. However, Herbert had to abandon his siege. Charles the Simple was returned to captivity and died a prisoner on 7 October 929. Herbert held on to Laon until 931 when Ralph campaigned against him. Many of Herbert's supporters then deserted, including Gilbert of Lorraine. Both Herbert and Ralph negotiated for the support of Henry I of Germany. Ralph took over Reims and Laon, though Herbert held the latter's citadel until 938. Hugh the Great supported Ralph in these efforts. Herbert's power diminished though he still had one card up his sleeve, making a useful marriage between his daughter Adela and Arnulf I of Flanders.

Ralph's position was far from secure in the early part of the reign. Among his allies, Herbert numbered the most powerful northern nobles including the count of Flanders. Hugh the Great was a relative by marriage whose allegiance might be won. However, the situation was volatile, and most lords looked first to their own interests. In the end Ralph was reconciled to Hugh the Great and successfully countered Herbert. Through Henry I of Germany, peace was established at Chelles in 935. Ralph returned possessions to the king taken by Hugh, much to the annoyance of the latter. The fact is that the king's position was held in the balance by the various lords. Ralph had done well in an awkward situation. He fought doggedly against a range of enemies and managed to win general recognition – but it took virtually all his reign to get that far.

Ralph's base was an unusual one in this period of West Frankish history, and explains his weakness in the north. His main interest was in the centre and south from a base in Burgundy. He faced rebellion in Aquitaine but it petered out. One notes that Seulf, archbishop of Reims, seen as a supporter of Herbert, accompanied Ralph's expedition to Aquitaine in 924 when the king invaded the lands of William II of Auvergne. William had refused to recognize Ralph as king but he submitted, though there was further rebellion in 926. Ralph returned to deal with it and was wounded during the campaign. William II's death in 927 eased the situation. His brother Effroi succeeded and recognized the king. In 923 Raymond III Pons count of Toulouse and of Gothia, recognized Ralph. Ralph I was unusually, even uniquely, a more effective king south of the Loire than north of it. He became ill at Auxerre in 935 and died on 14 January 936 with no direct heir. He was buried at Sens. His wife Emma died in 934 and his brother Boso in 935. Ralph's surviving brother Hugh the Black held Lotharingia and now received Burgundy. Ralph had fought against considerable odds with 'appreciable success'.[53] The struggle for the throne returned to a clash between Carolingians and Robertians.

LOUIS IV (936–54) AND HUGH THE GREAT

The Carolingians returned to rule West Francia with the accession of Louis d'Outremer as Louis IV.[54] Louis had been exiled in England with his mother and her family but was invited back to Francia and supported by the magnates in 936, elected 'by hereditary right'.[55] The Robertian, Hugh the Great or Hugh the White (from his pale face), was the son of King Robert I and brother-in-law of King Ralph, and undoubtedly the most powerful figure in West Francia, stronger in lands and wealth than Louis IV. Richer put into Hugh's mouth a somewhat unlikely explanation of why he supported Louis for the crown, declaring that his father had 'committed a great crime in reigning when one was still living who alone had the right to reign'. Richer makes Louis the hero king. He described Duke Hugh leading in a horse with gear bearing the royal insignia. Not waiting for aid, Louis leaped upon it with great agility.[56]

Hugh the Great was count of Paris and held Neustria with lands from the Loire to the Seine, except for areas lost to the Vikings. He held the counties of Paris, Étampes, Tours, Angers, Poitiers and Orléans, as well as the *pagi* of Blois, Chartres and Châteaudun. He was recognized as lord by the counts of Normandy, Vendôme, Dreux, Melun and Beauvais. He controlled lands in Berry and Maine. He was lay abbot or count-abbot of the Robertian monasteries, including

St-Martin of Tours, Marmoutier, St-Germain-des-Prés and St-Denis. Flodoard called him 'prince of the Seine' – which was the 'land of Hugh'. Richer saw him as 'duke of the Gauls', while Dudo called him simply 'the chief man of the whole kingdom'.[57] The king named him duke of the Franks. Hugh the Great was the first Robertian to be called Capet, said to relate to the monastic hood he wore (*chape* or *cappa*) as a lay abbot.

Hugh the Great did not seek the throne, according to Richer because he did not want to suffer his father's fate – no empty comment in the period.[58] Holding the throne was no great benefit to a prince with little authority beyond his principality. By becoming king, he took on troubles virtually beyond his power to deal with. The reigns of King Odo, King Robert I, and King Ralph I, hardly encouraged emulation. According to Richer, no great fan of the Robertians, Hugh was acting on the evidence of what had happened to his father, Robert I, who 'died on account of his arrogance' – that is for daring to become king.

In the event Hugh the Great initiated and supported the move to recall his nephew, the 15-year-old Louis, from exile in Aethelstan's England. Hugh realized that he himself could not expect support as king from other princes. Rival candidates were Hugh the Black of Burgundy brother of Ralph I, and Herbert II of Vermandois. The magnates of West Francia, including William count of Poitiers and Raymond count of Toulouse, could not agree on any one of their number to succeed. Hugh the Great's decision was to settle for the Carolingian. He sent for Louis and met him at Boulogne, where he swore fidelity. Louis was anointed and crowned at Laon on 19 June 936 by Artaud archbishop of Reims. Hugh accompanied Louis IV to Burgundy, when they besieged Langres whose garrison fled in the night. Hugh was rewarded with authority over northern Burgundy. Later Hugh received the title of duke of the Franks, that is, over Lesser France with command in the west. It was a position created by the king and seen as 'viceregal authority'.[59]

The late Carolingians have been called weak and useless. They are still seen as weak, essentially because they lacked possessions and wealth. As individuals, however, they were men of strength, ambition and determination. Modern historians have recognized their qualities and stressed that they were not puppets. In the tenth century 'not one of them was an effete or useless ruler'.[60]

Louis IV had experienced a difficult early life, with the long exile in England. At one point, even as king, Dudo says he was no more than a page in the household of William Longsword duke of Normandy. Louis was defeated by the Vikings and captured by them after the bit slipped on his horse. Richer says Louis accused Hugh of being behind this capture. Louis escaped and was captured again, finally saved from the Normans by Hugh the Great and able to regain some sort of security with help from the Ottonians. Henry the Fowler had died on 2 July 936 so that the red-bearded Otto I the Great came to the East Frankish throne in the same year as Louis IV became king in the west. Otto was in no position to intervene in the west, having to establish his own position, facing rebellion by his brother Henry duke of Saxony. There were also considerable threats from the east and Otto would become 'the Great' for his victories over Magyars and Slavs at the Lechfeld near Augsburg, and on the Recknitz. Otto was further diverted by imperial ambitions in Italy. He was crowned emperor in Rome on 2 February 962 but became embroiled in Italian and papal politics including the deposition in 963 of John XII, the very pope who had crowned him.[61] This allowed Louis IV a breathing space.

There can be no doubt that Louis still had to face considerable problems with no great resources. He proved a surprisingly tough king, keen to develop his position, willing to seek aid from Germany, and trying to balance his own lords by dividing them against each other. Louis demanded, and in the end received, homage from his leading magnates including Hugh the Great, Herbert of Vermandois, Hugh the Black, William Longsword, William Towhead, and Raymond Pons. Given his weak base position he did extremely well.

One dilemma for all the late Carolingians was how to juggle their powerful princes and retain power. They had two options – to side with the most powerful against the rest, or to form an alliance against the most powerful. Most often that powerful figure was the leading Robertian, as it was for Louis IV with Hugh the Great. Hugh had used his power to bring Louis to the throne, but Louis had no wish to be a puppet king. His case compared with that of all the late Carolingians, who usually ended by opposing the Robertians.

For Louis IV the alliance with the Robertian Hugh lasted only a year. According to Richer, Louis recognized that Hugh had supported his accession but complained that he had left him nothing but Laon.[62] From 937 Louis allied with Hugh the Black of Burgundy, thus 'freeing himself'.[63] Hugh the Black could have sought the throne in 936 but, once that opportunity was lost, his main concern was the growing threat of Hugh the Great to Burgundy. Louis also sought alliance with William Longsword of Normandy. Hugh the Great thus found it necessary to reorganize against the new royal coalition; he allied with Herbert II of Vermandois and came to terms with Otto the Great. After the death of his second wife, Eadhild sister of Aethelstan of England, Hugh the Great in 938 married Otto I's sister Hadwige. It is worth noting the Robertian copied the Carolingians with marital links to England and East Francia. Hugh now moved against Laon, which Louis had taken in 938, and now defended successfully.

Louis IV tried to improve his power base. His wanted to recover Reims and Laon, and to regain Lotharingia. This produced the constant dilemma. The Carolingians of West Francia needed a landed power base, and Lotharingia offered their best chance. But in seeking to win Lotharingia they antagonized the Ottonians, their best hope for powerful allies against the nobles. It was a round-about from which the late Carolingians could not escape with Lotharingia was the on the border between East and West Francia. Louis IV met Otto the Great in Lotharingia four times between 942 and 965.[64] Louis moved into Lotharingia in 938 in alliance with its duke, Gilbert, who had won Lotharingia in alliance with Henry of Saxony a rebel against Otto. Gilbert offered to recognize Louis IV as lord but was defeated by Otto I, who invaded Lotharingia in 939. When

Otto left, Gilbert rebelled again but was surprised by two Ottonian counts and drowned trying to escape over a river on horseback, leaving Otto in control of Lotharingia.

Herbert II of Vermandois and Hugh the Great made their move. They attacked Reims in 940, driving out Archbishop Artaud, and restoring Herbert's son. Hugh had been made archbishop as a child of four and thrown out in favour of Artaud, but he was now 20 and more acceptable. Louis IV needed new allies and turned to Otto I, increasingly influential in West Francia. Otto's sisters had married Louis IV and Hugh the Great. In 941 Hugh the Great finally defeated Louis, who was forced to take refuge with Charles Constantine in Vienne. Attempts to make Lotharingia the power base had the unfortunate result of drawing Louis' enemies together in opposition – West Frankish nobles, Ottonians and pro-Ottonian bishops. Louis had sought to escape the domination of Hugh the Great, now he felt similarly uncomfortable with Otto I. Louis therefore built a new coalition. Otto resolved the situation, temporarily, by joining Herbert and Hugh the Great. He invaded Louis' lands in 942 and captured Attigny, the old Carolingian base. Louis married Gilbert's widow, Gerberga, who was also Otto I's sister. Otto at first refused to recognize the marriage, fearing hostile intent, but in time they were reconciled. Through Otto, Louis was reconciled with Hugh the Great and Herbert at Visé in 942.

Another factor in late Carolingian politics was the lifespan of major players. Virtually every death of a king or prince brought crisis, and serious vulnerability for the realm or principality until a successor became established. In 942 William Longsword of Normandy was murdered by men of Arnulf of Flanders. At a conference between them, William was called back from the river to the bank, where he went carrying an oar, only to have his head sliced off by a sword. The deaths of William Longsword in 942 and Herbert II of Vermandois in 943, modified the situation – removing these major rulers from the chessboard of power in West Francia. Both were succeeded by minors. Louis IV had his illegitimate half-brother Rorico (bastard of Charles the Simple) elected bishop of Laon, and acquired the allegiance of the archbishop of Reims – the two traditional supports for the late Carolingians.

An unexpected event occurred in 944 when Louis IV was captured by the Vikings near Rouen. Perhaps unwisely, having offered Bayeux to Hugh the Great, Louis made terms with the Normans and withdrew the offer. Hugh then forced Louis to retreat. The Normans turned against the king and Louis was captured by the Vikings. Louis' rescuer was none other than Hugh the Great – but only to hand him over to his own vassal, Theobald count of Chartres. Hugh later yielded to pressure from the church, and ordered Louis' release – at a price – the surrender of Laon. Louis blamed Hugh the Great for his capture by the 'pirates' and if there is any truth in this, Hugh is less of a spotless hero than hitherto believed.[65]

In 946 Louis recovered Laon and Reims with the support of his father-in-law Otto. Archbishop Hugh fled to safety and Artaud was restored. Hugh the

Great remained a thorn in Louis' side. He besieged Reims again in 947 and 948 though he had to abandon the attempt. He laid waste the area around, with his 'thugs' carrying out 'disgraceful deeds'.[66] A number of magnates went over to Louis. Twice Hugh was summoned to a church council (at Verdun in 947 and Mouzon in 948) and twice failed to attend. He was condemned in his absence and excommunicated. A council was called at Ingelheim in 948. The reasons for Hugh's suspicions are clear. The 32 bishops attending were all from Germany and Lotharingia – only two came from West Francia and they were from Reims and Laon. Archbishop Hugh of Vermandois had been replaced for a second time by Artaud in 946. The council at Ingelheim ordered that Hugh should be deposed and excommunicated, and Archbishop Artaud restored. The conflict between the rival archbishops was finally settled. Artaud kept the see to his death in 961, though Hugh continued in vain to press his claim until his own death in 962. The council of Ingelheim also repeated Hugh the Great's excommunication.

Louis' position was improved by the decisions at Ingelheim, influenced by the presence there of Otto I. Even Hugh the Great felt obliged to yield to this coalition, though his immediate response was to burn Soissons and attack Reims. A council at Trier repeated the excommunication. Hugh finally submitted, though there was no likelihood of his being militarily defeated. The Robertians had always worked with the church, and benefited as a result. Hugh's backing down was diplomatic. Louis IV was not the only one who could manipulate the powers of the day in his own favour. Hugh made peace with the church and with his brother-in-law Otto.

By 950 Hugh controlled much of West Francia but then submitted and recognized Louis as his lord. In 953 Hugh repeated this recognition. By agreement, Hugh was to hold Laon while the king retained its citadel; Louis was to hold Reims. It had been a long and difficult struggle, but Louis had held his corner against powerful rivals and enemies. Unlike many of his predecessors, Louis IV tried to hold on to what he had. He made only two acts of donation. Louis also organized the succession of his son Lothar, and thus the continuation of Carolingian rule.

Louis IV's reign came to a sudden end. Approaching the River Aisne, he spotted a wolf and gave chase. His horse stumbled and Louis fell awkwardly. He was taken to Reims where his body seemed to inflate. He died on 9 September 954 and was buried in St-Remy. He had been king for 18 years but was still only 33.

LOTHAR KING OF WEST FRANCIA (954–86)

Lothar king of West Francia, the son of Louis IV, was 13 in 954. His mother Gerberga worked energetically to ensure his succession, contacting her brothers Otto I and Bruno archbishop of Köln, as well as her brother-in-law Hugh the Great. Bruno acted virtually as a regent for Louis, until his death in 965, but Lothar gained the crown because Hugh the Great again preferred to stand down in favour of a Carolingian. Archbishop Artaud crowned and anointed Lothar in Reims.

Lothar's reign is poorly covered by contemporary sources. What survives are the chronicle of Richer from 980, and the letters of Gerbert (later Sylvester II) – both hostile to the king. Richer was a monk at St-Remy in Reims, where Lothar was seen as a threat. Gerbert was politically involved, his allegiance switching from the Ottonians to the Robertians as best suited his career – though his main attachment was to the former.

Hugh the Great accompanied Lothar to Laon, parading him through Paris, Orléans, Chartres, Tours, Blois and Aquitaine – in much the way he had toured with Louis IV. Hugh was rewarded for his support. On the death without heir of Gilbert of Burgundy in 956, Hugh was named duke of Burgundy and Aquitaine. Hugh's son Otto-Henry married the heiress of Gilbert duke of Burgundy.[67] Hugh the Great's domination did not last long; the great Robertian died at Dourdan in June 956, possibly of plague. He was buried at St-Denis. He left three sons: Hugh Capet, Odo and Otto-Henry, all minors in 956 and taken under the protection of Richard I of Normandy. Bruno archbishop of Köln and duke of Lotharingia was the brother of Otto I and of Hugh the Great's wife. He was uncle to the three boys, and gave them protection.

With Hugh the Great gone, Bruno's influence increased. Hugh Capet, Hugh the Great's oldest son, was born in c.940. He eventually inherited his father's position, including power over Paris, Senlis, Orléans and Dreux and the great lay abbacies. In time Hugh Capet would prove equal to the demands of his inheritance. Early on, however, his future was uncertain and he struggled to maintain his position. The king prolonged his minority and Richard I of Normandy refused to recognize his overlordship. Bruno encouraged Lothar to take Burgundy and pass the duchy to Hugh Capet's brother Odo. When Odo died in 965, the younger brother Otto-Henry, previously destined for the church, succeeded in Burgundy.

There were rifts between Hugh Capet's vassal counts and Richard I of Normandy. Odo I of Blois married Lothar's niece Bertha, and stayed loyal to the king. Count Arnulf of Flanders, a man of 'viperish guile' and 'devilish deceit', recognized Lothar and was rewarded with the title of marquis (*marchio*).[68] In 965 Arnulf died, as did Archbishop Bruno, and Lothar took over Flanders. Lothar also took an interest in Aquitaine. In 982 he married his son Louis (V) to Adelaide, daughter of Fulk II of Anjou. Lothar proclaimed the couple king and queen of Aquitaine. Adelaide was 15 years older than Louis; the marriage failed, and with it Lothar's hopes in Aquitaine. Adelaide fled to William I count of Arles, whom she married.

Lothar's main hopes were, like those of all the late Carolingians, focused on Lotharingia. In 965 Lothar married Otto's step-daughter Emma of Italy. The marriage was successful and Emma's mother, Empress Adelaide, proved a useful support. However, Lothar's efforts in Lotharingia, as before, antagonized the Ottonians. Through Bruno it was East rather than West Frankish influence that gained a hold in Lotharingia, but Bruno died in 965, Gerberga in 969, and Otto the Great on 7 May 973. Otto was succeeded by his 18-year-old son Otto II, associated in rule as king since 961 and emperor since 967.

Otto II was well educated but less able than his father. In the difficult period that followed, Lothar strengthened his position in Lotharingia. In 969 Adalbero, son of the count of Verdun, was elected archbishop of Reims. Gerbert of Aurillac was a protégé of Adalbero, and was brought in to head the school at Reims. He proved to be another major political player. Adalbero and Gerbert made a formidable political team. Otto II's response to Lothar's attempts to regain power in Lotharingia was to encourage opposition to him. Lothar made a new expedition there in 978, accompanied by Hugh Capet, who was not enthusiastic. Lothar crossed the Meuse and Otto fled. Lothar entered Aachen and sacked the old imperial palace of Charlemagne. The West Franks pillaged the city and turned the direction of the bronze eagle of Charlemagne to face east rather than west. Lothar withdrew and Otto II sought revenge. He raided the west later in the year, taking Laon and firing the palaces at Attigny, Soissons and Compiègne.

Otto II's raid was more damaging than West Frankish chroniclers cared to admit, since it demonstrated the limitations of Lothar's recovery. Charles of Lower Lorraine had transferred his allegiance to Otto and handed Laon to him. Through Otto, Charles was proclaimed king of the West Franks, though he was never able to make it good and stalemate was soon reached again. Lothar struggled to make gains in Lotharingia, but his position in the west was reasonably secure. Otto II continued his raid towards Paris, which he viewed from the bank of the Seine, camping at Montmartre. Lothar fled to Étampes, but Otto's advance was blocked by Hugh Capet. Otto burned the region for three days and then abandoned the raid. During the retreat his rearguard was attacked by Lothar and defeated crossing the Aisne near Soissons. Lothar recovered Laon and prevented Charles of Lower Lorraine from establishing his claim to be king.

With the agreement of Hugh Capet, Lothar had his 13-year-old son Louis associated in the crown at Compiègne in 978, thus protecting the Carolingian succession. In 980 peace was agreed with Otto II at Margut-sur-Chiers. Lothar did this without consulting Hugh, who was annoyed more by the lack of consultation than by the outcome. Hugh complained that the king had forgotten his previous aid. In any case, the agreement simply underlined Lothar's weakness; he was reluctantly forced to abandon Lotharingia to Otto II.

Worryingly for the king, his policies followed that late Carolingian course and antagonized the leading Robertian, Hugh Capet. In c.980 Hugh transferred the relics of Saint Valery to St-Valery at Amiens, carrying them on his shoulders. It was said the saint appeared in a vision and promised his family the crown for seven generations. The Robertian reputation for piety and support for the church was beginning to pay off (though the story would have repercussions after seven generations). Hugh kept up the tradition of family piety, making pilgrimages, for example to the tomb of St Maïeul.

Hugh Capet built an alliance against the king. His sister, Emma's first husband, the duke of Upper Lorraine, had died and Hugh arranged a new marriage to Richard I of Normandy. Hugh himself married Adelaide, daughter of William III Towhead count of Poitiers, in c.970; her brother was Count William IV. Hugh and

Adelaide's son Robert (the Pious) was born in 972. Hugh Capet was concerned by Lothar's covert dealing with Otto II, which ignored his own position as leading counsellor. He feared what might have been agreed in secret. Hugh arranged his own meeting with Otto in Rome. An interesting episode occurred at the meeting when Otto II left his sword on a chair, and asked Hugh Capet to pass it to him. Hugh was about to do so when his companion Arnulf bishop of Orléans forestalled him, snatching up the sword and passing it to Otto. The point was that handing the sword could have been construed as making him Otto's vassal. Knowing Otto's stress on making Charles of Lower Lorraine a vassal encourages belief in the tale. However, Otto did not seem upset by the failure of his trick. He was openly reconciled with Hugh and now it was Lothar's turn to feel suspicious and worried.

Encouraged by Queen Emma, Lothar decided to attack Hugh Capet. He tried to have Hugh arrested during his return from Italy, while he raided Hugh's territory. Hugh evaded capture dressed as a servant with the baggage – though there was a crisis in a hostel when the game was given away by the manner in which the other servants treated him. Hugh, however, reached home safely. Lothar had attacked Neustria, anticipating that Hugh would be captured. Hugh on return recovered his lands, and peace was agreed – but there was no trust.

Lothar, again without consulting Hugh, married his son Louis to Adelaide widow of Stephen count of Gévaudan.[69] It was an attempt to increase power in Burgundy but failed. Adelaide was twice the age of her new husband and they 'hardly knew conjugal love' – in fact they probably never knew it at all.[70] The couple did not get on; they could not stand to be in the same room together, and slept in different hostelries. They did not speak to each other except in public, and then briefly. Glaber thought the lady tricked Louis into taking her home and then left him. She eloped with William count of Arles, which Richer saw as 'public adultery'. Louis quickly sought a divorce.

Otto II of East Francia was defeated in 982 by a combination of Byzantines and Saracens, and almost captured. He fled to Verona and then Rome, where he became seriously ill. The trouble was something worse than the indigestion Richer suggested (probably malaria), since on 7 December 983 Otto died in Rome at the age of 28. His son, who became Otto III, was only three. East Francia's problems were now multiplied by minority rule. The German court was dominated by two royal widows: Adelaide the former wife of Otto I, and Theophano the Byzantine wife of Otto II, daughter of Emperor Romanus II. Theophano remained regent for Otto III until her death in 991. Lothar of West Francia offered to protect the young Otto III but took the opportunity to enter Lotharingia in 983. Archbishop Adalbero's influence seemed stronger but he favoured an alliance with the Ottonians.

Lothar upset his friends by the attack on Lotharingia. He allied with Henry the Quarreler of Bavaria against the Ottonians. Henry was crowned as king of the East Franks. The Vermandois group, hostile to Adalbero, joined Lothar's coalition. Hugh Capet ignored the summons to assist Lothar – though two of his major vassals turned up. Lothar besieged Verdun for eight days. Lothar was wounded in the foot but Verdun surrendered and Lothar handed the city to his queen. Adalbero's brother, Count Godfrey, was imprisoned – henceforward known as Godfrey the Captive. Lothar kept Verdun for the rest of his life. Lothar went on to attack Liège and Cambrai, held by allies of Archbishop Adalbero, underlining the break with that prelate, whose brother was now his prisoner. Lothar accused Adalbero of treason for dealing with the Ottonians.[71] Lothar called an assembly at Compiègne in May 985 to try the archbishop for treachery. Hugh Capet decided the issue by arriving with an armed force to rescue Adalbero and disperse the assembly. Gerbert, echoing former opinions, wrote that Lothar was 'king in name only, Hugh is the real master'. Then Lothar fell ill at Laon. He lost his voice and shook with fever, while his stomach felt like fire. He died on 2 March 986, aged 44, and was buried at Reims. Again an early death proved a significant turning point. The chronicler of St-Maixent claimed that Lothar was 'poisoned by the queen, his adulterous spouse', but it was unlikely to be true.[72] Lothar had tried to build a solid Carolingian base, though without great success. He ended by antagonizing almost every major figure in his realm, as well as the Ottonians who had often propped up the Carolingians in the west.

THE END OF CAROLINGIAN RULE

LOUIS V (986–87)

In the view of Bordonove, when Lothar was buried at St-Remy, 'it was the Carolingian dynasty that was buried'.[73] Yet Lothar was succeeded by his son Louis V, who had been associated in rule since 978 and consecrated in 979. There was no inevitability about subsequent events. Glaber's comment, that Louis succeeded 'by hereditary right', shows how contemporaries viewed Carolingian and non-Carolingian rulers.[74] Some historians have labelled Louis as 'fainéant' (weak) – seeking a comparison with the late Merovingians.[75]

Louis V did not live long enough to make any great mark on events, so broad condemnation seems unfair. Nevertheless, during his short reign, he made three major errors – or rather continued to abide by errors made by his predecessor. These policies brought the final downfall of the Carolingians. Firstly the last Carolingian kings antagonized their greatest subject, the Robertian Hugh Capet. Secondly they lost the support of their main external prop, the Ottonians of Germany. Finally, they attacked and antagonized their most important ecclesiastical prop, the archbishop of Reims. To be fair, Louis did attempt to make some changes to these policies, but with little success.

Louis V was old enough to rule, but was he wise enough? His father's counsellors allowed him to continue as king despite their dissatisfaction with his father. Hugh Capet followed family tradition in supporting the Carolingian. Bordonove thinks that Hugh's chief merit was in knowing 'how to wait', but it is unlikely he anticipated becoming king, even in 986.[76] Louis made attempts to be reconciled with Hugh, who had allowed him to take the throne. Louis' mother

Emma also tried to help by making terms with the Ottonians.

The policy that Louis V did continue was hostility to Adalbero of Reims. The attitude of Hugh Capet here is puzzling. Was he now a loyal man of the king, or was he still the friend of Adalbero? Louis, apparently with Hugh's backing, besieged Reims. He summoned a new assembly at Compiègne for 987 to repeat the charge of treason against the archbishop. Hugh Capet had probably assured Adalbero of support, but there was another, if familiar, twist in the tale. The situation changed abruptly with Louis V's premature death on 22 May 987. He was hunting near Senlis when he fell. He bled from nose and mouth, suffered palpitations, and died aged only 20. The St-Maixent chronicler, persistent in his accusations, suggested another murder – this time by poisoned drink, and again unlikely.[77] Conspiracy theorists have nothing on medieval monastic chroniclers! Louis V was buried at Compiègne, the last Carolingian king.

Hugh Capet took command of the assembly and declared Adalbero acquitted. Adalbero then declared support for Hugh as king. Only the Vermandois group expressed opposition. A new assembly was summoned to Senlis to elect the king of West Francia. Hugh had only one major rival in Charles of Lower Lorraine, the last surviving Carolingian claimant. Charles throughout his life had been an outsider. He made few friends in West Francia, and few trusted him. In 980 when he had defended Cambrai after the bishop's death, Charles had taken his wife into the bishop's bed – an arrogant move not designed to win ecclesiastical favour, or any other much at that time. Charles supported Otto II against Lothar, then Lothar against Otto III so that now he lacked Ottonian backing. Charles had claimed that Queen Emma was an adulteress, and been exiled from West Francia, returning to the Ottonians. However in 987 the Ottonians had little reason to support his claim in West Francia; they could not trust him, and were not keen to set up a Carolingian rival. Charles wrote to Archbishop Adalbero, stating his hereditary claim, but he had hardly helped himself by supporting Adalbero's prosecution. Charles' flexible loyalties returned to haunt him now.

Archbishop Adalbero made his own views clear in a speech that damned the Carolingian. Charles, he said, was a troublemaker, a 'man without honour, without faith, without character'. Charles had married beneath him, the daughter of a lesser vassal, not a suitable match for a monarch.[78] The archbishop suggested that, under Charles, the country would not do well and if the West Frankish nobles wanted the country to prosper they should crown 'the illustrious duke of the Franks'.[79] The throne, Adalbero declared, did not depend on hereditary right – which was the basis of Charles' claim. Hugh, he believed, was a more suitable candidate. His support of the church, and of Cluniac reform, stood him in good stead. So did his family's position as defenders of Christian Francia against the Vikings. However, the St-Maixent chronicler's summary is shrewd, concluding it was not so much that Hugh was chosen as that Charles was 'rejected'.[80] Hugh Capet was elected king of the West Franks at Senlis. On 1 June 987, he was crowned at Noyon, and on 3 July consecrated at Reims. Thus began the Capetian era in West Francia, perhaps we might now say of France.

3

The new principalities, 800–1000

By the time the 'illustrious' duke of the Franks Hugh Capet came to the throne in 987, West Francia was a patchwork of principalities, large territorial units which recognized the monarchy (at least in theory), but were becoming increasingly independent.[1] The early Capetian monarchs therefore had limited authority over much of geographical France.

In order better to understand the rise of the Robertian prince to kingship, the status of the early Capetians, and the development of the French realm, it will be useful to examine the formation and nature of the principalities of West Francia. Before 987 one should still think in terms of the Carolingian Empire and its divisions rather than of national states like 'France'. Divisions were emerging but they were not yet permanent. What was happening in West Francia was occurring in East Francia, and in parts of the Carolingian Empire outside Francia proper, including Aquitaine, the Spanish March and Italy.

There is considerable variation in how these units were made up and how they operated. By the late ninth century six separate kingdoms had emerged, though still under the umbrella of the old empire. We shall concentrate on the units that became West Francia and later France. There was no single contemporary name for a unit or a ruler of a unit – not all were kingdoms. The term 'prince' (*princeps*) was used at times, and is a convenient term for us to employ. The only way to understand the situation is to view each principality separately.

Ironically as Carolingian kingship declined and collapsed, West Francia was recovering and prospering. The ninth century had seen economic disruption from the attacks by Saracens, Magyars and especially Vikings. Internal family divisions did not help the defence against these threats. However, in the meantime, certain families were accumulating lands – including the kings – and reaping the profits of the produce from those lands. Trade was also on the increase and towns were growing. By the 10th century the Carolingians had lost demesne land and so benefited less than they might have done from the economic growth. However, it is clear that they did not lose as much as was once thought – their grants were not chiefly of basic demesne. They also benefited indirectly through those lords who were loyal. The princes were in much the same situation as the kings, having to make grants to lesser men in return for loyalty. There is little doubt that magnates who held great cities like Paris, Orléans, Rouen, or Toulouse, gained as a result. The main threat to their prosperity came not from the crown (provided they were loyal) but from their own vassals – counts, viscounts, castellans, and lesser lords – who were seeking and sometimes obtaining the same independence from the prince that the prince was seeking from the crown. The same period saw the emergence of castles, not all belonging to royalty or great nobles. Some regions remained fragmented; some, like Berry, had virtually no public authority at all by the 10th century.[2]

In the period before 987, power moved from central royal authority to the princes. This can be exaggerated, since the Carolingian empire had been frequently divided and re-divided – in other words decentralization was not new. What now seems inevitable did not seem so then. The concept of a united empire lasted well after the appearance of principalities, and did not altogether disappear. Carolingian divisions of the empire are often seen as temporary arrangements, of sharing between the sons of a deceased ruler, but the divisions tended to follow similar traditional lines that helped form more permanent units. There was repeated recognition of regions with an identity – such as Neustria/West Francia, Austrasia/East Francia, Aquitaine, or Italy. This was apart from the ethnic divisions into, for example, the territory of Franks, Lombards, Aquitainians, Bavarians, Frisians, or Saxons. The lines of division were frequently defined as duchies, marches or subkingdoms. Some magnates accumulated greater territories and greater power. This often happened when kings appointed commanders to frontiers regions – the marquises and dukes. As Glaber saw it, writing of Normandy and Burgundy, 'these dukes surpassed all men in military might'.[3] But those who called themselves 'dukes' were rarely named as such by kings in the first place – Hugh the Great was an exception. Royal charters normally used other titles for their princes.

The principalities formed in different ways, and at different times, but the effect by 987 was a realm where the king held lands that roughly equated to a principality, and had little direct power in the other principalities. The change from the early Carolingian period has been exaggerated, but there was gradual movement in this direction. The royal 'principality' was on a level with other territorial principalities, together forming a kind of jigsaw of the realm. By 987 the jigsaw piece held by the Carolingian monarch had become smaller. The Carolingian ruler was about to be replaced by a prince who held a larger jigsaw piece. It must be said that through most of the period the princes were members of the Carolingian family – but this was about to change. One advantage for the new Capetian or Robertian king was that he held a major principality, including Paris, a major source of wealth, and was in some ways in a better position than the very late Carolingian kings. The metaphor of a jigsaw is of some value in viewing early medieval France and with the principalities France did become a sort of jigsaw, as described, but in the pre-Capetian period the situation was more fluid than that analogy suggests, perhaps more like floating patches that were forever moving and interchanging, and which depended on the personal power of individual princes rather than on precisely defined territorial units.

A second advantage for the new Capetian rulers was that the crown retained

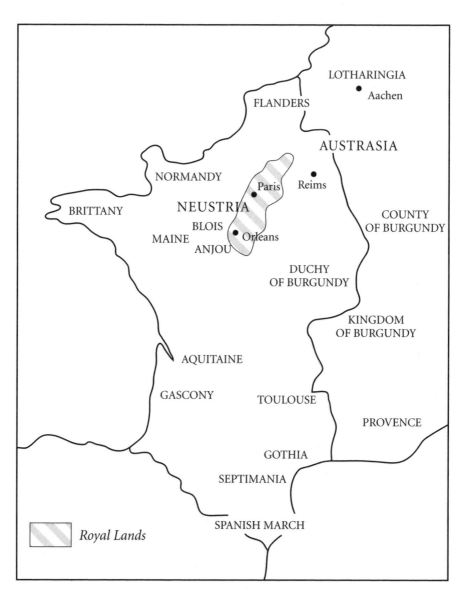

Western Europe in 987

theoretical superiority over the princes. The king was consecrated and had religious or even sacred attributes and a special relationship with the Frankish church. The Robertians brought their own contribution to this position, having carefully presented themselves over generations as protectors of the church, as well as being lay abbots and patrons of powerful abbeys. However much it might be ignored, the king had claims over the princes that they could not have over him – claims including loyalty and military support.

THE EMERGENCE OF PRINCIPALITIES

The relationship between king and princes was to play a major part in the history of the Capetians. Carolingian West Francia moved towards less centralized government, with stronger rulers in the component regions. For the most part those components remained in Carolingian hands – under different branches of the family. But, with the Carolingian family suddenly almost dying out, the princes chose one of themselves, Odo, to rule in place of the Carolingian king in West Francia. The throne had not been finally lost by the Carolingians, and shuffled backwards and forwards between Carolingians and princes. In 987 it went again to a prince, Hugh Capet – but this time it was permanent. The fact that Hugh Capet was a prince meant that the other princes saw him as one of their own, and made it more difficult for him to assume superiority. Early Capetian kings had difficulty in imposing their power outside their own principality – the other princes had anticipated a system where the king would be mainly interested in his own principality, and would have less power over them. In any case, at first the main problem for the Capetian king was to retain and enhance control over his own principality.

We may question the strength of the Carolingian Empire itself and the degree of centralization within it. The appointments that Charlemagne and his successors made, demonstrate limits on their powers in the localities. Charlemagne's attempt at centralization had a short lifespan. His agents, notably the *missi dominici*, became increasingly local rather than central figures, and from the death of Charles the Bald, almost disappeared altogether – though we still find at least one under Charles the Fat.[4] After that, with the division of the empire, the princes became more firmly ensconced. It became ever more difficult for kings to intervene in the principalities. For example, control of church appointments – a sign of where power really resided – was often assumed by the local prince. Control of the royal fisc in the principalities was taken over by the princes and with it rights that had been royal.

Even through the late Carolingian and early Capetian period, though, there was some royal intervention outside the demesne. Dhondt saw the change from empire to principalities as inevitable because the empire had become 'an anachronism', but this seems too determinist. Dhondt thought the change sudden, a revolution within 12 years, but in fact the development was far more prolonged. Dhondt also paints too catastrophic a picture of the rise and fall of kingship

– it never fell into complete disrepute; kings never altogether lacked power in their realms.

It must be agreed that there was a major change, resulting in a new structure for much of Europe. There emerged principalities, a dozen or more major units within East and West Francia. These gradually cohered into a pattern, the basis of kingdoms in France and Germany. This could not have happened had the cohering parts not acknowledged some overall power – if not the emperor then a king. West Frankish kings tended to appoint Franks to rule for them in the localities, especially Franks from the old Carolingian base of Austrasia – the Robertians in Neustria, the Bernards and Williams in Aquitaine. Thus the ethnic elements in the principalities – Norman, Flemish, Breton – were brought within a broader Frankish kingdom rather than becoming separate ethnic states. Most of the princely dynasties originated from Frankish Carolingians rather than local families. They usually began as royal representatives, though they increasingly sought independent rule. They took over royal lands, revenue and abbeys. One effect was that the princely dynasties became increasingly linked in their interests with the principalities rather than with royal concerns.

THE ROBERTIAN AND ROYAL PRINCIPALITY (NEUSTRIA)

The base of the royal principality in West Francia was what we have called Lesser France, around the Seine and the Oise, the land of the Franks between the Escaut and the Loire. The Île-de-France had been the last bastion of Roman Gaul. In the age of saints, such as Germain and Geneviève, it maintained Christianity during 'the swansong of Roman Gaul'.[5] Lesser France became the base of the new Frankish kingdom under the Merovingian kings from the sixth century, when the term Neustria came into common use. Neustria was the western Gallo-Roman region, in contrast to eastern and Germanic Austrasia. The great abbeys near Paris of St-Denis, St-Germain and Ste-Geneviève were founded by the new kings. Under the early Carolingians Neustria and Paris became less significant than Austrasia and Aachen, as a result of Carolingian concern with enemies to the east, but this was reversed under the late Carolingians and the dukes of the Franks.

From the late 10th century Lesser France, around Paris, became the base of the new Capetian kings, a reduced successor to ancient Neustria. It tended to split into two, Flanders separating off in the north. The royal principality was based on the two major cities of Paris and Orléans, smaller than Aquitaine or Burgundy but with considerable potential. Although Franks formed the basic population of the Robertian duchy, the principality was more an 'artificial creation of royalty' than an ethnic unit.[6] The ruler went under various guises through the period to 1000 – king, count, marquis of the Breton March, count of Paris, duke of the Franks, and eventually again king. Charles the Bald created it as a unit under the king, developing a lordship around Maine and Anjou as a frontier region against Bretons and Vikings. Robert the Strong, founder of the Robertians, appeared in historical records in 852 as a count, receiving lay abbacies from Charles the

Bald. He rebelled but was reconciled, given command against the Vikings, and named marquis of the Breton March. This gave him authority over the counties of Anjou, Touraine and Blois. The Breton March became part of the principality of Neustria.

After Robert the Strong's death, the Breton March was passed by the king to Hugh the Abbot. The Robertian family had made an impact on the region but their grasp was not yet hereditary. Only after the death of Hugh the Abbot did it return to Robert's son Odo as count of Paris. He led the defence of Paris during the Viking siege of 885–86. Paris then consisted of the fortified Seine islands, notably the Île-de-la-Cité, the original centre for administration of Roman Paris (Lutetia), plus settlements on either bank. The Vikings departed after an agreement with the emperor, Charles the Fat, who paid tribute and let them move on to Burgundy. They had to drag their ships overland to by-pass Paris, having been refused entry to the city or leave to pass the fortified bridge on the Seine. Having established himself as a successful warrior in the stamp of his father, Odo became the first non-Carolingian and the first Robertian king of West Francia in 888 after the death of Charles the Fat.

When the Carolingian Charles the Simple succeeded Odo as king, he appointed Odo's brother Robert as duke of Neustria in compensation.[7] Robert had power over the area between the Loire, the Seine, Burgundy and the sea. One gap in Robertian power was the establishment of Viking Normandy. Robert sought Norman acknowledgement of his overlordship, but without success. The Robertians supported the late Carolingian kings and were rewarded for it. Then in 922 Odo's brother Robert I was elected as king, though he lived only another year.

Robert's son, Hugh the Great, 'second to the king throughout the realm' (according to Louis IV), supported the Carolingians.[8] Ralph I (923–36) was related to the Robertian family through marriage to Robert I's daughter but Hugh sponsored the accession of the Carolingian, Louis IV, and accompanied him on a tour of his new realm, visiting the cities of his own lands in Neustria – Paris, Orléans, Chartres, Tours and Blois – before moving on to Aquitaine. Having given support to Louis IV, Hugh was made duke of the Franks in 943, but then came into conflict with that king.

Within four years of Hugh the Great's death in 965, his son Hugh Capet succeeded to the duchy. As a duchy Neustria only lasted until Hugh Capet became king (987–996); from then on it was the base of royal power. Hugh Capet's minority, however, had allowed the counties subordinate to the duke of the Franks – Anjou, Tours and Blois – to become more independent. Blois and Anjou developed into new principalities, though Hugh Capet was generally able to ally with one (usually Anjou) against the other. The duchy of Neustria was no more.

The Robertians, as counts of Paris or dukes of France, often had authority over even broader regions – for example as commanders of the Breton March against the Vikings. By 987 they could claim lordship over northern West Francia apart from Flanders, and had interests in the south. Their vassals included the counts of Chartres/Blois/Champagne, Anjou, Maine, and the Touraine. The power of the Robertians should not be exaggerated, since the authority of many of their vassals within their own counties and viscounties was becoming stronger, but the overlordship, however theoretical, retained significance. The Robertians fought their corner and, as Capetian kings, gained new interests in the Carolingian counties of the Vendômois, the Gâtinais, and Valois. They now possessed the Carolingian palaces at Attigny, Compiègne and Verberie. The collection of territories over which the Robertians claimed authority was the basis of their power. As Favier put it, one of the principalities had 'given birth to a new royalty'.[9]

One factor that helped the Robertians become kings, and as kings to rise above other princes, was their relation with the Frankish church. They held the episcopal counties of Reims, Laon, Beauvais, Sens and Châlons. Reims was the foremost of ten metropolitan sees in West Francia, commanding ten bishoprics. The Robertians were also lay abbots of major monasteries, including St-Denis, the two St-Germains in Paris, St-Martin at Tours, and Fleury. These monastic interests also spread Robertian power beyond their demesne and became an important means for expansion.

NORMANDY

Let us now look at the other principalities. The princes were roughly on a level with the Robertian governors of Neustria. Each principality could be a prop to the monarchy, or a threat. The Robertians had, for a time, a claim over Normandy. Hugh the Great played an important part in the formation of the Viking-ruled area around Rouen as a political unit – to become a 'fabricated duchy'.[10] In 911 Charles the Simple recognized Rollo, the Viking leader, as holding the region around Rouen. Dudo of St-Quentin exaggerated the event, as he did much else, in favour of the Norman rulers. He claimed, falsely, that Rollo had 'overrun the whole of Francia'. He exaggerated the lack of deference of the Normans, and depicted Rollo refusing to kiss the king's foot while one of his men seized the king's foot and tipped him over. In 911, Rollo had just been defeated by the Franks near Auxerre, so it was Charles who made the agreement from strength. Rollo had to promise to convert and to defend the Frankish kingdom against further Viking incursions.

Dudo also exaggerated the extent of the lands granted to Rollo, claiming not only the area around Rouen but the whole of Normandy and Brittany.[11] The creation of the core of Normandy, however, meant a reduction of the Robertian hold over Lesser France.[12] During Charles the Simple's reign other areas to north, west and south escaped from direct royal control, leaving only the region between the Seine and the Meuse. Even so the kings retained rights over the broader region. A new social structure was emerging and a different pattern of government – through allegiances and representatives rather than direct rule.

Rollo's son, William I Longsword (924–42), added control of the Bessin in central Normandy in 924, and the southern Avranchin and the Cotentin in 933. Normandy benefited from an enduring and long-lived Viking dynasty. Illegitimacy was not a bar to succession, and three of the first six rulers were illegitimate sons of concubines. Against expectation the Viking dynasty survived. They began to call themselves dukes, and endured well into the Capetian era, despite the assassination of William Longsword in 942. William was tricked by Arnulf of Flanders at a meeting on a Somme island, enticed on to a ship and murdered with swords. The assassination led to a crisis in Normandy, with a minor succeeding as Richard I (942–96). One effect was a temporary revival of Viking paganism.

Dudo of St-Quentin was at the court of Duke Richard I, who 'clasped me with love in his most affectionate arms'. He described Richard as pious, handsome and brilliant. Richard, as a minor in 942, had difficulty establishing himself. According to Dudo, he was a prisoner of the king, at one point 'dragged off in chains', but he became a major force in West Francia, though criticized for using Vikings as allies. Theobald of Blois was Richard I's major rival. Richard sent his agent, 'little Richard', to negotiate. Battle followed and Richard was victorious, regaining Évreux. Dudo gives a vivid picture of the duke standing 'on the raised platform at the entrance to his own house', with 'brilliant white hair, brilliant in eyebrows and in the pupil of the eye', a tall man with a long thick beard. Richard I made peace with Lothar in 965 but his major alliance was with the Robertians, an alliance that endured for a century and helped establish the Capetian dynasty. The alliance restored the former role of the Robertians as royal representatives in the region. Under Richard I Normandy began to appear as a territorial principality.

Richard I's piety extended to wearing a hairshirt, and going barefoot to the altar at Fécamp. Foreseeing his death, he commanded that 'so wicked a corpse' deserved burial only in the doorway of the abbey. He died the following night of 'apoplexy'.[13] Dudo remained at the ducal court of Richard II (996–1026), by which time Normandy was one of the best run principalities in France, its duke the 'most powerful of the great vassals'.[14]

FLANDERS

In the far north two other major principalities emerged. The first was Flanders which had to contend with West and East Francia both seeking control. Flanders was the Carolingian March between the Escaut, the Canche and the North Sea. The county that emerged contained a mixed population, including the Romanized people of Artois and Tournai, but in essence was the land of the Flemings. Thus it had a degree of ethnic origin but was never only ethnic in make-up. Like Normandy it faced Viking attacks. Flanders was largely forest and marsh, with much low-lying land, but had industrial and commercial prospects from its geographical situation. It became wealthy with the earliest major urban development in Francia. Flanders was a coherent unit from the time of Count Baldwin I Ironarm (Bras de Fer), appointed by Charles the Bald, despite the fact that Baldwin had seized and married Charles' widowed daughter, Judith. The marriage was eventually recognized and Baldwin given his county, founding an enduring dynasty.

Dhondt suggests that Flanders became the first real territorial principality under Baldwin I's son, Baldwin II the Bald, who succeeded in 879. He married a daughter of Alfred the Great of England. Baldwin II proved a ruthless ruler, not averse to having rivals assassinated – including the archbishop of Reims and Herbert I of Vermandois. Viking raids became so persistent that, despite Louis III's victory at Saucourt in 881, Carloman left the county to defend itself. Baldwin II constructed forts and emerged as the Christian saviour of the region. Both King Odo and Charles the Simple recognized his authority. Baldwin II has been seen as 'the true founder of the Flemish principality' – but one must beware of exaggerating the degree of independence.[15] Royal recognition still mattered.

Baldwin II died in 918 and was succeeded by his son, Arnulf I (918–65), named marquis in royal diplomas.[16] Arnulf came into conflict with Normandy and, following his father's example, had the Norman ruler William Longsword assassinated in 942. Arnulf survived the fury this roused. He compensated, to a degree, by introducing church reformers into Flanders. After Arnulf I's death, leaving only a grandson who was a minor, Flanders looked likely to disintegrate but was rescued by Arnulf II. There followed a further crisis on Arnulf II's death in 988, yet again leaving a minor heir. The Capetians made some gains at the expense of Flanders but Baldwin IV's rule (988–1035) proved 'one of the most important in the history of medieval Flanders'. The Flemish economy now took off. Baldwin IV supported Hugh Capet's accession and was rewarded for it. A marriage was arranged between Baldwin's widowed mother, Rozala (or Susanna), and Hugh Capet's son Robert – though the latter repudiated her in 991. Baldwin then rebelled but came to terms by which he kept Artois and Ostrevant. Baldwin IV was the first to move Flemish authority substantially eastwards over the Scheldt, when granted Valenciennes and Zeeland by the emperor, Henry II. Flanders remained a powerful principality through the Capetian period.

VERMANDOIS, BLOIS AND CHAMPAGNE

The other major Carolingian northern unit, Vermandois, was a growing power, the main threat to neighbouring principalities in the late Carolingian era, especially under the Herberts, but it failed to develop. Vermandois was ruled by a Carolingian family. By 889 Herbert I, a grandson of Pepin of Italy, held Soissons against the Vikings. Herbert I took St-Quentin and was named count of Vermandois but he was assassinated on the order of Baldwin II of Flanders. Herbert II, 'the tyrant', succeeded and expanded his territories, seizing lands from Lesser France and Champagne and taking Amiens, Valois, the Vexin and Laon.[17] He held a number of valuable towns, including Troyes, Meaux, Provins and Vitry. He dared to imprison the king of West Francia, Charles the Simple, and married the daughter of the Robertian King Robert I. He imposed his under-age son, Hugh, as archbishop of Reims. Herbert II was a major figure in West Francia in his time, though he found life more difficult after the accession of Louis IV. Herbert II died in 943 and was succeeded by his sons, who divided his lands. As a result the nascent principality of Vermandois did not develop.

Though beginning as viscounts of Tours, the descendants of the Herbertians were, however, founders of the later principality of Blois-Champagne. Herbert II's daughter, Liègarde, married Theobald the Trickster of Blois, and their descendants took over much of Herbert's land. Theobald gained the Touraine, the 'garden of France', from 942 and Chartres from 960.[18] Theobald the Trickster's son and successor was Odo I of Blois. One younger son, Herbert the Old, became count of Meaux and Troyes while another, Adalbert, became count of Vermandois and married Gerberga daughter of Gilbert of Lotharingia. Though Vermandois became less significant, Blois-Chartres expanded and remained powerful for centuries. Odo II of Blois (996–1037) sought the imperial crown, though he failed to gain it. Nevertheless, by the early 10th century, Odo II held Blois, Chartres, the Touraine, Champagne and Troyes.

ANJOU

Anjou was held by a viscount, and became a lesser county around the ancient *pagus* of Angers. It was 'only a small principality', part of the Breton March.[19] Anjou developed while its count was a vassal of the Robertians, aided by that connection. The count of Anjou was the most loyal of the Robertian vassals and benefited to the point where the county became a rival and a threat. Anjou gained from rule by long-lived and prolific counts who were able and energetic men – not unlike the Capetians. The Angevin counts were also excellent military commanders. Ingelger, a '*miles optimus*', won imperial favour, and was appointed count of Angers.[20] He was related through his mother to Hugh the Abbot. Ingelger's son, Fulk the Red, married Roscilla, daughter of Warnerius, thus making a Carolingian line. Fulk the Red was the first count of the Angevins. Fulk the Red's son and heir was Fulk II the Good (941–60), who also married a Carolingian as his first wife in Gerberga, daughter of the viscount of Vienne. Information on Fulk II's rule is thin. There was a tale that Louis IV laughed at Fulk for singing in the choir at St-Martin of Tours, to which Fulk responded with a note that an illiterate king was a crowned ass.[21]

Fulk the Good's son, Geoffrey Greygown (960–87), brought greater glory to Anjou, not least through victory over the Bretons at the first battle of Conquereux in 982. He made inroads into Aquitaine. We have information on Geoffrey and his successors from his descendant, Fulk IV le Réchin – who wrote a history of which a fragment survives.[22] Geoffrey married Adela of Vermandois, both a Carolingian and a Robertian. Their son, born after 15 years of marriage, was the most outstanding of the early counts, Fulk Nerra. Geoffrey Greygown forged a good relationship with Hugh Capet, and the young Fulk appeared at the royal court in 976.

Fulk III Nerra (987–1040) was the greatest and most successful of the counts of Anjou. He succeeded at the age of 16, in the year that Hugh Capet became king. His influence spread over Maine, Tours, the Vendôme and Saintonge. He pushed Angevin interests into Brittany, winning the second battle of Conquereux in 992. Fulk gained Loudun from Aquitaine and, after the capture of Herbert Wakedog, claimed overlordship of Maine. Fulk Nerra defeated Odo II of Blois, his prime rival, at the battle of Pontlevoy in 1016. The castles Fulk Nerra built on the border between Anjou and Blois are the earliest known in the west. He sought to compensate for a violent career by four pilgrimages to Jerusalem and a public flagellation. He avoided the wider ambitions that undermined the efforts of Odo II of Blois. Anjou's rise was gradual and continuous. The power of Anjou increased through the Capetian period, conquering Normandy under Geoffrey V le Bel, and ruling England under his son, Henry II.

BRITTANY

In the west, Brittany was ethnically separate with its own traditions, an example of the growing tendency in this period for ethnic groups to seek more independence and self-control – in reaction to weakening imperial authority. Brittany had a strong Gallic, Roman and Celtic past. In the Armorican peninsula the Romans had forced unity upon five Gallic tribes. In lower Brittany the Celtic language persisted. The Vikings destroyed the unity of ancient Brittany and forced the Franks to take defensive measures in the region. The Carolingians established a Breton March over the counts of Rennes, Nantes and Vannes with Robert the Strong as marquis. In the 10th century the counts of Rennes were recognized as dukes with the counts of Nantes as chief rivals. Brittany would be the last surviving independent principality. It remained largely outside the control of Frankish kings and dukes – though not beyond their ambitions and hopes.

Several strong rulers of Brittany emerged, not least Nominoë and his son Erispoë. Nominoë defeated Charles the Bald at Ballon near Redon in 845 and was recognized as ruling Rennes and Nantes. Erispoë was similarly successful at Jengland in 851, and in return was also recognized. Brittany, however, was open to outside intervention and often lacked strong central control. Charles the Bald allied with a rival to Erispoë, his cousin Salomon, who assassinated Erispoë in 857 and made himself duke – though he then joined the king's opponents. Salomon himself was assassinated in 874.

All of Brittany's neighbours – Normandy, Anjou, Blois and Lesser France – tried to take advantage of the disruption. There were further internal divisions, partly from the combination of Celtic Brittany with the Frankish centres of Vannes, Rennes and Nantes. Rennes and Nantes were ruled by counts and became Brittany's 'centre of gravity'. These counts were usually at odds with each other and a target for neighbouring principalities. Alan the Great (Barbetorte) ruled

Brittany to 952. He won victories over the Vikings and even called himself king. The Frankish additions to Brittany dominated the region and Brittany lost its Celtic character.[23] The counts of Rennes established some authority through Alan Barbetorte after his return from exile in England in c.937. He found the region in a dire state. Nantes had been abandoned and was in ruins. Alan fortified its church and built a new fortress. He established himself as count of Nantes, which became his capital. Through military campaigns he gained authority over six counties. Alan strove to emulate other Frankish principalities and gave homage to Louis IV in 942.

In Brittany, as elsewhere, hereditary castellan families appeared. On the death of Alan the Great there was a succession dispute and Brittany became a target for the neighbouring principalities. Blois supported the count of Rennes, while Anjou favoured the illegitimate sons of Alan. For a century from 952 Brittany lacked central authority and by the 11th century was struggling to equal neighbouring principalities. The duke accepted the necessity of paying homage to the duke of Normandy. William the Conqueror led expeditions into Brittany. The latter, like Normandy, came under Angevin and then English power. Brittany did not acknowledge the French crown directly again until the reign of Philip Augustus in 1202. It was the last principality to accept union with France, 'painfully accomplished in the late fifteenth century'.[24]

THE CENTRE AND SOUTH

Central and southern West Francia was even more unstable in the late Carolingian period than the north. Political units depended on personal holdings rather than territories with set boundaries. The south was separated from north of the Loire by tradition, custom, ethnicity, and even language – the Languedoc being, of course, the area of the *langue d'oc*, where 'oc' was the word for yes – and the 'home of southern civilization'.[25] Occitan, the *lengua romana* otherwise known as Provençal, was the language of about a third of geographical France.[26]

The region was seen as 'Roman', its dress and manners appeared shocking in the north. Aquitaine was hardly a united whole. It covered south-western France, from the Loire to the Pyrenees, the Rhône to the ocean. At its greatest extent it included Gascony, Poitou, Toulouse, Septimania (Gothia), and the Auvergne. It incorporated Gascons and Goths, and lacked ethnic unity, though all the residents were usually opposed to the Franks. What is sometimes called Occitania was a different world. Carolingian power was not strong in the south, almost non-existent by 987. Only one of Hugh Capet's charters concerned the area south of the Loire. One problem was the size of Aquitaine and the difficulty for its dukes (let alone the kings) of retaining power over the whole.

AQUITAINE, TOULOUSE AND POITOU

Aquitaine contained various ethnic groups and lacked cohesion. The eventual duchy was smaller than the original realm. The duchy was neither the Roman province nor the Carolingian realm.[27] In the seventh century dukes assumed royal powers and became independent of the Merovingians. It took several campaigns by Pepin the Short to bring Aquitaine within the Frankish realm. Charlemagne established six new counties based on the main *civitates* in Aquitaine. Frankish efforts were harsh and enduring resentment of Carolingian rule resulted. They were seen as outsiders and conquerors.

Charlemagne created a new kingdom of Aquitaine in 778, reorganizing it on Carolingian lines, with counties and marquisates. Aquitaine contained the counties of Poitiers, Auvergne, the Angoumois, Saintonge and Périgord – but apart from Poitiers they were almost independent. Charlemagne aimed to placate the people by increasing local control. In 817 Louis the Pious re-created the kingdom for his son Pepin I of Aquitaine. Pepin has not received much attention, largely because he died before his father while his son Pepin II did little to enhance his achievements. Nevertheless Pepin I's reign mattered.[28] He established his position and received a promise of further territories in Anjou and Neustria.

The kingdom of Aquitaine included Toulouse, Visigothic Septimania, and Gascony. The county of Toulouse was created to counter the threat of Gascony. No ruler over Aquitaine in this period had authority over the whole. The kingdom did not survive the problems of Pepin I's heir, who took over in 838. Pepin II was crowned king but Louis the Pious refused to recognize him and in 839 sent an army to enforce the succession of his son, Charles the Bald. Pepin II hung on with some support, notably in the March of Toulouse. Charles the Bald met considerable opposition. He made his sons kings of Aquitaine in turn – but neither Charles the Child (855–66), nor Louis the Stammerer (867–79), had much authority. Charles the Bald divided Aquitaine in three (Bordeaux, Poitiers and Toulouse), each with its military commander. Poitou went to the sons of Ramnulf I; the west to Bernard Plantevelue (Hairyfeet), the centre to Bernard of Gothia. Spanish counts disputed the east.[29] Bernard Hairyfeet did not seek a royal title and tried not to antagonize the Carolingians. He thus survived his two rivals and gained territory from them. Bernard of Gothia lost everything by revolt. Like Odo of Paris, Hairyfeet was loyal to Charles the Fat and allied with him against Boso (the brother-in-law of Charles the Bald). Bernard became a *fidelis* of Charles the Fat and emerged as the major figure in the region, as '*comes, dux et marchio*'. He founded the Carolingian duchy of Aquitaine, though it disintegrated on his death in 886 – the end of the Carolingian sub-kingdom.[30]

The major figures in Aquitaine were the counts of Poitiers and Toulouse, both Carolingian rather than Robertian in their sympathies. They ruled West Francia south of the Loire except for Gascony and Catalonia. Ramnulf II count of Poitiers was called 'duke of the greater part of Aquitaine' and tried to establish an independent realm.[31] He was called duke of Aquitaine by his death in 890. By c.900 there were five princes ruling divisions of Aquitaine, in Gothia, Toulouse, Poitou, Gascony and the Spanish March.

From 909 Bernard Hairyfeet's son, William the Pious, took over Aquitaine and Gothia, but Toulouse was split off under Odo son of Bernard of Toulouse. The duke of Aquitaine's demesne with a base in the Auvergne was larger than the king's and remained so until the 12th century. William the Pious called himself 'count, marquis and duke'.[32] William founded Cluny in 910 and remained the major magnate in Aquitaine until his death in 918, but still had to cede territory, including Toulouse and the Rouergue. He showed his piety by remaining celibate and hence producing no heir. He died in 918.[33] His nephew succeeded as William II but only lived until 927.

Berry rebelled and refused to recognize the new ruler. In 924 King Ralph I invaded the Auvergne. Aquitaine was broken up. The count of Poitou benefited most from the collapse of the duchy. William Towhead added the Auvergne to Poitiers and became the main power in central Aquitaine, but the old duchy was no more. William Towhead acknowledged the Carolingian king, Louis IV, and ruled until 963. William IV Firebrace, son of William Towhead, unlike his father claimed to be duke of Aquitaine, though he was not recognized by the king. Nevertheless, he ruled as his father had done until 995. Toulouse became a separate principality in the 10th century. Gothia went to Raymond III Pons of Toulouse, whose family retained it for centuries. Raymond Pons recognized King Ralph in 932. He was made prince of Aquitaine by a royal act in 941. Aquitaine passed briefly under the control of Toulouse, but Raymond died in c.950.

There were expeditions by Louis IV and Hugh the Great, but they did not destroy the southern princes. William IV held off a series of invasions, defeating Geoffrey Greygown of Anjou, the count of Périgueux, and the viscount of Limoges. In time control over the region passed to the counts of Poitiers. By the end of the Carolingian period, powerful separate principalities were developing in Poitou and Toulouse. Less stable units had also formed in Gascony and the Spanish March.

The Robertian, Hugh the Great, sought to increase his power in the south, including Burgundy. He briefly became count of Poitiers, having seized the county from the sons of Eblus Manzer. The latter's son, William Towhead, recovered Poitiers by 940. In 954 Hugh was granted Aquitaine by Louis IV but it remained an unsubstantiated claim. Hugh besieged Poitiers in 955, but failed to take it. Lothar tried to reconstruct the old sub-kingdom of Aquitaine for his son, but could not enforce it. The count of Poitiers then abandoned the Carolingian to support Hugh Capet in 987. Hugh recognized William IV Firebrace in 988. Under William V (995–1030), the grandson of William Towhead, Gascony became united to Aquitaine.

GASCONY

Gascony, like Brittany, had an ancient ethnic base, and resisted interest from all directions. It still does. Nevertheless, under Duke Lupus the Gascons recognized Carolingian overlordship from 769. Gascony lay between the Pyrenees and the Garonne. It was constantly weakened by internal rivalries. For a time there were two dukes of Gascony, one with internal support, the other recognized by the Carolingians. In the 10th century Gascony recovered lost territories in the Bordelais and the Agenais. Duke Garcia Sanchez divided his duchy into counties for his three sons, the eldest receiving the county of Gascony. When Gascony took over the Bordelais it acquired Bordeaux, which became the new capital. Gascony suffered from Viking and Muslim attacks, but overcame both. Gascony was joined to Aquitaine in the early Capetian period.

BURGUNDY

Other developing southern principalities were Burgundy and Provence. In the far south was also the March of Spain, not yet abandoned. Confusingly there developed three separate Burgundies – the kingdom, the duchy and the county. The duchy of Burgundy was part of the old Carolingian subkingdom including the counties of Autun, Beaunes, Avallon, Auxerre and Nevers. By the treaty of Verdun much of Burgundy went to Lothar, but Charles the Bald received 19 counties. Lothar's share was the basis of the kingdom of Burgundy, while Charles' share became the duchy. King Odo appointed Richard the Justiciar, count of Autun and brother of Boso of Vienne, as duke of Burgundy, while Boso took over the kingdom of Burgundy in 878, though his lands later became known as the county (Franche-Comté).

Charles the Bald's share became the duchy of Burgundy, the part of old Burgundy most attached to the Capetians. Like Flanders, Burgundy had divided loyalties, and divided claims to lordship from East and West Francia. Burgundy was divided internally between the East and West Franks. The kingdom was established by Rudolf I (888–911), great nephew of Empress Judith, on the death of Charles the Fat, whom he had supported. In 911 he was succeeded by his son Rudolf II, the king of Arles, who ruled to 937.

Geographically, the Saône divided French from German Burgundy. As well as the kingdom and the duchy, there also developed the separate county of Burgundy, later known as the Franche-Comté. The duchy of Burgundy formed around the county of Autun.[34] In 863 Charles the Bald appointed the count of Autun as *missus* over Burgundy. Richard the Justiciar succeeded his father as count of Autun in 880 and remained loyal to the Carolingians. He became duke of the Burgundians, known as 'the Justiciar' from his reputation for justice.[35] His base was around Autun, Sens, Nevers and Auxerre. He controlled at least 13 of the 19 counties of West Frankish Burgundy and founded the duchy of Burgundy in 890.[36] Richard's power was based on his military successes against pagans. He defeated the Vikings in 895 and at Chartres, and the Magyars in 911. By 916 he called himself duke. He died in 921 leaving two sons, Ralph who became king of West Francia, and Hugh the Black, who ruled the duchy of Burgundy. When Ralph became king, he passed most of his holdings in Burgundy to Hugh the Black. Hugh did not seek to follow his brother on the throne but held a considerable area. Hugh the Black did not recognize Louis IV as king and the duchy was ceded to Hugh the Great by Louis, after they invaded it together. Hugh the Black was defeated and lost Auxerre and Sens. After his death without sons in 952, the Ricardian dynasty's rule came to an end. Hugh the Black's son-in-law, Gilbert count of Burgundy, clashed with the Robertians and his duchy fell under the power of Hugh the Great.

The duchy of Burgundy went in turn to Hugh the Great's younger sons, Odo (956–65), and then Otto-Henry (965–1002), becoming Capetian. Odo married the Burgundian heiress Liétgarde, daughter of Gilbert. However, in 958 she was seized by the Burgundian magnate, Ralph count of Dijon, who made her his wife. The Carolingian Lothar attempted to take over Burgundy but finally recognized Odo as duke. Odo became the first Robertian ruler of Burgundy from 960, but it was a much reduced duchy. The count of Mâcon was one of several who ignored his authority. Various prelates, such as the abbot of Cluny, acknowledged the pope rather than the duke. It was no accident that Burgundy and Aquitaine played a major part in the development of the Peace of God movement, since it seemed the church was more likely to keep order than the lay powers.

When Odo of Burgundy died in 965, the magnates favoured his brother Otto-Henry, who ruled the duchy until his death in 1002. Otto-Henry held only three counties while his vassals controlled a further six. The duchy contained now only the 'central core' of Richard the Justiciar's Burgundy.[37] Otto-Henry died without a clear heir, which led to a war of disputed succession between his step-son Otto-William and his nephew Robert the Pious.

PROVENCE

Provence had been a significant region under the Roman Empire – Narbonaise Gaul or the 'Province'. It retained links to its Roman past in language and tradition. Charles Martel's victories had removed the Saracen threat and brought Provence safely within the Frankish realm. The early Carolingians divided it into counties. The Saracens wreaked devastation during the eighth and ninth centuries and established a base near St-Tropez. Provence came under the duchy of Arles, sometimes called the kingdom. By the 843 division at Verdun, Provence became part of Lothar's Middle Kingdom, which did not survive. A decade after Verdun Provence sought greater independence, becoming known variously as the kingdom of Provence, Arles, or Burgundy.

Richard the Justiciar's brother, Boso, became king of Provence in 879. He had been made *dux et missus* of Italy by Charles the Bald. Provence was outside the West Frankish realm, part of the kingdom rather than the duchy of Burgundy, acknowledging as suzerain the Holy Roman Emperor. Boso married Ermengarde, daughter of Emperor Louis II and proclaimed himself 'I, Boso, who am what I am by the grace of God' i.e. rather than by any earthly superior.[38] Boso's sister married Charles the Bald but Boso antagonized Charles the Fat, who confiscated his lands in 881. Boso died in 887, succeeded by his son Louis, crowned king of Provence in 890. Louis claimed the Holy Roman Empire and was actually crowned emperor in 901. However he returned to Provence after being defeated and captured at Verona. He was blinded in 905 – thereafter called Louis the Blind (L'Aveugle). He managed to rule Provence for a further 20 years, thanks to the efforts of his cousin, Hugh of Arles, who was rewarded with the titles of duke of Provence and marquis of Vienne. After Louis' death Hugh became king of Arles until his death in 948. The kingdom of Provence remained independent for a further century, becoming part of the Holy Roman Empire in 1032.

Saracen attacks still caused problems in the early 10th century when Fréjus was destroyed. Hugh of Arles won respect by his spirited defence, allying with Byzantium. On the death of Louis the Blind, Provence reverted to King Ralph I, and then to Rudolf II of Burgundy – though Hugh continued in control until his death. Otto I then took the lead against the Saracens, who were finally driven from Provence in 972. On the death of Rudolf III in 1032, Provence and the kingdom of Burgundy moved into the orbit of the Holy Roman Empire and to the 11th century remained imperial territory.

THE SPANISH MARCH AND ITALY

With Pepin the Short's success in Aquitaine, Frankish interest moved south. Charlemagne invaded in answer to an appeal for aid against the Saracens. His reverse during the return at Roncesvalles in 778 was serious but not permanent. The Franks invaded again in 797, when Charlemagne's son Louis the Pious restored some authority south of the Pyrenees. He besieged Barcelona, Tortosa, Huesca and Pamplona and established the Spanish March. Louis the Pious organized this region of north-eastern Spain into counties. The clash between Franks and Saracens continued in the 'forgotten war', when the Franks opposed the Saracens in the Mediterranean.[39] The Franks played a major part in defending the west against the advance of Islam.

The ninth-century count of Barcelona and the Spanish March, Wilfrid (or Wifrid) the Hairy, was probably descended from the Carolingian Visigothic count of Carcassonne. The March contained between six and nine counties. On Wilfrid's death in 897 his lands were divided between his sons but a modicum of unity was temporarily retained. The unity of the March foundered in the 10th century, leaving no strong principality in the region. There was little contact with the West Frankish realm, though the counts remained loyal to the Carolingians and hostile to the Robertians. Borel count of Barcelona was referred to in West Francia as the 'duke of Spain'.[40]

The late 10th century saw a new threat from Islam under al-Mansur. The late Carolingians could offer little aid, but neither could Hugh Capet. He did answer Borel's appeal, asking what route the army going south should take.[41] Hugh used the appeal as a reason for associating his son Robert, but had too much on his plate to campaign in the far south. Unity in the region of the March was not regained until the mid-11th century under the counts of Barcelona.

Italy was a fringe region for the Frankish world after a late and incomplete Frankish conquest. Local organization survived better than elsewhere. The cities retained their independence. Counts were less significant than elsewhere, but principalities developed more rapidly. Italy saw the emergence of localized principalities in Tuscany, Spoleto, Friuli and Ivrea. The southern Frankish rulers showed interest in northern Italy, still the home of the papacy and the western emperor. However control was unstable and German dominance was replaced at times by Italian-based or West Frankish kings of Italy and emperors. Hugh of Arles, for example, controlled much of northern Italy after 926. Berengar of Friuli rebelled against Hugh, who retired to Francia. Berengar was elected king of Italy in 950 and associated his son Adalbert. These Italian and southern contenders held power when the German ruler was busy elsewhere but they could rarely confront him. When Otto I turned his full attention to Italy he established himself by force and was crowned emperor on 2 February 962, the beginning of a new era in European history. It established the German Holy Roman Empire, a major player in European politics throughout the rest of the Middle Ages.

CONCLUSION

By the end of the 10th century France was recognizable as a realm. Its components would modify over the centuries but kept some continuity. The personal holdings of major individuals, mainly under royal lordship, transformed into major territorial units under magnates whom we refer to as princes – whether called dukes, marquises, counts, super-magnates, sub-kings, or kings.

The principalities formed in a variety of ways and were not equivalent to each other in government, relation to the monarchy, degree of unity, or in any other way. They do, however, represent the emergence of a new political system depending more on personal relations – between king and prince, between prince and subject lord, between lesser lords and their men – than on territorial integrity. The pattern of the principalities makes sense of the new social scheme that we call feudalism. It was a political system that depended on the social glue of protection, fidelity, loyalty, homage, vassalage, obligation, and duty. It was a relatively decentralized system, giving a fair degree of power to the lesser lord in every relationship, generally reliant on land granted (as a fief) by a master to its holder, with duties promised in return. This is not to say that society or politics was systematized or that every relationship was the same as any other – there was enormous variation in the possibilities and the actualities, but a new emphasis on how things worked had emerged. The period of change from West Francia being part of the Carolingian Empire to becoming the realm of the Capetian kings, was the age that saw the emergence of a France composed of principalities. The change was not as dramatic as some historians have made it, either in speed of development or in degree – but it happened.

Charlemagne's empire was less centralized and less strong than some have made it. The later Carolingian Empire was neither so weak, nor so decentralized, as some have made it – or at least not so dismembered. Charlemagne was a powerful ruler but the Carolingian Empire was a frail construct. It was brought together through military effort, conquest and forcible conversion. The conquered regions always sought separation or greater independence; it was unlikely that the enormous empire would long survive its creator. The weakness of the structure of Charlemagne's empire has not always been recognized, and has led historians to underestimate the abilities and achievements of his successors. In recent times there has been a revision of the post-Charlemagne period. Louis the Pious, Charles the Bald, even Charles the Fat, have found defenders.[42] In older versions, the pre-Capetian period was 'anarchy'.[43] The empire of that period was called 'a patchwork of scores of petty states'.[44] We may now suggest, however, that the empire was separating into more manageable units, including West and East Francia, whose kings were generally able and effective rulers. It has also been argued that the Carolingian collapse was not caused by a 'rise' of the aristocracy (which had always been powerful) – but by a simple succession problem.[45]

Charlemagne and his successors tried to govern their kingdoms by appointing their own men to govern more localized units – notably the counts, and later marquises, dukes and lesser agents such as viscounts. Up to 1000 these units became established in geographical terms, but the appointees remained royal representatives to the end of the Carolingian period. There was an increase in the number of territorial units in the old empire, and in West Francia, about 29 separate territories at the end of the ninth century, and no less than 55 by 1000.[46] The transformation of leading figures into territorial lords was a slower and later development than once thought.

The emergence of principalities was not necessarily a weakening of Western Europe, or even a diminishing of royal power. The principalities only slowly moved from areas under royal representatives to more cohesive territorial units, partly ethnic. The subject populations came to be ruled, in time, by men they respected and saw as *their* princes. These units came under the umbrella of one of the greater kings, as the Carolingian Empire transformed into the beginnings of national states. Thus one group of principalities began to see themselves as belonging to West Francia (France) or East Francia (Germany), and their subjects to see themselves as French or German. The princes may have sought power for themselves, and tried to exclude aspects of outside control, but they still acknowledged the king of France, or the German emperor.

Inevitably the border regions were less certain in their allegiance and hesitated over acceptance under one umbrella or the other – as with Flanders, Burgundy, or the Pyrenean lands. Nevertheless, as with atoms, the principalities tended to group around one nucleus as their natural position in the order of things. Once peoples and princes saw themselves as belonging to France, then France was a stronger kingdom.

The princes were seen increasingly as defenders of their principalities and their people, receiving the 'consent of the local population'.[47] The principalities often represented the best hope of political stability. The weakness of royal power, either of the late Carolingians or the early Capetians, has been over-emphasized. Enough account has not been taken of the change in the political structure, which emphasized allegiance to the king from the principalities. It has been common to see the early Capetians as weak kings but we shall approach them, from the start, as rulers of a burgeoning and flourishing kingdom.

It is well before we close this chapter to remember that early Capetian France was not only divided into principalities, but also into metropolitan sees. There were ten metropolitan sees, eight of which were royal including Reims as the foremost. The metropolitan see of Sens had eight bishoprics of which seven, including Paris, were royal. The king also had authority over many abbeys. It is also true that in some areas royal power over the church was weaker and in five ecclesiastical provinces with 43 bishoprics there were none that was royal at all.[48]

Like other nobles the kings had influence over appointments to their own bishoprics and abbeys. Even sees and abbeys that were not royal might look to the king for support against an unpalatable local lord. All in all, the royal role in the French church gave greater power throughout the realm than the relation between king and princes might suggest. According to Richer, Hugh Capet was able to call 'a meeting of all the bishops of Gaul' – even if all did not attend.[49] The royal role in the church would play a significant part in the growth of Capetian power.

4

The first Capetian kings, 987–1031

We have queried the degree of powerlessness of the late rulers of West Francia, both Carolingian and non-Carolingian. It is true they were frequently dependent on support from East Francia, but they were not mere puppets. To a point, government was a combined royal Frankish effort, maintaining at least some concept of overall empire. These late rulers all had close Ottonian relatives. Both Louis IV and Hugh the Great, for example, married sisters of Otto I.

It is also true that the various lords – dukes, counts and castellans – sought to improve their powers and with some success, but this too can be exaggerated. It would be impossible to find a period when such ambitions did not exist. And even the princes' power never extended to complete control over the kings. The key point is to note the changes that were occurring, rather than to overstress royal weakness – as earlier historians have done. The main change that we have identified was the move from a ruler dependent upon personal representatives such as *missi*, counts and other agents, to a pattern of government where territorial principalities developed their own administration. The king still received some respect throughout what we may begin to call France, and power partly depended on personal links with the princes.

The main change was that the localities now had a different kind of government and a different attachment to the monarchy. The jigsaw of emerging principalities was not set in stone, and lesser lordships were still forming and re-forming. Under the early Capetians new lordships emerged such as Meulan, or the house of Montmorency, the castellanies of Gallardon, Nogent-le-Roi, Montfort l'Amaury and Epernon.[1] However, the major divisions of the Carolingian Empire had largely been settled by 987, and the new units were no longer governed only by Carolingians. France and the Holy Roman Empire were emerging as separate kingdoms, each containing a patchwork of principalities. France, it has been suggested, consisted in 987 of some 15 major 'demesnes' and this was 'the apogee of the seigneurial regime'.[2]

The whole of the former Carolingian Empire was now divided into a few large territorial principalities. Some came directly under the rule of the king of France and others attached themselves to him. There were still regions disputed by the emerging monarchies, including Lotharingia and Burgundy, but there was little effort to restore a united empire. The major invasions from outside – Viking, Magyar, Saracen – were now mostly over.[3] Regrouping, recovery and growth in the new political pattern could proceed with less interruption.

The Earlier Capetians

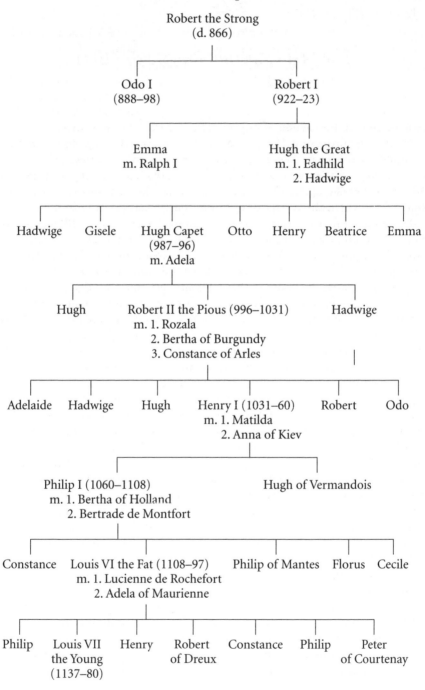

Robert the Strong
(d. 866)

Odo I
(888–98)

Robert I
(922–23)

Emma
m. Ralph I

Hugh the Great
m. 1. Eadhild
2. Hadwige

Hadwige Gisele Hugh Capet Otto Henry Beatrice Emma
(987–96)
m. Adela

Hugh Robert II the Pious (996–1031) Hadwige
m. 1. Rozala
2. Bertha of Burgundy
3. Constance of Arles

Adelaide Hadwige Hugh Henry I (1031–60) Robert Odo
m. 1. Matilda
2. Anna of Kiev

Philip I (1060–1108) Hugh of Vermandois
m. 1. Bertha of Holland
2. Bertrade de Montfort

Constance Louis VI the Fat (1108–97) Philip of Mantes Florus Cecile
m. 1. Lucienne de Rochefort
2. Adela of Maurienne

Philip Louis VII Henry Robert Constance Philip Peter
the Young of Dreux of Courtenay
(1137–80)

THE REIGN OF HUGH CAPET (987-96)

THE SITUATION IN 987

Hugh Capet was born in 938 but only became king in 987, largely because he twice declined the position in favour of Carolingian claimants. His father, Hugh the Great, had died in 950, so Hugh Capet had long experience of governing the family territories. Richer suggests there was stronger support for the Carolingian, Charles of Lower Lorraine, than previous historians have thought.[4] Charles was the surviving brother of King Lothar, 'the sole survivor of his father's line', who claimed 'by hereditary right', being from the 'just line of royal offspring'.[5]

There was hesitation in late 10th-century society over accepting non-Carolingians as kings. Glaber saw the new Capetian kings as 'men of common blood'.[6] This attitude was probably the greatest obstacle that faced the first three non-Carolingian kings (Odo, Robert I and Ralph), and the reason that Hugh Capet had avoided taking the crown. The situation confronted him again in 987. Hugh was the eldest son of Hugh the Great, duke of the Franks, and Hadwige. Hugh's mother and wife were Carolingian and it seems odd that later Capetians could be seen as non-Carolingian.[7] Hugh Capet married Adelaide, sister of William IV duke of Aquitaine, in c.970. He treated his Carolingian wife with respect and she brought additional strength to his position; he named her 'associate and participator in our realm'.[8] By 987 Hugh and Adelaide had an adult son, Robert. In effect, from the very beginning the Capetians had Carolingian blood in their veins. In addition, through his father, Hugh Capet was the grandnephew of King Odo, and the grandson of Robert I king of West Francia. On his mother's side Hugh Capet was descended from the Ottonians of East Francia. Descent from Carolingians, Ottonians and Robertians – it was not exactly the genealogy of a butcher! Hugh succeeded his father as duke of the Franks in 936, taking over Paris, Orléans, Senlis and Dreux, as well as several lay abbacies. Hugh Capet was not in direct line of Carolingian descent, but he was of noble blood, from the greatest magnate family in West Francia.

The by-name 'Capet' is normally used to distinguish our first Capetian king. His father, Hugh the Great, had also been called Capet, but the name is most commonly associated with the founder of the dynasty. As mentioned earlier 'Capet' may have come from 'chapet' (a short cloak) or more likely from the word for a monastic cape or cloak – associated with, and presumably worn by, the Robertians as lay abbots. Little is known about Hugh Capet as an individual simply since the contemporary sources are thin, and for this reason he has often been belittled. Richer, the major source for the reign, was a Carolingian sympathizer. Lesser sources are even more critical, including that from the later southerner, Adhémar of Chabannes. There are barely a dozen surviving charters to balance the chronicle accounts. There is no detailed description of Hugh's looks and no close information on his private life. Hugh de Fleury did say he was 'the image of his father', but it is not certain he meant in looks.[9] Later medieval writers tried to fill the gaps by inventing a fictional Hugh Capet – son or uncle or nephew or grandson of a butcher who made good, or a former butcher himself who impregnated a knight's daughter, or even a not very good butcher 'who knew very little of the trade'.[10] Most later medieval references to Hugh were critical, despite the fact that the Capetians became established on the throne. A canon at St-Victor in Paris claimed that Hugh had usurped the throne. William of Malmesbury called him 'a squire who had no great name'.[11] Dante presented him as the son of a butcher, having his own political reasons for criticizing the French monarchy.[12] Hugh was the hero of a 14th-century *chanson de geste*, which presents an impoverished youth, participating in tournaments, conducting amours, producing bastards – but there is little fact amid the fiction.[13]

Hugh Capet was at least conventionally pious; he dressed in clerical vestments as a lay abbot.[14] Richer declared that he had 'great piety'.[15] Hugh was once shocked on his way to church at St-Denis by a couple making love. He threw his fur cape over them and entered the church to pray for their souls.[16] At another time, moved by compassion, he gave his cloak to two poor fishermen to keep them warm. He was accustomed to pray for the poor and consistently favoured church reformers and holy men. Hugh went on pilgrimages, as to the tomb of St Maïeul at Souvigny. He went barefoot carrying the reliquary of St Valery on his shoulders. It was in 1050 that the story emerged of St Valery appearing to Hugh to promise the throne to his heirs, but only 'until the seventh generation'. This became significant when the seventh generation approached.[17] At any rate Hugh earned a reputation for piety and was called 'the best defender of the church of God'.[18]

Richer of Reims, son of an official of Louis IV, wrote the major narrative source for the reign of Hugh Capet.[19] It survives in the original and much revised manuscript – found at Bamberg in the 19th century. Richer was a canon and cantor in the cathedral at Reims and became a monk at St-Remy. He dedicated his work to Gerbert of Aurillac (later Sylvester II), who may have asked him to undertake it. Richer's political sympathies changed over the years.[20] He was a moderate man, occasionally caught up in turbulent events. In general he was favourable to the Carolingians, yet not violently hostile to Hugh Capet. Richer noted that Hugh did not know or understand Latin – which had to be translated for him.[21] We may take it that Hugh was probably not highly educated, in contrast to most of his successors. Richer also saw 'France' emerging as a unit in Europe, though he called it 'Gaul'.[22]

Reims was the centre of attention for Hugh Capet's relatively brief reign. Our knowledge for events elsewhere is thin or non-existent. Reims was an important city, between the East and West Franks, and a target for both. It was an important archiepiscopal see. The two major sources for Hugh Capet's reign relate to Reims: Richer was a monk there, Gerbert of Aurillac, whose letters survive, became its archbishop. Neither was unbiased. Gerbert was even more involved in the politics of his age than Richer. He sought career advancement and later became pope as Sylvester II with Ottonian support. Gerbert arranged the collection of his letters and presented a deliberate slant on events. He resented Hugh Capet's choice of the Carolingian Arnulf as archbishop of Reims, a post he expected for himself. Gerbert did work as secretary to Archbishop Arnulf but was arrested by Charles of Lower Lorraine when he captured Reims. Gerbert was taken to Laon and decided to give allegiance to Charles, now calling Hugh and his son 'interim kings', and Charles the 'legitimate heir'.[23] Gerbert then made another volte-face, returning to Hugh's allegiance – he was far more flexible in his loyalties than the much condemned Ascelin bishop of Laon. Gerbert acted as Hugh's secretary. After the capture of Charles, Gerbert was made archbishop of Reims by Hugh, but without papal assent.

Hugh Capet had royal ancestors and relatives in Odo I, Robert I and Ralph I yet he had pursued the traditional Robertian practice of supporting Carolingians for the throne. Hugh the Great had died in 956 when his son Hugh Capet became count of Paris – as well as Orléans, Senlis and Dreux. Hugh inherited Neustria from his father and was made duke of the Franks in 956. In 985 Hugh defeated a rebellion against the Carolingian King Lothar. However Hugh moved into the Ottonian camp in 981, allying with Otto II against Lothar. The last Carolingian king, Louis V, died in 987 after a short reign, leaving an uncertain succession. Hugh Capet had widespread support for the crown in 987. His acceptance was aided by his previously modest behaviour. He had not sought to oppose the succession of the last Carolingian kings but his links with the family had weakened by 987. His opportunity came after the early and unexpected deaths of Lothar and Louis V. Only a few politically significant figures opposed Hugh's election in 987. Baldwin IV count of Flanders (988–1035) supported Hugh's accession and in return was recognized as count of Flanders. The counts of Blois and Anjou were vassals and supporters of the Robertians and, in 987, were content to accept Hugh as king. Normandy from its beginnings had a close relationship with the family. There was a direct Robertian connection with Burgundy. Most West Frankish magnates hoped to gain from the downfall of the Carolingians and rule by a fellow prince. Only the count of Vermandois rebelled but, as Glaber noted, many who at first accepted Hugh's accession later 'became traitors'.[24] Nevertheless, there was general acceptance of Hugh's accession. Ottonian Germany had its own problems. The new emperor, Otto III, was only seven. East Francia had a regency government under Otto's mother, the empress Theophano, until her death in 989, and then under his grandmother Adelaide to 994. Some suggest these two women played a major part in the west during Hugh's reign.[25] At any rate, in 987 the Ottonians, the Empress Theophano, the magnates – none opposed Hugh – apart from the count of Vermandois and Charles of Lower Lorraine.

Charles of Lower Lorraine was the only surviving Carolingian candidate for the West Frankish throne, but his past actions had earned him many enemies and few friends. He had supported Otto II against his own brother Lothar, and then Lothar against Otto III. Many retained some loyalty to the Carolingians, but few trusted Charles or were prepared to take up arms for him. He wrote to Adalbero archbishop of Reims, stating his hereditary claim, but received no sympathy. Adalbero recognized his own debt to Hugh Capet, who had blocked

Carolingian efforts to bring him to trial and rescued him. Hugh had thus saved the archbishop's office and freedom. He was also responsible for the release of Adalbero's brother, Godfrey of Verdun. Adalbero repaid the debt with a decisive speech to the assembled magnates and prelates, rejecting the claims of Charles, whom he averred was unsuitable through his 'perjuries, sacrileges and evils of every kind'. The archbishop supported the claim of Hugh Capet, 'the illustrious duke'.[26] Church support proved vital and as the later chronicler of St-Maixent thought, 'God chose a better prince'.[27]

There followed an assembly of magnates at Senlis before the end of May, which elected Hugh as king of the West Franks. Little opposition was voiced. Hugh was aided by being not the first but the fourth non-Carolingian king. The idea of a non-Carolingian was less of a shock than previously. Nor had Hugh seized the throne at his first opportunity – rather the reverse – he had avoided taking it on two occasions when he might have been expected to do so. Now his accession was widely welcomed. Hugh Capet was proclaimed king and crowned by Adalbero archbishop of Reims at Noyon on 1 June 987. In his coronation oath he promised 'as best I can' to preserve canonical privilege, law, and justice, and to act justly to every bishop in the realm.[28] He was consecrated at Reims by Archbishop Adalbero on 3 July 987 with the holy oil once used for Clovis. Hugh had become God's representative in the kingdom of West Francia. This divine approval was important to Hugh and his successors. It was only with the Capetians that it became common practice for the archbishop to consecrate the new king at Reims.[29]

Hugh Capet's achievements as king have generally been belittled. There was only muted opposition voiced in 987, but not everyone was comfortable with his accession. There was some support for the claims of Charles of Lower Lorraine, despite reservations about his character. This preference was not easy to express once Hugh had been crowned, but it continued in the background – as one can see in the ecclesiastical chronicles. Still in the 14th century Hugh was called a usurper, and this may be one reason why there was never a second Capetian King Hugh. Reservation about his right to the throne has persisted through the ages. Many modern historians have seen him as taking rather than accepting the throne – there was an adult Carolingian candidate in Charles whose claims were overruled. Hugh's accession has been seen by some as a political trick, or even a 'coup d'État'.[30] Nor, in modern times, has there been much admiration for the first Capetian. Hugh is presented as a weak king, a territorial prince with little authority beyond his principality. He was an 'unimposing figure' who only survived through the 'incompetence' of his opponents.[31] He was a 'mediocrity', a 'man of little initiative' with 'a ducal mentality'.[32] He was 'weaker by far' than any of his princes, with only 'an illusory suzerainty', as 'a nominal king'.[33] It was an 'inglorious reign', 'brief and without prestige'. He was 'a conditional monarch', a mere 'kinglet' of the Île-de-France, a king 'by default'.[34] The achievement of the early Capetian kings in general has been called 'utterly insignificant', as has the figure of Hugh himself. The age has been viewed as one of 'decadence', not worth studying until the time of Louis VI.[35] It has been claimed that Hugh Capet's main aim and achievement was to survive – but he did survive and that was no mean feat.[36]

HUGH CAPET AND HIS REALM

In 987 Hugh Capet retained part of the former Robertian principality, and gained part of the former Carolingian demesne. Some historians have argued that his possessions were small – only 'the debris' of former holdings.[37] There is some truth in this. Hugh was not as wealthy and powerful as his successors would become. It was not easy for him to dominate the princes. But the duke of the Franks had not been unimportant or weak – arguably the strongest of the princes – and kingship added rather than subtracted power and wealth. Hugh kept the region around Paris, Étampes, Orléans and Melun, and received Compiègne, Reims and Laon.

Hugh did cede Melun to Bouchard the Old of Vendôme, a loyal follower, and he recognized church authority in Laon and Reims – so even in his demesne he did not keep all that he received. He was prepared to make some concessions in order to gain or keep loyalty and support – often as important, or even more important, than direct landholding. Royal power deriving from the demesne was a complex mix of rights and resources, including strength through vassal support, possessions other than land, profits from such as fishing or vineyards, rights from such as hunting, woodland and forest, services in transport, rights of justice, rights to hospitality, rights concerning the church, and many others.[38]

Nor was royal power restricted to the demesne. Kings had a special religious position, a unique role in the realm, demanding allegiance and respect from all subjects. Kings held a special position over abbeys and bishoprics, not only those they controlled directly, but as protectors of all within the realm. Kings were also often seen as the main protectors of towns. They had a special role in freeing the population from serfdom. They had the right to demand aids and to summon military service for national defence. Royal residences, castles and palaces, were valuable possessions. These various powers existed in 987 and were not lost.

At best, it has been said, Hugh Capet survived, but we believe he achieved more than this. We cannot be certain of his aims but it seems likely that he set out to retain the crown in the family – and he succeeded. It was no accident that one of his earliest acts was to associate his son Robert as king on 30 December of the very first year of his reign. Hugh persuaded the papacy of the need for this in case he had to leave his realm to defend Christendom against the Saracens. An appeal reached Hugh when Borel count of Barcelona (part of the Carolingian world) sought aid against the Saracens. Borel's appeal had been ignored by the Carolingians but Hugh made a positive response in a letter that has survived, and may have genuinely intended to bring aid, though he never actually set out.[39] His reason given for not doing so was Charles of Lower Lorraine, who threatened Laon. Another source suggested that Hugh associated his son because 'he was failing somewhat in strength' – but since he lived nine years after the event, that seems unlikely.[40] That Hugh made efforts to bring the church onside suggests that the association was his own idea and that his prime intention was to ensure the succession of his son. Hugh won church approval for the association. Given that Archbishop Adalbero's speech supporting Hugh's accession had argued that Hugh's claim rested on election rather than heredity, church support was not certain. However, Hugh's move worked. Association had occasionally been used by the Carolingians and now for two centuries it became the normal Capetian practice to ensure succession within their family. Robert was associated as king at Orléans on Christmas Day 987.

Less successful was Hugh's plan for his son's marriage. First he sought a Byzantine wife, an example that later Capetians would follow – but this effort failed. Nevertheless it suggests the ambitions Hugh had for his family – stressing royal and even imperial status. Hugh then arranged to match Robert with Rozala (renamed Suzanne in France), daughter of Berengar II king of Italy. Like many Capetian brides she was of Carolingian descent. She was the widow of Arnulf II count of Flanders, and her son was the current count, Baldwin IV. Robert was 16 at the time of marriage in 989 while his wife was over 30. Robert never accepted his fate happily and the marriage failed by 991 – causing problems with the church. Rozala returned to Flanders but Hugh kept her dowry of Montreuil-sur-Mer in Ponthieu, giving the Capetians their first direct access to the sea. With the breakdown of the marriage, Flanders was ready to join the opponents of Hugh Capet.

The major political problem for Hugh Capet was the existence of the adult Carolingian rival Charles duke of Lower Lorraine. One of Hugh's early measures was to abandon Verdun to the German emperor, seeking to counter Ottonian support for Charles. Charles' first hostile effort was to move on 'the Carolingian town' of Laon, where he had some support.[41] Hugh lacked the expected aid from Fulk Nerra of Anjou, who was distracted by events in Brittany. Fulk had become count at the age of only 17 and needed to establish himself.

Laon stood on a mount and would not be easy to take. Charles approached it cautiously in 988, hiding men among the vines and behind hedges. Allies let him in. Bishop Ascelin tried to escape but was captured – though some thought his 'escape' was an attempt to hide his treachery, and that he had arranged things for the duke. His subsequent escape suggests this was untrue. King Lothar's widow, Emma, was among the prisoners. Charles occupied Laon and improved the fortifications. He set up regular patrols to guard the walls, heightened the towers, dug new ditches, and prepared throwing engines for defence. Hugh Capet called a church synod to declare Charles and Arnulf excommunicated. He tried to recover Laon in 988. His siege engines did some damage but it was soon repaired. The German empress, Theophano, attempted to reconcile the rivals and Hugh agreed to accept her mediation but Charles refused. A sortie led to Hugh's retreat – abandoning the siege. He then sought to build an alliance against Charles, but with little success. Bishop Ascelin escaped by sliding down a rope from the tower.

Hugh pardoned him for any offence and returned to Laon with a new army in the spring of 989 but rain hampered his efforts. The citizens made a sortie and again Hugh withdrew. Richer's critical account stresses the damage Hugh caused, including burning down an old woman's hut.[42]

HUGH CAPET AND THE CHURCH

Hugh's relationship with the church helped to bring him to the throne and to keep it. Archbishop Adalbero's alliance with the king provoked some opposition. Séguin archbishop of Sens was jealous of his ecclesiastical rival, having expected to consecrate Hugh. He now condemned the king as Adalbero's creature but Hugh kept the support of most French bishops – even winning over Séguin. Hugh's wife, Queen Adelaide, helped through her efforts at church building. Hugh won papal support for his expressed intention of fighting the Saracens – though he never went. Hugh also maintained his family's reputation as church patrons, noted for piety and pilgrimages. Helgaud of Fleury said Hugh favoured the abbeys, encouraging reform. Hugh used the church in the fight against his prime enemy, Charles of Lower Lorraine. A church council was called at which Charles was again excommunicated.

There was, however, a problem with the papacy over Reims. When Archbishop Adalbero became ill in 989, the citizens of Reims sought aid from the king. Gerbert of Aurillac, the friend and supporter of Adalbero, expected to succeed. It seemed a good move for the king too, who could expect continued support from Gerbert. Hugh Capet came to Reims as soon as he heard of the archbishop's condition, arriving on the day Adalbero died, just too late to see him alive. Adalbero had held his see for 20 years and his support had been vital to Hugh; the choice of a co-operative successor was vital.

Hugh Capet rashly decided to have Arnulf installed as the new archbishop – though he claimed the decision was made by the people of Reims. Arnulf had been a canon at Laon and was the illegitimate son of the Carolingian King Lothar, and nephew of Charles of Lower Lorraine. Arnulf was presented with an agreement in the form of a chirograph, by which he promised fidelity to the king. According to Richer it was the bishops who insisted on this move rather than the king.[43] Arnulf made his oath of fidelity, swearing on the Eucharist. Hugh presumably hoped to placate Charles by the appointment of his nephew Arnulf, but the move was risky – and it failed. Richer suggested that Arnulf always favoured his uncle and 'cared for him'.[44] Arnulf soon betrayed his oath and the king's choice backfired. Arnulf let Charles into Reims at night. A priest, Adalgerus, later said, 'I opened the gates on his [Arnulf's] orders'.[45] Arnulf thus betrayed Hugh's trust and handed Reims to Charles. Charles was now master of Reims, Laon and Soissons, and Hugh's position was much weakened. Arnulf compounded his treachery by giving fidelity to Charles. Lorraine now supported the duke, while the Ottonians ignored Hugh's requests for aid. It was the major crisis of the reign. The new king's future looked very dubious.

Hugh's support of Arnulf at Reims had also antagonized the previously friendly Gerbert, who had expected to succeed. He was ambitious and Hugh had frustrated him. The support of the see of Reims and the church was vital to Hugh's position. Now both Gerbert and Arnulf moved into Charles' camp. Gerbert, in a letter, now referred to Hugh's family as 'intermediary kings'.[46] He did not expect the dynasty to survive. Hugh seemed to have made a catastrophic mistake. Gerbert, however, soon thought better of his support for Charles, and adopted a less committed position.

By 991 Hugh had come to regret his choice of Arnulf, and now preferred Gerbert as archbishop when Arnulf was disgraced. Gerbert with Hugh's support held the see until 998. Ironically his method of gaining Reims brought opposition from the papacy. Arnulf was deposed by a French council of bishops, not a method the papacy could countenance. John XV denied the council's right to make the decision, and reversed it. Eventually Gerbert yielded and in 997 left Reims. He went to the Ottonian court and received support for a bishopric in Italy.

This period saw the foundation and rise of the great abbey of Cluny in Burgundy. This was not the work of Hugh Capet, but it was an important development of his age, and received his support. Abbot Odilo of Cluny took over in 994 and in a long rule (to 1049) oversaw the spread of Cluniac reform through much of France, building a 'monastic empire'.[47] Hugh Capet encouraged the reform and asked Maïeul, when abbot of Cluny, to reform St-Denis. Maïeul died on his way in 994. The work of reforming St-Denis was carried out by his successor, Abbot Odilo. One finds some criticism of Cluny and the king, not least from Ascelin bishop of Laon. Secular ecclesiastics resented the success of Cluny and its houses in escaping from episcopal control. The waspish Ascelin suggested 'it is no longer the king who rules ... our master is King Odilo of Cluny'. He saw the king as 'King Hugh the monk'.[48] Reform was not completely successful. Glaber reckoned that the kings chose 'unworthy men' for church appointments, men 'corrupted by bribes', presumptuous, avaricious, and who failed to stem the lustful and incontinent behaviour of laymen. The comments have the ring of an embittered man, but presumably had some foundation in fact.

This period also saw the emergence of the Peace of God movement, notably in Aquitaine and Burgundy. It began on a local level, largely where the church stepped in because neither central nor lordly power was sufficient to keep order. A programme was drawn up for keeping order, to be enforced by lay support. Guy II, count-bishop of Le Puy, was responsible for the first move in 975 when he received his see. He called a meeting near Le Puy to seek an oath from local lords to keep the peace.[49] A scheme for the Peace of God was put to a meeting of the bishops of Aquitaine under Gombaud archbishop of Bordeaux at Charroux in 989. Three major decrees were issued – that churches should not be entered by force, that soldiers should not steal from peasants or the poor, and that those who attacked clerics should be excommunicated. A similar assembly followed at Narbonne in 990, making similar points and stressing that nobles should not seize church land. An assembly at Le Puy in 994 offered protection to merchants through oaths taken over relics.

Assemblies began to suggest, and then demand, respect for the church and the poor, threatening excommunication for failure to observe their promises. The assemblies sought a more committed response from the local lords, through oaths. The Peace of God idea spread to become virtually a national movement. It sparked the idea of the Truce of God, an attempt to limit war in the Christian world by forbidding it at certain times and on certain days. Both movements were led by the church but received lay and royal support. The king became the main hope of enforcing the movement. It was an opportunity for the king to intervene beyond the demesne in order to keep order with church approval.

HUGH CAPET AND THE MAGNATES

Charles of Lower Lorraine gained support from a number of leading figures in France, including Conrad king of Burgundy, Herbert count of Troyes and Odo I of Blois. Charles' area of control increased and threatened Hugh. This situation was the major crisis of Hugh Capet's reign. Odo I of Blois seized Marmoutier and rebelled against Hugh, but was defeated and reconciled when Hugh offered him Dreux. Dreux was handed over in 991 but Odo did not remain loyal. He may have hoped to become duke of the Franks with help from Otto III of Germany. He did not give further aid against Charles but seized Melun, 'almost surrounded by the Seine', for himself.[50] He also plotted with Ascelin bishop of Laon against the king. Hugh built a new alliance with Richard I of Normandy, William IV of Aquitaine and Baldwin IV of Flanders. The allies recovered Melun after a siege.[51] The people of Melun turned against the count and opened their gates. It was arguably the most important moment of the reign.

Hugh had survived a major rebellion but his position remained precarious. There had always been questions over his right to the throne. The almost universal acceptance at his accession did not last. Glaber wrote that Hugh 'found his authority ignored by men who had shortly before submitted to him' – though the chronicler also admitted that the king tackled rebellion with 'vigour of body and spirit'.[52] Hugh was fortunate that the opposition was rarely united – partly through his own efforts to split it. With Odo of Blois in the opposing camp, Hugh could ally with Odo's rival, Fulk III Nerra count of Anjou (987–1040). Fulk Nerra had been associated with Hugh before the latter's accession. Their alliance was of mutual benefit. Hugh's descendants were to rule France for centuries; Fulk's family became the most powerful princely dynasty in France (and kings for centuries in England).

Odo of Blois again made peace with the king in 996. Hugh also made deals with William V of Aquitaine and Richard I of Normandy, both acknowledging him as king. Odo I of Blois' death, leaving only young sons in Odo II (996–1037) and Theobald, eased Hugh's position – but too late to take much advantage. Other magnates died at about the same time, William Firebrace of Aquitaine in 994,

Herbert II of Maine by 995, Henry of Burgundy in 996. Richard I of Normandy died on 21 November 996, succeeded by the young Richard II (996–1026). The latter part of Hugh's reign saw the accession of new and young princes, who were not in a position to do much harm to the now established king, but who would play a significant part after Hugh's death.

Hugh Capet could not keep direct control over all the lands of his father. The counts of Blois and Anjou had been vassals of the duke of the Franks. The relationship was not forgotten, but they expanded their own territories and power. The counts, as rising men, had been content to be vassals. Their rise to princedom on a par with Burgundy or Flanders altered their attitude. Hugh's authority could no longer operate in Anjou, Tours, Champagne, or Blois without the relevant count's cooperation. The king's best plan was to exploit rivalry between the two, and make sure one of them was always his ally.

With the rise of these principalities and the general changes in France, Hugh's demesne was a reduced region, mainly the land around and between Paris and Orléans. From this the monarchy had to resource itself. At least it was a profitable region. Lemarignier claimed that what the king lost in 987 was not recovered until the 12th century, but this seems incorrect with regard to the extent of late Carolingian control, and to Hugh's 'losses'. Neither the late Carolingians, nor the early Capetians, had an enormous demesne but they had the advantage of divine favour, royal authority, and rights that complemented their demesne wealth. Lemarignier thought 987 brought a loss of authority, especially in the south – but any change was gradual.[53] Very little land or authority was lost in the immediate transfer of dynasty, though the rivalry between the families did cost something during the ninth and tenth centuries. If anything the Robertian lands, plus surviving Carolingian demesne, meant an *improved* royal base in 987.

It was often the case that, as with Anjou and Blois, the kings could no longer command former vassals without question and had to rely on personal allegiance. Hugh Capet did, however, generally manage to play these counts against each other. Anjou was generally loyal, in particular if it meant opposing the count of Blois. Richard II of Normandy had supported Hugh for the crown and continued to be loyal. The duchy of Burgundy went to Hugh Capet's brother, Otto-Henry (965–1002), making another valuable ally.

One of Hugh's major supporters was Fulk Nerra of Anjou, who succeeded Geoffrey Greygown in 987. Fulk had considerable military experience and used it to expand his territory. Anjou emerged as a major principality. It was an inland county with potentially hostile neighbours. Fulk had to fight the forces of Normandy, Brittany, Aquitaine, and especially Blois. Alliance with the king was welcome.

Walter, a viscount appointed by Bouchard of Vendôme to administer the county of Melun caused problems. He thought the king 'incapable of reigning' and joined Odo of Blois, handing over Melun. With Norman aid, the king recaptured Melun and hanged Walter before its gate.[54] Walter's wife, who had encouraged the rebellion, was hanged by the feet, to the jeers of the soldiers as her clothes fell to reveal her naked body. Both died. The loss of Melun was a blow to Odo of Blois and a reminder that Hugh was no feeble king.

Brittany also caused trouble, again involving Odo of Blois. Here Hugh had support from Fulk Nerra. The war between Blois and Anjou swayed one way then the other. Fulk attacked Nantes in 992. In the battle of Conquereux fought near Nantes, Fulk defeated the Bretons under Odo's ally, Conan of Nantes.[55] Fulk was unhorsed, but saved by his mail armour, though his standard bearer was killed. Fulk retreated and re-assembled while Conan withdrew into undergrowth and removed his armour to take a breather. In one account, a man of Fulk's spotted Conan and ran him through with a sword.[56] In Glaber's chronicle, Conan's right hand was severed before he surrendered. We have no way of knowing which version is correct, but there is no doubt that Conan lost the battle. Fulk Nerra marched on Nantes, which surrendered. The citadel resisted but then surrendered. Fulk appointed Viscount Aimery of Thouars as count of Nantes, later replaced by Judicaël. It was a vital victory for Fulk, and equally useful to the king.

The struggle with Odo of Blois continued, with success going one way then the other. Hugh, in alliance with Fulk Nerra, fought a further three-year war with Odo. Fulk had built the castle of Langeais by 994 at the junction of the rivers Roumer and Loire – the second oldest known castle in Europe. Odo took Langeais and Fulk appealed to Hugh for aid, but Hugh had become ill while in the Auvergne. Hugh did arrive belatedly, and a truce was agreed. Fulk went on to recover Langeais, another victory for Fulk and the king. This conflict ended when Odo developed a sore throat and then probably a heart attack. He belatedly entered the abbey of St-Martin at Marmoutier, seeking pardon for his many sins. He died on 12 March 996. Fulk Nerra was able to move into the Touraine.

Early in the reign Hugh faced opposition in the south, where his accession was questioned. Most southern magnates neglected to recognize him openly. Their chroniclers (mostly writing later) treated Capetian claims to the throne as illegitimate. The count of La Marche, when summoned by the king, asked 'who made you king?' The house of Poitou did form an alliance with Hugh, and the fall of Charles of Lower Lorraine led to wider acceptance of Hugh.

In examining Hugh Capet's relation with all the magnates, we need to examine the royal demesne, which gave the king more power than is sometimes acknowledged. Apart from the region around Paris and Orléans, the demesne included such important and growing towns as Senlis, Melun and Corbeil. The Robertian demesne provided sufficient wealth to support a powerful prince. To it had been added the surviving Carolingian demesne. It was once thought that this had virtually vanished, but recent study suggests the late Carolingians were more powerful than was believed. It is now realized that charters and other documents reveal a more extensive late Carolingian wealth, including vital *villae* or residential royal palaces.[57] Hugh took over the late Carolingian palaces at Attigny, Compiègne and Verberie. There were also regalian rights, including economic rights over lands and men and commercial transactions. Newman's comment, that one should not confound the royal demesne with the full extent of royal power, is relevant. Further wealth and power came from royal rights in the church, as in lay abbacies, and sees within royal territories. The king had received unction and was in a position that no other lay person in the realm could attain. Hugh did cede parts of the demesne to vassals, notably restoring Melun to Bouchard of Vendôme – but all kings had to balance wealth with keeping vassals loyal. Bouchard was also father-in-law of the king's major ally, Fulk Nerra. When Odo of Blois captured Melun in 991, Hugh recovered it with the aid of Fulk and Bouchard. It should be noted that Hugh's limited grants from the demesne were all recovered in time.

HUGH CAPET AND THE OTTONIANS

Hugh had to make concessions in order to keep his throne. These included giving up Verdun 'without any blood' to the German emperor.[58] At about the same time, Godfrey the Captive count of Verdun was released, after payment of a ransom. These acts helped reconcile France and the empire. The release of Godfrey was also a favour to his brother, Adalbero of Reims, a vital royal supporter. To make peace with the empire, Hugh was prepared to abandon the Carolingian position in Lorraine, but from temporary necessity rather than as a permanent loss. That the German kingdom was largely supportive to the French king was a significant part of establishing the dynasty.

After the death of Archbishop Adalbero, the unwise appointment of Arnulf to Reims and its consequences proved less damaging than it might have been, thanks to the actions of Ascelin bishop of Laon. Gerbert and Richer portray Ascelin as untrustworthy – though he was more consistently loyal to the Robertians than they were! Historians have followed them in seeing Ascelin as a 'deep-dyed … old fox' who committed many acts of treachery.[59] Thus Ascelin plotted with Odo count of Chartres, according to Richer, to hand West Francia to the Ottonians, which seems unlikely. Ascelin generally kept faith with Hugh Capet and advised him in a letter against the appointment of Arnulf as archbishop of Reims – advice he would have done well to follow. Like others, Ascelin survived difficult political swings – Laon was in the same region and in much the same situation as Reims – caught between the ambitions of France and Germany. Ascelin's action may be seen as underhand, but it was in line with his previous friendly advice to Hugh. Ascelin was a northern ecclesiastic with family links to the Ottonians and it is probable that his compatriots saw his attachment to Hugh Capet as treachery – though others followed when it suited them. Ascelin called a conference in Laon with Charles of Lower Lorraine and Arnulf archbishop of Reims. Ascelin must have decided in advance to pursue the interests of the French king. On the night of Palm Sunday, 29 March 991, Ascelin sat down to dinner in the duke's palace with Charles of Lower Lorraine and Archbishop Arnulf. Charles had his suspicions about Ascelin. He offered a cup of wine to the bishop, saying he should refuse it if he were Judas. Richer presents this in terms of the Last Supper, placing Charles in the position of Christ![60] Ascelin, like Judas, did not hesitate to drink. Charles asked him to swear fidelity, which he did, and then went to bed. Ascelin hid a sword under his cloak and took command of the town gates. In his own city Ascelin, 'the old traitor', roused his men and had Arnulf and Charles arrested.[61] The two leapt from their respective beds but neither had a weapon to hand – Ascelin had hidden their swords. Charles threw himself at the bishop but was surrounded, pushed on the bed, and held down. Ascelin said that he desired vengeance for his previous exile. Ascelin, 'as Judas delivered Christ, delivered Charles'.[62] Ascelin certainly looked like a treacherous customer to anyone who supported Charles but he had acted well in support of his king – not normally seen as treachery. Arnulf, Charles of Lower Lorraine, his wife Adelaide, his son and two daughters, were all sent to Orléans. They were shut in the tower and later moved to Senlis. Charles died a prisoner in 991, his son Otto succeeding to Lower Lorraine. Whatever his motives, Ascelin's arrest of the king's enemies, and especially of Charles, was the most important single event in allowing Hugh Capet's reign to survive, continue and prosper.

The act also resulted in the handing over of Laon to the king in 991. Thus both Reims and Laon were now under Hugh's control. The council held in the abbey of St-Basle at Vierzy in June 991 was attended by French bishops. It demonstrated that Hugh Capet was not without wider powers, could still summon a church assembly for his realm and expect most of his bishops to attend. Archbishop Arnulf was tried for treason. He was asked, 'Did you not open the gate to Charles?' When no answer came, one bishop shouted, 'Speak, wretch!'[63] Arnulf produced little defence, was found guilty, and deposed. As Gerbert wrote, Arnulf 'convicted himself'.[64] He pleaded for mercy, prostrating himself before Hugh. Arnulf was granted mercy but Gerbert was elected to replace him as archbishop of Reims.

Pope John XV was not impressed by a French synod deposing and appointing archbishops. The pope had little direct authority in France but applied pressure elsewhere, persuading Otto III to call a German assembly in 992. The French supported Gerbert; the Germans declared for Arnulf. Hugh Capet, in a letter to the pope, compared Arnulf to 'the ancient traitor Judas', calling him the 'partisan of a tyrant' (i.e. Charles) and a 'lost man' – but the papacy was adamant.[65] Hugh called a new council at Chelles in 993, defying the pope and confirming Arnulf's deposition. The dispute over the archbishopric continued to the end of the reign, with a French synod at Reims in 995 confirming Gerbert's election, followed by a German one denying it at Ingelheim in 996. The main protagonists, John XV and Hugh Capet, both died in 996. Gerbert bowed to pressure, abandoned Reims, and moved into the imperial camp. The Ottonians promoted his career in Italy – to an archbishopric and finally to the papal throne as Sylvester II.

Charles of Lower Lorraine's family was released but he himself died in prison, some said of poison. His son joined Otto III. He was proclaimed duke of Lower Lorraine but died young without heirs, and thus the direct Carolingian line came to an end. Glenn's point that Charles had greater public support than previously thought, suggests also that Hugh's achievement in overcoming that rival deserves greater praise than it has received. Bishop Ascelin later did act treacherously against Hugh and went over to Otto III of Germany, probably hoping to gain the archbishopric of Reims. Perhaps he was disappointed not to receive Reims from Hugh after his capture of Charles. He was never to gain it.

THE END OF HUGH CAPET'S REIGN

As if Hugh had not enough problems with his magnates, he also had trouble from his son Robert – despite his association as king at an early age. Robert was called 'the Pious' but ironically caused problems through his sexual desires and marital arrangements. He repudiated the wife, Rozala, his father had found for him. He desired marriage with Odo I's widow, Bertha. His father opposed the plan and the liaison created problems with the church. Bertha was older than Robert, though not by as much as Rozala. We shall return to this matter as it affected Robert's own reign. At any rate the difference between father and son soured Hugh's final year.

Hugh became ill in 996 when returning from pilgrimage to the tomb of his former friend Saint Maïeul. Near Tours Hugh felt worse and pustules broke out over his body, probably smallpox. He died at Melun on 24 October 996, aged about 55, and was taken for burial to St-Denis. This proved to be another significant example for the line that he founded, as St-Denis became the dynasty's necropolis.[66] Hugh left three legitimate children, his son and heir Robert, and two daughters, Hadwige and Gisela. There was also an illegitimate son, Gozlin, fathered by a concubine. Gozlin became abbot of St-Benoît-sur-Loire (Fleury) in 1004, and archbishop of Bourges in 1012 – in both cases through his half-brother King Robert.

Hugh Capet's achievements were greater than once thought. His horizons were less narrow than has been claimed – he was no mere ruler of just a principality. He asserted some authority over the princes throughout France. He overcame the threat from Charles of Lower Lorraine. He successfully combated Odo of Blois. Hugh also dealt with the church in France and in Rome as a king, calling assemblies and defying the pope. Hugh also corresponded with Theophano the Byzantine princess who had become empress in Germany, and the Byzantine emperor himself. He sought the Byzantine emperor's 'friendship' and a possible marriage for his son Robert – it was a route that later Capetian kings would follow.[67] Hugh had his eye on a wider world, the world of kings and emperors. The fact that he founded a great dynasty was more than an accident. He had arranged the succession of his only son in a way that would become common practice.

THE REIGN OF ROBERT II THE PIOUS (996–1031)

Robert was an experienced ruler when he came to the throne. He had been associated as king from the age of nine and was now about 24. He was born, baptized and brought up in the Robertian city of Orléans – 'the second capital', where he was associated as king and first crowned. It has been suggested that he was more 'Orléanais' than Parisien.[68] Before his accession Robert had sought independence from his father, most notably in choosing Bertha as his wife rather than Rozala.

We know a little more about Robert as a person than we do of his father. Helgaud of Fleury tells us that he had been seriously ill as a child, when his parents feared for his life.[69] Hugh and Adelaide made offerings to the church of Ste-Croix for his recovery. However he grew to be an able man of war who 'excelled in the military arts'.[70] Robert was tall and good-looking, with high shoulders, smooth hair, a well grown beard, a fair complexion, a prominent nose, a gentle mouth and a humble expression. He was 'affable and pleasant'. On horseback Helgaud said his big toe nearly touched his heel, suggesting possible deformity.[71] Robert enjoyed singing in church and hunting, and was constantly reading holy works – at prayer all hours of day and night. He carried a library around with him. He frequently pardoned sinners and thieves, as well as conspirators against his life. Once he reversed a death penalty, simply instructing the guilty not to do it again![72] Two chroniclers speak of Robert's *imbecillitas*. There is some dispute as to the meaning of this term but a reasonable translation is 'simplicity'.[73]

We are slightly better off for sources on Robert's reign than his father's. There are more charters and several relevant chronicles, including those by his contemporaries William of Jumièges, Adhémar of Chabannes and Fulbert of Chartres. William was a monk at Jumièges who continued the work of Dudo of St-Quentin before attempting an account of events in his lifetime from his Norman outlook. Adhémar was a monk at St-Cydard in Angoulême, who wrote after having a vision of Christ. Fulbert was consecrated as bishop of Chartres in 1006 when nominated by Robert. He wrote several letters to the king, mostly to excuse himself from councils, usually on grounds of health, or once because not given sufficient advance warning.[74] Glaber remains an important source, dying in c.1046.

The most important single source is a life of the king, the *Vita* by Helgaud, a monk at Fleury under abbots Abbo and Gozlin, who were both close to the king. Helgaud knew the king whom he saw as a father. He described the king's concern when Helgaud got into danger crossing the Seine – the king prayed and tears flowed down his face until they came safely to shore.[75] The *Life* was hagiographical, that is, largely uncritical praise of the 'glorious king of the Franks', 'this perfect king' who is treated like a saint, and is about the significance of religion in his life rather than an account of his daily doings.[76] It also breaks into sermons on piety and humility but does contain anecdotes about the king with the fullest information we have on him. Helgaud criticized the king's second marriage and 'the faults which he has committed', though he forgave him because he repented.[77] Helgaud had his own political stance which we need to understand in order to appreciate his work. His role at Fleury was guardian of the relics and treasure, as well as precentor with an interest in music. He also wrote poetry and was responsible for building at least one church (which he calls 'modest but charming') and rebuilding another of which he may have been the architect.[78] Helgaud records the king's visit to this church. Helgaud became a priest some time after 1022. He was at Fleury but not greatly favoured by Abbot Abbo (who was murdered in 1004). Helgaud supported Abbo's controversial replacement, Gozlin, who was nominated by Robert the Pious and was the king's illegitimate half-brother. Glaber called Gozlin 'the son of a prostitute'.[79] Helgaud, however, praised Gozlin and respected him. Helgaud's work was written soon after Robert's death almost in the form of a funeral oration.[80] We are fortunate that it survives in its original manuscript with corrections made by the author.[81]

The main problem for historians is that in contrast to Hugh Capet's reign, where the main sources were hostile, the major works on Robert the Pious are extremely favourable. The fact that Robert is known as 'the Pious' shows the rather uncritical attitude of those who thus described him.

ROBERT'S MARRIAGES, THE CHURCH, AND HIS 'PIETY'

Robert's first wife was Rozala (renamed Suzanne), 12 years older than him – he called her his 'old Italian'.[82] She was the daughter of Berengar II of Ivrée, ruler of Italy, widow of Arnulf II count of Flanders, and Carolingian through her mother. Robert repudiated her in 992, causing political problems for his father, as we have seen. He then fell for Bertha, widow of Odo of Blois, and caused even more problems by insisting on marrying her. He may have had political reasons, knowing that the widow needed – and indeed asked for – protection from Fulk Nerra of Anjou. Richer said she 'took King Robert as her defender of affairs and advocate'.[83] Bertha was the daughter of Conrad II king of Burgundy and descended from the Welf family. Archambaud archbishop of Tours married them in the presence of several French bishops who were prepared to accept the match, though others opposed it.

Robert upset the papacy by this second marriage, but in other ways upheld the Robertian tradition of support for the church, thus earning his nickname of 'the Pious'. Thietmar of Merseburg called him 'a man always ready for peace and respectful to all'.[84] He was a generous benefactor of churches, colleges and abbeys. He often gave aid for ecclesiastical buildings, as for the collegial church of St-Aignan in Orléans after a fire. He practised his religion assiduously in private and in public, frequently on his knees, praying in church. He loved to chant psalms and sing hymns, and even composed hymns. He was generous with alms for the poor – lay and clerical. He took 12 poor men with him at all times, picking up a new man to replace one who died. They were treated with royal benefits in food and living.

Helgaud has many tales of Robert's generosity, including secretly passing food to a poor man under the table from which he was eating at Étampes.[85] Crowds of the poor were frequently fed, watered and clothed by him. Once he insisted on washing the feet of over 160 clerks with his own hands and drying them with his own hair, in emulation of Christ.[86] He did not turn from lepers in horror but kissed them, read scripture to them, and entered their houses. Touching them took away all their sadness, says Helgaud. Robert was the first Capetian said to heal by touch or through a miracle, inspiring the later medieval belief that French kings could cure scrofula by touch. Once when Robert washed his hands, a blind man asked to have the dirty water thrown over him; the king obliged and the blind man saw.[87]

Robert liked to 'suffer the little children to come unto him' and tell them about saints, such as St Aignan, whose tomb he rebuilt. Robert was keen on relics, and presented many to churches. He several times carried saintly remains on his shoulders, for example those of St-Aignan in Orléans in 1029, as earlier he had done with those of St Savinien in 1028. He commissioned the New Testament illustrated by the Lombard Nivard, the only surviving manuscript of this type from France at this time.

The label of 'Pious' may nevertheless seem strange, since one of the most notable facts of his life was his rejection of Rozala in favour of Bertha, whom he desired – despite family and church objections. Hugh Capet had opposed the match and Gregory V condemned it. The result was a long dispute with the papacy. Bertha was the widow of Odo I of Blois, by whom she had five children. Apart from having a wife, Robert had been godfather to one of Bertha's children – a reason for the church to reject his attempted marriage. They were also within the proscribed degrees for marriage as second cousins in the third degree. Gregory V, encouraged by Otto III, condemned the match at Pavia. Robert was excommunicated and bishops who had supervised or encouraged the marriage were censured. Even Helgaud called it an 'illicit copulation', one from which 'the law separates him doubly' – though he omitted to name the lady concerned.[88] The archbishop of Tours, who conducted the marriage, was deposed by the pope. The situation for Robert improved in 999 with the election of Gerbert of Aurillac as Sylvester II. Sylvester had a history of links with the Capetians, and had tutored Robert. He sought reconciliation. Helgaud said Robert was pardoned because he became penitent and 'confessed his fault'.[89]

Bertha produced no royal offspring, and from c.1000 was no longer treated as queen. In 1004 Robert abandoned the marriage, presumably seeking an heir. His choice fell on Constance of Arles (or Provence), daughter of William the Liberator count of Provence and Adelaide of Arles (widow of Louis V).[90] She was the granddaughter of Fulk the Good of Anjou. Robert did not entirely end the relationship with Bertha, and problems continued between his partners and their respective relations and supporters. The marriage to Constance was approved by the church, and quickly produced offspring – four sons and two daughters – but was not altogether happy. For a start it aroused political hostility, especially from Bertha's relations including Odo II of Blois and Hugh of Beauvais. Hugh was a favoured companion of King Robert and sought to influence him against Constance, 'sowing trouble between them'.[91] The marriage represented a political shift for the king from alliance with Blois to alliance with Anjou. The committed chroniclers reflected the attitude of their lords. It is difficult to trust every word they wrote against Constance, but she certainly provoked their venom. Fulbert of Chartres wrote a letter to his friend Hildegar, noting that Hildegar had 'incurred the queen's bitterest hatred by opposing her' over her preference for the succession.[92] Fulbert of Chartres thought her 'quite trustworthy when she promises evil, as is proved by her many memorable deeds'. Glaber, a misogynist, said it was 'soft petticoat rule' and called her 'a haughty spouse', adding that if a man wanted something, a woman would not agree.[93] It was said she was domineering, caused rebellion by her sons, and interfered in the succession arrangements.

Nor did the churchmen approve of her southern background and the people she brought to court with their unfamiliar and lax manners. William of Volpiano condemned the southern ways, though he came from Italy. Glaber described their detestable habits, luxurious life and odd haircuts; 'flippant and vain, with strange manners and clothes ... like actors in indecent hose and shoes, [men with] clothes too short for them', who 'jump rather than walk'.[94] One might feel that clerics were easily shocked and southern clothes were not the only ones criticized at the time – note Thietmar of Merseburg's comments on women's clothes, which 'reveal to all their lovers whatever they have to offer'.[95] Constance's southerners also upset the court's ideas of religious practice. It is not clear what they did exactly, but it was said to show lack of respect for religion and was 'the mark of the devil'.[96]

Helgaud said the king called his wife 'Constant the inconstant', and contrasts her character to the king's.[97] When a thief cut a valuable pendant from the king's clothing, Constance called him 'an enemy of God', but Robert commented that God had wished him to take the object as he had more need of it than they did. Helgaud thought she 'never joked', but always said what she meant. Much of the criticism of Constance comes from monks with little sympathy for women, southerners, or Angevins. Modern historians have mostly followed the chroniclers seeing Constance as 'an impossible virago', 'a dreadful queen, cantankerous, miserly and jealous'.[98] Pfister thought 'the evil that Constance did to her country was incalculable'.[99] Fliche, with a little more benevolence, said at least her 'fecundity compensated for her bad character'.[100] Robert then tired of Constance and sought another divorce, going to Sergius IV (1009–12) in Rome for that purpose in 1010. His appeal was denied and he accepted the status quo, dismissing Bertha from court. Constance had been lodged at Theil while Robert was away. She claimed to have been visited at night by Saint Savinian with news of her liberation. When Robert returned and resumed their relationship, she believed the vision had come true. It was claimed that Robert now 'loved his wife more' – not very difficult given the amount of love shown to date![101]

We note other of Robert's faults, and wonder about his 'piety'. He was no saintly ascetic. It has been said that 'Pious' was applied by his chronicler or hagiographer, Helgaud of Fleury – as mere fawning. But other contemporary sources used the same term, including Fulbert of Chartres who wrote to the 'pious king'.[102] Adhémar of Chabannes thought Robert had 'great piety', as did

Glaber.[103] Odorannus said he was 'extremely attached to religion'.[104] There can be little doubt that Robert was genuinely interested in supporting religious establishments and was a respecter of relics. In a letter to Robert from Fulbert of Chartres, it is clear that the king was worried by the 'omen' of a 'rain of blood' in his kingdom, as reported to him by William of Aquitaine, who saw it as a portent. It was impossible to wash the 'blood' off anything but wood. It was probably in fact carried by the wind from the Sahara. The king approached Fulbert with his fears about the phenomenon, and the latter gave him a considered response, including a repetition of the views of Gregory of Tours on a similar occurrence in earlier days.

Theis makes two points on why Robert was known as 'Pious', suggesting that support of the church was inseparable from political leadership, and that Robert's reign coincided with the millennium and its religious connotations.[105] Robert frequently made public demonstration of his religion – praying, attending services, reading holy works, singing hymns and psalms, respecting relics and saints. It is probable that 'pious' did not mean quite the same as it means now, but reflected his general support of the church. The supposed 'piety' also resulted from his learning at the feet of such masters as Gerbert of Aurillac, which allowed him to read scripture and the work of the fathers, as well as to understand and debate intellectual matters with leading clerics in a way that many laymen, including his father, could not. According to William of Jumièges, Robert was 'the most devout king, a man well versed in letters, who had been educated by the monk and philosopher Gerbert', and received an education 'worthy of a cleric'.[106] He could sing hymns with clerics and even wrote hymns. He held various abbeys and was patron to others. He supported Cluniac reform, founded abbeys, built churches, and encouraged the development of colleges of canons regular. Prelates welcomed his support and he encouraged the development of count-bishops.[107]

Robert supported the Peace of God movement. During his reign assemblies proclaimed the Peace, and the movement spread through France. The enforcement of the Peace against laymen who broke it became the king's role as protector of church and people. Robert, like Hugh, has been called weak, yet in France he was the prime mover against lords who oppressed the church. Tackling lesser lords and castellans was relatively easy and within his powers, but he was also prepared to tackle greater lords, destroying Arnulf's castle at Yèvre, and opposing Odo of Blois for the monks of Massay. To the Peace movement was added the Truce of God, the agreement of Christian knights not to attack other Christians at certain times. The council of Elne in 1027 announced the programme: to ban fighting from Saturday evening to Monday morning. The idea of a truce was extended from Thursday to Sunday. It was again proclaimed at Arles in 1041, and Pope Nicholas II extended the idea to the whole of Christendom in 1050.

Robert was active against heretics and Jews, which suited the contemporary church. Fulbert of Chartres said the king should be praised when he 'aids Christians and harms heretics'.[108] Robert thus earned favour among French

clerics, part of the reason he was named 'the Pious'. The Jews could expect some
protection from kings, but Robert permitted persecution of the Jews in Sens
– praised by Glaber as 'proper vengeance' against these 'arrogant, envious, and
insolent' people.[109] Jews were expelled from other cities and there were killings
in Orléans after a report, probably false, that a Jew from Orléans had betrayed
Christians in the Holy Land to the Muslims. The accused man was burned alive
outside the city walls.

The emergence of heresy as a threat was a notable development. This was an
age that saw questioning of traditional beliefs. There is a story of a curate called
Leutaud at Vertus near Châlons in 1000.[110] One day this poor man, when supposed
to be working in the field, fell asleep and had a vision of bees entering his body
and giving him orders (messages from Satan according to Glaber). He went home
and repudiated his wife, destroyed the crucifix in the local church, and preached
against tithes – winning followers. He was convinced of his error by the local
bishop, Gebuin, and committed suicide, throwing himself headfirst into a cesspit.
Such radical ideas were often found in heresies – though we have no details of
this individual's beliefs or where they came from.[111] Some influence came from
beyond France – particularly Italy. Glaber says heresy was brought by an Italian
woman who 'seduced whoever she could'.[112] He also mentioned Sardinia and
Spain as sources of heresy. Adhémar of Chabannes reported groups of Manichees
arriving in Aquitaine, Toulouse and Limoges, between 1015 and 1020.

Heresy arose at about the same time in several places. 13 heretics were burned
in Orléans in 1022 on royal orders – the first official execution of heretics in the
west. They were clerics from Orléans. Richard II of Normandy alerted Robert
to the problem, having been informed of it by a clerk. At an assembly called by
the king, the clerics in chains were accused of opposing baptism and marriage,
questioning the Biblical version of creation, the virginity of Mary and the dogma
of the Trinity. They were accused, as most heretics were, of sex orgies and worship
of the devil. A debate before the king lasted nine hours. One of the accused was
Stephen, a former confessor of Queen Constance. The accused were found guilty,
unfrocked, and handed to the secular power. They were sentenced to death by
burning. As they came out Constance flew at Stephen, brandishing a staff with
which she knocked out one of his eyes. Robert's anti-heresy actions were praised
by ecclesiastics and chroniclers. It seems, however, that some had sympathy for
the clerics and tried (in vain) to rescue them. Others sought to kill them, and
Robert told Constance to go outside, believing she could prevent the clerics being
killed. One of the accused retracted and was pardoned. Thirteen or fourteen stuck
to their beliefs and were executed on 28 December 1022 on a large fire. A heretic
who had died before the scandal broke was exhumed and his remains thrown
into dung. This was the first punishment of the kind handed out to heretics in the
west. Robert dated one of his charters in 'the year when the heresiarch Stephen
and his accomplices were condemned and burned at Orléans'.[113]

It has been suggested that the church at Orléans was closely associated with
the king and queen, and that their harshness was an attempt to clear themselves

of any part in the heresy.[114] It is ironic that the same people who condemned the heretics, including the king, could hold an assembly in Paris to dispute the position of St Martial (a third-century bishop), and decide that he was one of the apostles![115] A brave Benedictine from Italy did stand up and argue that Martial had not been an apostle, but to no avail. At Tours they found a sandal of Christ's, while at St-Jean d'Angely they possessed the head of John the Baptist! Only *some* odd beliefs got you burned!

Robert earned a good reputation with clerics by supporting churchmen in disputes against laymen, but found difficulty balancing disputes between ecclesiastics, notably between bishops and abbots. His natural alliance was with the bishops, who generally supported him and were often counts as well as bishops. Robert's 'piety' in no way prevented him from intervening in church appointments. Many bishops had a close association with the crown and played a part in political decisions – as at Hugh Capet's accession.

A problem for the king was that papal reform aimed to release monks from lay control, with Cluny as the model. Robert's gifts to abbeys and support of reform overcame some of the opposition. He sided with abbeys against local lay lords, thus increasing royal influence. Robert extended the privileges granted to Cluny, to all the abbeys that depended on the great house.[116] He protected Cluny by forbidding the building of a castle close to it.

The chronicler Fulbert of Chartres sought aid from the king against the threat to his church from Geoffrey viscount of Châteaudun. Geoffrey had rebuilt his castle of Gallardon, previously destroyed by the king, and built a new castle at Illiers which posed a threat to Chartres. Fulbert did not receive immediate aid, either from King Robert, his son Hugh, or from Odo of Blois – and had to repeat his appeal because 'our church is oppressed'.[117] Royal intervention did not always win unanimous church approval. The canons of Chartres were not pleased with the king's choice of a successor to the bishopric in 1028, and complained to the archbishop of Sens. They wanted their dean Albert to be elected and did not want 'the king or any of our brethren of less sound judgement' to favour someone else – not a very laudatory comment on the king's judgement. When the king continued to oppose their man, they felt he was acting 'with no regard for what we said.'[118]

Robert was praised by chroniclers for his personal generosity. On one occasion he noted the silver decoration of a lance which Constance had presented to him. He asked a poor man to remove the silver and gave it to him to keep – but said not to tell the queen! Constance turned up later and was astonished at the state of the lance. The king claimed he had no idea what had happened – so he was not always truthful![119] Once Robert saw a man stealing a gold ornament, but allowed him to keep it. When Constance rebuked him he replied that the man 'needed it more than we do'. In a similar story, Robert found a clerk called Ogier stealing a candelabrum from the altar, but refused to tell on him. Constance was furious, swearing by the soul of her father to torture the men guarding it, remove their eyes, and do shameful things to them if they did not catch the thief – but Robert gave the clerk money to help him escape.[120] The king afterwards commented, 'God has made a gift of it to one of his poor'.

THE CLASH BETWEEN ANJOU AND BLOIS

One of the main problems for Robert the Pious was to manage the clash between his two most powerful vassals, the counts Fulk Nerra of Anjou and Odo II of Blois – both 'swollen with pride' according to Glaber.[121] These counts had been vassals of the dukes of the Franks but now ruled major principalities. Their rivalry had been significant under Hugh Capet, who had mostly allied with the Angevins against the Blesevins. The alliances were more mobile under Robert the Pious, after he repudiated his first wife to marry Bertha. Bertha was the widow of the count of Blois and the king's liaison with her meant a closer relationship with that principality. There may, indeed, have been political intent in Robert's marriage, distancing himself from the powerful Fulk Nerra. Royal policy underwent an abrupt about-change. Robert began to oppose Fulk's efforts to take the Touraine, and Fulk was forced to retreat. A further blow to Anjou was Robert's alliance with William count of Poitiers, until the latter made his peace with Fulk in 1000. This was a 'radical shift in Capetian policy'.[122] Odo II of Blois took advantage of the change to move against Anjou, especially when Fulk Nerra went to the Holy Land. Both sides sought to maintain their gains by building new castles, as now Odo built Montrichard on the Cher, and Montbazon.

The counts of Blois in the period were clever and ambitious but they met their match in the powerful and ruthless Fulk Nerra of Anjou. His ruthlessness is illustrated by the treatment of his wife Elizabeth. Having accused her of adultery and heresy, he ordered 'combustio comitissae' (the burning of the countess)![123] Robert the Pious may have wished to counter Fulk's power – though that was probably not his main motive for marrying Bertha. The situation altered radically again when the king married for a third time. Again there must be a suspicion that Robert had political aims. He did not abandon Bertha immediately, and did not abandon Blois altogether, but his new queen, Constance, was a cousin of Fulk Nerra and relations between the king and the count of Anjou then improved. By 1006 king and count were reconciled. Fulk took the opportunity to advance east at the expense of Blois, building castles as he went.

Fulk Nerra was powerful but at times he overstepped the mark. The most obvious case was his treatment of Hugh count of Beauvais, an ally of Odo of Blois favoured by King Robert. The killing of Hugh was condemned by Fulk's enemies, and by the church, and led to new hostility from Robert. Hugh was said to have influenced the king against Constance, turning Robert's mind back towards Bertha and the Blesevins. When the king was hunting in Hugh's company in 1008, a dozen men suddenly appeared, set upon Hugh, and killed him. Helgaud said King Robert was saddened by the death.[124] Fulbert of Chartres accused Fulk of being responsible for the 'dreadful' and 'monstrous crime', and guilty of treason for protecting the killers.[125] Fulk was threatened with excommunication, and it led to one of his four pilgrimages (that of 1010) to Jerusalem to seek forgiveness. Robert sought to renew his marriage to Bertha, going to Rome for approval. Fulk returned from pilgrimage, made his peace with Rome, and built a new monastery in penance. Robert gave up his plan to re-marry Bertha and restored Constance. Robert broke with Odo II of Blois over Sens and was reconciled with Fulk in Rome in 1016.

War broke out between Odo II and Fulk again in 1016 when Fulk allied with Herbert Wakedog of Maine and tried to take Tours. Odo came to its relief and they fought at Pontlevoy on 6 July 1016. Fulk was unhorsed and knocked unconscious, but Herbert came to the rescue. He charged Odo's left, which scattered, leaving Odo and his infantry surrounded. Pontlevoy gave Fulk the advantage over Blois on his eastern border, and was a vital event in the struggle between the principalities. Odo tried to move into Touraine in 1021 but was forced to retreat. Fulk made new advances and, among his successes, captured Doué-la-Fontaine.

In 1021 the future of the counties of Meaux and Troyes became uncertain on the death of Stephen of Vermandois without heir. Many major figures had a claim, including Odo II, Fulk Nerra and the king. Odo refused to abandon his claim and ignored a summons to court. One cause of dispute was a difference between Odo and Richard of Normandy but it was the claim to Meaux and Troyes that was at the root. Robert had at first accepted that Odo should have them, but now had second thoughts about allowing Odo control over lands on both sides of the Capetian heartland. There followed a five-year war.

Odo was furious at losing royal favour. He wrote hotly to the king with his advice – 'if you will deign to listen'.[126] Odo had not come when summoned, but still rebuked the king for making a decision 'without hearing my case'. He reminded Robert that, when in favour, he had served him 'at home, in the field, and in foreign parts'. He resented the discord 'that you have caused' and appealed to the king to stop persecuting him. He sought reconciliation. What this letter shows is that Robert's power was considerable and that even an aggressive and powerful prince like Odo needed to be on good terms with the king.

Robert was able to call on the aid of Fulk of Anjou against Odo. Fulk was only too happy to seize disputed border lands with the king's acceptance. In 1026 Odo II besieged Montboyau and Fulk countered by taking Saumur winning a victory near Amboise. Eventually terms were made, whereby Fulk kept Saumur and Montboyau was razed to the ground. It was a significant step in the advance of Anjou into the Touraine.

In the latter part of Robert's reign Fulk sought gains in the south, at the expense of Aquitaine. By 1020 he held much of northern Poitou and built the castle of Moncontour to maintain his power there. He also moved into Berry, an area of royal interest. Anjou was becoming Greater Anjou, a threat to the crown once more. The switch of royal alliance from one count to the other made much sense. It was not only necessary to split potential opposition but to balance comital expansion in territory and power.

ROBERT THE PIOUS AND HIS SONS

Robert ended his battle with the church over Bertha in order to have sons. The marriage with Constance was difficult but provided sons in abundance – perhaps too many for the stability of the realm. Royal sons always had ambitions, and younger sons were often resentful if they received less than hoped for. Constance provided Robert with four sons: Hugh, Henry, Robert and Ralph. Their daughter Adela was betrothed to Baldwin (V) of Flanders 'while she was still in her cradle', and in 1028 became the wife of this important prince.[127]

Robert followed his father's example by associating his eldest son, Hugh, in his rule in 1017. Helgaud thought Hugh 'a young man of great merit', liked by all.[128] Hugh, however, died young on 17 September 1025, leading to a dispute over the succession, generally blamed on Queen Constance. However, hints in the chronicles suggest she was not alone in believing her third son, Robert, would make a better king than the second son, Henry. In a letter, Hildegar wrote to Fulbert of Chartres calling Henry 'a hypocrite, lazy, weak, and ready to take after his father in having no regard for what is lawful' – but otherwise he was OK! Hildegar added there was disagreement among the bishops over the succession which was 'causing discord'.[129] Robert however had his way. He associated the eldest son, Henry, who was consecrated on 14 May 1027 – with Odo's agreement. This was obtained by accepting Odo's tenure of Champagne. Henry's association was a cause of trouble with Constance, who favoured the younger son, Robert. She showed her 'feminine animosity' and rode off in a fury immediately after the ceremony.[130] Others also opposed Henry's succession, which did not bode well for his reign. There seem to have been genuine doubts about Henry's abilities. Probably some nobles were doubtful about establishing the dynasty with the third Capetian in a row. There followed rebellion by the sons Henry and Robert in 1030, according to the hostile chroniclers backed by Constance with her 'feminine machinations'.[131] At the time the queen was with her husband in Burgundy, and one must doubt any direct role in the rebellion. What is mysterious is the motive of Henry, already recognized and associated. In any case, the ageing king soon made peace with his sons.

BURGUNDY

Robert's provision for his sons was not considered sufficient by them, and there was a series of rebellions, possibly backed by Constance. Robert did make attempts to provide for his sons. In turn, Hugh and Henry were associated as kings. Robert's greatest acquisition for the monarchy was the duchy of Burgundy, where he named his then second son Henry as duke in 1017. When Hugh died and Henry became heir to the throne, the third son Robert was named duke of Burgundy in 1027. We have to cope with the history of Burgundy without aid from Helgaud, who said he left it to historians to deal with – if you could find one, and if that one could write something of sufficient length![132] We have to cover Robert's greatest achievement through the eyes of less favourably inclined writers, such as Adhémar of Chabannes and Ralph Glaber.

Robert had shown an interest in the south from the beginning. He was active south of the Loire, campaigning in Poitou and Berry in 997 against the viscount of Bourges. He led an expedition to Aquitaine in 1019. Robert intervened several times over southern church appointments, naming abbots in Berry. On the death of his uncle the Robertian Henry duke of Burgundy in 1002, Robert saw the possibility of gaining the duchy. He opposed the claim of Otto-William count of Mâcon. Duke Henry had ruled Burgundy for 37 years but left no sons, only a stepson, Otto-William, whom he had given the county of Nevers and adopted as heir. Otto-William now passed Nevers to his own son-in-law, Landry, and occupied the duchy. Robert's motive for opposing may have been fear that Otto-William would unite the county with the duchy and take it under imperial control.

Robert the Pious raised a force with support from Richard II of Normandy. Richard had his own problems in Normandy and was glad to ally with the king. They invaded Burgundy in 1003. Robert received local aid from Hugh of Chalon. He failed to take Auxerre but ravaged Burgundy to the Saône, firing the abbey of St-Germain at Auxerre. When Robert and Richard besieged Avallon, Otto-William came to make his peace. Robert took Avallon and Auxerre, though Sens did not yield until 1015 – when Dijon also fell. Opposition was overcome and the king took over the duchy.

Robert used his position as protector of the church to support the bishop of Sens against the local count, Rainard II. The count acted with disrespect to the church, which he despoiled apparently claiming that he was 'King of the Jews', while Glaber bluntly called him 'the Mad'.[133] On one occasion, turning from the archbishop at mass, Rainard presented his backside for the kiss of peace, and then spat at the archbishop.[134] For some unclear reason, when the king took Sens, the count was naked when he fled.

Otto-William was the son of Gerberga and represented imperial interest, so Robert's move into the duchy of Burgundy was important in the current and subsequent clash of France and the Holy Roman Empire over Burgundy as a whole. The death of Bishop Bruno was followed by Otto-William's withdrawal. He submitted, as did his ally and son-in-law Landry of Nevers. The kingdom and county of Burgundy remained imperial, but the duchy kept its French connection. Over the next decade Robert recovered Sens and Dijon. His marriage to Constance of Arles was a further extension of southern interests. Their second son, Henry, was named duke of Burgundy. When Henry became heir to the throne, his younger brother Robert was given the duchy. Burgundy remained a strong base of Capetian support. King Robert detached Auxerre from the duke of Burgundy's control, thus making a direct gain for the crown.

ROBERT AND THE PRINCES

Robert, like his father, was no mere puppet in the hands of the princes. He had to cope with a series of difficult problems, including the rivalry of Blois and Anjou, and the need to intervene in Burgundy. Throughout the reign Normandy was a significant ally, especially under Richard II, but relations were not always easy. The dukes kept links with their Viking relatives, and Normandy had its own problems, including a peasant revolt in 997. Sometimes, through Normandy, the Vikings were employed as allies by the king, but it was a link that brought criticism. William of Jumièges notes that Robert himself was worried about Viking influence, 'fearing that France might be destroyed by them'.[135] It was why he called the rival rulers of Blois and Normandy together at Coudres, hoping to bring peace.

Flanders was an occasional royal ally. The county was closely involved with Robert's interests in Lorraine, and his relationship with the German rulers. Robert's repudiation of Rozala soured relations with her son, Baldwin IV. Robert II tried to revive the French claim to Lorraine. His father had abandoned those claims to keep in with the German emperor and reward Archbishop Adalbero for support. Robert sought to recover the duchy, invading in 1006 and 1019, albeit without final success. Robert did marry his daughter, Adela, to Baldwin (V) of Flanders, developing a greater link with that principality which supported the monarchy in the next reign. When Henry II of Germany invaded Flanders in 1020 he did so with Robert's backing but gradually relations improved, cemented by the marriage to Adela, who was brought up in Flanders until old enough to consummate the match in 1028. Flemish interest moved eastwards. Like Burgundy, Flanders was not entirely French. Its links with the German kings was as great. Robert's situation was eased by division within Flanders leading to war between Baldwin IV and his son, which led to the former taking refuge in Normandy. On his return, with Norman aid, he came to terms with his son, and they agreed on joint rule.

ROBERT AND THE CASTELLANS

Lesser lords holding fortresses became a significant power in the west, gaining independence they had not possessed previously. Such lords emerged in the royal demesne as elsewhere. This is reflected in royal documents, where demesne lords appeared more often than princes as subscribers. The castellans included the lords of Gallardon, Nogent-le-Roi, Montfort l'Amaury and Épernon. Already, however, we see the king countering this development. Robert demolished several seigneurial demesne castles, including those at Yèvre, Déols and Gallardon.

Historians have pointed to a change in government in the latter part of Robert II's reign.[136] It was marked by a move from royal decisions through diplomas with the assent of major princes, nobles and clerics, to a more private type of charter with the assent of local lords. This has been seen as showing a decline in the court with greater men no longer attending, 'a degradation in the nature of the royal acts'. But Robert, at regular intervals, continued to meet greater lords and prelates. It is more likely that the change in the documents represents business done by the king in a more personal manner, in the presence of a few chosen men. One finds that the assent of the queen and the sons was more commonly noted on the charters, what Lemarignier calls 'a kind of family government'.[137]

One major fact, often overlooked, was the effect of economic difficulties brought about by natural causes. Robert's reign saw a series of famines – in 1001, 1003–8, 1010–4, 1027–9, and in his last year. A man caught selling human meat in a market was arrested and executed. A succession of bad harvests could not but have a detrimental effect. Robert's piety through alms and generosity was particularly well timed to counter hostility.

Robert the Pious settled the last rebellion by his sons Henry (now his heir) and Robert in 1030. Henry, Robert, and their mother Constance were reconciled and travelled with the king to Poissy. The marriage had not always been easy, but it had endured for 30 years. In June there was a partial eclipse of the sun – always an omen. Robert suffered a fever and died on Tuesday 20 July 1031 aged 61. He was buried at St-Denis before the altar of the Holy Trinity. Queen Constance survived into her son's reign, to 1034, when she too was buried at St-Denis, the first Capetian queen to be thus honoured.

CONCLUSIONS

Like his father, Robert the Pious has not always been credited with his considerable achievements. One historian sees the first four Capetian reigns as 'long and ineffective'; another as 'the nadir of the French monarchy'.[138] Favier says Robert was 'a king of France who could not go without risk from Paris to Orléans'.[139] Yet Robert strengthened the royal resources, not least by the acquisition of Burgundy. He held his own against the Ottonians, the fate of the duchy of Burgundy being the best example. He generally pursued a policy of friendship with the German king and avoided war – seeking agreement over several disputes. In 1006 Baldwin IV of Flanders attacked Valenciennes, but Robert did not join him, and agreed a peace with the German king, which was then forced upon Baldwin. Robert's meeting with Henry II by the Meuse in 1006 was the first between a Capetian king and a German ruler.

Robert also avoided involvement in Italy, leaving the field to Henry II. Both kings supported Cluniac reform. In 1023 Robert agreed to a meeting with Henry II. They came to opposite sides of the Meuse – Robert on the left bank, Henry on the right, and met as 'equals'.[140] They exchanged presents, both offering expensive gifts, but each accepting only modest ones. Henry made the first approach, crossing the river. The following day Robert crossed to the German side. They issued a joint diploma in favour of an abbey. In 1025, when the Lotharingian nobility turned to Robert for aid against Germany, he did not respond. His sister married Rainier IV count of Hainault, a further link with the Lotharingian nobility.

Robert should be credited with not overreaching himself. He sought Burgundy, but was not prepared to risk more distant adventures. He was offered the crown of Italy in 1024 by the opponents of Conrad II (successor to Henry II), but refused it for himself and his son Hugh, allowing the German emperor to employ his energies there. Hugh probably resented this decision on his behalf, and it contributed towards his rebellion. Conrad received the Italian crown at Milan in 1026 and was crowned emperor in 1027.

The accession of Robert meant father to son succession, the first of a very long line. The Capetians ruled until 1328 but the following kings of France were also descendants. The descendants of Hugh Capet ruled France for eight centuries under 32 kings.[141] Karl Leyser claimed that the accession of 987 was 'important above all in retrospect', suggesting that it was rather less important at the time.[142] There may be truth in this, and one winces a little at some more recent comments on 987, seeing Hugh Capet as 'the creator of our country' and so on.[143] Had the Robertians not held on to the crown for more than one reign our perspective would have been different. But in a sense all history is retrospect – we can only look back on the past and we must to an extent see it from our own point of view – so being important in retrospect does matter. In Aquitaine at least, by the end of Robert's reign the continuation of the Capetian dynasty was more readily accepted.[144]

The first two Capetians retained the Robertian patrimony. Hugh made concessions to establish his position but Robert recovered Dreux and Melun, and won control of Burgundy. When Helgaud listed the palaces where Robert gave alms to the poor, what is impressive is the number and importance of the locations, including Paris, Senlis, Orléans, Dijon, Auxerre, Avallon, Melun and Étampes.[145] Robert was *not* a poor king, as witness his frequent gifts of alms, food and drink to crowds of poor, lay and clerical – on Helgaud's evidence on a daily basis – of bread, fish, wine, vegetables and money. Nor was Robert as narrow in his interests, geographically, as one might suppose from the frequent comment that the early Capetians were only minor princes. Robert was active, as shown by charters and other evidence, in Flanders, Aquitaine, Burgundy and Normandy.

We should not underestimate the problem of uniting France in this period. In the 11th century there were major differences between the principalities, and not only in political terms. The language of north and south was different. The cultural and social differences were great – note the hostility in the north to the southern ways of those who accompanied Constance to the court of Robert the Pious. It may, nevertheless, reasonably be claimed that by 1031 the kingdom of France had been firmly established. The Frankish and German principalities had threatened to become independent, but within France that had not happened. The princes of Normandy, Aquitaine, Blois, Anjou and Flanders were powerful men with much authority in their principalities, but they were part of a kingdom whose king they recognized. At times they sought his approval, his confirmation of grants, or his support. They saw themselves as belonging to France.

5

Successful failures, 1031–1108

We have already seen Henry I (1031–60) and Philip I (1060–1108) branded with the first two Capetians as weak and ineffective kings. One contemporary called Henry 'the present kinglet', who had 'not deviated from his father's worthlessness'.[1] We have seen that neither Hugh Capet nor Robert the Pious was truly a feeble or poor king, and that each made reasonable achievements. Yet at least those first two kings have earned some praise over the centuries, if only because Hugh founded the dynasty and Robert was pious. It is difficult to think of any similar way in which the next two kings of the dynasty have been noted for any achievement at all. Yet, as this chapter heading implies, like their immediate predecessors, they deserve better of historians.

One reason for belittling their reigns in England is that they lived in the age of the Norman Conquest. William the Conqueror rose to power during the reign of Henry I, and conquered England during that of Philip I. Such an achievement might be thought to dwarf whatever the French kings managed, particularly as the Norman expansion seemed at the expense of the French monarchy. The Norman dukes from William became kings and could compete with their overlords.

To continue the historical onslaught via modern historians one might quote, for example, Hallam – that Henry I was 'too much a territorial prince, too little a king'.[2] Or De Castries, who condemns him for being 'the least known of all the Capetian kings', and – on the grounds that no chronicler gave him much space, and records from the reign have been destroyed – 'a mediocre man'.[3] Bautier called him 'the very feeble king of the new Capetian dynasty'.[4] To Koziol he was 'the weakest of all Capetians'.[5] Dhondt thought that in the principalities 'royal authority was nil'.[6] Fliche believed Henry was not very intelligent.[7] Petit-Dutaillis considered that signs of royal development only appeared with Philip I, while under Henry, defeated at Varaville, 'royal power was weaker than ever'; that the monarchy had made some advance under Robert the Pious but under Henry I 'it now seemed condemned to stagnation'; that anarchy in France now 'reduced the Capetians to impotence'.[8] In general the view of historians echoes that of Lemarignier – the decline continued.[9]

It is, however, with Henry I that the modern historical pendulum begins slowly to swing in favour of the Capetian kings – in Henry's case modestly. Dhondt showed Henry's renewal of French interest in Lorraine; the king's confirmation of charters was welcomed in Anjou; he had some influence in Brittany. His relations with the German emperor, his Russian marriage and his links with Poland show a broader interest. Jean Dunbabin thinks that at least the central part of the reign was a 'time of solid achievement'.[10]

The lack of evidence is a major problem. Dhondt found Henry 'a phantom to the historian', and a tyrant to the church.[11] But the lack of material can be exaggerated. What is lacking is a major friendly source. Henry I had no apologist to compare with Helgaud for Robert the Pious. This inevitably means a less friendly press than most members of the dynasty. He does, however, appear at reasonable length in some contemporary sources, including Hariulf of Fleury and Ralph Glaber. He features in Anglo-Norman sources, including William of Jumièges, William of Poitiers and Orderic Vitalis – all with a Norman viewpoint.[12] The chroniclers of Jumièges and Poitiers dedicated their works to the Conqueror and wrote later. Henry also featured briefly in the *Life of King Edward*, probably by a monk at St-Bertin. We therefore see him from an external and usually critical viewpoint – especially when he was in conflict with the lord where the chronicler was based.

Hariulf was born near the abbey of St-Riquier in Ponthieu in the year of Henry I's death, placed in that abbey as a child. He became a scholar who wrote lives of saints, books of miracles, poetry and history. His main work, for our purposes, was his *Chronicle of the Abbey of St-Riquier*. He was the abbey archivist with access to diplomas, charters and letters – some of which were destroyed in a 12th-century fire. The work survives in an autograph manuscript, beginning 'I Hariulf, a monk of St-Riquier'.[13] He became abbot of Oudenbourg near Bruges. He thought Henry covetous, because the king wanted a villa that Hariulf thought belonged to his abbey. A slightly more positive note is struck by Ralph Glaber, who said Henry was lively in mind, active in body, generous to the church, 'vigorous in arms' and worthy of his realm – but his praise is fairly conventional. The *Life of King Edward* also gives conventional praise to Henry as 'a man admired for his military courage and goodness'.[14] William of Jumièges also praised Henry's military skill.

Henry I was born in c.1007 and made duke of Burgundy by his father in 1015. Despite his own mother's opposition, he was associated in rule with his father in 1027, after the death of his older brother Hugh. Despite opposition, Robert the Pious had kept firmly to his own choice, and Henry succeeded to the throne on Robert's death in 1031.

HENRY I (1031–60) AND FAMILY REBELLION

We may question the bad press of Henry I in many respects and see him as another early Capetian who has deserved better of history, but there is no doubt that in the first part of his reign his position was 'precarious'.[15] His mother Constance received a bad press from a biased group of clerical writers. William of Jumièges called her 'his most wretched mother', and said the king was 'afflicted by the step-mother like hatred of his mother Constance' who 'made an effort to dethrone Henry in favour of Robert'.[16] She has not fared much better from historians – Dhondt calling her a 'femme noire'.[17] There is some exaggeration in the attacks on her but she does seem to have engaged in family politics. She was condemned for encouraging rebellion by the sons against their father and blamed for favouring one son over another. After the death of her eldest son Hugh, she opposed the choice of her second son, Henry, as heir, riding off after Robert associated him in rule. Then and later, she favoured the third son, Robert. Chroniclers also expressed doubts over Henry's suitability to rule, though it is difficult to pin down the fault. There is hesitant criticism of Henry's character or personality – did he seem weak, or weak-minded? A study of his reign does not bring out any fault that would disqualify him from kingship. Bautier accuses him of misogyny.[18] A recent suggestion, and only a suggestion, is that he might have been homosexual. This is an attractive idea because it would fit the hints against his character lacking any definite nature. It is a possibility but there is no direct proof. Nolan suggests that Constance may have been at odds with all her sons, wanting more control, or perhaps to protect her dower.[19] Glaber commented that on Robert the Pious' death there was 'cruel discord', not just with Henry, but between Constance and her sons.

On King Robert's death, Constance took over a number of important towns – Senlis, Sens, Béthisy, Dammartin, Le Puiset, Melun and Poissy – apparently on behalf of her younger son, but these were her dower lands, to which she had a claim. It showed distrust of her son Henry and was virtually rebellion from the first moment of the reign. When Henry I appointed a new bishop of Sens, Gelduin, in 1032, he was opposed by Odo II count of Blois. Henry besieged Sens but had to abandon the attempt. In the following year, part of Sens was handed to Odo by Constance, seeking his protection from her son. Odo occupied Sens and Henry fled to Fécamp to seek aid from Robert I of Normandy, 'according to the fealty the duke owed him'.[20]

Henry recovered from this early reverse. He was welcomed in Normandy, receiving aid from Duke Robert, as well as from Fulk Nerra of Anjou and Baldwin V of Flanders. Constance was besieged at Poissy and fled. Henry refused to agree terms and waited until she was forced to seek pardon – which was granted. Constance died in 1034 and was buried at St-Denis. Fulk Nerra's role was vital. Bachrach claims that he saved Henry I's throne.[21] There were other factors, but it is true that the support of the count was vital, especially against Odo of Blois. Fulk defeated the Blesevins at Gournay and Clairvix, and Odo had to seek peace.

Baldwin of Flanders became the king's brother-in-law and allied with him and Godfrey duke of Lower Lorraine against the emperor Henry III. Godfrey's father had been duke of Upper and Lower Lorraine, but the German ruler opposed him succeeding to both regions. Henry I and Baldwin V supported Godfrey, showing again that the early Capetians had not lost interest in Lorraine. Godfrey submitted to Henry III in 1049, but trouble broke out again in the 1050s. Probably Henry I pressed his rights in Lorraine at his final meeting with Henry III in 1056. In many ways the reverse of Capetian weakness is the truth; the accession of the new dynasty deprived the *East* Frankish ruler of power in the west. It was the Capetian who now influenced episcopal elections in Lorraine. The Germans had previously influenced late Carolingian successions to the West Frankish throne; that power was now lost.

The situation in the north leads one to question the general belief in Henry I's weakness. Some of the princes at least thought him capable of rule. He also saw the need to divide the princes against each other. If one prince or one group of princes proved hostile then he sought alliance with their natural enemies. Henry quickly regained Poissy and Le Puiset, and Constance abandoned her rebellion – if such it was. Henry granted the duchy of Burgundy to his brother Robert, previously known as 'Lackland'. It had been Capetian policy to keep the duchy in the family. Henry himself had held Burgundy for a considerable period and gained experience of rule there. Handing it to Robert has been treated as weakness, 'a political error', but it was the move most likely to win Robert's cooperation.[22] The result was an enduring alliance between the Capetian dynasties of France and Burgundy.

RELATIONS WITH NORMANDY

Normandy provided a safe haven for Henry I after the rebellion by Robert. He found help in recovering the lost towns and restoring his authority. Duke Robert I welcomed him at Fécamp and gave military aid. In return the new king granted the French Vexin to Robert, a potentially serious loss to the crown. The Vexin lay between the Andelle and the Oise and was commonly divided between the monarchy and Normandy at the River Epte. Henry I's grant to Normandy was later recovered but it left a claim that Normandy would repeat.

Through Normandy, Henry I developed a good relationship with Edward the Confessor during his exile. The 'virtuous kings' met and Edward visited the French court.[23] It was claimed later that Edward picked up some ideas while there, including his decision to attack usury. When Edward acceded to the English throne in 1043, Henry sent an ambassador with congratulations. When Edward exiled Godwin of Wessex, Henry with Baldwin of Flanders contacted Edward on the earl's behalf. Relations with Normandy fluctuated, as they did with Blois and Anjou. During the minority of William the Conqueror, a bastard and unsure of his hold on the duchy, Henry acted as his protector.

The first difficulty came through Henry's difference with Waleran I count of Meulan. The king chased Waleran into Normandy and received Norman aid against him. It led, in 1040, to Henry besieging Tillières-sur-Avre, a Norman outpost against Blois held by Gilbert Crispin, who refused to surrender to Henry, who took and destroyed it. Then in 1043 Henry entered Normandy through the Hiémois against rebels from the Île-de-France who had taken refuge there, including Waleran. Henry took Argentan with Norman aid, and fired it. He allied with Thurstan Goz, lord of Toutainville and viscount of Exmes and they seized the Hiémois. William the Conqueror saw this as invasion. Thurstan was exiled and

Henry returned to France – but he rebuilt and garrisoned Tillières. Henry made a point of facing any of his princes who seemed too powerful. In Normandy he became known as 'the castle-grabber' – his usual policy in the principalities.[24]

The Conqueror needed the king's aid against internal opposition and probably did homage to him.[25] Henry knighted William in c.1044 and assisted William against rebellious subjects in 1047. William only survived his minority thanks to 'crucial assistance' from the king.[26] Richard II had been a loyal supporter of the Capetians and was generally 'pacific'.[27] Duke Robert I had not been able to keep a firm hold over the duchy and the situation worsened with the accession of an illegitimate minor in a situation akin to 'anarchy'.[28] The trouble in Normandy turned into rebellion against the young duke in 1046, partly caused by resentment of the activities of William's uncles, William count of Arques and Mauger archbishop of Rouen, who had strong influence. The latter was unpopular, reputed to dabble in necromancy. However, information on the uncles comes largely from hostile chroniclers and probably both men should be seen in a kinder light.[29] William of Arques was a patron of the church, and the building of Arques was hardly a crime. Mauger encouraged the Peace of God in Normandy and introduced the Truce there in 1047.

The 1046 rebellion was fired by the barons of Lower Normandy, including the 'two arrogant viscounts' of the western regions – Nigel I Falconhead of the Cotentin and Ralph I of the Bessin, 'who had conceived a hatred' for the duke.[30] Magnates from the Cinglais joined as well as cousins of the duke, including William count of Eu. Another cousin, Guy of Burgundy, led the rebellion. Guy was a younger son of the Conqueror's aunt, Adeliza, and her husband Reginald count of Burgundy. In Normandy Guy received the castles of Brionne and Vernon, but was apparently not satisfied. He was accused of seeking the dukedom for himself. The rebels tried to capture young William at Valognes but he escaped at night to Falaise. 'Forced by necessity' he went to Henry I and threw himself at the king's feet, requesting aid.[31] Henry I responded, 'at last remembering the support once given to him by the duke's father'.[32]

Henry entered Normandy in 1047 and camped between Mézidon and Argences. A number of Norman supporters of the duke joined him. They advanced to occupy the river bank, facing the rebels and battle followed on flat ground at Val-ès-Dune beside the River Orne. When the armies met, 'the entire earth shuddered and trembled'.[33] Henry was struck on the shield, unhorsed, and helped back into the saddle. He then 'frequently made himself visible' to counter any news about the mishap.[34] He won the battle and the duke's enemies fled. Loose horses galloped around and many rebels drowned in the Orne – the mills at Borbeillon were blocked by bodies floating into them. The battle was 'won by the king rather than by the duke'.[35] William of Jumièges saw it as a 'happy battle', since the result was to 'ruin so many fortresses of criminals and houses of evil-doers'.[36] Guy of Burgundy shut himself in his castle of Brionne, which the Conqueror besieged from 1047. Guy surrendered in 1049 and was pardoned, returning to Burgundy. William of Eu was forced into exile.

William then had to cope with Geoffrey Martel of Anjou in southern Normandy and Maine, 'a treacherous man in every respect', though modern historians suitably detect 'a very great political intelligence'.[37] Geoffrey seized the city and county of Tours from Theobald I of Blois-Chartres and then defeated and captured him at Nouy in 1044. Tours, Chinon and Langeais were recognized as Geoffrey's in return for Theobald's release. Geoffrey went on to occupy Le Mans. He did homage to the king for his acquisitions but Henry began to fear his growing power. William of Poitiers claimed that William of Normandy served the king 'with devotion and fidelity', and that the king preferred his advice above all others.[38] At any rate Henry turned to this powerful rival of Geoffrey, who joined him in an attack on Anjou, capturing Mouliherne near Angers in 1049.[39] Geoffrey retaliated by taking Ste-Maure. The conflict was balanced rather than decisive (as often presented) and was prelude to a new peace.

William turned his attention to the southern strongholds of Domfront and Alençon, controlled by the Bellême family and not yet Norman. The Bellêmes were descended from the Creil family, vassals of the Robertians.[40] In the 1020s they extended their power north into Normandy where Yves Bellême became bishop of Sées. Geoffrey Martel provoked the Conqueror by taking over these castles on the southern border of Normandy in alliance with the Bellêmes. The garrison at Domfront favoured Anjou rather than Normandy, allowing Geoffrey to enter without a fight. William advanced to Domfront, where he learned of an opportunity to take Alençon. Leaving a force to blockade Domfront, he moved to Alençon. The garrison of the outpost he attacked, jeered from the walls, waving skins and calling 'pelterer' – mocking his illegitimacy and his family that prepared human skins for burial.[41] When William captured the outpost he had the hands and feet of 32 mockers hacked off. The brutality persuaded Alençon and Domfront to surrender. William's growing success posed a new threat that the king could not ignore and he now turned again to Martel, but William defeated the allies at Varaville.

THE THREAT FROM BLOIS

It has been recognized by most historians that during the first half of Henry I's reign, and until c.1044, the main threat came not from his mother Constance, or his brother Robert, both of whom were fairly easily reconciled, but from Odo II count of Blois. Henry sought alliance with Conrad II of Germany, while Odo now attempted to detach Henry's youngest brother, another Odo, from the king. Henry met Conrad II at Deville on the Meuse in 1033 and agreed a marriage between Henry and Conrad's daughter, Matilda. She was however an infant, born in 1027, and died in 1034 at Worms.

There was intermittent fighting between the king and Odo. Their earlier clash had ended in peace but trouble soon broke out again in 'a second civil war' from 1034–39, mainly rising from Odo's ambitions.[42] Odo II's lands were in three main blocs: a western region including the Touraine and Blois; a northern wedge including the Beauvaisis; and the eastern area including Troyes. In short, Odo posed a considerable threat to the royal demesne. He sought further territories that would have completely surrounded the demesne. Thanks to Henry he failed. Henry won the support of enough vassals to contain Odo, who tried to win Dreux but failed. In 1037 Odo II died in Lorraine at the battle of Bar-sur-Aube.

Odo II's lands were divided between his sons, Blois going to Theobald I, and Troyes and Meaux to Stephen. Both sought to make the youngest Capetian, Odo, an ally. Rebellion came in 1041 with an attempt to depose the king. Powerful magnates were also involved, including Ralph IV count of Amiens, Valois and the Vexin, Waleran I count of Meulan, and the lord of Mortain. Henry fought off the opposition, capturing brother Odo who was imprisoned along with the count of Vermandois. The king made gains for the royal demesne. On the death of Rainard count of Sens, an ally of Odo of Blois, Henry also restored the Sénonais to the demesne.

The tables were further turned by the advance of Anjou against Blois-Chartres and the victory of Geoffrey Martel at Nouy in 1044, leading to the takeover of Touraine. The growth of Angevin power under Geoffrey Martel was considerable. The county of Anjou tripled in size and became a major principality. Henry had already begun to back off from his alliance with Geoffrey Martel. The Angevin move to an imperial alliance was a direct provocation to the king. He made one more attempt at reconciliation with the count but relations had broken down by 1044. Theobald of Blois' step-daughter Agnes married Henry III in 1043. She was also related to Geoffrey Martel (daughter of his wife Agnes by William V of Aquitaine). Dhondt saw this as Geoffrey moving towards an imperial alliance, while Guillot suggests the marriage made Geoffrey 'the most redoubtable enemy of Henry I'.[43] The death of Henry's wife Matilda in 1044 broke the last link in friendly relations between France and the Empire. Henry then married Anna of Kiev, recently rejected as a wife by the Salian.

Henry I now allied with magnates in Lorraine, notably Godfrey the Bearded duke of Upper Lorraine. Lorraine had long been disputed between the East and West Franks. Godfrey had been denied Lower Lorraine by Henry III and Baldwin V of Flanders but was defeated and imprisoned, losing his lands. On his release in 1046 he again rebelled. In 1046 Henry I invaded Lorraine while Henry III was in Rome, but abandoned the attempt. Nevertheless he continued to spend much time on his northern border, probably trying to pressurise Henry III.[44] The two met again at Ivois in 1048 and issued a treaty of friendship. Henry I had broken up the threatening alliance between the Empire and Anjou. Henry could now take the offensive against Geoffrey Martel.

Henry I's position was stronger by the 1050s. He made an agreement with Henry III, confirming his retention of part of Lorraine. 1054 saw another twist in the alliances when Theobald of Blois did homage to Henry III. Henry III now turned hostile to the French king and even challenged him to single combat. As always, it was refused, but they parted on bad terms, the first open break between France and the Empire since 1033.

When the count of Sens died in 1055, Henry I took over that city. Theobald turned to Germany against the Capetian, and the emperor turned to Pope Leo IX. Henry I's problems with Leo only ended with the latter's death. In a dispute over the succession to the bishopric of Langres, Henry had to abandon his preferred candidate, a double defeat, since the bishop was also count. The clash with the pope also led to hostility from ecclesiastical chroniclers. Henry III's death in 1056 eased Henry I's position. He had gained little in his relations with the emperor, but he had held his own and established a claim on Lorraine. He had also seduced Geoffrey Martel from his imperial alliance.

THE THREAT FROM ANJOU

Anjou had proved an ally early in the reign, happy to join the king against the old foe, Blois. In the 1040s the situation altered. Odo II of Blois died in 1037 and his sons faced problems. Alan III of Brittany died in 1040. William the Conqueror was not yet firmly established and Normandy still unstable. Baldwin V showed more interest in eastward expansion and Lorraine than elsewhere. The king's brother was not yet firmly established in Burgundy. Geoffrey Martel had quarrelled with his father, but they were reconciled and Fulk, though nearly 70, embarked on his fourth and last pilgrimage to the Holy Land, leaving Anjou under his son. Fulk underwent the most violent penance, dragged naked with a rope round his neck, and beaten on the back with a stick. Perhaps not surprisingly he did not survive long. He returned to Europe but died at Metz on 21 June 1040, when Geoffrey succeeded. The series of deaths made life easier for the king.

Geoffrey's accession did not weaken Anjou, since he was already ensconced in power and Anjou was 'stronger than it had ever been in its history'.[45] Geoffrey was master not only of Anjou but of Aquitaine, the Agenais, Bordelais, Vendômois and Maine. Dhondt saw 1043 as 'a turning point in the history of Henry I'.[46] By this time the king had dealt with the early opposition. He had twice beaten his Blois/Champagne opponents. He had received support from Anjou against that principality's 'natural enemies'. In Bachrach's view Anjou had played the 'decisive role' in the king's success to that date.[47] Henry had co-operated with Anjou in the early part of his reign but Geoffrey now looked a bigger threat than Blois. Dhondt argued that Geoffrey Martel initiated the change in alliances of this period, from ambitions of expansion, seeking an imperial alliance against the French king. Henry tried to block the move by meeting Henry III at Ivois in 1043 but his initiative was rejected and he was forced to oppose Geoffrey.

Henry had given some support to Angevin advance but became worried as Geoffrey took over the Touraine and Vendôme from Theobald I. Henry encouraged Geoffrey Martel's interests during Fulk's time, as an ally. Fulk had been guardian to the young Bouchard count of Vendôme, and Geoffrey's overlordship was accepted by the king, providing that his own right was recognized. Angevin power in the region increased while the king's motive was to counter the interest of Blois.[48] Bouchard died and Martel took over the county directly, a usurpation to which the king 'shut his eyes'.[49] But when Geoffrey captured Tours in 1044, Theobald turned to the king for help, hoping to separate him from Anjou. Henry I now feared Anjou's interests in Aquitaine and Gascony. Geoffrey sought to further his interests by alliance with the German emperor.

THE ALLIANCE SWITCH

The Norman chronicles veer in their assessment of Henry as he turned from an ally to an opponent. The fault was not on one side – though the Normans and most English historians have blamed Henry. Crouch points out the previous close relationship between the duchy and the Capetians, and sees Henry's change in 1052 as a 'dubious decision' that weakened the monarchy.[50] Yet Henry was pursuing a consistent policy, seeking to contain any prince who threatened to become over-powerful, switching alliances to keep the balance. Henry I consistently insisted on his powers within the principalities. Note, for example, the number of charters issued to Norman abbeys – which clearly valued royal support. The chroniclers played down the fact, but Henry called on Norman troops when required – and received them. Even in Normandy the clerks named the king before the duke in their prayers.[51]

William the Conqueror, as he matured, sought to expand the duchy, partly at the expense of the king. Henry in return wanted to restrict William's activities. Dhondt shows a change in royal policy from c.1044. The first half of the reign had focused on the demesne and the threat from Blois. Now Henry turned his attention to containing other princes, notably Geoffrey Martel of Anjou and William of Normandy.

In 1050 Geoffrey Martel repudiated his wife Agnes and ended that link with the empire. From 1052 there was a change in the political pattern in France when the king 'radically reversed his system of alliances'.[52] Martel, a strong opponent of the king in the middle years of the reign, became the king's strongest ally – until both died in 1060. At the time Geoffrey was threatened by Normandy, Aquitaine and Blois, and needed to restore relations with the king. The changeable alliances of Henry I were not simply the result of royal caprice, but of fluid political situations. It should be noted that our main sources are Norman and now become hostile to Henry as they had always been to Anjou.

Dhondt thinks that the alliance between Anjou and the king, which dominated the end of the reign, was initiated by the count. Bishop Gervase had been forced to flee from Le Mans by Martel who refused to let him return. The dispute caused trouble between the count and the papacy. Now Henry helped Geoffrey to find a solution. They supported Gervase as archbishop of Reims, and the papacy dropped its hostility to Geoffrey. Geoffrey now favoured church reform and restored monastic lands. He agreed to return the Vendômois to the heir, Fulk l'Oisin (the Gosling meaning Nincompoop!). Henry and Geoffrey met at Tours in 1057 and went on to Angers, where Henry was able to call Geoffrey his 'fidelis'.

From 1052 Henry allied with Geoffrey against the growing power of Normandy, an alliance that strengthened in the following years. The Normans had been Capetian allies since 987 so this was 'a momentous change'.[53] The Conqueror's campaign against Domfront and Alençon played a major role in causing the change. Henry reversed his policy with Normandy, partly forced on him by William's actions. According to Orderic Vitalis it was 'Satan, who never ceases to molest the human race, [who] now stirred up great enmity between the French and the Normans'.[54]

Henry received encouragement from discontented Normans. William of Poitiers names magnates who went over to the king during the siege of Arques.[55] William of Jumièges says that Roger Montgomery went to Henry in Paris 'because of his perfidy', while his five sons committed crimes in Normandy.[56] The rebels inflamed the king with 'their insane provocation'.[57] Normandy had shown increasing interest in Brittany and Maine. Another threat to the king was the effort of William to improve relations with the emperor, Henry III, and an interest in Lorraine.[58] The Conqueror did approach Henry I in 1052, probably seeking reconciliation, but if so the attempt failed.

Maine was surrounded by principalities and was of interest to the Capetians. The key figure was the lord of Bellême, who established a proto-principality. The Bellêmes had striven to win Maine from its count, Herbert Wakedog. With William the Conqueror a minor, the Bellêmes acted. Maine was divided between Hugh IV, son of Herbert Wakedog, and Geoffrey Martel. Hugh IV's marriage to Bertha, daughter of Odo II of Blois and widow of Alan of Brittany, was 'catastrophic for the influence of the count of Anjou in Maine'.[59] The Bellêmes supported Hugh, but he was defeated and captured by the Angevins. The young Herbert II count of Maine, son of Hugh IV who died in 1051, was controlled by Martel who took over the county. Hugh was probably kept by Martel and unable to go to Normandy until some years later.[60]

In 1051 William the Conqueror married Matilda of Flanders, daughter of Baldwin V and niece of Henry I. The church opposed the match since William's uncle had been married to Matilda's mother – though the marriage had not been consummated. The marriage went ahead and was eventually accepted by the church in return for each partner sponsoring the building of a church. The alliance between Normandy and Flanders, the greatest northern principalities, was a threat to the monarchy, and part of the realignment of alliances.

The Conqueror declared his interest in Maine by moving into the county. In 1054 he built a castle at Ambrières in northern Maine, posing a threat to Geoffrey of Mayenne, who was pro-Angevin. The Conqueror attacked his castle and Geoffrey of Mayenne sought aid from Martel that was not forthcoming. Geoffrey of Mayenne surrendered and did homage to William. Henry I supported Martel in Maine while Bellême turned to Normandy for aid. The Bellême heiress, Mabel, daughter of William Talvas by his first wife, married the Norman lord, Roger II of Montgomery, viscount of Exmes, in c.1050. Mabel was a domineering woman, criticized by several chroniclers. She often visited Orderic's abbey of

St-Evroul, always with a large retinue that strained the abbey's resources. The abbot asked her to moderate her habits but she ignored him. The chronicler thought it was the abbot's curse that made her ill with sharp pains in the chest which she could only relieve by having a baby suck her nipples. (The baby died but Mabel recovered.)

William garrisoned several border strongholds, including Domfront, Alençon and Bellême. Yves of Bellême, bishop of Sées, may have joined his niece Mabel and her husband in 1057, though Guillot believes he stayed loyal to Henry.[61] By 1060 Mabel and Roger, and hence Normandy, were possibly in control of the old Bellême lands – though Guillot argues that Norman power there was never great and Martel remained overlord of the Bellême lands until his death. We are inclined to accept Guillot's view over this difference in historical interpretation.

In 1052 Henry reversed his policy and allied with Anjou against Normandy. William of Poitiers blamed 'the counsel of perverse men'.[62] William of Jumièges agreed that Henry was 'roused by malicious and envious suggestions of some men at his court', but the change was the result of more complex causes, primarily fear of the Conqueror's growing power. Geoffrey had suffered most from William's expansion. He had also lost his link with Germany after repudiating Agnes of Aquitaine in c.1049.[63] The marriage had given Geoffrey interests in Burgundy and the Nivernais; its end meant the abandonment of those hopes. Geoffrey then married Grécie from the family that held Langeais, part of the new relationship bringing king and count together.

In 1053 Henry I supported the rebellion against the Conqueror by his uncle, William count of Arques, 'a very fierce and a good, bold knight'.[64] The Conqueror had abandoned his former advisers in favour of younger and lesser men. William of Arques was granted the county of Talou but remained dissatisfied, and built his castle of Arques in defiance of the duke.[65] The Conqueror's uncles felt ignored in the new regime and justified rebellion by pointing out William's illegitimacy. The Conqueror besieged Arques. Henry I entered Normandy 'with a powerful army, wreaking havoc among the Normans'.[66] He aimed to relieve Arques but his allies were beaten at St-Aubin-sur-Scie. The Normans 'as if in flight', drove the French into an ambush and then turned back on the enemy as they pursued.[67] Henry thought of getting supplies into Arques, but eventually retreated to St-Denis, 'shamefully' according to William of Jumièges.[68] William of Arques surrendered and was exiled to Boulogne, where he died. His brother, Archbishop Mauger, retired to his estates in Guernsey, and later drowned near Cherbourg.

In 1054 Henry I and Martel invaded Normandy again with two armies – north and south of the Seine. The king's younger brother, Odo, led the northern force. He moved through Neufchâtel-en-Bray to Mortemer in the Norman Vexin, choosing comfortable lodgings and not expecting attack. The Norman chronicler accused the French of being 'very arrogant, very cruel and very destructive' – laying waste, taking booty, preoccupied with arson and rape.[69] During the night they drank wine and caroused. They were attacked at dawn by Robert of

Eu in a battle that went on until noon, and Odo was beaten. Guibert of Nogent's father, Evrard, had fought for the French and his son described how 'it was my father's fate to be taken prisoner'.[70] Guibert claimed that William was not given to releasing prisoners and preferred 'captivity for life', though Evrard was later released.[71] Guy I of Ponthieu was another captive, and became William's vassal. After the battle William sent Ralph of Tosny to shout the news into the king's camp from a nearby tree (or hill in another account).[72] He called 'Frenchmen, Frenchmen, get up, get up! Be on your way, you are sleeping too much! Go and bury your friends who have died in Mortemer'.[73] Henry was in bed when the news came. The invasion was abandoned

In 1057 Henry and Geoffrey invaded Normandy yet again, this time from the south. The royal army laid waste as it progressed towards the sea. Part of the royal force was defeated at Varaville near the coast when attempting to ford the Dives, 'weighed down by the plunder they had taken'.[74] William attacked the rear part of the royal force, stranded on the right bank when the tide turned, 'the sea rose and the waves were high'. Henry I climbed a hill 'and saw his men being destroyed' becoming 'filled with anger and sorrow'. The king was persuaded to retreat. William made gains in the wake of the battle, recovering Tillières in 1058, and taking Thimert after a siege.

Although the Conqueror emerged successful from the conflict, he had played a defensive role during Henry I's reign. William faced severe threats and had to beat off serious invasions. Maine stayed in Martel's grasp until his death. Varaville did not end the conflict and a further forgotten campaign followed in 1059. It was only the death of Henry I and Martel within months of each other in 1060 that gave the duke much needed relief. Both were succeeded by minors. William was able to turn his attention to England. The king's death, however, did not give William immediate triumph (as the Norman chroniclers imply).[75] His victories had been defensive; there was no peace for a further seven years.

HENRY I'S MARRIAGES

In 1033 a marriage was arranged between Henry I and Matilda, daughter of the emperor Conrad II but she was a child and died in 1034. Henry's first marriage was to another Matilda, the niece of Henry III of Germany. The marriage was short-lived. The second Matilda was a child, of ten, and not able to marry until 1043. They produced a daughter but Matilda died in 1044 and the child only survived four years. Henry's second marriage was the exotic match to Anna, daughter of Jaroslav the Wise grand duke of Kiev.[76] Most chroniclers could not get her father's name right – he appears as Georgius, Juriscloth, Juliusclodii and Buflesdoc.[77] There had been several recent matches between Kiev and European powers, including Hungary and Norway. For a king in this period, especially one without an heir, there was a long gap between the death of Matilda and this second marriage. There were no reports of mistresses and historians have hinted at 'some more intimate problem', and possible homosexual leanings – though there is no real evidence.[78] The nearest is the comment of Fulbert of Chartres, that he was 'effeminate' (*mollis*).[79]

Anna's father was Jaroslav grand duke of Kiev, her grandfather St Vladimir. Jaroslav's conversion to Christianity made possible links with the West. Henry sent two embassies to Kiev, the first in 1049 arranged the marriage, the second to escort the bride to France. She brought gifts rather than land, including Anna's Hyacinth, a gem later presented by Louis VI to St-Denis. The marriage probably occurred in 1051. Anna was intelligent and active. Unusually for the period for a woman she was able to sign her name. She was the first French queen known to employ a tutor for her family, in Enguerrand '*pedagogus regis*'.[80] Henry and Anna's son, Philip, was born in 1052 and two other sons followed in Robert and Hugh, though Robert died young in 1063. One result of the match was the introduction of a new family name for their son Philip, which became a well-used name for the dynasty. It was Greek rather than Russian, but entered France through Anna. We shall resume Anna of Kiev's colourful career after she was widowed in 1060.

HENRY I, THE SOUTH AND THE CHURCH

There is not a great deal to record of Henry's efforts in the south. Robertian and Capetian interest in Burgundy was sustained, but elsewhere royal interest had declined. Evidence for the reign in general is slight and for the southern region very slight. The grant of Burgundy to Henry's brother Robert has been criticized but had beneficial results – the ducal dynasty remaining staunchly loyal. Robert was succeeded by his grandson, Hugh, noted for piety, opposing the Moors in Spain, and ending his life as a monk at Cluny.

Henry continued to develop royal relations with southern churches. Henry supported the Peace of God movement and encouraged the Truce of God. 'On the advice of King Henry' Aimon archbishop of Bourges called the peace council at Bourges.[81] The movement was pushed forward there and at Limoges, knights now to be punished if they failed to take the oath of peace. Oath taking was extended from knights to all men over 15. The archbishop of Bourges organized a diocesan militia to enforce the peace. In 1037 the movement met a serious setback in a clash with Odo of Déols. The archbishop's 'plebeian multitude' was slaughtered by the knightly troops. The peasant force, including 2000 on asses, panicked and many drowned in the river. Berry was left in disorder and castellan independence increased.

In 1041 at Arles the Truce of God programme was proclaimed fully. The extended days on which it should apply were defended: Thursday in memory of the Last Supper, Friday for Good Friday, Saturday for the day Christ's body was placed in the Holy Sepulchre, and Sunday for the Resurrection. In 1050 the Truce received the backing of Pope Nicholas II who declared it should apply to all Christendom. As one historian puts it, 'the Peace was to protect some Christians all of the time, the Truce was to protect all Christians part of the time'.[82]

Henry supported church building and endowments, especially in the demesne. He endowed St-Martin-des-Champs near Paris and supported monastic foundations, chiefly on the model of Coulombs. With the reform of houses of canons, new foundations were made such as St-Martin-des-Champs. Anna of Kiev was also generous, as with gifts to St-Vincent at Senlis.

HENRY I'S ADMINISTRATION

This reign saw significant development in making government records with the emergence of diplomas, both royal diplomas with multiple subscriptions and non-royal subscribed by the king. Fifty-two of the first type are known, and 29 of the second.[83] One of the most obvious conclusions is that royal approval of local agreements mattered. It may be partly from survival rates, but surely not entirely, that there was a considerable increase from 1043 – only two multiple diplomas survive before that date. One sees the emergence of a royal bureaucracy. Until this reign large assemblies had produced the main acts of government but that process waned and was replaced by a more intimate group around the king. The main focus for those receiving diplomas and those signing was Paris and the demesne. Witness by the great was not common though it did occur, and showed the occasional presence at court of practically all the leading lords. However, the main evidence is for subscription by middle-ranking individuals, a working bureaucracy operating under royal instruction.

THE END OF HENRY I'S REIGN

Henry I did not associate his son Philip until late in the reign, partly because Philip was very young. He was finally associated on 23 May 1059 at Reims, still only seven. When Henry became ill in 1060 he asked for a potion to prolong his life and was given a purgative. He suffered pains in the stomach with extreme thirst and, in the doctor's absence, demanded water and took a drink too soon, so that the purgative poisoned him. Orderic casts doubt on the abilities of the doctor, John of Chartres, whom he says was nicknamed 'Blockhead' (Surdus).[84] Henry died at Vitry-aux-Loges near Orléans on 4 August 1060.

Like all the early Capetians, Henry was a greater success than the chroniclers allowed. Modern historians have sometimes been kinder, seeing him as a 'realist'.[85] He had succeeded where it mattered. The major threat had come from Blois in the first part of the reign. Henry dealt with that successfully. Anjou then presented a major threat but Henry again coped and previous enemies became his allies. Henry has been blamed for not containing Normandy but that was hardly for want of trying and the success in England did not come until after Henry's death. Henry pursued a familiar Capetian policy, combating threats at home and not becoming involved in distant matters. Letting princes pursue their interests beyond France was generally a successful policy – it kept them busy and often caused their downfall. The later wars between England and France have a complicated causation and one can hardly blame Henry I. Had his invasions of Normandy been more successful, William might have failed in England – but it is an uncertain theory. In reality there was not much Henry could have done to foresee or prevent those later developments – except accidentally.

Nor was Henry an inward-looking princeling. He married a Russian princess in 1051 and his political interests included Germany, Byzantium and Poland. Casimir of Poland came to Paris in 1034 when he needed refuge. He entered Cluny but was recalled to Poland in 1041, when his vows were reversed by Benedict XI. He returned to Poland as King Casimir I and married Jaroslav of Kiev's sister, another link to Henry.

Perhaps Henry's main achievement was to strengthen his position in the old Robertian principality, now the royal demesne – particularly in the Île-de-France. The crisis facing him probably posed the most serious of all the threats to the continuation of Capetian rule during the first four reigns, a combination of attacks from powerful princes, and from a coalition of lords in the Île-de-France. Early on Henry suffered losses – forced or granted – including the Vexin, the Vendômois, Perche, Valois and Meulan. By the end of the reign he had recovered all except Langres, which Dhondt reasonably calls 'a good result'.[86] Henry stood firm against Blois and prevented its greater expansion. He stood against Anjou's attempt to bully him through alliance with the emperor and the papacy, and here too survived. He faced a formidable list of princes in Odo II, Geoffrey Martel and William the Conqueror, but came through, looking considerably stronger in 1060 than he had in 1031.

THE REIGN OF PHILIP I (1060–1108)

Henry I's son Philip was born to Anna of Kiev in 1052. His naming is a little mysterious but came from the Russian connection though of Greek origin. Jean Dunbabin investigated the matter thoroughly but without a certain conclusion.[87] The oddity in the first place is that the Franks normally used restricted family names. For the Robertians or Capetians one would have expected Robert, Hugh or Odo. Historians assumed that 'Philip' came from the Russian connection, which seems likely, but no known member of Anna's family was called Philip, though it was a name used in Byzantium. There are other theories, none proven. Perhaps it was a bid to appear more imperial. It is interesting that both Philip I and Philip II used the addition of 'Augustus' in charters. Perhaps it was a harking back to Philip of Macedon father of Alexander – but then why not 'Alexander'? Perhaps it looked back to the Roman emperor Philip the Arabian (244–49), which sounds unlikely though he was said to be the first Christian Roman emperor. He and his son, also called Philip, were martyrs in Decius' persecution. The most likely theory is that the name harked back not to an emperor but to the apostle Philip. There were claims about his part in the conversion of the Russians (or Scythians – respected in Kiev), and it was claimed of the Gauls. The name was probably suggested by Anna of Kiev, who after Henry I's death married into the

Bar family which also began to use the name Philip. The name also linked to an interest in classical literature and the unlikely (but believed) idea that Frankish rulers had Trojan ancestors. The obituary of Philip I claimed: 'this king was of the family of great Priam'.[88] Whatever the reason, and we cannot know for certain, it was an 'eccentric' choice but proved enduring. Other Philips followed in the family, including one of Philip I's sons by Bertrade.

Philip I was not associated as king until Henry was ailing on 23 May 1059. He was consecrated at Reims by Archbishop Gervase, confirmed by church, lords and people – though it was an affirmation of rights and not an election.[89] Philip was only eight at his accession in 1060, and his uncle Baldwin V acted virtually as regent – Hariulf called him custodian or guardian.[90] It is slightly surprising that Baldwin rather than Robert of Burgundy took this role. Robert was the former king's brother, while Baldwin was merely his brother-in-law, through marriage to Adela. Fliche thought Henry I made the decision to make Baldwin regent, in association with Anna of Kiev.[91] In a charter Baldwin was called 'the head of the royal palace'.[92] Bautier suggests the term 'co-regent', in harness with Anna.[93] Baldwin kept the king close, travelling with him around the royal demesne – to Dreux, Paris, Senlis, Étampes and Orléans. Baldwin also took Philip to Compiègne, Reims and Flanders. Some acknowledgement was made of Anna's position. In a charter Philip states, 'I assume royal power conjointly with my mother'.[94] Anna's disappearance from the royal court coincided with her decision to make the criticized marriage to Ralph of Crépy.

There was no serious opposition to the succession, despite Philip's tender years – a sign that the dynasty was now established. Philip reached his majority and took over in 1066; Baldwin V died the following year. Philip was the last of the quartet of early Capetians who have been condemned as weak and unsuccessful – but we shall continue to insist that he no more than his predecessors deserves this reputation. Guibert of Nogent criticized Philip – 'a man most mercenary in what belonged to God' who had 'squandered' church goods during vacancies.[95] Guibert was a troubled soul, losing his father when only eight months old, dominated by a mother he admired but feared, who spent her later life in a hairshirt. He confessed to wickedness in youth, without providing details. He was tutored by a man whose learning he did not respect and who beat him unmercifully and unjustly. Guibert was of knightly class, connected to Clermont, but chose to enter the abbey of Fly (or St-Germer), becoming abbot of the small house of Nogent in 1104. His father had been unable to consummate his marriage for years, until experiencing sex with another woman. The editor of Guibert's *Memoirs* suggested the author might have been a repressed homosexual – a common modern suspicion.[96] Guibert's major works were biblical commentaries, an account of the First Crusade, and the autobiographical *Memoirs*, though he confessed to writing poetry on the model of Ovid, works 'bereft of all decency'.[97] Nevertheless he condemned sexual misdemeanours, rounding on Jean count of Soissons for only attending church to eye a beautiful woman with whom he would later pass the night. The *Memoirs* are vivid and provide unique information, such as an account of a storm that hit his abbey, damaging its structure and possessions. One effect was that some monks had their pubic hair scorched! Guibert supported papal reform and criticized simony, married priests, absentee priests, and other sins of the age. It is not surprising that this man who condemned minor sexual transgressions with great vigour should criticize the king.

Orderic Vitalis called Philip 'indolent, fat, and unfit for war'.[98] Anglo-Norman chroniclers were critical. William of Malmesbury described him as 'belching from his daily surfeit of food', preferring cash to war so that he could 'return to his gluttony'.[99] Nor was Philip popular with the papacy. Gregory VII, the great reforming pope, called him a tyrant possessed by the devil, a perjurer, and a robber.[100] There were a few friendly comments; the chronicler of Morigny, whose abbey benefited from royal generosity, thought Philip 'wise', having 'admirable prudence and depth of spirit'.[101]

One can again marshal a host of critical comments about the king, but in terms of modern assessment the tide begins to turn, with some historians – most of whom utter much criticism – offering faint praise. For one, Philip was, of all the incompetent and weak early Capetians, 'the worst of them'.[102] It was 'an obscure reign' whose ruler had an 'un-Christian attitude'.[103] Luchaire commented that it was one of the longest reigns in the history of France, 'but also one of the most empty', and 'one of those that brought least honour to the dynasty'.[104] He adds that no king had a more limited effect on events or men. Many criticize his looks and behaviour – 'fat, sensual and greedy', 'a somewhat distasteful figure' with 'largely negative qualities'.[105] To Calmette under Philip 'royal power is so feeble that there is virtually no point in the sovereign pretending to examine all the rights which come to him through suzerainty'.[106] Barlow called him 'a prince of the lowest reputation'.[107] Fawtier thought him 'the Capet who has been most severely judged both by his contemporaries and by latter-day historians', 'unattractive, earthy, sordid, gross', a 'fat monarch … resented for his gourmandizing, his sensuality, his greed' but adds reluctantly that he was 'a practical man and a realist'.[108] Barber sees him as 'overweight and inert' and in later years thinks he 'lost the capacity to rule'.[109]

Nevertheless there has been a movement in historical opinion and Philip has his defenders, even admirers. Lemarignier wrote that although things did not develop until Louis VI, there were signs of improvement under Philip.[110] Luchaire commented that most have made 'a judgement of extreme severity', seeing 'a glutton, debauched and lazy, a ravisher of women', but this 'appears to us to accord little with historical truth'.[111] Luchaire adds that Philip's vices were hardly worse 'than the common measure', and it was only in his last years that he grew obese and inactive. He attributed the obesity to 'a malady' shared by several of the family – not least Philip's son Louis. The historian concluded that this monarch had political ability, successfully led armies, and was 'far more active than tradition allows'.[112] In evidence he pointed to the many expeditions of Philip – to Flanders in 1071, Corbie 1074, Poitou 1076, Brittany 1076, the Vexin against Normandy over many years, as well as numerous military efforts against local lords and castellans. Luchaire saw him as 'an intelligent prince, practical, and endowed with political sense'. Hallam believed that under Philip royal power began 'very slowly to make a comeback'.[113] We see a shift towards some praise for a Capetian monarch, albeit often lukewarm. Petit-Dutaillis saw the first signs of a stronger monarchy, though still condemning Philip for shameless simony and scandal.[114] The expansion of the demesne and the development of royal administration have won over a number of historians. Most favourable is the author of the only major work on Philip's reign, Augustin Fliche, who saw this as 'one of the most important [reigns] in the Middle Ages'.[115]

FLANDERS

Philip was active in Flanders in the early part of the reign. As a minor he had to accept decisions by Count Baldwin V (1035–67). Baldwin's most significant act as regent was not to act against his son-in-law, William of Normandy, encouraging the conquest of England. Fliche rightly saw that Conquest as 'malheureuse' for the future of France.[116] The failure to stop William may have had unfortunate consequences for the monarchy but it is far from certain that opposition would have been successful or more productive. Given Baldwin's relationship to William one could hardly expect him to be hostile. In many ways avoiding involvement benefited the gradually growing strength of the crown.

Baldwin V died on 1 September 1067. On the premature death of Baldwin VI in 1070, Philip supported his son, Arnulf III (1070–71), aged 15. The succession was disputed by the boy's uncle, Robert the Frisian, younger brother of Baldwin VI, who entered Ghent and seized power. Arnulf's mother, Richildis, appealed to the king and Philip took an army to Flanders. Robert left Cassel and battle was joined on 22 February 1071. The best accounts describe a Flemish charge that proved successful.[117] It was not a decisive defeat for Philip, who withdrew, but the young Count Arnulf was killed in the conflict and his mother captured.

Philip continued the war and Robert of Frisia was captured. There was a rising in St-Omer in favour of him and he was released. Philip sacked and pillaged St-Omer with some violence, but both sides then agreed peace and Richildis was released. Philip showed his political sense by recognizing Robert as count, in return for the cession of Corbie. Philip now married Bertha of Holland, Robert the Frisian's step-daughter, in c.1072 though there were no children until 1081 – not a unique situation with the Capetians who were often not prolific sires. Robert of Frisia in 1103 agreed to provide military service for Henry I of England but 'saving his fealty to Philip king of France'.[118]

PHILIP I AND NORMANDY

After the death of Henry I relations between the monarchy and Normandy seemed good. Wace saw the duke as 'a very close friend' of Philip – but not for long.[119] During the minority Baldwin of Flanders allowed and even encouraged the Norman Conquest of England. As a minor Philip cannot be held responsible. William's conquest succeeded and he became king of England. William was a vassal of the French crown but he and his successors were now an obvious threat to their overlords.

When Philip came of age he tried to counter the Norman accumulation of power. William, according to Wace, sought out the king at St-Germer and offered to be his vassal for England in return for alliance, but Philip consulted with his advisers and refused. He spent his reign seeking to contain Norman power, with some success in Brittany. Brittany was already a target for the Conqueror, and now became a centre of opposition to Normandy. It was a divided region and its powerful neighbours had ambitions there, including Anjou, Flanders and the monarchy. Count Conan died in 1066 and was succeeded by Hoël. Ralph de Gael, with family interests in England (as earl of Norfolk) and Brittany, rebelled against the Conqueror in 1075. He was beaten in England but fled to Brittany. There he survived and joined an alliance against Count Hoël. The latter went to attack Dol, which Ralph had made his base. The Conqueror besieged the castle and Philip led an army to relieve it in 1076. Ralph had support from other Norman rebels, and from Fulk of Anjou. Philip's relief succeeded and a battle was won against William outside the stronghold – a victory ignored by Anglo-Norman chroniclers but 'the first major military setback of his [William's] life'.[120] The Conqueror lost 'men and horses and incalculable treasure'.[121] William abandoned the siege, leaving baggage and treasure, and Norman power in Brittany declined. Philip had succeeded in halting the Norman advance. The victory also confirmed Philip's seizure of the French Vexin.

Philip allied with Norman rebel lords, several of whom took refuge in Norman border castles, and gave aid to William's enemies in England. Edgar the Aetheling was offered refuge at Montreuil-sur-Mer 'so that he could do daily harm to those who were not his friends'.[122] Montreuil was a potential base for invasion of England, between modern Dieppe and Boulogne, close to Flanders, and a threat to Normandy. However, Edgar's fleet was caught in a storm at sea and he only reached land with difficulty, returning to Scotland and later making terms with the Conqueror.

Philip's most obvious ploy was to divide the Norman ducal family. William's eldest son Robert Curthose had become discontented, expecting more independence and power in Normandy and Maine. Curthose seems a resentful and disappointed man, short (hence the nickname – Curthose or shortstockings), and yet another fat prince. William tried to satisfy him and from 1077 Robert began to call himself duke of Normandy. There was also trouble between Robert and his brothers William Rufus and Henry, leading to an unseemly brawl at Laigle in 1077. Philip encouraged Robert's ambitions and supported rebellion against his father. Curthose tried to take Rouen but his father drove him from Normandy.

The divisions within the ducal family weakened Norman hopes of expansion. Norman rebels established a base at Gerberoy, where some of Philip's knights joined the garrison. The Conqueror came there after Christmas when the garrison made a sortie, and Curthose defeated his father in the ensuing battle in January 1079. William was unhorsed, wounded in the hand by his son, and humiliated. He then abandoned the siege and retired to Rouen. By 1080 father and son were reconciled and Curthose was recognized as heir to Normandy, but remained dissatisfied. In 1083 he rebelled again and Philip supported him, leading to the fatal episode of Mantes.

Philip had little part in events in Maine but they worked in his favour. Maine lacked strong central authority, its count failing to become a major prince. Disputes and the ambitions of neighbours made Maine unstable.[123] The number of castellanies began to increase noticeably. There was a popular rebellion in Le Mans in 1070, caused by the unpopular domination of William of Normandy, though aimed against his vassal Geoffrey of Mayenne. The citizens formed a commune, albeit of brief existence. The Conqueror quelled the rebellion. In 1072 the citizens appealed to Fulk IV le Réchin of Anjou, who entered Maine and expelled Geoffrey of Mayenne. The Conqueror returned in 1073 and restored Norman authority. In 1077 Fulk attacked La Flèche; the Conqueror came to its relief and Fulk was wounded and withdrew. They made an agreement, but it was unlikely to last. Fulk had a further success against the Conqueror in 1081, this time capturing La Flèche. William made a new agreement, reverting to the former position. Curthose was to hold Maine but he recognized Fulk as overlord for the county. As Douglas notes, the French king was 'the real victor'.[124]

The main arena for conflict between the Normans and Philip was the Vexin, north of the Seine between the Oise and Andelle. It contained vital centres such as Mantes, Meulan, Pontoise and Gisors. It divided the royal lands from Normandy and had been shared between them, an obvious bone of contention. Philip's father had ceded the French part of the Vexin to Duke Robert I. Now Philip sought to recover it. Simon count of the Vexin inherited as a minor. The shock of seeing the disinterred naked body of his father made him decide to become a monk, handing his lands to the king. Simon was betrothed to Judith daughter of the count of Auvergne but on their wedding night they took a vow of mutual sexual abstinence. She remained a virgin for life and he entered the abbey of St-Claude in the Jura. Philip took over the French Vexin, which he later passed to his son Louis. It advanced the Capetian demesne to the Epte.

Philip invaded Normandy during the Conqueror's absence in England in 1086 with support from Curthose, raiding around Évreux. William in reply tried to recover disputed territory in the Vexin in 1087, claiming Pontoise, Chaumont and Mantes. Bates has queried whether the grant by Henry I to the Conqueror was ever made, suggesting that the Conqueror's claim to the Vexin was 'dishonest'.[125] Philip, it was said, then jeered at the Conqueror's fatness – for a man who became obese he was oddly keen to note others' corpulence – considered a possible spur to William's expedition. Fliche suggested that the reason for William's fatal expedition against Mantes was that Philip had used it as a base for raids into Normandy.[126]

William prepared a large expedition, crossing the Epte to ravage the Vexin, killing two hermits before entering and firing Mantes. The English chronicler thought it 'a miserable thing he did, and more miserable was his fate'.[127] In one version, the Conqueror's horse reared up at flaring embers and he was forced on to his pommel which ruptured him. Badly ill and suffering from the heat, he was taken to the priory of St-Gervase just west of Rouen. There he died on 9 September 1087. His son Robert Curthose was at the French court. Philip had divided the Conqueror's territories: England went to Rufus and Normandy to Robert.

Philip continued to support Curthose and encouraged opposition to William Rufus, a policy threatened by occasional reconciliations between the brothers. In 1091 they agreed to attack Le Mans, not good news for Philip. He was saved for a time by the discontent of the younger brother Henry, who attacked his siblings and fortified his strongholds in western Normandy. Philip gave some aid to Curthose against Rufus, but let Rufus buy his neutrality. In 1092 Rufus persuaded Philip to leave the siege of Aumale, 'either for love of him, or for his great treasure'.[128] Again at Eu Philip decided to withdraw. Philip's aid to Curthose remained half-hearted. The brothers were reconciled and declared Philip to be 'far above all their princes in wealth and generosity'.[129]

When Curthose went on crusade, Rufus added Normandy to his English lands. He repeated the Conqueror's claim to the Vexin which he invaded in 1097, besieging Chaumont. The defenders resisted and with bows killed 700 of the attackers' horses; 'the dogs and birds of France were gorged to repletion on their bodies'.[130] A truce was agreed after Philip's son Louis had repelled the Anglo-Normans. The French Vexin remained in royal hands. Rufus famously was killed hunting in the New Forest in 1100.

The Anglo-Norman threat however did not end. It was perhaps unfortunate for Philip that he had backed the least dependable of the three brothers. Rufus had got the better of Robert and now the youngest brother, Henry I, won England. The possibility of encouraging division between the brothers remained but was now less effective. Curthose failed to establish a claim to England and Henry I invaded Normandy to win a decisive victory at Tinchebray in 1106, when Curthose was captured. Philip had been happy to leave the brothers to sort out their own conflict but probably came to regret not giving aid in 1106. Curthose was imprisoned for the rest of his life while Henry established himself as duke of Normandy, reuniting England and Normandy, and restoring that threat to the Capetians. Philip's only hope was to take up the cause of Curthose's son, William Clito, who had taken refuge in Flanders.

THE REST OF THE REALM

Our problem with other regions is lack of information but there were no major problems involving the monarchy. There was a crisis in Burgundy in 1075 on the death of Duke Robert I. Robert wanted his younger son Robert to succeed rather than the heir by primogeniture, Robert's eldest grandson Hugh by his deceased son Henry. Eventually the duchy went to a younger brother of Hugh, called Henry – but it was an internal problem. Order was restored and Hugh entered Cluny as a monk, leaving the duchy to his brother.

Luchaire, though critical of Philip, admitted that he had shown more interest than his predecessors south of the Loire, where he sought to restore former Robertian influence, as in Sologne and Berry. The acquisition of the vicomté of Bourges in 1101 with the castellany of Dun-le-Roi was a significant gain.[131] The houses of Blois and Anjou had interests in Berry which clashed with Philip's, further underlining the significance of Philip's gain of the Gâtinais early in the reign and Berry towards the end.[132]

Philip kept contact with southern churches – at Autun, Mâcon, Flavigny and Tournus. He was patron of various southern abbeys, including Charroux, and St-Jean d'Angely. In 1076 he was at Poitiers to dedicate the church of Moutierneuf. In 1077 he was at Orléans for an assembly that included two dukes, eight bishops and three archbishops over monastic arrangements. The duke and bishops of Burgundy appeared in the royal entourage and signed his charters. Other southern princes appeared at court, including the counts of Nevers and the Auvergne, the lords of Bourbon and Beaujeu.

THE SCANDAL OF BERTRADE

Philip suffered over his choice of partner in a strangely similar way to his predecessor, Robert the Pious, and attracted even harsher criticism. Philip's first wife was Bertha of Holland, 'noble and virtuous daughter of Florent count of Holland, and step-daughter of Robert the Frisian'.[133] The marriage in 1072 was part of the reconciliation between Robert and the king. She produced no offspring for nine years until 1081 but then bore two children – Constance, and Louis (VI). Nevertheless she was repudiated in 1092 for unclear reasons – possibly preceding his interest in Bertrade. Chroniclers suggest different reasons and it is not easy to decide between them. William of Malmesbury said the king complained she was too fat – which given his own growing obesity seems a bit rich, but tallies with his remarks about the Conqueror.[134] Bertha was retired to the castle of Montreuil-sur-Mer, part of her dower land.

Bertrade de Montfort had married Fulk le Réchin count of Anjou four years before.[135] Fulk had at least two previous wives. He had to fight to gain and keep his county. His older brother Geoffrey the Bearded became count of Anjou in 1060 but proved a poor ruler. Fulk rebelled, defeating and capturing his brother twice. On the first occasion he released him under pressure from Pope Alexander II and King Philip. Fulk then rebelled again and defeated his brother at Brissac in 1068, imprisoning him at Chinon. The king again tried to get Geoffrey released but abandoned the attempt. Fulk IV (1068–1109) was recognized as count in return for passing the Gâtinais and Château-Landon to the king. The papal legate declared Geoffrey insane and absolved Fulk from fault. These events weakened

Fulk's position and made it easier for Philip to cope with the usually powerful principality of Anjou.

Fulk le Réchin is an interesting figure, responsible for writing a unique chronicle of which part (the *Fragment*) survives. He was accused of starting a fashion for shoes with long points or 'scorpion's tails', according to Orderic because he had deformed feet. After the reconciliation with the king, the count remained loyal and supportive. Even the scandal over Bertrade did not greatly disturb the alliance. Orderic says that Bertrade was actually responsible for the reconciliation. Before Fulk's death the king recognized his son, Fulk (V) the Young as prospective ruler of Anjou, the heir acknowledging that he held the county from the king – the first overt admission in over a century.[136]

The scandal began in 1092 when Philip repudiated Bertha and married Bertrade de Montfort. Chroniclers presented different versions of events. It is not certain whether Philip seized Bertrade by force or if she chose to leave her husband, Fulk. The latter seems more likely. Orderic says she wanted to avoid being deserted, so sent a message to Philip, 'the weak prince', who accepted the offer from 'the cunning woman'.[137] Orderic also claimed 'no good man praised [her] except for her beauty'.[138] Fulk was noted for his multiple marriages, 'given to polygamy'.[139] Bertrade was by various accounts his third, fourth or sixth wife. One said she left him because he was planning to repudiate her anyway, so she sought protection from the king. Guibert of Nogent confirms this, saying she would have been 'sent away like a whore'.[140] Hugh of Flavigny claimed Philip acted 'without regard for the reputation and majesty of the throne ... all France will raise its voice and the whole West cannot ignore Philip's crime'.[141] Duby though has suggested the match was a useful political union, 'a good choice', bringing the king the support of the Montfort family which held 'a key fortress'.[142] She also bore Philip three children, two of them male.

The official church view was presented by Orderic, claiming the king 'rotted away shamefully in the filth of adultery', but saving his chief blame for Bertrade – women were always worse sexual offenders to medieval monks. Orderic condemned them all: 'the unruly concubine left the adulterous count and clung to the adulterous king'![143] Yves of Chartres was closer to the king but refused to accept the match. He wrote: 'I cannot approve ... I cannot assist at solemnizing this marriage' ... 'you will not see me in Paris'. He argued that Philip could only proceed if a general church council approved the divorce, and swore he would never accept the marriage as things stood; 'I would rather be plunged into the depths of the sea tied to a millstone'.[144]

The papacy was scandalized, others probably less so. It is clear that many in France were prepared to accept the marriage. Philip received support from many prelates, including the bishops of Troyes and Meaux. Bishops were prepared to oversee and attend the marriage and coronation, resisting papal threats. At Reims two archbishops and eight bishops confirmed the marriage. In 1094 at the council of Autun the papal representative, Hugh of Die, declared Philip excommunicated – the first French king to suffer this humiliation. The archbishop reversed the decision of the council at Reims permitting the marriage. There was a gap between the reforming church's views on marriage and the general practice of royalty and aristocracy. Many wives were repudiated, many men took several wives, but the sentence was repeated at the council of Clermont-Ferrand in 1095. The ecclesiastical view was hardening and several clerics criticized Philip. Bernold of St-Blasien accused him of 'uniting himself to the wife of his vassal', committing adultery and incest. Yves of Chartres pointed out that Bertrade was the king's cousin.[145] Chartres became a centre for reform and opposition to the marriage. Yves was a prolific writer of pamphlets and letters and put much energy into attacking the liaison. The king ignored papal condemnation 'like the deaf adder which blocks its ears to the voice of the charmer'. Philip ignored Yves' criticism and imprisoned him – though he was released fairly soon in 1093. Yves continued to support the papal position, refusing to send troops to aid the king in 1094 with Philip under excommunication and the realm under interdict – giving as reason the 'illicit' liaison.[146] Bertrade's former husband, Fulk, joined the protests against the marriage but only under papal pressure and without conviction. Urban II then went to Angers, recognized Fulk, and presented him with a golden flower – possibly broom rather than a rose and the origin of the nickname Plantagenesta.[147]

From 1094 to 1104 there was a succession of excommunications, in 1095 at Clermont, 1096 at Tours and 1101 at Poitiers. The country was placed under interdict in 1097. Chroniclers say that church services were halted when Philip appeared. Bertrade reacted furiously when this occurred at Sens, ordering that the closed church doors should be broken down and mass celebrated by her own priests. The king was able to ignore papal condemnations for 12 years until he decided to seek reconciliation. He may even have benefited financially since he halted his grants to churches. Reconciliation was made easier when Paschal II sought refuge in France in 1106 and met Philip at Nîmes. Bertha died soon after the new match, which simplified affairs though the papacy continued to condemn the marriage for incest. Twice more Philip took oaths to repudiate Bertrade, but went on living with her. Fliche thought Philip 'hoped that the pope would close his eyes'.[148]

Philip was excommunicated again in 1099 at the council of Poitiers, when William IX duke of Aquitaine broke up the church assembly. He entered the church with soldiers and declared they were in a town he held from the crown, and if they dared to go ahead, 'I swear to you by the faith that I have vowed to him, that you shall not leave here with impunity'.[149] One of the duke's men threw a stone at a cardinal. It missed but hit a clerk, who was killed. The duke then begged pardon and was forgiven. A new papal representative, Richard bishop of Albano, introduced a more conciliatory tone from 1102. In Paris in 1105 Philip again presented himself as penitent, going barefoot and taking an oath 'never again to have contact with this woman except in the presence of trustworthy persons'.[150] Again he was cleared and again he ignored his promise. The pope permitted Lambert bishop of Arras to absolve the king. Philip promised 'I shall no longer have any illicit relations with Bertrade'.[151] The king ignored his promise but the pope did 'close his eyes'. Fulk's attitude was shown when welcoming his former wife and her new husband in Anjou in 1106. Churchmen, however, were less forgiving. Philip suffered for his sins with 'decaying teeth and scabies and many other infirmities and ignominies according to his deserts'.[152] Bertrade, having given Philip two sons (Philip and Florus) and a daughter (Cecilia), ended her days in the abbey of Fontevraud.

PHILIP I AND THE CHURCH

Philip's relations with the church were damaged by his marital arrangements. He has also been accused of resisting church reform in a way that seemed alien to the attitudes of his predecessors. Partly this may be from a change in papal rather than royal views. Gregorian reform placed secular rulers in a difficult position, threatening their rights, powers and income. The Peace movement made headway but Philip took little part in it. Philip was king at the time of the First Crusade, but took no part in its planning or execution; he could hardly participate while under excommunication. Had Philip gone on the Crusade he would have been its leader, which the papacy could not countenance. When Urban II proclaimed the First Crusade at Clermont in 1095 he repeated the excommunication of the king.

Nevertheless the First Crusade and the early stages of the crusading movement occurred during the reign of Philip I. He can be given no credit for the development (and equally no blame). It was fundamentally a 'French' development. Urban II appealed to 'the Franks', 'to you our sermon is directed and to you our exhortation is extended'. Participants came from Normandy, Flanders, Blois, Lorraine, Toulouse, Provence, and virtually every French region, including the royal demesne. The first knights to reach Constantinople were led by Hugh of Vermandois, the king's brother. French prelates were involved too, not least the original leader of the Crusade, Adhémar bishop of Le Puy. Philip did not discourage the crusade and did fund some of the participants, in return for rights in their property.

There was a parallel movement in Iberia, against Muslims. Appeals were made to Christian Europe and especially France. Some French knights and lords participated in each of the three counter efforts, including Odo duke of Burgundy in 1087. It was arguably the turning point in the Christian versus Muslim struggle in medieval Iberia. Again Philip had no personal or direct involvement. He pursued the typical early Capetian policy of avoiding involvement in distant parts.

Philip has been accused of opposing Gregorian reform. Historians have gradually shifted their views. The reform movement sought to remove lay power over the church and clerics, especially over appointments to bishoprics and abbeys. No ruler could easily yield to this, since it would remove vital powers. One only needs to list bishoprics at question – Lyon, Tours, Sens, Reims and Bourges – to see how far the movement threatened royal power. These were largely sees in provinces where only tentatively did princes recognize royal authority, and where influence over the church was the monarchy's first hold. The rise of the monarchy was due partly to cooperation with the church, and naming loyal and sympathetic men to key offices had been vital – and still was.

Philip received considerable support from his bishops – the natural result of the system. While bishops received office from royal support they were likely to repay it with loyalty and support. The new bishop of Paris, for example, was none other than Bertrade's brother. He was unlikely to repeat papal criticism of the liaison. Many other French bishops owed a debt to the king – in receiving office, grants, or royal approval for their acts. By and large they backed the king. Among the most vocal in their support were Walter bishop of Meaux and John bishop of Orléans. Philip's interventions are of interest. He deposed uncooperative bishops – including Yves of Chartres, Guy of Beauvais and Renaud of Langres. He became involved in battles over appointments, as when the pope deposed Manasses II of Reims, whom Philip defended. Without sympathy from the French church, Philip and his realm could hardly have survived 13 years under papal interdict virtually unmarked. Philip continued to intervene in significant church appointments, as when Arnulf bishop of Le Mans died in 1081. William the Conqueror nominated one of his household clerics, Hoël, but Le Mans was in the ambit of the see of Tours. Philip and Fulk IV opposed Hoël and pressured the archbishop, who refused to consecrate him. William had the bishop consecrated at Rouen in 1085. It was not exactly a triumph for the king but it shows continued lay involvement.

Philip was intransigent over the investiture dispute, defined by Gregory VII in 1075 and promoting free elections to ecclesiastical offices. Philip allowed some local church elections to stand. He settled for a broader agreement between church and state on this issue – church elections (often of the royal candidate) and church consecration of the elected, but homage to the king for temporalities. Philip and Pope Paschal II made an agreement over investiture at the council of Troyes in 1107. The king abandoned the practice of investing prelates, and receiving homage from them, but was to receive an oath of loyalty and keep control of temporal possessions – so that he could, for example, dispose of church wealth during vacancies.

Another aspect of reform was against corruption over church appointments. Philip is often accused of simony, the buying of church office. What Philip was doing was what all rulers had been doing for years. It was the church, for understandable reasons, that was seeking change. It wanted good men, the best men for the task, chosen for merit not cash. Philip was accused of taking money from the church. This was hardly new. He profited from money for appointment to bishoprics and other offices.

Heresy appeared intermittently during the 11th century. Philip's reign saw further examples, most notably in the ideas of Berengar of Tours, who was born in Tours and studied under Fulbert of Chartres. He returned to the abbey of St Martin at Tours in 1031 and later became an archdeacon at Angers. He emphasized reason and came into conflict with church orthodoxy, especially over the Eucharist. His ideas were condemned at councils in Rome in 1050 and Paris in 1051. In 1079 he signed a confession of faith in Rome. He returned to France to retire to the island of St-Côme, where he died in 1088.

Philip, despite his later reputation, continued to support the church in the demesne and the realm. He had the usual Capetian respect for the church and religion, especially for relics and saints. He supported Cluniac reform, made grants to Cluny, encouraged reform at St-Magloire in Paris, and refounded St-Martin-des-Champs as a Cluniac priory in 1079. He made various grants to other houses, including Fleury, where he chose to be buried.

PHILIP I AND THE DEMESNE

Philip was as roundly condemned by chroniclers as any of his predecessors – perhaps more so. He has also received a pretty bad press from historians. In recent times however, he has found more defenders than the first three Capetians. One reason is the realization that he was actually quite successful, not least in adding to the demesne. Fliche initiated this change, declaring that Philip had 'inaugurated this policy of systematic annexation' for the dynasty.[153] Luchaire agreed, believing the increase in demesne was deliberate, 'a policy of annexation'.[154] Philip was the first Capetian not to alienate *any* of his demesne.[155]

Philip extended the demesne and protected the Capetian core lands. He acquired the Gâtinais in 1068, the French Vexin in 1079, the Vermandois, Valois, the towns of Corbie, Sens and Melun plus the vicomté of Bourges in 1101. By the end of his reign, the crown controlled Pithiviers, Le Puiset and Corbeil. Paris and Orléans were no longer the only major towns in the demesne. Philip took over the castellanies of Château-Landon, La-Chapelle-la-Reine, Lorrez-le-Bocage and Lorris. As in the north, so here, the acquisition had significance in linking Capetian territory in the Senonais to Orléans. Philip had played a major part in consolidating and protecting the royal demesne.

Corbie had been restored to royal control in Philip's deal with Robert the Frisian after the battle at Bavichove near Cassel in 1071. It is an example of how far royal neutrality or support was valued by the princes. Corbie was an important gain, a thriving trading town on the border between Lesser France and Flanders. Philip was prepared to defend the acquisition by arms in 1074, forcing the residents to swear fidelity. In 1107 Philip improved his hold on the town by granting privileges to its merchants.

On the death in 1074 of Ralph of Crépy, count of the Vexin, Valois, Amiens, Bar-sur-Aube and Vitry, Philip again recovered lands. Ralph had a chequered marital history. He accused his second wife of adultery and repudiated her for Anna of Kiev. The match to Anna was condemned for consanguinity, bigamy and because the queen abandoned her children. The new marriage was 'contrary to human law and to divine law and for it he [Ralph] was excommunicated'.[156] The couple were excluded from court until c.1070. On Ralph's death there was a succession war between his son Simon and his son-in-law Hugh. Ralph's budding principality broke up. Philip seized part of his lands and passed some to his younger brother Hugh, establishing another Capetian dynasty, which as in Burgundy, remained loyal to the crown for many years. Philip invaded the French Vexin, which now became part of the royal demesne. Simon entered a monastery in 1077, consenting to the king's possession of his father's lands including the Vexin. The move may have been forced by the king but there is no direct evidence. The Vexin was passed to Philip's son Louis and Vermandois to his brother Hugh, known as Hugh the Great like their great ancestor – the start of another Capetian dynasty. The acquisition of the Vexin, Vermandois and Valois was a tremendous gain for the crown, providing a buffer region against Normandy and Flanders.

As for Anna of Kiev, her gifts to the church did something to restore her reputation, for example founding a house for canons in Senlis by 1069. She confirmed a royal gift in 1075 as '*mater regis*' and then disappeared from the records. She probably died in 1078 but all we know is that she was dead by 1089, when Philip made a gift for the rest of her soul.[157]

Philip purchased the vicomté of Bourges, in c.1101. The manner of his acquisition and the extent, have been questioned.[158] Philip did not go on the First Crusade but he gained from it. Many of the lords who went needed cash to fund their expedition. One such was Odo Arpin viscount of Bourges, whom Philip paid a sum of uncertain total.[159] Odo passed the viscounty with its capital and the castellany of Dun-le-Roi to the king. These lands remained in royal hands after Odo's return. He was believed dead but had in fact been captured on crusade and was released after a long imprisonment. On return he was unable to repay the loan and entered Cluny, later becoming prior of La Charité-sur-Loire. His wife entered a convent. Philip twice returned to assert his claims, taking over Bourges and Berry and making Orléans safer for the Capetians. In Bautier's terms 'Berry for the first time since the accession of the dynasty had become a base for launching a major political effort towards the centre of the realm'.[160]

Philip's territorial gains were of great importance to the dynasty. The core possessions were now better protected and royal wealth considerably increased. It was a 'significant moment' in the formation of the Capetian state, and one that has not been sufficiently recognized.[161] Most of the gains did not come by chance but through diplomacy and the employment of royal force in support of legal claims. Philip left all his acquisitions to his heir along with the inherited demesne. This was a new practice since previous kings had passed acquisitions to cadet branches. It is a further sign of increasing royal power as well as a significant increase in direct royal wealth.

Criticism of Philip centres on his relations with the lesser lords in the demesne. The contention is that Philip was so weak he could not control even the lesser lords in his own lands. The main event quoted is the king's defeat in 1079 by one such lord, Hugh of Le Puiset, 'the most intractable and bellicose of the castellans', aided by William of Normandy.[162] Philip sought aid from Burgundy and besieged the Le Puiset stronghold near Yèvre-le-Châtel. Hugh made a sortie and scattered the royal troops, pursuing his enemies and capturing several lords he later ransomed. Luchaire called this 'the most dishonourable [defeat] that the Middle Ages remembers'.[163] It was a defeat but it was not representative of events of the reign, and too much has been made of it. Philip increased the royal demesne and royal authority within it. This advance is often credited to his son Louis, active for his father before becoming king. It seems unjust to give no credit to the king. There was no division between father and son over the issue; whatever Louis achieved was for his father. Castellans now regularly attended court, surely recognizing royal authority rather than the reverse.

Prince Louis' first move was against the lords in the demesne north of the Seine, partly directed at assisting the abbey of St-Denis whose lands were threatened by Matthew I count of Beaumont, Dreux de Mouchy, and Bouchard IV lord of Montmorency. The latter was summoned to court to explain his actions but refused to come. Louis with aid from Robert the Frisian then attacked Bouchard and his allies. Montmorency was besieged and surrendered. In 1102 Louis burned Dreux de Mouchy's castle. Matthew of Beaumont besieged Luzarches, was summoned to court and refused to come. Louis took Luzarches and returned it to Hugh. A storm hit Louis' force when besieging Chambly against Matthew, causing him to withdraw. He tried again the following year and forced an agreement on the count. There was another clash with Ebles de Roucy, who was harassing the church of Reims. Louis went against him with 700 knights in 1102. There is a clear policy behind these minor campaigns. The monarchy was protecting the church against baronial threats, using a judicial approach to put the lord in the wrong. The king, represented by his son in these years, enforced the legal decisions – mostly with success.

There were similar conflicts in the demesne south of the Seine. Philip was troubled by the castellan of Montlhéry and his Rochefort relatives. There were complaints about the conduct of the lords of Montlhéry (Miles the Great and then Guy Troussel), who acted as brigands, using the castle as a base. They caused trouble for anyone travelling to Orléans, including the king. Philip tried to take Montlhéry but at first failed. He gained the castle in the end by marrying Philip, his son by Bertrade, to the heiress Elizabeth, daughter of Guy Troussel. Later the castle passed to Philip's son Louis. The First Crusade provided some relief for the king in this region, when several of the problem lords went to the Holy Land, including Guy Troussel and Miles the Great. When Guy the Red count of Rochefort returned from crusade he accepted the royal gains in return for becoming seneschal. Miles viscount of Troyes, younger brother of Guy Troussel, then tried to recover the castle but Louis beat him off and the castle was razed. When Anselm Garlande recovered the seneschalcy, Guy the Red rebelled. A planned marriage between Prince Louis and Guy's daughter Lucienne was dropped. War broke out again when Guy's son Hugh rebelled. Louis besieged his island castle at Gournay, attacking with a fleet. He took the castle and handed it to the Garlandes.

Louis attacked several Rochefort strongholds, including Methisy, Chevreuse and Brethencourt. The conflict continued beyond Philip's reign. Louis also campaigned on the borders of the Limousin and Berry, in 1107 against Humbaud lord of Ste-Sévère – who submitted and was imprisoned, and whose troops were hanged. There is no clear division between the reign of Philip and his son in their demesne policy. The foundation of royal success was well established by the time of Philip's death.

When Montlhéry was taken Philip explained the problems it had caused him in the past: 'it was impossible to go from one to the other [Paris to Orléans] without the permission of my enemies or under the strongest escort'.[164] Suger wrote that on his deathbed Philip made a point about this castle to Louis, 'Beware my son, keep watch and guard that tower well; the grievance I have suffered from it has made an old man of me before my time; the evil and perfidy of those who reside there has never allowed me a moment of rest'.[165]

PHILIP I'S ADMINISTRATION

One reason Philip's reputation has gradually recovered is the recognition of his role in royal administration. This has become clearer as records have been discovered, studied and printed. We now realize this period saw the emergence of the prévôt (*praepositus/praefectus*) and changes in the personnel of royal administration. Prévôts first appeared under Robert the Pious but now the office became regular, permanent, and more clearly defined. Prévôts represented the king in the demesne, now divided for administrative purposes. They appeared at Orléans, Paris, Sens, Étampes, Poissy, Mantes, Senlis and Bourges, and probably Pithiviers and Compiègne.[166] The prévôt acted for the king in local justice and supervised the collection of taxes and tolls.

We now find an arch-chancellor, chancellors, seneschals, chamberlains, butlers and constables as well as a royal chapel staffed by clerks.[167] These officials begin to appear under Henry I and are found regularly under Philip I subscribing to royal documents. The arch-chancellor Gervase of Reims consecrated the young Philip. His office was honorific and died with its holder in 1067. The others however – chamberlain, seneschal, constable and butler – were active administrators. A handful of major officers become the main subscribers to royal documents, representing the palace. The chamberlain controlled the household and its personnel; the seneschal supervised the prévôts and commanded the military; the constable was in charge of the stables, the butler of food and drink. The chamberlain was generally the head of this little group, with the seneschal second but of increasing importance.[168] However it was not a system set in stone; the significance of individual officers varied, and there was no fixed hierarchy. Their importance is shown by their attestation of royal documents. They formed 'a distinct and all powerful association'.[169] They were the royal counsellors and by the end of the reign the most important figures at court. The chancellor was usually the final subscriber to documents. He was responsible for producing charters and head of a chancery. The arch-chancellor was honorific and the chancellor did the job with staff including vice-chancellors and notaries, most if not all being royal chaplains. The chancellor sealed diplomas and held the royal seal. The palace also required marshals, cooks, pantrymen and so on – in total a sizeable group travelling around the demesne and the realm with the king. In the view of Lemarignier the dominant court figures were from the families of castellans and knights of the Île-de-France, men such as the seneschal Guy the Red, the butler Walter of Senlis, or the chamberlain Waleran from the Riche family.[170]

The king visited his palaces with an impressive entourage that often included major prelates and princes. The fact that bourgeois and obscure persons appeared in the records has been pointed to as a decline but only meant the employment of lesser men in a more centralized bureaucracy. There was also a growth of royal administration in the localities. Prévôts were no longer part of the royal entourage but attached to regions. There was a shift in the social background of those who prepared royal documents and administered government. The process began under Henry I but is clearer under Philip, and gathered pace. Government was no longer in the hands of the princes, lords and prelates but of lesser men – castellans and clerks. This has been interpreted as showing royal decline in that great men were not at court. This view does not however stand up. Great men did still come to court, perhaps rather more often. They were also called to great assemblies. What we do see is royal government taken more firmly into the king's hands and those employed by him for the purpose. Some of Philip's documents show personal royal orders (commands or mandates) given without any subscribing lords or officials.[171] Under Philip the process moved on but was not complete. There were still some great lords and fairly powerful castellans involved, but the change is evident. *Fideles*, notably lesser lords of the Île-de-France, became of major importance – such as the counts of Meulan, Dammartin and Beaumont. The role of counts declined and virtually ended in Philip's last decade. There were still members of lordly families such as the Rocheforts and the Garlandes but there were many from ordinary knightly families such as the Neauphles and the Ridels. In the late reign the permanent figures in the palace took over, a move from the court to the palace at the heart of royal government.[172]

An interesting example of royal support given to a royal official for church office occurred in 1100 when the chapter at Beauvais was divided over the candidates. A minority favoured Stephen of Garlande, the king's chancellor – and so did Philip. The majority favoured Galon, who received papal support, but Stephen was elected – a sign of royal power. The Garlande family was of major significance in the administration for years to come. This period may have seen the 'decomposition of the Carolingian state' but only in the sense that it was replaced by a new order.[173]

PHILIP I'S DEATH

Philip died at Melun on 29 July 1108, suffering from toothache. He had chosen to be buried not at St-Denis, for which he was condemned by Suger, but at Fleury. His tomb was placed between the choir and the altar and rather oddly became a cult centre. It was destroyed during the French Revolution. There was an attempt at restoration in 1830 when a body was found of a very large person, but probably not Philip. Bertrade, 'still young and beautiful', entered the convent of Fontrevaud.[174]

GENERAL CONCLUSIONS

Thalamas is right to see 'seigneurial' as a better description of society in this period than 'feudal'. We have seen the rise of principalities and within them of castellans. But these two reigns saw a gradual reversal, as princes gained more control over castellans and kings gained more recognition from princes. This change was not complete, but it had begun, and was a major success for our two kings.

Recent work on this period has reached interesting conclusions on social rank. Historians seem agreed that, however you define it, nobility was always recognized. Timothy Reuter has stressed how rank might be recognized through appearance, speech or food.[175] We might suggest that in much the same way royalty was also recognizable. Men bowed to a superior in society. The princes might have become more independent but they still recognized virtue in royalty. Philip I consistently referred to himself as 'King of the Franks' and to his kingdom as 'the realm of the Franks'.[176] Most princes came to court, gave homage, and provided troops when the king demanded. The rituals of coronation and consecration marked kings as superior to their subjects. There were rebellions against both the kings we have examined in this chapter, but by and large they were recognized and treated as kings. Each in turn made the Capetian dynasty that bit stronger.

6

The Fat and the Young, 1108–80

From 1108 to 1180, through most of the 12th century, France was ruled by two kings called Louis – the first known as Louis the Fat, his son as Louis the Young. It is generally agreed that the period saw an important move forward by the French monarchy. However, we have pressed the point that the first four Capetians were more successful than generally acknowledged and to a degree we must see these two kings as less significant – or rather that the nature of their significance needs to be re-defined. One certainly does not feel like accepting the assessment of either as 'a second-class king'.[1]

SUGER AND THE KINGS

The main reason for previous emphasis has been the importance attached to a major source for both reigns, the work of Suger, born in 1081 and abbot of St-Denis from 1122 to 1151. He was 'little in body and little in race', 'such a little person as me', with black eyes in a thin face, and becoming bald.[2] William, a monk under Suger, wrote a life of his master, describing his great heart in a frail body. Suger lived simply, sleeping on straw and occupying a bare cell. He was a careful and able administrator and a hard worker. He was well educated, an accomplished Latinist who could quote chunks of classical works, as well as the Bible and the Fathers. His interests included the arts and architecture.

Suger was promoted to *praepositus* or abbot's deputy over the St-Denis house at Berneval-le-Grand in Normandy, and then later at Toury in Beauce (1107–12). His administrative abilities were soon demonstrated and he increased the income of Toury from 20 *livres* a year to 80.[3] Suger then turned to diplomacy, acting for the king, meeting popes and attending councils in Italy and France. As abbot he was responsible for a major rebuilding of St-Denis that contributed to the beginning of Gothic.[4] He also brought a collection of valuable objects to his abbey.

Suger wanted the world to remember him; the work in the abbey displayed his name no less than 13 times.[5] He confessed to sins, 'the enormity' of his crimes, being 'an irreligious man' – but one suspects exaggeration.[6] He was conservative but had friends among the leading reformers, not least St Bernard, who was at first critical of St-Denis but came to respect Suger. He made a ponderous pun that the abbot had learned to suck (*sugere*) the breasts of Divine Wisdom rather than the lips of flatterers.[7] There has been recent revision of Suger's significance, notably by Lindy Grant.[8] Oddly enough he was not greatly enamoured of either king (Louis VI or Louis VII) though he did much to boost their reputations. He criticized Philip I for his marital arrangements ('carried away by lust for the married woman he had snatched away'). After the marriage Philip 'did nothing worthy of royal majesty'.[9] Suger preferred to exaggerate the virtues of Louis VI.

Suger distorted history to suit his own agenda – seeking to benefit his abbey. He emphasized the historic role of St-Denis, including the importance of Saint Denis himself. The achievements of at least three persons called Denis (or Dionysius) were melded into one fabled figure.[10] Suger became angry when Abelard questioned this fiction. The abbey became the royal necropolis and the church for coronation. Suger rebuilt the abbey magnificently. He increased and made more profitable the abbey's holdings and was certainly a successful abbot.

We shall need to return to Suger often during this chapter but suffice to say that a revised view of his work leads to a revised history of these two reigns. We shall argue that the work of these two kings continued in the vein of their predecessors, with modest achievements in face of considerable difficulties. We do not wish to condemn either king but simply to play down a little their achievements. It is equally necessary to play down Suger's role in the development of the monarchy.[11] He has been seen as the creator of the theory of the monarchy, and of 'France'. In fact he was no great political or original thinker. His main contributions were attempts to inflate the importance of St-Denis.

Suger's work on Louis VI is *The Deeds of Louis the Fat*.[12] This is ironic since Suger wished to portray his master as Louis the Glorious (*gloriosus*).[13] By the end of the 12th century, after Suger's death, *gloriosus* was altered to *grossus*, 'the Fat'! Louis was indeed fat but Suger had not intended to make that the title of his work. So far as one knows, since Suger, no one has called him Louis the Glorious while everyone knows him as Louis the Fat. Fatness was a characteristic of many Capetians, probably an inherited trait. In few if any cases does it seem to have incapacitated them though Louis' mobility was further hindered by a leg wound received in 1128, leaving him hardly able to drag the leg about.[14]

Suger's work on Louis VI is of greater depth than that on Louis VII, which is unfinished. It used to be believed that Suger and Louis VI were educated together at St-Denis, but this now seems unlikely.[15] The relationship developed later. Louis had a close feeling for the abbey where he was educated, but his connection with Suger began on professional lines. Suger became a royal servant, a diplomat, and then a counsellor. His major employment was on embassies – to England, Scotland, Sicily and Rome. When Suger was elected abbot of St-Denis on the death of Abbot Adam in 1122, the king was actually annoyed. Louis imprisoned the unfortunate messengers from St-Denis because the election had been 'without royal assent'.[16] Suger was absent on an embassy and was apprehensive about facing the king, but Louis met him on his return and accepted the election, releasing the messengers. St-Denis was a major abbey, and Suger was now bound to be a figure of importance in the realm. He was not an agent for the monarchy, so far as we know, before 1118 – and then as a minor diplomat. Even with his election he had no great influence until after the fall of Stephen Garlande in 1128. Then he became an important counsellor and later regent during Louis VII's crusade. Perhaps the most interesting information about Suger comes from the life of him by one of his monks, William. After Suger's death William was sent, apparently out of favour now, to the priory of St-Denis in Vaux where he wrote the life of his former master.

LOUIS VI (1108–37)

Louis VI was the son of Philip I and his first wife Bertha of Holland, born in c.1081. As a youth he was slim and tall, though now for ever to be known as Louis the Fat. Orderic already thought him fat by the time of the council at Reims in 1119. His weight partly came from the 'formidable appetite of a hunter'.[17] Writing of 1122 Suger says that 'by now his body was heavy ... with folds of flesh'.[18] By the age of 46 he was unable to mount a horse though he had earlier loved hunting. He was Philip I's recognized heir, and associated in rule in c.1099, though he was neither consecrated nor crowned then but known as *rex designatus*. After Philip I's death Louis was consecrated and crowned at Orléans by Daimbert archbishop of Sens during a dispute with the archbishop of Reims, whose task it was traditionally.

There were claims that Bertrade tried to poison her stepson, who was ill for several days, unable to eat or sleep. Louis recovered but retained a pallid countenance for the rest of his life – it was said from the poison. We are inclined to dismiss the claim that Bertrade was a poisoner, a common medieval way of damning a person and unlikely often to be true – but no doubt Louis did look unusually pale after his illness. According to Orderic, Louis was eloquent. At least three chroniclers mention his simplicity, including Suger, who said he was 'cheerful, pleasant and friendly ... some even thought him simple'.[19] One has the impression that to look at Louis appeared a simpleton. Guibert of Nogent mentioned less attractive traits such as greed and cupidity, but this seems related to his method of government more than his personality.[20] Yves of Chartres, though generally complimentary, accused Louis of being illiterate, a gambler and a lover of women.[21]

Louis had two half-brothers, sons of Bertrade, Philip and Florus. Both Philip I and Louis were generous to them and they proved no threat to Louis's succession, though some chroniclers hinted that their mother Bertrade had ambitions for them. Philip married Elizabeth, the daughter and heiress of Guy Troussel of Montlhéry and received the county of Mantes with the agreement of Louis. Philip I never budged from his initial choice of successor in his oldest son. Louis was a 'loyal lieutenant' to his father.[22] Philip the step-brother later joined an abortive rebellion – according to Suger encouraged by Bertrade.[23] Louis went reluctantly to deal with him, besieging his castle and the rebellion collapsed.

Louis VI is seen as responsible for 'the revival of royal power' in Lesser France and France as a whole.[24] Thalamas saw a transformation in royal power.[25] To

Luchaire he was 'the happy star of the dynasty', entitling a chapter 'The Revival of Royalty'.[26] Following Suger, he makes the young Louis responsible for royal activity in the last decade of Philip's reign; Louis is king 'in fact from 1100, in title from 1108', when 'the real feebleness begins to diminish'.[27] Recently Gobry has called Louis 'the restorer of the Capetian dynasty' who 're-established the image of monarchy'.[28] Similarly, Delperrié de Bayac sees the reign coming after 'two centuries of defeats and decline'.[29] Even so, Louis VI does not receive an entirely favourable press. Hallam thought him an 'unpromising' hero, except in contrast to Philip I![30] She points out his ill health, obesity and gluttony. Dunbabin sees Louis VI and Louis VII as 'military failures', and 'unchivalric figures'.[31] She points out Louis' difficulty in defeating local castellans, requiring two campaigns against Thomas of Marle and three against Hugh du Puiset.

Louis' marriage record was not exemplary. He was betrothed to Lucienne from the castellan family of Rochefort, daughter of Guy the Red. Paschal II annulled the match, stressing the unsuitability of such a low ranking wife. Louis did not marry until 35 – a very late age for a king needing a successor. His sexual habits were not exactly saintly and he produced nine illegitimate children, but these did not ensure the succession. He married Adelaide of Maurienne and, though late beginners, they had eight sons and at least one daughter. The oldest son was Philip, born in 1116 and associated in 1129. Philip died as a young man in 1131 when his horse fell over a pig and he struck his head on a stone. The second son, Louis, was then associated and eventually succeeded.

ROYAL ADMINISTRATION UNDER LOUIS VI

Luchaire and Bournazel made detailed studies of Louis' administration.[32] We are well informed on the composition of the royal entourage and household, the major officials and courtiers. The trend mentioned under Philip I continued, and great princes play a lesser role at court or in witnessing acts. There was a move away from great lords active in administration, with new personnel emerging.[33] The most prominent of these were from lesser families as were the signatories to royal documents, most from the Île-de-France.[34] Three families dominated – those of Rochefort, Senlis and Garlande.

The seneschal was the chief official, leading the royal army among other tasks. Second was the butler, followed by the constable, chamberlain and chancellor. The constable was responsible for the stables and commanded the cavalry. The chamberlains supervised the royal chamber and finance. The chancellors dealt with writing tasks. There were also lesser officers such as the clerks, notaries, chaplains and minor chamberlains.

The number of names in the documents overall is misleading; it is clear that many appeared only for a single occasion, perhaps of local interest. Only a few, such as Suger, were regularly present. Suger stresses his own humble birth but he was from a lesser knightly family – much as other administrative figures of the reign. Suger exaggerated his own importance and we should not see him as a chief minister. He came to royal notice while a humble monk, through his legal knowledge – 'the best lawyer in the royal hall'.[35] He was chiefly useful as a diplomat, especially to the papacy.

We know something of the major figures in administration, notably Suger and members of the Garlande family, even more significant than Suger. They descended from obscure figures, father and son, Adam and Aubert – though Adam may have been vicomte of Corbeil and seneschal. The Garlandes dominated Louis' court for 20 years, headed by Stephen Garlande, chancellor, and from 1120 seneschal. His brothers Anselm and William were seneschals, while Gilbert also played a part. Anselm also married into the powerful Rochefort clan. As they rose they married into the well known families of Gallardon, Montmorency and Beaumont. They also made territorial gains from royal generosity – such as the grant of Gournay-sur-Marne.

The Garlandes made enemies, including Yves of Chartres who called Stephen illiterate, a gambler, a womanizer and an adulterer.[36] The Morigny chronicler commented: 'it was said he [Stephen] ruled rather than served the king' – not meant as a compliment; he was the one 'by whose counsel the whole of France was ruled'.[37] The archbishop of Tours said to Stephen, disparagingly, 'you sit as first among the palatins and dispose at your pleasure of the whole kingdom'.[38] St Bernard criticized Stephen as a cleric who was also chancellor, seneschal and leader of the royal army.[39] He accused him of seeking profit from religion.[40]

Stephen Garlande's niece, Agnes, daughter of William, married Amaury de Montfort. Stephen promised Amaury he would succeed him as seneschal. Louis was enraged that his official should take so much upon himself, particularly as he was seeking to limit heredity in office. Amaury was also a vassal of the duke of Normandy, who had fought the king and opposed Clito, so Louis had good reason for not wishing him to have powerful office. The Garlande reaction to this crisis underlines the problem for the king over the appointment. Stephen joined a rebellion against Louis, supported by Theobald IV of Blois, and Henry I of England. The war lasted three years. Louis attacked the Garlande castle at Livry in Brie, where Louis' relative Ralph of Vermandois lost an eye when hit by a missile from a catapult. The king's leg was wounded in the same way. The castle was taken and destroyed. The dispute led to a break between the king and the Garlandes. Louis removed Stephen from office and ordered the destruction of his property in Paris. Stephen made his peace and was reinstated as chancellor in 1132, though lacking the former trust and dominance. A royal ploy to prevent office becoming hereditary was to keep them vacant for a lengthy period, thus breaking the succession and a new seneschal was not appointed for four years.

The Garlande rebellion was a turning point in the reign.[41] Two new figures emerged to prominence, the king's relative Ralph of Vermandois (later seneschal), and Suger. Both showed the vital quality, missing in Stephen Garlande, of consistent loyalty. Suger has been accused of manipulating Stephen's fall, but it is unlikely since he had been close to him. The power of these royal bureaucratic families was 'precarious'.[42] They provoked opposition, especially from those of higher social rank who saw them as 'vile persons' risen above their deserts.[43] Royal power was not inconsiderable, and the king could make or break apparently powerful families.

Administrative methods continued steadily from the previous reign. Prévôts remained important in local government, collecting taxes and tolls in the demesne, while central administration became more organized. There is an increase in the number of charters surviving – from 3.6 a year to 12.1.[44] They were now prepared in the royal office rather than in the recipient's location. They went to a wider geographical area, including Toulouse. One should not however make the organization seem *too* fixed. Terms which later had precise meaning were often employed more vaguely. One cannot always distinguish between curia, council and entourage, or between the roles of *fideles*, *curiales*, officers and counsellors. Newman's view that 'there was no uniformity in justice' stands well for a general comment on administration.[45]

It is usual to see the curia as the king and those around him giving justice. But the translation as 'court' incorporates the other sense of a royal grouping. Sometimes, especially in the 12th century, the curia consisted of the king and his greater officers. Increasingly royal justice distanced itself from feudal justice, though the king had a role there too. The king tried to reserve to himself a variety of cases. Louis VI listed homicide, treason, theft and rape as subject to royal judgement. He also sought involvement in cases of usury, forgery and areas that affected crown rights – such as fishing in the Seine.[46] The increasing scope of royal justice meant an increase in royal income. As well as 'curia', we meet the term 'palace'. Bournazel suggests three contemporary meanings of palace: the royal residence, the personnel that served the residence, or a group around the king.[47] There was clearly an overlap between the meaning of the terms curia and palace.

It is difficult to define how the king took advice. We hear of councils and counsellors but the very uncertainty of their role as assemblies, or individuals, suggests no permanently organized system. The process depended on the king's will – what groups or individuals he chose to consult and when. Louis VI did constantly seek advice before acting, calling magnate and church councils for the purpose, and summoning individuals to give their views. Over the appeal to aid Christians in Barcelona in 1109 there was an assembly when the king spoke 'to his council' before responding.[48] There are many examples of church councils, for instance to look at the separation of the bishoprics of Noyon and Tournai in 1114 at Reims, or to support Innocent II or 'Anacletus II' at Étampes in 1130. It was up to the king how much he followed such advice but it is likely Louis noted opinion and did not often go head on against it. Over the papal dispute, Suger and St Bernard both declared for Innocent, as did the assembly, and Louis accepted the decision – despite a personal preference for Anacletus.

We see a gradual decline of great lords in attendance upon the king. They could not participate regularly in government and administration. Those closest to the king came from the knightly families of the demesne. We see the emergence of a curia or palace, of familiars or *fideles* – the terms vary but the fact is of a fairly close knit group from lesser families in daily attendance upon the king assisting in all matters of government, administration and business by executing necessary tasks and giving the king advice. We also see, through the example of Stephen Garlande, the king preventing individuals or families gaining dominance. The king used lesser men but also made his own role greater.

LOUIS VI, LESSER FRANCE AND THE LORDS OF THE DEMESNE

Luchaire admits that Louis' policy for the demesne followed that of his father, to augment the demesne through purchase, exchange, confiscation or conquest.[49] Within the Île-de-France the monarchy now held more land than any other lord. Louis VI completed the Capetian effort to control the castellans within the Île-de-France.[50] He pursued his policy by force when necessary, an active military man, 'above all a man of war'.[51] However, even within the demesne, royal control was not complete or always effective. Lords and castellans could still act with a degree of independence. Suger noted the problem of travel between the royal cities of Paris and Orléans, disrupted by lords with lands and castles alongside the route. It can be argued that the policy of control was undertaken by Philip I, and achieved by Louis VI – though we bear in mind the difficulties.

Royal activity followed a pattern that one can present as deliberate policy. The king sought a legal reason to intervene, to protect the church, or oppose unjust activity by the lord. He then summoned the offender to solve the matter by judicial means. This commonly failed and the king then made threats. If these also failed, he took to force. Royal power was now generally superior to that of the local lords – though a group could resist, at times with success. Louis VI as well as Philip I suffered occasional defeat. But more often royal power triumphed and the lord submitted. Castles increasingly became subject to royal command. Our information about this is mostly from the royal point of view, notably from Suger. The respective lords are condemned – men like Hugh du Puiset or Thomas of Marle. It is likely that such men were no worse than the average but for opposing the king were criticized and condemned.

A dilemma for clerical chroniclers was how to deal with Christian crusaders who returned and came into conflict with the crown. Suger gave an account of Louis' efforts during his father's reign as part of his own (Louis') success, and the division between his period as son and sole ruler is not always easy to distinguish. Louis' work began under his father and continued after 1108. He tackled a series of troublesome nobles in the demesne or nearby, including the lords of Boves, Coucy, Montmorency, Mouchy-le-Châtel, Beaumont, Corbeil, Pomponne, Montlhéry, Roucy, Meung and Mantes. Under Philip I, Prince Louis campaigned against these lords, mostly with success. He employed tough military tactics, where necessary laying waste, besieging castles, burning, and destroying. He was prepared to accept surrender and grant mercy, but on occasion could be harsh. Suger, with admirable Christian sentiment, gloried in Louis' punishment of Ebles de Roucy (in 1102): 'what a splendid deed ... the torturers tortured with the same or even more pain than they had used to torture others'.[52] Against Geoffrey Borel at Meung in 1103, Louis used fire so the defenders leapt from the tower for their life, only to fall on waiting lance points or be shot by archers, to 'carry off their miserable souls in sorrow to hell'.[53]

Many of the troublesome families were interconnected through marriage. When these connections can be traced, they show a complicated network of family links. The Montlhéry clan controlled a range of castles, including Chevreuse, Rochefort, Châteaufort and of course Montlhéry. Through marriage they had connections with even more strongholds.

The southern part of the demesne on the left bank of the Seine created much trouble for the king. The castellan opposition received aid from the king of England and Theobald of Blois. The families concerned included those of Maule, Rochefort and Montlhéry. There were problems with various strongholds, including Chevreuse, Rochefort, Châteaufort and Corbeil – though Montlhéry was the kingpin. The Montlhéry family controlled lands in the south of the demesne with castles at Rochefort, Châteaufort, Gometz and La Ferté-Alais. They also allied with the Le Puiset family with lands to the south-east.

Hugh I du Puiset had fought and beaten Philip I – commonly seen as a great defeat, though not so different from what happened to Louis VI. Hugh I married Alice, sister of Guy of Rochefort. Their son Evrard died on the First Crusade. His brothers, Hugh II and Guy, held the lordship in turn. On the death of Guy his nephew Hugh III inherited. Hugh III proved as troublesome to the monarchy as had Hugh I, 'a worthless shoot', 'more feared than loved'.[54] In the demesne Hugh was a major, perhaps *the* major, threat to royal authority. His main holdings were south of Chartres, his position made stronger by marriage to Agnes, daughter of Stephen-Henry count of Blois. Hugh allied with his brother-in-law Theobald of Blois – a major opponent of Louis, but the allies quarrelled between themselves. Hugh attacked Chartres, seized church land, and ignored excommunication. He attacked Toury in Beauce, belonging to St-Denis, supervised by Suger. Hugh took refuge in his castle at Le Puiset, 50 miles south of Paris. His victims, led by Theobald of Blois, attended a royal council at Melun in 1111 and appealed for action. Suger joined those baying for blood, calling Hugh a mad dog. Suger was asked by Louis to fortify Toury as a royal base against Hugh.

Louis summoned Hugh to court but he refused. His possessions were declared forfeit but he refused to surrender his castle. Louis besieged Le Puiset, with Suger present, producing carts filled with a mix of wood, dried blood and animal fat to be lit and rolled against the defences, 'a sort of incendiary black pudding'.[55] A bald and poor priest from Guilleville climbed up to remove pieces of the wall. He called on others to follow suit and the royal forces broke in. Hugh retreated to the keep but the castle fell and was destroyed. Hugh was wounded, captured, and chained in the tower at Château-Landon. When released under oath in 1112 Hugh ignored his promises, rebuilt his castle, and joined Theobald of Blois. Louis was defeated in battle near Le Puiset and his forces were scattered, though Ralph of Vermandois saved them from complete disaster. Louis finally beat Hugh and his allies in 1118 at Janville, seen as 'the decisive blow'.[56] Theobald of Blois was wounded and retreated. Le Puiset was taken, destroyed, and its wells filled. Louis had broken the power of the Rochefort-Montlhéry clan. Hugh III went on pilgrimage to the Holy Land, during which he died. Louis now controlled the areas around Chartres and Orléans.

The problem of control of the demesne families was increased by their intermarriages, as between Garlande and Rochefort, Garlande and Senlis, or Senlis and Montfort. The Montlhéry clan, including the lords of Montlhéry, Rochefort and Montmorency, was broad and powerful in and around the royal demesne with connections to the lords of Breteuil and Gallardon, and the counts of Meulan and Beaufort.[57] They possessed a string of castles. Guy the Red count of Rochefort returned from crusade to take up his former post as seneschal.[58] He died in 1108. His daughter Lucienne was betrothed to Prince Louis, though the marriage never took place – leading to resentment against the Capetians. Guy the Red's son Hugh de Crécy, 'a skilled and valiant young warrior', succeeded as seneschal, and caused trouble for the king from 1105 to 1118.[59] Hugh strangled his cousin, Miles of Bray, and imprisoned Odo of Corbeil, whose men appealed to Louis for aid in 1108. Louis had an initial success when Anselm Garlande entered Corbeil at night but there was fighting in the streets – the small royal force was thrown back, and Anselm was captured. Eventually Hugh threw himself at the king's feet, seeking pardon. He became a monk! Louis took castle after castle, and marked his successes with new royal fortresses at Montchauvet, Lorrez-le-Bocage, Grez, Corbeil and La Ferté-Alais.[60]

Thomas of Marle was the most renowned of Louis' demesne enemies, a 'wild beast', 'the vilest of men and a plague to God and man alike', an 'unbearable madman', 'like a wolf gone made'.[61] Thomas upset the ecclesiastical chroniclers and perhaps he was not the nicest of men. Guibert of Nogent described him torturing peasants and captives, hanging them by the testicles, beating and starving them to death. Thomas even came to blows with his father, Enguerrand de Coucy, and cut the throat of a relative, Walter archdeacon of Laon.

Thomas of Marle supported the citizens of Laon in their rising of 1112, when the bishop was killed. The leaders were sheltered by Thomas. One bishop declared a crusade against him, promising indulgences and absolution. Thomas was excommunicated in 1114 and condemned in the royal court – but continued his activities for 30 years. Louis joined the forces against him on behalf of the church. He took two castles and Thomas surrendered, begged the king's pardon, and received it – hardly suggesting behaviour quite as beyond the pale as the chroniclers imply. As with Hugh du Puiset, Louis reached an accommodation whereby Thomas offered compensation and the royal force was dispersed.

It was however more than a decade before Thomas ended his turbulent activities. He ignored his promise to the king. In 1130 Ralph of Vermandois, for Louis, organized an expedition against Thomas. Louis went though now hampered by obesity. At Coucy Ralph's men caught him. Ralph pierced him with his sword and handed him to the king. He made a long confession, was imprisoned, and soon died. Royal troops still had to enforce order in the region in 1132, when Thomas' son Enguerrand caused some trouble. Peace was finally made and Enguerrand married the niece of Louis' cousin Ralph of Vermandois.

The detailed accounts of Louis' struggles against the castellans show that he did not have an easy passage. He was no more consistently victorious than Philip I, with occasional setbacks and defeats. The leading castellans took decades to subdue; Suger minimized the difficulties. The king's victory was gradual, through '34 years of incessant war'.[62] However, it can be claimed that in the end disturbances were quelled and royal power made firmer.[63]

Louis followed a consistent policy in dealing with the castellans – legal justification, court settlement, force if necessary, and was consistent in his follow-up. He emphasized the obligations of defeated lords as vassals. He sought to maintain order through control of castles, condemning 'illicit construction' without royal consent. He garrisoned or destroyed captured castles. Louis could be ruthless in punishing opponents and traitors. When one of his castellans was killed at La Roche-Guyon, the killers and residents were mutilated, disembowelled, and thrown from the tower on to lances with their points upwards. The leading killer's heart was torn out and impaled on a stake.[64] Children were cast headfirst on rocks, and bodies thrown into the Seine to float into Normandy as a warning.

Louis' successes meant the spread of royal administration, especially in the demesne and Lesser France. New prévots were placed in Montlhéry, Châteauneuf, Moret, Sanois and Yèvre-le-Châtel. Essential routes to Paris and Orléans were now controlled by the king. The defeat of the lords of Le Puiset secured the route to Chartres. The taking of Ste-Sévère, Meung, Château-Renard and St-Brisson gave safe access to the Loire and Berry. The struggle between king and castellans was partly about the benefits from justice and tolls – now royal profit was much greater.

The consequences of Louis' victories over local lords can hardly be exaggerated. The demesne was as much 'a collection of rights' as a territorial unit. Expanding the demesne meant increased rights and profits.[65] The king was now safer in his base and could tour his principality with ease. Administration and profits were tightened and increased, the roads were improved, trade grew and (perhaps most vital for the future) Paris benefited enormously. Great improvements were made in the city, including new bridges, and a new market at Champeaux.

LOUIS VI AND THE PRINCIPALITIES

Louis' policy for the demesne was pursued outside it too, often in response to church appeals for protection. Sometimes appeals to the king were made in disputes between lords. We should not underestimate royal power outside Lesser France; Suger noted that 'kings have long arms'.[66] Louis was soon involved in activity beyond the demesne, in his first year over the inheritance of Archambaud IV lord of Bourbon between his son Archambaud V and the boy's uncle, Aimon II Vairvache – who seized the lands. Aimon had antagonized the priory of St-Pourçain, and Louis took up the cudgels on the priory's behalf. Aimon was summoned to court but refused to come. The king marched on Berry and besieged Aimon's 'well fortified' castle at Germigny-sur-l'Aubois.[67] Aimon surrendered, throwing himself at the king's feet. He agreed to restore priory lands, and returned with Louis to Lesser France as a prisoner.

Louis 'ever prompt to aid churches' went south in 1122 to defend the bishop of Clermont against William VI count of Auvergne (1096–1136).[68] Louis besieged the count's castle of Pont-du-Château. The count was forced out but planned revenge. He again attacked the bishop, who sought the king's aid. Louis, nothing if not persistent, returned in 1126, in the company of Charles the Good of Flanders, Fulk V of Anjou, Conan of Brittany, and a contingent of Norman knights. They besieged the unfinished castle at Montferrand. Suger, for safety, slept in a tent under his shield. The castle fell and those captured had their hands cut off. William X duke of Aquitaine (1126–37) brought a force to intervene on behalf of the count, annoyed that the king was dealing directly with a vassal who 'holds the Auvergne of me'.[69] In the end he backed down and accepted an agreement, recognizing Louis as overlord, and leaving him to settle the matter.

Louis' last expedition south was in 1135 against St-Brisson-sur-Loire, a key stronghold near Gien, 45 miles south-east of Orléans. Its lord had been attacking passing merchants. The wider aim was control of Berry. The castle was taken and fired. By the end of the reign Louis controlled Ste-Sévère, Germigny and St-Brisson, all important points on the border of Berry. As Bautier sees it, 'Berry for the first time since the accession of the dynasty had become a base for launching a major political effort towards the centre of the realm'.[70]

At the end of his life Louis made a potentially great step forward for the monarchy. William X, duke of Aquitaine died in 1137. He had named Louis as ward for his daughter, Eleanor. The king arranged for her to marry his heir, Louis. It seemed that the great principality of Aquitaine would be added directly to the royal lands. This was not to be permanent but it was an ambitious move.

FLANDERS

In Flanders Louis received aid from Robert the Frisian, Baldwin VI, Baldwin VII, and Charles the Good, notably against Henry I of England. Robert was crossing the Marne on campaign with the king, when he fell from his horse and was trampled on by others. Baldwin VII died young in 1119, hit on the head by a lance at Eu, leaving no direct heir. Charles the Good acquired Flanders (1119–27) with Louis' support since Charles' mother was his own aunt – Adela of Flanders sister of Bertha of Holland. The murder of Charles in the church at Bruges on 2 March 1127 was a shocking event that gave Louis an opportunity to intervene. Charles was attacked when praying prostrate on the floor in St-Donatien at Bruges. The count had provoked the family of Erembald de Furnes, which provided major officials in the county, led by the brothers Bertulf, Lambert of Reddenbourg, Didier Hacket and Wilfrid Knop. Bertulf was prévôt of St-Donatien and chancellor of Flanders, and Didier was castellan of Bruges. Charles had antagonized them by punishing Didier's son Burchard for his part in a feud.

Thirty conspirators entered the church and blocked off all the exits. They attacked Charles, Burchard cutting off his head as he looked up. Louis avenged the count, punishing the murderers in a manner seen by some as 'heavy-handed'.[71] He called an assembly at Arras to decide the succession. The major claimants were Thierry of Alsace, William of Ypres and Baldwin IV count of Hainault. Thierry was Charles' cousin but was not present. William was also a cousin and present, but he was illegitimate. Louis named William Clito son of Curthose as count.[72] Clito had failed to gain Normandy, but Louis had found him useful a pawn against the Anglo-Normans. Clito was married to Jeanne de Montferrat, Queen Adelaide's sister. Clito was elected and accepted by most of the major cities of Flanders. Louis acting as overlord, confirmed Clito's charters, named castellans and aided Clito against William of Ypres, who disputed the succession. William was captured and imprisoned at Lille. The murderers of Charles the Good were arrested and executed, Wilfrid Knop and 21 others hanged from the tower of Bruges. Burchard had fled but was captured, tied to the top of a great wheel and left to the crows. His eyes were torn out and his face ripped to shreds by birds. He was made the target for every manner of weapon and died 'a vile death'.[73] His remains were thrown into a sewer. Berthold fled but was handed over by his own men and hanged from a gallows with a dog tied to a pole. The dog ate his face and defecated on him. Most of the other conspirators were given pardons but then taken one by one and thrown from the top of the tower of Bruges, breaking their necks.

Clito proved unequal to the task of ruling Flanders, lacking sufficient local support. Thierry of Alsace, the son of Gertrude of Flanders and grandson of Robert the Frisian, contested the succession and won wide backing. He married Fulk IV of Anjou's daughter, Sybil, whose marriage to Clito had been annulled for consanguinity. Fulk had been so angry that he arrested the papal ambassadors and burned off their hair and beards (for which he was excommunicated). Clito alienated many by his unnecessary brutality and angered major cities by denying their privileges. Many rebelled, beginning with St-Omer in 1128, soon followed by Ghent and Bruges, who turned to Thierry. In 1128 Clito allied with William of Ypres, who was released. Opinion in Flanders swung against royal involvement: 'the king has no right to impose a count on us by force', and he should 'mind his own business'.[74] Louis had Thierry excommunicated and besieged him in Lille but abandoned the attempt after six days. Clito was wounded in the hand by an arrow at Alost; it turned gangrenous, and he died. Thierry defeated William of Ypres and was recognized as count in 1128. Louis had little option but to accept. William went to England and became chief lieutenant to King Stephen. Louis' actions in Flanders have been seen as a failure, 'one of the follies of the reign'.[75] Luchaire suggests that Clito failed because Louis came to his aid too late, delayed by the Garlande crisis.[76] It was nevertheless, however briefly, a step forward in royal ambitions. Louis had controlled the succession to a major principality even if the candidate failed.

NORMANDY AND ENGLAND

Louis' greatest problem with his principalities came in Normandy, now under a duke who was also king of England and unwilling to be treated as anything but a king. At Tinchebray in 1106 Henry I defeated and captured his brother, Curthose, who remained in prison for the rest of his life until 1134. As a result England and Normandy were reunited, and under a determined and able ruler.

Henry I now seized Gisors on the Epte, claiming a right to it through Pagan of Gisors who had, however, been a *fidelis* of the French king. Louis demanded that Henry give up Gisors and marched with allies including Robert of Flanders, Theobald of Blois and William of Nevers. They attacked the lands of Henry's supporter, Robert of Meulan. After a confrontation across the Epte, Louis went to Gisors. Henry agreed to destroy the castle within 40 days – but failed to keep his promise, and fighting continued. Henry I wished to withdraw from being a vassal to Louis and 'protected [the Norman border] by an impressive line of new castles'.[77] The French accounts describe Louis' successes, while the Norman note those of Henry I; it was in fact an indecisive struggle.

From the start Louis faced a threat from Normandy to Lesser France, both depending on the Seine for communication and wealth from trade. The two held territories either side of the Epte, dividing the Norman from the French Vexin. Henry I pressured Louis by alliance with Theobald IV count of Blois, his nephew. Theobald's younger brothers, Stephen count of Boulogne, and Henry who was promised to the church, were welcomed in England. Stephen eventually succeeded his uncle as king, and Henry became abbot of Glastonbury and bishop of Winchester. Theobald's power increased after 1125 when he united Blois with Champagne. The family's lands on either side of the royal demesne posed a major threat to the Capetians.

Louis VI's next clash with the Anglo-Norman state was the prolonged war from 1109–13. Henry I was joined by Theobald of Blois, the count of Flanders, and several castellans from the Île-de-France, including Guy of Rochefort, Hugh du Puiset and Hugh count of Troyes. Louis pursued the old policy of dividing the Anglo-Norman family by supporting Curthose's son, William Clito. Louis defeated the opposing castellans but achieved little more in this first clash. In 1113 he backed down and recognized Henry I as holding Maine and Brittany.

Clito failed to gain Normandy but still received Louis' support and war broke out again from 1116–20. Louis took Gasny on the Epte but was then threatened by Henry's two counter castles, one called Malassis or 'badly sited', which Louis attacked.[78] Henry became nervous about security, always protected by guards at night with shield and sword at his side. A counsellor who betrayed Henry was 'mercifully' condemned to have his eyes and genitals removed.[79] Henry's nephew Stephen held Alençon for him and was besieged by Fulk V of Anjou, encouraged by Louis. Henry attempted relief and was brought to battle in 1118. Fulk made a sortie and Henry's force fled. Henry's ally Theobald of Blois was wounded in the forehead by an arrow and Alençon surrendered to Fulk.

In 1119 Henry I gained his revenge and Louis suffered defeat at Brémule. Louis VI and Fulk V had invaded Normandy in support of Clito, hoping to gain Gisors. Henry I was supported by Theobald of Blois. He posted scouts on the hill at Verclives, overlooking the plain at Brémule. The scouts warned Henry when they saw the French emerging from the woods. Seeing the size of the enemy army, Bouchard of Montmorency advised Louis to avoid battle and retreat, but he refused. William the Chamberlain gave the same advice to Henry I, with the same response. Louis ordered a cavalry charge led by the Norman William Crespin. The sources are agreed that it was a disorderly charge and responsible for the defeat – even Suger called it 'a bold but careless attack'.[80] Eighty French knights were killed. The king ordered a second charge which also failed, though Henry I was struck on the head – saved by his mail. The French broke and were pursued into the forest of Musegros. Louis VI lost his horse and his banner, isolated among the trees. He was saved by a peasant, who led him to Les Andelys. Henry returned to victory celebrations in Rouen. The French invasion of Normandy had failed. Louis burned Ivry and Chartres and besieged Breteuil. He complained about Henry and Theobald as disloyal vassals to a church council at Reims – but it was scant compensation for humiliating defeat.

The main blow to Henry I came not from Louis but in the unhappy fate of his son. William the Aetheling was Henry's only legitimate son, though he had numerous illegitimate offspring. In 1119 William married Matilda, daughter of Fulk of Anjou. In 1120 William performed homage to Louis, who agreed to cede Gisors. William and a gang of drunken youths set out for England from Barfleur in the White Ship under its captain, Thomas. They took over the vessel and sank it. Several notable figures went down with it, including William's brother Richard, their sister Matilda, a sister of Theobald of Blois, and Thierry the nephew of the emperor Henry V. Only one man survived to tell the tale. Henry I was now without a clear heir, a situation that swung the political pendulum back in Louis' favour.

Louis continued to support Clito and to receive aid from Fulk of Anjou and Waleran of Meulan. Waleran had been imprisoned by Henry I for rebellion and then released. A third war broke out in 1123. On the death of the emperor Henry V, Henry I arranged a new marriage for his daughter Matilda (Henry V's widow) to the son of Fulk V of Anjou, Geoffrey le Bel. The death of Clito meant the loss of Louis' major ally in Normandy. Henry I's most likely heir was either his daughter Matilda or one of his Blois nephews – in neither case likely to favour Louis. Henry I's death in 1135 brought these factors to a head. His nephew Stephen seized the English throne and became duke of Normandy. Matilda's Angevin husband, Geoffrey V, began his conquest of Normandy, and Matilda planned to invade England with the backing of her half-brother, Robert earl of Gloucester. Henry I's death eased the situation for Louis, followed as it was by the challenged succession of Stephen, and internal war in England and Normandy. Stephen was too concerned with his own difficulties to offer any threat to Louis. To conclude that Louis did not defeat Henry I and his Blesevin ally but 'held them at bay' seems fair.[81]

LOUIS VI AND THE EMPIRE

For much of his reign Louis was at odds with the Holy Roman Emperor. Henry V married Matilda, daughter of Henry I of England, a consistent enemy to Louis. Louis' position was eased by the imperial concern with the papacy. The expectation that relations between empire and papacy would improve after the death of Henry IV proved false. Henry V continued the clash and was excommunicated in 1116 and 1119. It was not until 1122 that he made terms with the papacy. Louis kept on good terms with the papacy, on occasion offering refuge to popes forced out by imperial opposition.

In 1124 Louis faced a major invasion from the Empire, possibly exaggerated by Suger. Encouraged by Henry I of England, the emperor Henry V raised a large army to attack Lorraine. Louis' response to the news was (presumably in French) 'Tpwrut Aleman'.[82] Louis received the standard from St-Denis, and rallied his forces. The response showed that royal power was not confined to Lesser France; it was a French army in the broader sense. It is true that most came from the north, and that some southern troops arrived late, but men came from Paris and Orléans, Reims and Châlons, Étampes, Laon, Troyes and Soissons, the northern principalities including Flanders, Vermandois and Blois. They came from Aquitaine, Poitou, Burgundy, Nevers, Brittany and Anjou.

Louis' right was commanded by Ralph of Vermandois, the van by Hugh duke of Burgundy and William count of Nevers, the rear by Charles the Good of Flanders. The only major vassal of the crown not present was the duke of Normandy (Henry I of England). The army was formed for battle though no fighting ensued. The imperial force was sufficiently discouraged and turned tail. Suger boasted of 'a grand and prestigious victory'.[83] Henry V had little opportunity to take up the cudgels again with trouble from Hungary, Bohemia and Holland. He became ill at Utrecht and died in 1125.

LOUIS VI AND THE CHURCH

Louis' relationship with the church, like so much else, has been seen through the eyes of Suger, and again we need to be aware of distortion. Suger presented the abbot of St-Denis as head of the French church – but this was never the case. His claim was based on a charter forged at the time.[84] He emphasized every connection between the king and his abbey. His agenda included playing down the role of his rivals, such as the archbishop of Reims, or the bishop of Paris. St-Denis benefited from Suger's relationship with the kings, through land grants and rights. Louis VI granted the famous hyacinth from Anna of Kiev to St-Denis.

Suger emphasized the royal role in the Christian world. Several historians have detected a far from complete admiration for Louis VI, but it suited the chronicler to stress his role in the French church and his connection to St-Denis – gifts such as the crown of Philip I, positions confirmed, the royal standard kept and granted in the abbey. This *vexillum*, the banner of the counts of the Vexin, was the standard of the abbey's saint and known as the oriflamme.[85] It was a red silk banner with a green fringe on a silver-gilt staff with green tassels. The original banner stood on one side of the altar at St-Denis with a replica on the other side, which was probably the one taken on campaigns. Suger wove a fiction of the king holding lands from the saint. Suger thought the king should not be a vassal to any other human but invented the idea that he was subject to the saint for abbey lands in the Vexin. In 1127, when Louis invested Clito with the Vexin, no mention was made of St-Denis; it is unlikely that the king saw the situation in the same light as Suger. The abbot's line on the standard was an attempt to link the king, the nation, the church and the abbey – Saint Denis leading the royal army. Suger's spin worked and the standard became the oriflamme of legend, fictitiously linking the Capetians with Charlemagne, and the monarchy with the abbey. It became practice that the king received the standard from the abbey whenever the nation went to war.

Suger condemned Philip I's liaison with Bertrade de Montfort, Louis' 'sycophantic stepmother'.[86] He presented Louis as a contrast to his father. He was hardly a saint but Suger's presentation makes him seem not far off, including his association with miracles. Guibert of Nogent also referred to Louis curing scrofula by touch – a sign of the power the king received from God via the church at consecration. Suger's relationship with individual popes aided a good relationship between the papacy and France. The papacy hoped for aid during Philip I's reign in its conflict with the empire, a hope undermined by the marriage problem. Hostility between papacy and empire had not abated. French support for the crusades helped improve relations and there was no marital dispute with Louis VI. In 1118 Gelasius II fled to France. Calixtus II had an even closer link, as uncle of Louis' wife Adelaide, while Innocent II owed his very position to French support.

A policy that was the king's rather than the abbot's was to support the church beyond Lesser France, winning political footholds. Time and again Louis made protection of the local church his reason for intervention in disputes. Thus he supported bishops in Nantes, Burgundy and Languedoc against secular attack. Louis VI was no blind supporter of church reform like former kings defended royal rights, especially in episcopal elections. Louis was prepared at times to oppose the papacy. He had his coronation at Orléans rather than Reims, to avoid accepting its new archbishop, Ralph the Green. Louis did later yield over this, but only on condition that Ralph swore fidelity. Louis' determination to preserve royal rights led to disputes with the papacy over elections at Laon, Auxerre, Orléans and Arras. He did not approve the election of Stephen of Senlis as bishop of Paris and Stephen had to seek refuge with the Cistercians.

Louis opposed subordinating the diocese of Sens to the see of Lyon, protesting he would rather see the realm burning and himself doomed to death than Sens come under Lyon.[87]

There were then clashes between king and papacy but the latter was undergoing a period of difficulty, unable to sustain its position in Rome. The hostility of the emperors necessitated dealings with the French king. On more than one occasion the emperor supported an anti-pope. Innocent II was faced by Anacletus II and forced to leave Rome. He sought aid in France.

We may also credit Louis VI with a policy that differed from Suger's in supporting the new monasticism. It is true Suger knew St Bernard and developed a good relation with him, but Suger opposed any challenge to the supremacy of Benedictine St-Denis. Louis, however, was sympathetic and supportive to Cluny, Cîteaux, Prémontré, Tiron and Fontevraud. Fontevraud was founded by Robert of Arbrissel and reformed; Bertrade resided there until her death. Vital of Mortain founded Savigny in 1112; Tiron was set up in 1114 by the hermit Bernard. The Cistercians prospered with 41 houses founded in France in the reign. Louis also favoured canons regular, another new organization, founding St-Victor in Paris in 1108 under William des Champeaux. Louis granted St-Victor privileges in a charter of 1113 and his personal physician, Obijon, left his wife to join the order. St Norbert of Xanten founded his order of canons regular, the Premonstratensians. The Augustinians also prospered and were recognized. Louis assisted in the foundation of various other houses, such as Hautes-Bruyères in 1112, Chaâlis a Cistercian house in 1136, and made many gifts to houses.

On the other hand Louis was not very sympathetic to Gregorian reformers who wished to diminish royal power in the church. Yves of Chartres put the kernel in a nutshell to Henry I of England, 'terrestrial power must be submitted to ecclesiastical government'. It was a view that no contemporary king could accept, including Louis, who found himself in opposition to Hildebert of Lavardin archbishop of Tours, Yves of Chartres and Stephen of Senlis bishop of Paris. Yves spent some time in prison; Hildebert was exiled for several years; Stephen sought refuge with Theobald of Blois and appealed to the pope against 'the new Herod'.[88] Nor was Louis always in accord with St Bernard. Suger glossed over these differences except where it suited him.

One cannot leave the reign without noting the importance of schools, learning and major literary and cultural figures. Paris and other cities developed important schools attracting scholars, such as Anselm, Abelard and William de la Porée. Abelard was an original thinker whose contribution would have been great in any age – it is doubtful if he would have been as safe in any other western state as in France, where he received some protection, not least from Louis VI, Theobald of Blois and Louis VII (if not from the relatives of Heloise!). We may reasonably conclude that like almost all the Capetians Louis VI was a devout Christian who did his best to support the church and keep on good terms with the papacy. He supported the new monasticism. According to Yves of Chartres, Louis was 'a simple man, devoted to the church, and full of good will towards the apostolic see'.[89]

LOUIS VI AND THE ECONOMY

The 12th century was an important period in the development of France – politically, economically and culturally. Louis only played a certain part but it is not to be ignored. He took a lead in enfranchising serfs and granting privileges to towns. Urban growth brought wealth and political power. The policy of giving privileges to merchants and citizens became increasingly important. One begins to see an alliance between king and bourgeoisie. Louis used this alliance to counter difficult castellans and lords. It provided a second string to the royal ambition for greater power; the king had not only the church but also the mercantile element as potential allies throughout the realm, seeing the monarchy as their chief hope of political support. Louis' attitude had some qualifications; he was not prepared to recognize rights that harmed his own position, opposing new privileges for Bourges and Paris, suppressing customs that restricted the powers of royal agents.

The period saw the emergence of organized urban groups seeking greater control. The usual aim was to establish a commune allowing control by the leading citizens. Communes emerged in the later 11th century and appeared with greater frequency in the 12th, as at Laon and Amiens. Many nobles saw commune development as dangerous and even revolutionary, often accompanied by violence that added to their fears. Nevertheless the movement offered an opportunity to the king. Communes needed protection against local lords who were usually opposed to them. The obvious protector was the king and Louis VI has been called 'the father of the communes'.[90] Support for the crown from towns that were growing in economic value was a vital part of Capetian development. The act of recognizing a commune usually brought immediate financial reward in the form of a payment by the town – as at Amiens.

Towns also sought recognition of mercantile rights, and again turned to the king. The count of Flanders granted a charter of commercial privileges to St-Omer in 1127, confirmed by the king. Similar privileges were granted to Arras, Valenciennes and Lille. Louis supported a degree of urban independence – but not within the demesne. There he was more prepared to recognize privileges than communes – as at Paris, Mantes, Chelles, Corbie, Étampes, Bourges and Soissons. Various new markets were agreed, including Les Champeaux in Paris.

The rising at Laon caused much concern. The city was an episcopal seat. Bishop Gaudry, who allied with Henry I of England, was an eccentric cleric who employed a negro servant as executioner. The citizens were antagonized by him and established a commune which Louis VI recognized in 1111. The bishop appealed against this and in 1112 Louis revoked his decision and suppressed the commune. This led to a revolt, virtually a general strike with shops and inns closing. On Good Friday citizens marched on the episcopal palace. Some of the bishop's men were killed defending the palace. The bishop dressed as a servant and hid in a cask in the cellar. He was discovered and pulled out by the hair. His head was split with an axe so that blood and wine flowed together. The body was dragged naked through the streets and dumped in the market place. Thomas of Marle earned his vile reputation by supporting the rebels in Laon – which few nobles or clerics would dream of doing. He used the opportunity to deal with his own enemies, hanging some by their private parts until they ripped off. Peasants looted the town. The king ended the commune in 1114 – though it was re-established in 1128. Louis restored order but he earned criticism for initially supporting the commune.

This was an important period in the freeing of serfs. The royal charter to Lorris in the Gâtinais was issued, which became a model for such charters. It granted privileges, the freeing of serfs and protection to the fair and markets. In 1115 Louis supported Amiens against the 'tyrant' Adam, though he had to besiege the place and was wounded in the attempt. The keep surrendered and was razed. Louis was more inclined to confirm grants made by others than to apply freedoms in his demesne but several such confirmations are recorded in charters, as at Laon, Beaune and Janville.

THE DEATH OF LOUIS VI

When campaigning against Theobald of Blois in 1135, Louis became seriously ill. After taking St-Brisson, he set out for Paris, reaching Meraër (Châteauneuf-sur-Loire) in November. He had diarrhoea and dysentery; doctors administered potions and bitter powders which only made him worse. He feared imminent death, made confession and expressed his desire to be buried at St-Denis. He insisted on reconciliation between Ralph of Vermandois and Theobald of Blois to ensure peace after his death. He then recovered but 1137 was a hot summer and he fell ill again in the forest of Yveline near Melun. He moved to Béthisy in June, 40 miles from Paris. There he heard of the death of William X of Aquitaine. The king agreed to the marriage of his son Louis to the eldest of William's two daughters, the heiress Eleanor. Suger and an escort went with young Louis to claim his wife and the unexpected prize of the duchy of Aquitaine.

Louis' health deteriorated further when back in Paris. He wanted to die as a Christian and made frequent confessions, including to Gilduin abbot of St-Victor. He donned a monastic habit and ordered a carpet to be laid on the ground with ashes spread on it in the shape of a cross. He was laid on this cross, emulating it with arms spread, and thus met his end on 1 August 1137 at the age of 56. News of the death was sent to Prince Louis in Aquitaine. The body was taken to St-Denis for burial.

Louis' successes have been recognized and his reign seen as the time when the monarchy recovered, yet the pattern of the reign was very similar to that of his father's. Louis suffered military defeats, by Hugh du Puiset and his allies in 1112 and by Henry I at Brémule in 1119. His eventual success was hard won and restricted in extent – though none the less important for that. Louis VI may be best known as 'the Fat' but he was also called 'the Justiciar' and 'the Battler'. Perhaps the best summary of his achievements was expressed by a French book-seller called Sebastien who posted me a copy of Delperrié de Bayac's *Louis VI*.

Enclosed with the book was an unexpected friendly note hoping that I would travel in medieval France and noting that Louis 'fought all his life to build his little kingdom'.

LOUIS VII (1137–80)

Louis VI's eldest son, by Adelaide of Maurienne, was Philip. Louis associated Philip in 1129 at the age of 13, but the latter was killed in 1131 when his horse stumbled over a pig in a Paris suburb. He was thrown, his head hit a stone and the horse fell on him. He was carried to a nearby house but died in the night. Philip was buried at St-Denis. Louis VI's second son, Louis le Jeune (the Young), had been aimed at a church career – evident in his later conduct. He was now 11 and was associated in rule in a ceremony conducted by Pope Innocent II at Reims on Sunday 25 October 1131. He was taken in procession to the abbey of St-Remy and escorted to the cathedral by Innocent II. There Louis was consecrated with the oil reputedly used to baptise Clovis.

When Louis VI thought he was dying he declared, 'I Louis who am a sinner, believe in the one true God'. Suger was in tears and the king responded, 'Do not weep for me, my dearest friend, be glad that I have been able to prepare myself'. He then handed a ring to Prince Louis, and made him promise to watch over the church, the poor and orphans, and guard the rights of his subjects, relying on God 'through whom kings reign'.

William X of Aquitaine's suggestion that his daughter and heiress, Eleanor of Aquitaine, should marry Louis was a bonus for the monarchy, and taken up promptly. Louis VI organized the party to escort his son south. It included Suger, Theobald of Blois and Ralph of Vermandois. The marriage was celebrated in the cathedral of St-André in Bordeaux in 1137. Prince Louis was 17, his bride only 15. It cannot have been altogether a joyous occasion since the bride's father had recently died, and the bridegroom's father had fallen ill again – to expire soon afterwards.

Louis VII on his seal of 1137 appears as a young man with hair to his shoulders. He was educated in the cathedral school of Notre-Dame in Paris. He was genuinely pious and organized the first royal crusade. Despite its military failure he insisted on staying to see the Holy Places. During the crusade he never forgot mass or the hours, whatever the military conditions or the weather.[91] His first wife famously declared that being wedded to him was like marriage to a monk. Later when ill at the siege of Nonette Louis was offered a young girl to enter his bed and speed his recovery. He primly refused, 'if nothing else will cure me, let the Lord do his will by me, since it is better to die ill and chaste than live as an adulterer'.[92] He was unusual in his age for showing tolerance to the Jews, appointing a Praepositus Judaeorum to protect them. His reign saw a significant increase in the freeing of serfs, encouraged by the church and the king. In a charter he declared 'all men having a common origin were endowed from birth with a kind of natural liberty. It is given to our royal majesty to raise them anew to this liberty'.[93] He was a gentle and modest man, noted for 'kindness and simple mildness'.[94] Walter Map described an occasion when Theobald of Blois found the king sleeping in the forest, guarded only by two knights. He scolded him for risking his life. Louis replied, 'I sleep alone and safe because no one envies me'.[95] Walter Map recorded Louis' comment on the wealth of England, remarking that 'we in France have only bread, wine, and the enjoyment of life'.[96]

The young Louis, now married, returned to Paris. The coronation occurred at Christmas in Bourges. The queen mother, Adelaide, attempted to control affairs through Ralph of Vermandois, but Suger stepped in and Ralph retired. Adelaide married a noble of the second rank, Matthew of Montmorency. Historians have condemned Louis VII as a weak and unsuccessful king, cowardly, a poor politician and strategist.[97] Luchaire saw him as dominated by the church, 'a fearful and maladroit politician who humiliated the crown before the Plantagenets'.[98] Gobry suggests that Louis was more unlucky than maladroit – in his preparation for kingship since he was not expected to inherit, in marriage for who could have foreseen the problems and consequences of the match. Louis seemed most unlucky in his offspring, that after marriage to three fertile women he produced no son between 1137 and 1165, which much influenced politics in the period. In more recent times Pacaut, Duby and Sassier among others, have gradually resurrected his reputation.

Louis VII is possibly the most difficult of the dynasty to sum up. Chroniclers and historians have differed over his character, his abilities and his achievements. We can only tackle the problem of assessment by examining his efforts and asking a series of questions. Was Louis responsible for the failure of his first marriage, and how disastrous was that failure? Was Louis responsible for the failure of the Second Crusade, and how disastrous was that? Was Louis to blame for the rebellion by his brother Robert, an exception to the normal family loyalty of the dynasty? How far was Louis to blame for allowing the formation of the Angevin Empire which posed such a threat to France? These are not the only questions, but they outline the debate we need to enter.

LOUIS VII AND THE CHURCH

Louis has been portrayed as dominated by the church. He was certainly pious and listened to ecclesiastical advice, though he did not always take it. He respected clerics and counted among his correspondents John of Salisbury ('my most dear friend') and Thomas Becket – who studied in Paris and later found refuge in France.[99] With one or two spectacular exceptions, Louis behaved as a good Christian and added to the Capetian reputation for piety. He lived a simple life, like a priest, with the canons at Notre-Dame in Paris. He kept to a diet of bread and water every Friday. One cannot but make comparisons with St Louis.

While on Crusade, Louis agreed that his regent Suger should co-operate with the papacy over governing the French church. He supported the Peace and Truce of God. In 1155 at the Council at Soissons he proclaimed he would enforce 'peace

for the whole realm' – offering security to churches, peasants and merchants.[100]
The king declared a ten-year peace and persuaded the princes and prelates to
accept it by oath, with himself as the final enforcer. A sculptor produced a bas
relief of Louis in 1171, holding a church in his hand and inscribed the 'peaceful
king'.[101] Louis maintained the Capetian tradition of gifts and support for the
church. 177 charters were donations or concessions to the church; 275 charters
confirm gifts by others. Building and rebuilding was patronized, including work
on Notre-Dame in Paris.

Louis did, however, follow the other Capetian tradition of protecting royal
rights against the church. Pacaut's investigation of episcopal elections has far-
reaching effects on our assessment of Louis.[102] Pacaut suggests that the three
main contributions of a king in the election of a bishop were to authorize the
election, to confirm it and to hold the regalia during a vacancy. The king also
granted the regalia to an elected bishop. Louis' position, without compulsion,
was similar to that agreed between papacy and empire at Worms in 1122 – the
clergy should elect, the church consecrate, but the king should give the regalia.
Louis accepted that elections should be made by the church, by cathedral canons
and other relevant clergy. The 12th century saw a gradual move from a general
clerical election towards one by cathedral canons only.

In his first year as king Louis clashed with the pope over the election to Langres,
initiated not by secular interference but by a difference between the clerical
electors. Some chose a Benedictine monk, but he was opposed by St Bernard
and the Cistercians. Louis, persuaded by Peter the Venerable abbot of Cluny,
confirmed the initial choice and conceded to him the regalia. For the vacancy at
Bourges, Louis favoured his household official, Cadurc, but the canons preferred
Peter de la Châtre, archbishop of Agen. The electors had failed to notify the king
and he refused to confirm their choice. Innocent II intervened to reject Cadurc as
unsuitable – an unusual and provocative step. Louis' reaction was to shake with
anger and declare that so long as he lived Peter would not be allowed to take up
the post. The pope placed an interdict on all places where the king resided. Both
Innocent II and St Bernard blamed the clash on hasty action by a young and
rash king – 'a child' wrote the pope. Louis did not act in this fashion again. The
situation over Bourges eased with Innocent's death and his replacement by the
more conciliatory Celestine II in 1143, and then a series of brief papacies due
to deaths – of Celestine within three months, and Lucius II after 11 months. In
1144 Louis agreed to yield on condition that Peter swore fidelity.

There were other similar if lesser disputes, as when Grimoald was elected
abbot of Alleux and consecrated by the archbishop of Bordeaux. Louis refused to
recognize him because his assent had not been sought. He forbade Grimoald to
enter Poitiers. St Bernard commented 'unhappy is the land whose prince is only
a child', but Louis refused to budge. The matter was settled by Grimoald's death
in 1141. As Pacaut makes clear, although there were disputed and problematic
elections under Louis VII, at most three were caused by the king.[103] Only at
Bourges was the cause a blatant intervention by the king on behalf of a favoured

royal candidate. Most candidates favoured by Louis proved acceptable and proceeded through the normal channels. Among them were members of the royal entourage (usually excellent administrators), royal relatives, and relations of royal favourites or allies, and some notable men such as John of Salisbury to Chartres, Peter Lombard and Maurice de Sully to Paris and Gilbert de la Porée to Poitiers. In other words royal influence could often have an excellent result. The most common cause of difficulty was a dispute between ecclesiastical electors; more through St Bernard trying to introduce Cistercian candidates than by Louis seeking to impose his will. St Bernard was involved in most of the disputed elections before his death, though often it must be said in order to find a solution.

One aspect of Louis' reign was increased contact with the south. Louis had political reasons for championing southern churches against local lords. In 1140 Peter the Venerable abbot of Cluny claimed that his region was 'without king, without duke and without prince' – but the situation was changing and would continue to change as royal intervention increased.[104] Louis' marriage to Eleanor gave one excuse for action, but it did not halt after the breakdown of the marriage. Another motive was to balance power against Henry II by making new southern alliances. Louis made personal contacts in the south, notably with lords who accompanied him on crusade, such as the counts of Mâcon and Forez. Louis became active in church matters in Burgundy, Languedoc, Aquitaine and Toulouse. He dealt with secular opposition to the church in Clermont and Le Puy in 1163 and in the Mâconnais in 1166 and 1171. He declared, 'we intend to help all the churches established in our realm'.[105] Louis expanded the number of 'royal' churches, bringing in those of Narbonne, Agde, Lodève and Maguelonne. The bishop of Cevennes recognized Louis as 'our good master, our defender, and our liberator'.[106]

Pacaut argued that it is hard to define a 'royal church'.[107] In theory all churches were royal but in practice various princes and lords held secular authority over a see. Pacaut's solution was to examine all the bishoprics and decide where royal power was 'effective', where the king was able to exercise the rights claimed. There can be no question of the royal prerogative over the sees of Sens, Reims and Bourges. About half the sees were effectively royal but a considerable number, largely in the west, came under the authority of the new Plantagenet king. No prince could rival the two kings. Bordeaux came under Louis VII when he married Eleanor, but was lost after the dissolution of the marriage and her attachment to Henry II. The Capetian used his right to protect all churches so that ever more churches became effectively royal. In the province of Lyon, where all the sees except the archbishopric itself were royal, there was expansion at the expense of the empire. Pacaut calculated that only 16 sees were effectively royal in 1031, but that increased to 26 sees under Louis VII.[108]

The intervention of the king to enforce justice and keep the peace by supporting churches that appealed for aid, had a further consequence in pariage agreements, giving the king a share. Fawtier noted that royal churches outside the demesne were treated as 'Capetian advanced posts'.[109] The practice of allowing free elections to bishoprics and abbeys, with provisos over informing the king of the intention and waiting for his approval afterwards, had no doubt begun from weakness but increasingly came from strength. Louis permitted Suger and the pope to act for him during the Crusade. It became Capetian policy and allowed a more relaxed relationship with the papacy than developed in England or the Empire. Henry II was referred to, in contrast to Louis, as 'the hammer of the church'.[110] This did not prevent Louis from favouring candidates from his family and household, who usually succeeded.

A key moment was the dispute between the king and Theobald of Blois over the marriage between the king's cousin Ralph of Vermandois and Eleanor of Aquitaine's sister Petronilla. Ralph met Petronilla at court and fell for her. He was older than her and had lost the sight of one eye. Nevertheless Petronilla acquiesced in the match. Ralph was close to the king and seneschal but the couple were too closely related for some in the church. Worse, Ralph still had a wife in Eleanor, daughter of Odo III of Troyes and niece of Theobald of Blois. Ralph eloped with Petronilla and repudiated his wife. Complaisant bishops, led by Ralph's brother Simon who happened to be bishop of Noyon, declared the old marriage invalid on the grounds of consanguinity. Theobald protested and Innocent II sent a legate who condemned the repudiation. Ralph was ordered to leave Petronilla and take back his first wife. St Bernard in his usual restrained manner declared Ralph an 'adulterous tyrant'.[111] The second marriage was declared illicit and Ralph was excommunicated. St Bernard tried to reconcile the parties. The excommunication was to be dropped but Innocent II refused to budge. Only the deaths of the pope and Ralph's first wife, allowed the situation to be resolved.

Louis in revenge upon Theobald of Blois now chose to recognize the rights to Troyes and Champagne of Odo of Champagne, son of Hugh count of Troyes and nephew of Louis. Theobald claimed that Hugh, who had become a Templar, was impotent and Odo must be a bastard and disqualified from the succession. Theobald claimed Troyes for himself while Louis declared Odo the rightful heir, and war followed. Louis attacked Vitry held by one of Theobald's vassals, firing the church in which 1300 people were taking shelter. The pope condemned the act. When Louis realized what had happened he burst into tears and clearly regretted the act – his decision to crusade was partly an act of contrition. He lost heart in the campaign and an agreement was reached. However Innocent II ordered Ralph to resume his first marriage and excommunicated him again. The situation eased with the death of Innocent II in 1143. Eugenius III decided that Ralph's first marriage was invalid and the second marriage was recognized in 1148, after the death of the first wife.

Louis VII maintained a generally good relationship with the papacy. France remained the chief refuge for popes needing shelter from the emperor or the Romans. Both Eugenius II and Alexander III sought protection in France. Alexander faced a challenge from the anti-pope 'Victor IV', supported by Frederick Barbarossa. Alexander finally prevailed with Louis' aid. Louis also welcomed

Thomas Becket in flight from Henry II in 1164 – despite Henry demanding that he deny refuge. Louis tried to reconcile the king and his archbishop. The papacy could not fail to contrast Louis with Barbarossa who encouraged anti-popes and drove the pope from Italy, or with Henry II deemed responsible for the murder of Becket.

Not that Louis was subservient to the popes, as some have thought. When Alexander III took no action against Henry II for seizing Louis' daughter Margaret as future intended wife of Young Henry, Louis brought him up sharply by initiating negotiations with Barbarossa. Alexander knew on which side his bread was buttered and came to heel; the negotiations halted. Later Alexander granted Louis a golden flower in recognition of his contribution to the church. Louis showed his respect for religion, often in public. Apart from crusading, he undertook several pilgrimages not normally on the agenda of French kings, including to Canterbury and Compostella.

While Barbarossa favoured anti-popes, Louis supported Alexander III, formerly Cardinal Roland Bandinelli. Alexander's chief rival was 'Victor IV'. Louis ordered the French bishops to recognize Alexander but was not subservient to the pope, rather the reverse since Alexander needed his aid. In 1163 over the vacancy at Châlons, the pope wrote to the archbishop of Reims that they should wait to discover Louis' view before acting. Alexander was forced from Rome and took refuge in France. Clerics close to Louis still obtained major bishoprics in France, including his brother Henry who was bishop of Beauvais and then archbishop of Reims, and his nephew Philip of Dreux who became bishop of Beauvais in 1175.

If Louis showed less than wholehearted support for Alexander III, it was because Frederick Barbarossa continually harassed him to support Victor. Louis was non-committal and escaped direct conflict when given an escape by the arrogant behaviour of the emperor's representative, Rainald Dassel archbishop of Köln. In 1163 Alexander rewarded Louis with a golden rose as 'the most Christian king' – a title the Capetians retained. 'Victor IV' died the following year. Another anti-pope was elected as 'Paschal III', but he had less impact than Victor. Alexander III retained the papal throne for 22 years.

When French churches needed protection against local lords, Louis VII was their first choice – and he usually responded, often with positive results. A number of lay lords in regions where royal power had previously been ineffective also now preferred to seek protection from the king. Thus the lord of Bresse offered himself as a vassal, 'come into this region where your presence is necessary to the churches as well as to me'.[112] Among southern nobles who sought Louis' aid were the viscountess of Narbonne and Roger Trencavel.

THE SECOND CRUSADE

The burning of Vitry moved Louis to consider a pilgrimage to the Holy Land. He also felt strongly the early death of his brother, Philip, whose vow to go to the

Holy Land Louis wanted to fulfil. Louis wanted to show repentance for his action at Bourges which had led to a papal interdict. St Bernard advised him to go on pilgrimage and events transformed it into a crusade. The news of the fall of Edessa in the Kingdom of Jerusalem in 1144 brought a strong reaction in the west.

On Christmas Day at Bourges in 1145 Louis VII announced his intention to take the cross, revealing 'the secret in his heart'.[113] He is thus seen as 'the initiator of the Second Crusade'.[114] Pope Eugenius III planned the expedition and St Bernard preached it. Another Cistercian, Rudolf, preached the crusade in Germany, provoking anti-semitic feeling which St Bernard tried to counter. Many flocked to join the crusade, according to Bernard, leaving 'widows whose husbands are still living'.[115] St Bernard preached to an assembly at Vézelay where there were so many people that it was held in a field outside the town. Bernard might be imagined as a powerful and robust figure, but Odo of Deuil described him here as elderly and frail, a small weak man – though with all his old vigour. St Bernard spoke from a specially erected wooden platform. The demand was so great that Bernard ran out of prepared crosses, and tore up his own clothes to make more. Louis VII took the cross there on 31 March 1146.

Louis went on to a leper colony outside Paris, which he entered with only two of his men and stayed a long time. As so often, one detects the model for St Louis in his predecessor. On 11 June 1147 in the presence of Eugenius III, Louis prostrated himself before the altar of St-Denis, was given the pilgrim's scrip or wallet by the pope, and received the oriflamme. Many leading nobles took the cross, including Thierry of Flanders, Raymond of Toulouse, Henry of Meaux and Yves of Soissons. The king's wife and mother were in tears. On the same day Louis departed from Paris in the company of Eleanor.

Contemporary accounts of the Second Crusade are few. The two main commentators, Odo of Deuil and Otto of Freising, both left incomplete works. Odo was a monk at St-Denis who accompanied the king as a chaplain. His account is in a letter sent back to his abbot. Later Odo would succeed Suger at St-Denis. Odo's letter described Louis' journey to and through the Holy Land but finished before the siege of Damascus. Possibly Odo, like Otto of Freising, had no wish to retail the failures that followed. Otto bishop of Freising in Bavaria was Conrad III's brother and in his history skimmed over the disastrous crusade. There are fuller accounts, but none with the knowledge of events that these two possessed without utilizing. William of Tyre gave a fuller picture, but wrote well after the event.

The emperor Conrad III was reluctant to crusade, but decided to participate. Phillips argues that in the end the German force was 'the largest contingent'.[116] The French and German armies travelled separately. Louis considered a sea voyage and was promised aid from Roger II of Sicily. However Roger was at war with Byzantium and not on good terms with the emperor or the pope, so Louis decided to go overland. The plan was to meet in Constantinople. According to French chroniclers the Germans, who went first, left a trail of destruction and bad feeling so that the French were met with considerable suspicion and every step was made difficult. Louis went to Metz and on to Worms. His force crossed the Rhine in boats, and travelled through Bavaria, Hungary, Bulgaria and the Balkans to Constantinople. Louis wisely avoided involvement in the political divisions in the city. The Byzantine emperor, Manuel I Comnenus, wanted him to move on rapidly, but Louis made time to tour the city, which much impressed the Franks, especially the 'almost matchless beauty' of the gold and marble Blachernae Palace.[117] Odo of Deuil thought the city surpassed others in wealth, and in vice. He described the meeting between the two rulers, 'almost identical in age and stature'. They embraced, kissed, conversed through an interpreter, and parted 'as if they were brothers'. But Odo doubted the emperor's sincerity.[118] He had few compliments for either Germans or Greeks, blaming one or other for the failings of the crusade: 'the Germans were unbearable, even to us'.[119] The Greeks hampered rather than helped, intriguing with the Muslim Turks. Odo tells how the Greeks purified any altar the French had used, because they thought them defiled.[120] The French came to see the Greeks as not really Christians at all.

The Germans moved on to Asia Minor and suffered a defeat at Dorylaeum from which the Crusade never recovered. The remnants of the force either went home or joined Louis. Conrad survived but had been wounded by two arrows and hit in the head. After joining Louis briefly, he returned to Constantinople. The French did little better. Louis took the coastal route and marched via ancient Ephesus, seeing snow on the mountains. They won an initial victory but then the van under Geoffrey of Rancon, disobeying orders, allowed the Turks to occupy high ground between the divisions of the army at Laodicea. For this failure, says Odo, Geoffrey 'earned our everlasting hatred'.[121] On 7 January 1148 the Turks trapped and destroyed part of the French army. The survivors crossed the mountains, climbing a difficult way that 'seemed to touch heaven'.[122] Horses and men slipped and fell. The ground was impossible for cavalry. Many knights were left without mounts and baggage transport was difficult. The king was involved in fighting and had to climb a rock by grasping tree roots to escape and fight off attacks. He survived and proceeded but the Crusade now had little hope of success. Among the dead were the counts of Tonnerre and Dammartin and the earl of Warenne.

Odo makes it clear that there had been failings in the march. Louis now adopted the Templar method, keeping contact between divisions and protecting the flanks, maintaining position under harassment. They had to eat horses as food grew short. There were four more clashes with the enemy but the Franks beat them off. The survivors reached Atalya on 20 January 1148. The Greeks provided ships 'at an outrageous price'.[123] The Franks landed at Antioch on 19 March. The damage suffered during the journey was fatal to the prospects of the crusade.

Further problems emerged during their stay in the principality of Antioch. Its ruler was Raymond of Poitiers, younger brother of William X of Aquitaine and uncle of Queen Eleanor. Zenghi, ruler of Aleppo and Mosul, took Edessa in 1144 but died in October 1146. Raymond wanted to lead the crusade against Zenghi's son and successor, Nur ed-Din, but Louis refused. Raymond tried to change his mind via Eleanor. Uncle and niece held long private conversations, and malicious rumours spread about their relationship. John of Salisbury reported 'familiarity' between the two. Whether an affair or just gossip, it annoyed Louis, who decided to move on to Jerusalem, his main goal. Eleanor refused, which was an unheard of reaction from a wife. Rumours about her and Raymond increased and Louis carried her away at night – the eventual failure of the marriage was clearly predicted.

Conrad III had returned to Constantinople but now came to Jerusalem. The rulers met and planned further action. They attended the High Court of Jerusalem and a meeting at Acre on 24 June 1148 with Baldwin king of Jerusalem. There was less than total local support; the counts of Antioch and Tripoli did not attend. The assembly's decision seems questionable, even 'stupid'.[124] It decided to attack Damascus, an important town, but not seen by historians as a threat to the Kingdom – quite the reverse, it had been an ally. The real threat was thought to come from Nur ed-Din, who was delighted to find a new ally in Damascus – and came to its relief.

However the crusaders had reason behind their plan. Edessa had been attacked and destroyed; there was little hope of success there. Damascus had been friendly but it was already moving towards alliance with Nur ed-Din and posed a new threat.[125] The Kingdom could not afford to let Damascus fall to Nur ed-Din; it was a 'feeble principality' that appeared easy pickings.[126] In other words the crusading siege may have failed but it had a justifiable aim. The military campaign proved disastrous. Christian delays allowed the Muslims of Aleppo and Mosul to reach Damascus. The crusaders camped amid orchards and gardens that provided food and water, but also cover for enemy archers. On the advice of local Franks, the Christians moved to open country to the east but were then short of supplies and without water. The siege had to be abandoned after a mere four days.

A new assembly was held and the decision taken to attack Ascalon, but it did not proceed because of local opposition. Conrad III and most of the other leaders decided to go home, including Louis' brother Robert. Louis chose to remain and visit holy sites. In France there were political problems for the regent Suger, the most dangerous from the return of Robert of Dreux, who left his brother on bad terms. Taxation to support the Crusade had provoked resistance. Suger begged the king to return and Louis eventually sailed in the summer of 1149 – he in one ship, Eleanor in another. Eleanor's ship was captured by the Byzantines but she was rescued by Sicilians. Louis arrived in Calabria on 29 July, Eleanor later in Palermo. They travelled together through Italy where Eugenius III tried to save their marriage. He persuaded them to share a special, large bed. They returned to France together. The rebellion of Robert of Dreux was soon dealt with. Suger's care of the kingdom had been good, and resuming control was not difficult for Louis. Neither Geoffrey of Anjou nor Theobald of Blois had taken advantage of his absence. Suger's agreement with the pope in advance of the regency had proved wise and problems with the church were not great.

Louis planned for a new crusade immediately and discussed a joint effort with Henry II. Nothing came of it and war broke out between the kings. Louis had not been a successful crusader but his reputation gained rather than diminished. The effects of the crusade were not good for the Kingdom of Jerusalem but neither were they disastrous. It was only later that the situation worsened drastically and the Kingdom really declined after the defeat at Hattin in 1187.

THE MARRIAGE TO ELEANOR OF AQUITAINE

Louis' marriage to Eleanor of Aquitaine in 1137 had seemed a great leap forward for the Capetians. The future looked rosy for the young couple. She was the recognized heiress to the duchy, where Louis was able to intervene in a way previously not possible. Soon after his accession there was rebellion in Poitiers and he moved at once to suppress it. He led a further expedition south in 1141. Louis began to offer protection to southern churches and received homage from southern lords.

Famously, however, the marriage went wrong. The couple proved incompatible. Louis seemed besotted by the beautiful young girl from the south, though her southern habits caused some upset at court. She was less taken with Louis, later comparing her marriage to life with a monk. By 1143 'a dislike had sprung up' and there was talk of separation before the crusade.[127] Gervase of Canterbury recorded discord between them, though he thought it best passed over in silence.[128] The Second Crusade brought matters to a head through Eleanor's flirtation or affair with her uncle, Raymond of Antioch. William of Tyre accused her of adultery, though this remains uncertain.[129] Possibly worse was her refusal to obey Louis' order to leave Antioch for Jerusalem. Medieval husbands did not expect such refusals. Eugenius III tried to reconcile them and broke into tears when they left. The reconciliation did not endure. There was a further consideration – after 15 years of marriage Eleanor had produced no sons, only two daughters, Marie born in 1145 and Alice born after the crusade.

Eleanor was the less enthusiastic member of the pair but Louis took the initiative to end the marriage. The question of consanguinity had already been raised and offered a way out. Louis wanted to have the match annulled. Eleanor may in the end have run off and found a new partner, but only *after* her husband had chosen to end the marriage. The question was put to an assembly of French prelates at Beaugency in 1152 which supported an annulment on the grounds of consanguinity; both were descended from Robert the Pious, cousins in the fourth and fifth degree. One account said Louis did not wish to keep his wife 'against the Catholic law'.[130] One wonders how honest this was, since both his second wife Constance of Castile, and his third Adela of Champagne, were related in the fourth degree. At Beaugency there was no serious opposition to a separation. The annulment was proclaimed on 21 March 1152.

Louis has been condemned for this separation as 'a political fault of the gravest kind', 'a political error that could not be justified'.[131] The implication is that Louis should have taken alternative action. He could have kept his wife, perhaps locked her up as her second husband was to do. But in 16 years Eleanor had not provided Louis with a son. Given their now cold relationship, the prospect of producing further children seemed unlikely. If Louis wanted a new wife and a son, he must let Eleanor go. There was then no way he could control her movements or prevent her remarrying. That Eleanor should produce five sons and three daughters by her new husband was an irony too far.

It was impossible to know in advance that she would attach herself to Henry of Anjou, 11 years her junior. Walter Map did accuse her of 'casting her unchaste eyes upon him'.[132] There were hints that when Geoffrey V and his son Henry were in Paris, Eleanor had an affair with Geoffrey. Others thought she might then have begun a relationship with Henry – no more than malicious gossip. Geoffrey was now dead. Her flight to Henry may have been motivated by her desperate need for protection. Before she latched on to Henry, Eleanor had to elude two attempts to catch her and force marriage on her. The first was by Theobald V of Blois, newly come into his inheritance and unmarried. He offered marriage but she refused and fled at night. (Later Theobald married her daughter!) Then Henry of Anjou's younger brother, Geoffrey, made a bid but she also escaped his clutches. The link to Henry was by no means a certainty until it happened. Few ambitious men would turn down a marriage to the heiress to Aquitaine, though the duchy would be difficult to hold and govern, and would remain a French principality. That Henry of Anjou would become king of England was no more than a possibility at the time. Perhaps Louis should have been more careful but the risk was not as clear as it seems with hindsight. Louis' main motives – to lose an uncongenial wife, to marry one better suited, to produce a son – in the end all came to fruition. Perhaps it was not such a political error as most have assumed. At any rate Eleanor attached herself to Henry. Neither saw any reason to delay. They married at Poitiers on 18 May 1152, only two months after the annulment. Thus Henry, count of Anjou and duke of Normandy, acquired Aquitaine where they now went to establish his claim. Within two years the couple also ruled England.

LOUIS VII AND THE PLANTAGENETS

The re-marriage of Eleanor of Aquitaine to Henry of Anjou was the key moment for relations between France and the Plantagenets in Louis' reign. Louis had not shown great interest in England. He was content to let Blois and Anjou settle their own disputes. Thus Geoffrey V took Normandy from Stephen by 1145, and made his son Henry its duke. Louis saw the Empress Matilda fail to win England from Stephen in civil war. He watched her son Henry make a claim to England, at first with little success. Stephen kept England and had two sons, Eustace and William, to follow him. Henry's chances did not look strong. Militarily he made little impact. It seemed that England would stay under the house of Blois, and Normandy under Anjou – a division that suited the French king. Louis married his sister to Stephen's son Eustace.

However, events can be surprising. Louis had welcomed Geoffrey and his son Henry in Paris, when Henry was recognized as duke of Normandy – the first time a duke of Normandy did homage in Paris. This was the occasion of rumours about Eleanor's relations with father – and son. On Geoffrey V's death in September 1151, Henry became count of Anjou as well as duke of Normandy, a powerful prince. Then came the opportunity to marry Eleanor and the claim to Aquitaine – though Louis continued to claim it for his daughters by Eleanor. Louis, angered by his wife's marriage, invaded Normandy but soon retreated. Henry then defeated the rebellion of his younger brother Geoffrey. Louis continued to harass Normandy and cause problems for the young duke.

Meanwhile in England there were drastic changes. Many nobles were prepared to accept Henry of Anjou so they could keep lands in Normandy and England together. Stephen was forced into an agreement with Henry, the treaty of Winchester of 1153. Stephen's son Eustace, not party to the agreement, died in August 1153. His younger brother William, for reasons unknown, was disregarded for the succession. In 1154 Stephen died and Henry took the throne with little opposition. The threat to Louis was only too clear. The territories of Greater Anjou were now added to Normandy, England and possibly Aquitaine, making a very powerful rival. The Angevin Empire would pose problems for France for years to come.

Louis claimed that Henry had 'violated feudal custom'.[133] He declared Henry's French holdings forfeit; it was a declaration of war and a situation that bedevilled the rest of Louis VII's reign. Henry was ready to acknowledge the French king's suzerainty of his French lands, and did homage in 1151 and 1169. His sons would follow suit. Louis had to accept the outcome in England and recognized Henry as duke of Normandy and king of England. In 1156 they made peace and Louis restored what he had taken in Normandy. Henry did homage for his French lands. The peace was never secure, but it was renewed in 1158 when the two made a pilgrimage to Mont-St-Michel and attended mass by abbot Robert of Torigny.

However, when Henry sought to take Toulouse in 1159, Louis decided on renewed military action, and intermittent war continued through the reign. Henry claimed Toulouse as duke of Aquitaine but Louis left his brothers to harass Normandy while he marched south and entered Toulouse. He beat Henry to it, and was joined by the threatened Count Raymond V. Henry sent his ally, Theobald of Blois, to defend Normandy. With a weakened force, Henry decided against fighting his overlord, and retreated. It was a vital moment, demonstrating the attitude of both kings. Raymond told Louis, 'it is in you, after God, that we put all our trust'.[134] Louis may have seemed outmanoeuvred over Eleanor's flight, but his position in the south had not disintegrated. Events at Toulouse marked a halt in Henry's advance. Louis found lords in Aquitaine ready to ally against Henry. Henry's increase in power worried other princes who were now prepared to side with Louis. In 1160 the kings made a new peace at Chinon. Louis recognized Henry's rights over Normandy and Aquitaine, but omitted to settle the Vexin question.

Henry found more problems in his own family than did Louis. In 15 years Eleanor gave Henry three daughters and six sons, perhaps too many sons! Certainly Henry found it difficult to satisfy the ambitions of his surviving male brood – Young Henry, Geoffrey, Richard and John. They envied each other, fought each other, and allied against their father – with their mother's encouragement. The disappointed queen ironically allied with her first husband against her second, through her sons. Louis exploited these divisions to play one Plantagenet against another.

A constant problem for Henry II was that his lands were not a unity. His sons expected a share. Thus Aquitaine, Normandy, Brittany and Anjou came into the hands of one or other of the sons. Louis could claim overlordship and demand homage. When the sons quarrelled with their father, it was inevitable that they should seek Louis' support. The brothers were also jealous of each other. When Henry II tried to set up John with Chinon, Mirebeau and Loudun, Young Henry was angry. He set off with his father to Chinon but in the middle of the night departed to join Louis. Together they besieged Rouen but Henry II came to its relief and Louis abandoned the attempt. The point is that divisions among the Plantagenets gave Louis opportunities to oppose Henry in one region after another.

Plantagenet divisions increased with the dramatic events around Thomas Becket. Becket's father had been sheriff of London and gone on pilgrimage to Jerusalem where he was said to have been captured by Saracens and enslaved. He escaped with the help of the daughter of the house, now called Matilda. She was presumably Islamic and middle-eastern. They married and their son was Thomas. He went into the church and became royal chancellor, representing the king on embassies, including one to Paris. He was befriended by Henry II, who forced his election as archbishop of Canterbury in 1161. Becket wished to abandon his secular functions and quarrelled with the king, refusing to accept the Constitutions of Clarendon. At Northampton Becket was condemned and his goods confiscated. He fled at night disguised as a pilgrim into exile to be protected by Louis VII. Louis questioned Henry's right to depose an archbishop, insisting that he would not have acted in the same way, referring to Becket's 'loyalty and sanctity'.[135] Louis knelt before the archbishop for a blessing, and welcomed him to the realm. After his return to England, Becket was murdered in his own cathedral on 29 December 1170 by four of Henry's knights. Henry II was at the mercy of the church and his enemies. Louis was among the critics, declaring that St Peter's sword would avenge 'the martyr of Canterbury'.[136] Whether the knights had been ordered or encouraged to kill the archbishop is unlikely, but Henry still seemed at fault. He had to admit this and show repentance. There was genuine shock over the event throughout Europe, ammunition for Henry's enemies and a factor in causing the 1173–74 rising.

Louis VII encouraged the serious filial rebellion against Henry of 1173–74. Eleanor felt humiliated by her second husband and actually joined forces with her first husband. Henry's sons, Young Henry, Richard and Geoffrey, joined Louis in Paris. There were revolts against Henry in Aquitaine, Anjou and Brittany, as well as England. The Scots joined the alliance. However, the rebellions lacked unity, allowing Henry to tackle the regions in turn and defeat the rebels one by one. William the Lion, king of Scots, was captured. Louis besieged Rouen but abandoned the attempt on news of Henry's approach. The sons submitted to the father and sought pardon.

Henry survived the rebellion but the threat did not altogether disappear. Henry trapped Eleanor at Faye north of Poitiers. She tried to escape her second husband (making a habit of it) dressed as a man, but was caught and locked up at Chinon and then Salisbury through the ten remaining years of the reign. Gerald of Wales saw the reconciliation as 'more shadowy than real'.[137] Young Henry rebelled again in 1183 though he died soon afterwards. Richard did not prove any easier an heir. Louis and Henry patched up another peace in 1177, when they agreed on a new crusade, though it never happened.

Richard's initial share was to hold Aquitaine under his father but he saw it as succession to his mother, and resisted attempts by father and brothers to remove him. Richard allied with the Capetians against his father. Louis had done well in limiting the damage caused by his divorce. He lost a direct hold on Aquitaine but his power there increased rather than decreased by the end of the reign. The Plantagenet divisions did not end with Louis' death. Under Louis' son, Henry II would end his reign in humiliating defeat by a French alliance with his son Richard. Beyond that, under the younger son John, the Angevin Empire would crumble to a quick end.

LOUIS VII AND THE OTHER PRINCIPALITIES

In Louis VII's reign the power and wealth of the monarchy climbed above that of the princes – with the obvious exception of Henry II. For the first time the Capetian monarchy became a genuine power in the south of France. Even within the Angevin principalities royal rights were recognized. Henry II and the sons who held principalities did homage to Louis. The role of magnates in the royal entourage had been shrinking. The entourage was composed of members of castellan families from the Île-de-France, and lesser men. As the king re-established direct relations with all the princes, there was a need to associate them with major political decisions. What emerged in the 1140s were major assemblies to which the princes came, both secular and ecclesiastical. Such assemblies met at Vézelay and Étampes in preparation for the Second Crusade. There appeared, at the king's behest, a wide range of French archbishops, bishops, abbots, princes and counts, including those from the south. The crusade was a special case but national assemblies occurred regularly under Louis VII, as in 1155 and 1173. Louis' reign saw the appearance of another concept with enduring importance with the first mention, in 1171, of 'peers of the realm'. This was thought to be copying the system of Charlemagne and his 12 great lords, largely a literary fiction, but becoming reality under Louis VII.

The English chronicler, Ralph of Diceto, saw Louis' power as 'transcending the majesty of his predecessors'.[138] The French king was now more of a match for the emperor. In Flanders, Champagne and Burgundy king and emperor maintained a lively interest. If anything Louis prospered more than his rival. A factor in France's favour was Louis' relation with the church. There was also a sea change in relations between the king and the house of Blois-Champagne, allied against the growing power of the Plantagenets. Blois, which had been the main threat to the king, became an ally. The division of Blesevin family lands was also helpful to the king, since none as individuals were as powerful as the previous count. Louis received support from Theobald V of Blois, who was appointed seneschal, Henry the Liberal count of Champagne, Stephen count of Sancerre, and William who became archbishop of Reims. The brothers Theobald and Henry married the daughters of Eleanor, Marie and Alice. Flanders joined the alliance against Henry II, and Louis's son Philip married the count's niece Isabelle of Hainault.

Marriage brought a new link with the south when Louis' sister Constance married Raymond V count of Toulouse in 1154. In 1162 Raymond declared 'I am your man, and all that is ours is yours'.[139] It was another useful alliance against Henry II. It is true that later the marriage fell apart and Raymond for a time went over to the Angevins, but he then supported Richard against Henry II, and by 1176 had returned to Louis.

TOWNS

The growth of royal power moved in parallel with that of the French towns. Louis VII recognized privileges for trade groups in Paris, including the watermen, the butchers and the bakers. Paris was becoming a major European capital, an important cultural centre with developing schools that attracted the foremost minds of the day. There was a concomitant achievement in literature and thought, and a music school at Notre-Dame. The period saw the rise of Gothic architecture. The structure of the city was becoming more recognizable to us with the building of the great church of Notre-Dame under Bishop Maurice de Sully. In 1177 a visitor declared, 'the choir of the church is now finished with the exception of the roof of the middle aisle ... there will be no church to compare with it this side of the Alps'.[140]

Other towns grew in significance, with their populations, as throughout northern Europe, expanding. Trade increased and with it wealth. This encouraged hopes for greater independence for the cities. The king was the obvious person from whom to seek protection against the demands of local lords and of the church. Louis VII provided charters to many towns, guaranteeing privileges, and in return gained loyalty to the crown. Communes became more common and were often given royal protection. The Auxerre Chronicle commented that 'all towns where a commune was established belonged to him'.[141] Louis also confirmed or granted rights to hold fairs and markets, and extended the length of various fairs. Several new towns emerged. Adelaide the queen mother founded Royallieu near Compiègne in 1153 while the king was involved in the development of Villeneuve-le-Roi in 1163, and later Villeneuve-d'Étampes. Louis VII granted charters to southern towns, as in Berry in 1175. It should be noted, however, that he was not prodigal in granting new communes, and refused permission as often as he gave it. Louis gave some support to communes when it resulted in a closer link between the town and the crown, often with financial benefits, but he was less favourable if it was at his own expense.

Royal interest spread to lesser settlements. Louis VI set an important example with the grant of customs to Lorris-en-Gâtinais. In his reign however it was only rarely copied. Under Louis VII there was a major change and the king granted the same or similar customs to many villages in and around the demesne and elsewhere – often naming the Lorris customs as the model. In 1174, during a vacancy in the bishopric, Louis renewed the charter to Laon and extended it to 17 settlements in the neighbourhood.

ADMINISTRATION UNDER LOUIS VII

At the start of the reign Suger was still a dominant figure. He saw Louis VII as a model administrator, fitted 'by nature as well as by application'.[142] Suger took the leading role in royal administration during the king's absence on the Second Crusade. Suger was not without rivals and opposition, as from the Queen Mother and Ralph of Vermandois. Suger handed over a sound administration when Louis returned from crusade. Most commentators thought royal administration improved rather than declined after that moment. Suger was important early in the reign and during the crusade, but his role lessened between 1140 and the crusade, and after it. Officials from the previous reign disappeared by death or change. Algrin the chancellor was disgraced in 1139. New men appeared, notably Cadurc, who became chancellor in 1140. Louis did not allow one official to dominate. Cadurc lost prominence for a time and was replaced by Suger's nephew Simon. Suger died in 1151, when the king attended his funeral. In the following year Hugh de Champfleury was appointed chancellor.

Louis VII has been criticized as weak in control of the administration. Increasingly this seems a mistaken view. Much depended on the views of hostile Anglo-Norman chroniclers. Thus Walter Map described conflict at Louis' court between lay and clerical members. The poet Waleran of Yèvre wrote a verse against three officials 'set up over the whole of France', who were cheating Louis 'in his simplicity' – keeping a share of the takings for themselves. These three forced the king to banish the poet from court and he was only restored through the efforts of Henry II. Map admits that the three officials were found out and punished.[143]

Our knowledge of administration is far from complete, causing dispute over financial details. The extent of Louis' income is uncertain. Conon prévôt of Lausanne overheard gossip about how much Louis left when he died. Even if his figures were correct, the meaning is unclear. Was it gross or net income? Was it income from the demesne or in total? The evidence is generally taken to mean that Louis' income was relatively small and the royal revenue much increased by Philip Augustus. However, it seems that royal income was already considerable.

The royal entourage was now composed of lesser folk, such as knights or ordinary clergy. Walter the chamberlain was 'more noble in his actions than in his birth'.[144] Louis, like his father, had counsellors from ordinary backgrounds, in what he called 'the council of those who surround us'.[145] Louis used ordinary members of his entourage to represent him. Josbert Briand acted 'in place of the lord king' in a judgement over the abbey of St-Germain-des-Prés. Thierry Galeran went to Aquitaine to preside over a local assembly for the king. Louis extended the use of prévôts. Sixteen new prévôtés were created and others reorganized. At the start of the reign there were some 25 prévôts and by the end about 40. Louis increased his own authority by limiting family grasp on offices, declaring 'hereditary right is completely forbidden'.[146] One development in the entourage was the emergence of legal specialists and trained lawyers, increasingly important for dealing with business. Their rise parallels the growth of the new schools and universities. Giraud of Bourges was a royal notary who wrote a treatise on law in 1163.

The role of the great officers – seneschal, chancellor, chamberlain, butler and constable – continued to develop. Magnates and prelates who held such office were now often nominal and honorific. The trend towards lesser social figures in office continued. Louis kept the loyalty of almost all his officials, rewarding them with gifts, not of demesne land but of offices and promotions. Clerks could hope for a good appointment in the church. Louis once told the bishop of Paris to reserve the next vacant benefice for the royal clerk, Barbedon. The belief in specialization of the great officers has been exaggerated, and they were often flexible in their functions. For example, chancellors and butlers could deal with justice as well as the seneschal, or the chancellor could command the army.[147]

Nevertheless the major office was still that of seneschal, and held by major figures during part of this reign, in Ralph of Vermandois and Theobald of Blois. Louis, like his father, pursued a policy of 'vacance' – leaving offices vacant.[148] This diminished the frequency of hereditary succession and demonstrated that office depended on the king's choice and that even the greatest officer was not essential. During a vacancy the function was continued by others in the entourage. Ralph of Vermandois was only appointed seneschal in 1131 after a four-year vacancy. Ralph died in 1152 and no new seneschal was appointed for two years. When the chancellor, Hugh of Champfleury, was disgraced in 1172, no new appointment was made for seven years. When Matthew of Montmorency died in 1160, there was a vacancy in the office of constable until 1164. Between 1149 and 1154 all the main officers except one were replaced not by sons but by men chosen by the king. As Sassier concluded, it all points to a 'decline of the great officers'.[149]

THE DEATH OF LOUIS VII

Our general thesis becomes clear as we examine the early Capetian kings in turn. Many were seen as weak, poor and unsuccessful kings. Yet, when each is looked at in more detail, we find mitigating circumstances and an element of success. The case of Louis VII is perhaps the most notable. Here is a king who has been widely criticized and condemned yet, when we examine his reign, the balance falls on the positive side. Louis has been called 'a colourless nonentity', 'almost silly', 'a weak, pious and shifty king', and a slave to the church. He was condemned for losing his first wife and with her the duchy of Aquitaine.[150] Worse, it is alleged that he allowed Aquitaine to be acquired by his great rival who thus founded the Angevin Empire and posed a major threat. Louis VII has been compared unfavourably with his great contemporaries, Henry II and Frederick Barbarossa, as well as with his father Louis VI, and his son Philip II.

In his relation with Eleanor though, Louis' behaviour comes out better than hers. His wife may have had one affair, or several. Apart from rumours about her relations with Raymond of Antioch and Geoffrey of Anjou, she was reported to have had affairs with the troubadour Bernard of Ventadour and various other individuals, though the evidence is never foolproof. A German poet wanted England's queen to lie close in his arms.[151] Another rumour connected her with Ralph de Faye. If she was not guilty of adultery, she obviously appeared as an attractive woman who flirted enough to cause gossip. There is no evidence that Louis was other than faithful to his three wives. In 1154 he married Constance of Castile, daughter of Alfonso VII. She was 18 and the marriage took place in Orléans. Soon afterwards Louis went on pilgrimage to St-James of Compostella, when he met Alfonso VII, as well as Raymond-Berengar IV of Barcelona and Raymond V of Toulouse. Constance died on 4 October 1160 in childbirth with her second daughter. Louis was still without a son and hastily arranged a third marriage to Adela of Champagne, younger sister of Theobald of Blois. The wedding occurred only a month after Constance's death. Louis was a good father to his children by the marriages: two daughters from Eleanor of Aquitaine (Marie and Alice), two from Constance of Castile (Margaret and Adelaide), and finally in 1165 a son by Adela of Champagne (Philip), and another daughter (Agnes).

Few historians would guess that the individual referred to by a monk at St-Germain-des-Prés as 'the most glorious King Louis' was Louis VII.[152] It was Louis who adopted the fleur-de-lys as the Capetian symbol. The modern restoration of his reputation began properly with Pacaut's study of the reign. Others, such as Duby and Sassier, have been persuaded. The study of non-narrative sources has helped to sway opinion. One sees more clearly the active side of his administration, his running and development of the demesne, the operation of his court, his greater involvement in the south and areas beyond the demesne. A re-examination of his relation with the church was badly needed. It is now clear that he was no mere servant to the popes, especially Alexander III. If anything the boot was on the other foot. Alexander needed Louis more than the French king needed him. Louis was pious, like virtually all the Capetians. He respected the church and the papacy, but he was prepared to make a stand on issues that mattered. Louis' relation with the papacy was of great benefit to his kingdom. One only needs to compare the situation in France with that in the England of Henry II and Thomas Becket, or the empire of Barbarossa with its defeat in Italy and schism with the papacy.

After his birth in 1165 there was never any question that Philip Augustus was his father's heir. Possibly *because* there was no doubt, Louis did not hurry to associate his son. It was only in 1179 that Louis went ahead with this Capetian tradition. Philip was to be associated on the Feast of the Assumption, on 15 August. Ironically this did not happen even then because Philip himself became ill after an unfortunate experience when hunting boar in the forest near Compiègne. Louis was severely troubled. He wept and prayed, sighing night and day. He was said to have seen the murdered Thomas Becket who proclaimed, 'Our Lord Jesus Christ sends me as your servant, Thomas the martyr of Canterbury, in order that you should go to Canterbury if your son is to recover.'[153] Louis decided to make a pilgrimage to Becket's tomb. He sailed from Boulogne, the first Capetian king to visit England. Henry II welcomed him at Dover and escorted him to Canterbury, where he spent two days in prayer. The trip seemed to have worked and Philip recovered so that a new coronation could be planned.

Philip recovered but the journey had taken a lot out of the ageing Louis, who fell ill on returning to Paris. He suffered a stroke that paralysed his right side and left him unable to speak. The association of Philip went ahead at Reims on 1 November 1179, but without his father. Philip assumed the reins of power. The old king died on 18 September 1180. He had chosen to be buried not at St-Denis, but at his own foundation, Cistercian Barbeaux. An inscription was placed on the tomb that read like an instruction to his son:

> You who survive him are the successor to his dignity;
> You diminish his line if you diminish his renown.[154]

Louis VII's tomb was opened in 1566 by Charles IX, when it was said the remains were intact. In 1817 the remains were transferred to St-Denis on the orders of Louis XVIII.

7

Philip the Great

The Briton Gerald of Wales was a student in Paris in 1165. He later recalled a Saturday night in August when woken by a great roar outside with trumpets blaring and flickering torches. He wrote, 'through all the great city there was such a noise and clanging of bells, such a multitude of tapers kindled through all the open spaces of the town, that not knowing what such a racket and abnormal disturbance could mean, with such a blaze of light in the night, it was thought the city was threatened by a great fire'.[1] Gerald peered out of his window. Two old women were passing by with torches and told him that at last the old king had a son. Louis VII had married a third time, to Adela of Champagne. All his wives had been fertile but in 28 years of married life he had fathered only daughters. Now at last his first and only legitimate son was born. One of the women said the baby was 'Dieudonné' (Godgiven). Philip's birth was in August and hence he was known as 'Augustus'. Some later called him Philip the Great and, in our view, he was the greatest of the Capetian kings, not as saintly as Louis IX, not as good a warrior as Louis VI, and certainly not without faults – but great in his achievements.

Louis VII received a report of the birth when at matins the following morning. The infant was baptized the next day. Louis said the child was 'of a more noble sex', for which perhaps we can forgive him, considering the significance for the succession. The name Philip seems ordinary enough now, and had been given to the Capetian king Philip I, but was of Greek origin brought through the marriage to Anna of Kiev, and still rare in the West.

English historians have found Philip II uncongenial. Hallam thought him 'in many ways an unattractive figure'.[2] He was a tall and well-made young man, a good rider and trained in combat. His 'arm was powerful in the use of weapons'.[3] To William the Breton he was 'a young lion'.[4] After the Third Crusade, during which he lost his hair, one chronicler described him as 'a fine man, well proportioned in stature, with a smiling countenance, bald, a ruddy complexion, inclined to eat and drink well, and sensual'.[5] Some historians have thought he lost an eye, but this seems unlikely.[6] He was earnest, even as a youth, and noted for his piety. He introduced a rule against swearing at court; for blasphemy 20 sous must be given to the poor or the offender was thrown in the Seine. He ordered that prostitutes be removed from the Church of the Innocents. He agreed with the church view against tournaments. He showed little interest in the arts, music or literature. He had a reputation for meanness; one tale had a beggar asking for alms in the name of his royal forebears. Philip asked 'the forebears on which side?' He replied on the side of Adam. The king gave him a small coin, at which the beggar stared and asked 'Is that all your forebears are worth?' Philip replied, 'If I gave you a coin for every ancestor from that line, I should not have much left.' He was not, however, always glum and was noted for his cheerful looks and fresh face. He was fond of alcohol and demanded wine against medical advice when ill. He was nervous and fearful of attempts on his life.

Philip was the obvious heir. He was not associated as king until Louis VII was dying, but probably because there was no dispute over his claim. Louis decided to associate Philip in 1179, arranging a ceremony for 15 August. Philip went hunting boar near Compiègne, was separated from his party, and became lost. He spent two days in the forest before being found by a charcoal burner who led him back to civilization. Philip was badly affected by the incident, in a state of collapse and unable to speak. The coronation was postponed and his father decided to go on pilgrimage to Canterbury for Philip's sake. On his return Louis found his son recovered but he himself fell ill. The coronation went ahead two months after the original date, without Louis. Philip's mother was also absent, at her husband's bedside. The ceremony was conducted by William Whitehands archbishop of Reims, Philip's uncle. Louis was incapable of governing and Philip took over immediately.

THE EARLY REIGN

Philip was only 14 and had need of advice. One measure that was soon decided was his marriage. Philip of Flanders arranged a match, which Louis VII had previously approved, with Isabelle of Hainault at Bapaume on 28 April 1180. She was the daughter of Baldwin V count of Hainault, who became Baldwin VIII count of Flanders (1191–94). Her mother was Margaret, sister of Philip count of Flanders. She was only 10 in 1180, described as tall and beautiful. She brought the advantage of Carolingian descent, was discreet, and 'a most holy woman'.[8] A new coronation ceremony was performed for the couple in May 1180 at St-Denis. Four months later Louis VII died on 19 September and was buried at Barbeaux.

Given his age, it is not surprising that Philip's mother, Adela of Champagne, continued to influence the new king. Her brothers constituted a powerful political group: Henry the Liberal count of Champagne, Theobald V count of Blois and Chartres the seneschal, Stephen count of Sancerre, and William Whitehands archbishop of Reims. Their younger sister, Mary, was married to Hugh III duke of Burgundy. Their lands surrounded the royal demesne. Philip, however, was no meek and mild boy and soon quarrelled with his mother. He believed, probably correctly, that his mother was planning treachery and ordered her personal lands to be seized. She took refuge with Theobald of Blois.

Philip needed to counter the Blois bloc and turned for aid to Philip of Alsace count of Flanders, uncle to the new queen. He had organized the marriage and

The Later Capetians

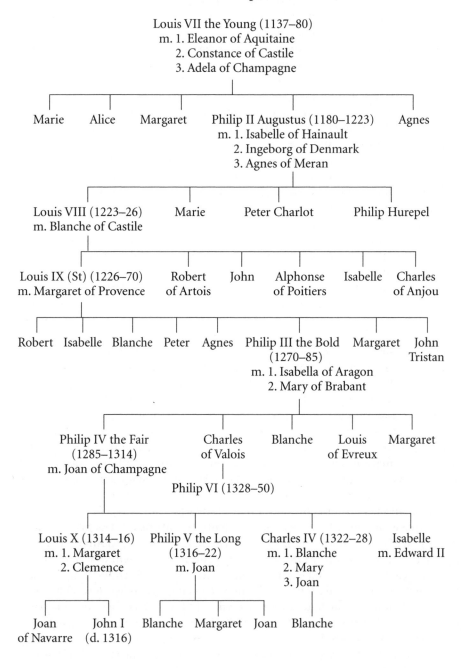

Louis VII the Young (1137–80)
m. 1. Eleanor of Aquitaine
2. Constance of Castile
3. Adela of Champagne

Marie   Alice   Margaret   Philip II Augustus (1180–1223)   Agnes
m. 1. Isabelle of Hainault
2. Ingeborg of Denmark
3. Agnes of Meran

Louis VIII (1223–26)   Marie   Peter Charlot   Philip Hurepel
m. Blanche of Castile

Louis IX (St) (1226–70)   Robert   John   Alphonse   Isabelle   Charles
m. Margaret of Provence   of Artois   of Poitiers   of Anjou

Robert Isabelle Blanche Peter Agnes Philip III the Bold Margaret John
(1270–85)   Tristan
m. 1. Isabella of Aragon
2. Mary of Brabant

Philip IV the Fair   Charles   Blanche   Louis   Margaret
(1285–1314)   of Valois   of Evreux
m. Joan of Champagne
Philip VI (1328–50)

Louis X (1314–16)   Philip V the Long   Charles IV (1322–28)   Isabelle
m. 1. Margaret   (1316–22)   m. 1. Blanche   m. Edward II
2. Clemence   m. Joan   2. Mary
3. Joan

Joan   John I   Blanche Margaret Joan   Blanche
of Navarre   (d. 1316)

was brother-in-law to Baldwin of Hainault. The count of Flanders became the king's guardian but the friendly relationship did not last. When the count's wife Elizabeth of Vermandois died, the count claimed her lands but the king opposed this at first, though conceding later. Then the count married Matilda, daughter of Afonso I of Portugal, declaring that she should have lands to which the king had a claim. The count turned to the German emperor until this too was settled. Further trouble occurred over Philip's marriage to the count's niece Isabelle in 1184, when Philip considered an annulment. At Senlis he announced his intention to end the marriage. Isabelle emerged from the palace in a shift, barefoot, and carrying a candle. She toured the churches, kneeling at the altars, weeping and praying. She blamed the king's 'evil counsellors'.[9] She begged for support from the people, a highly unusual move. Politics may have been involved; Philip was pressuring her father to drop his alliance with Flanders in favour of a closer royal link. Philip took back his wife and in 1185 Hainault allied with him against Flanders. Philip then marched against the count and forced him into submission. On 3 September 1187 Isabelle bore Philip a son, his later heir, Louis (VIII), his only legitimate son to survive. Isabelle died in childbirth in March 1190; the twin sons she bore lived only hours and were buried with her at Notre-Dame.

In the early part of the reign Philip established a better relationship with the Plantagenets, mainly from a change of attitude by the ageing Henry II. They met between Gisors and Trie in 1180 to agree peace. Philip's new attachment to Flanders rather than Blois aided reconciliation. Henry encouraged reconciliation between Philip and his mother. Philip did not repay Henry with co-operation for long. He took up the old ploy of supporting the sons against the father: Young Henry in 1183 (though he died later that year), and then Geoffrey, whom Philip made his seneschal. On the death of Young Henry, Philip demanded the return of Margaret's dowry – the Vexin and Gisors. Philip also encouraged rebellion against the Plantagenets in Aquitaine. Geoffrey died young, in 1186, when wounded at a tournament in Paris. Philip then made overtures to Henry II's heir apparent, Richard. A marriage was arranged between Richard and Philip's sister Alice, with Gisors and the Vexin as dowry. The delay over celebrating this marriage (which never took place) became an issue. There was a rumour that Henry II had seduced the girl being brought up at his court.

In 1187 Philip invaded Berry against Henry II with Richard as his ally. Later in the year Philip attacked Plantagenet territory along the Loire. After an unsuccessful attempt at peace in 1188, Philip chopped down the elm that marked the meeting place, under which Henry II had rested in the shade while Philip was left in the burning sun. Henry II had exclaimed as he sat in the shade, 'when I lose this tree, I shall agree to the loss of all this land'.[10] Philip ordered it felled. Henry II then attacked Mantes, which Philip saved. At the subsequent conference, Philip demanded that Richard be recognized as Henry's heir. Henry refused to answer and Richard angrily did homage to Philip and left the meeting with him. The war continued but Henry was ill. At Le Mans Henry was forced to flee. Philip captured his baggage, and ate his abandoned dinner. There was a further conference at Ballon where Henry was barely able to sit on his horse. He had to make the humiliating capitulation of Azay, paying 20,000 marks 'compensation'. Henry was carried away to Chinon where he learned that his favourite son, John, had joined his enemies. He suffered a stroke and died soon after on 6 July 1189.

During the first decade of the reign Philip made significant additions to the demesne. Montargis was acquired from Peter de Courtenay. In 1185 he added the Amiénois, the county of Montdidier with 65 castles, Roye, and then the county of Tournai in 1187. The increased demesne and more efficient administration led Philip to increase the number of prévôts from 35 to 52 by 1190. By the same date royal revenue had increased by 22%. New officials called *baillis* were introduced by 1184. They operated in small, itinerant groups to keep a check on the activities of the prévôts. Philip continued to restrict the power of major officials by allowing vacancies. When the chancellor Hugh died in 1185, he was not replaced for a year.

Louis VII had been unusually tolerant and protective of the Jews; Philip proved less so. In 1180 he issued an edict that led to arrests, confiscation of property and demand for ransoms. In 1182 Philip 'ejected all the Jews from his own towns and castles', which had been their main area of safety.[11] This led to short-term gain but in the long run proved an error and a loss. Later he relented and recalled the Jews.

Philip's early years saw disturbances in the kingdom, largely from troublesome castellans. Bands of unemployed soldiers – virtually brigands – roamed about offering themselves for paid service, or seizing what they needed, and posed a new threat. These were the *cottereaux* or *routiers*, widely unpopular but difficult to oppose without considerable force. Accusations included taking captives for ransom, sleeping with captives' wives, flogging, killing, destroying holy objects and setting fire to churches. In the 1180s some localities suffering in this way and receiving no help from the authorities, formed associations for their own protection. A carpenter, Durand, led one such group, wearing uniforms with white hoods and known as *capuchons*. In the Auvergne they fought the routiers and killed some 3,000. In the Rouergue a mercenary leader called Courbaran was caught and hanged with 500 followers. The nobility, however, came to fear the power of the associations and accused them of heresy. They were hunted down and suppressed.

Philip's first decade as king saw important decisions about Paris. The work on Notre-Dame was complete. The first college in Paris, the Dix-Huit, was set up in 1180, and statutes were issued for the new university. In 1183 Les Halles were constructed for trade. Rigord described the king strolling through his palace and gazing from the window at ships on the Seine.[12] He noticed the poor state of the muddy road, and the stench from open sewers. In 1186 Philip ordered the streets of Paris to be paved in stone, work that took 10 years to complete. Paris was still the smaller city of some 25 acres within its Roman walls. Now Philip built a new encircling wall, enlarging the enclosed city to 625 acres. In 1190 he ordered a wall with towers and gates for the right bank. The market of Les Champeaux was enclosed and a new castle built – the Louvre.

PHILIP AUGUSTUS AND THE CRUSADES

Philip Augustus was the second French king to crusade, following in the footsteps of his father, Louis VII. As the fall of Edessa had spurred the Second Crusade, so now even more dramatically the battle of Hattin in 1187 and the fall of Jerusalem inspired the Third. Philip also played a role in the Fourth Crusade and the Albigensian Crusade, though he did not participate in person. Philip's crusading role has been underestimated, largely because the sources of the Third Crusade were hostile, and because crusade historians have shown more interest in Richard than Philip.

The survival of the Latin Kingdom of Jerusalem was in the balance by the 1180s. Saladin had built a new Ayyubid Empire incorporating Egypt and Syria, and threatening the diminished Kingdom. In 1186 Guy of Lusignan became king, but he could not count on the loyalty of all his subjects. Rainald of Châtillon had provoked the Muslims by attacking caravans and killing pilgrims returning from Mecca. He also broke the peace agreement by attacking Damascus. Saladin besieged Tiberias, which brought King Guy to its defence, leading to the battle of Hattin in 1187, a major disaster for the Franks. The Christians lost the True Cross and with hardly any resistance the Muslims took over Sidon, Beirut and Acre. Then Saladin attacked and took Jerusalem. The only major city to survive was Tyre, thanks to Conrad of Montferrat. Tyre's archbishop, Joscius, set off to the west to seek aid. Urban III drew up a crusade appeal, but died before it could be issued.

The main rulers of the Christian west responded favourably, including Philip Augustus and Frederick Barbarossa. The latter set out in 1188 but died on the way in 1190. Some Germans continued to the Holy Land. Henry II and Philip Augustus had contemplated crusading in 1185, and levied the infamous Saladin Tithe – which Philip abandoned after strong opposition. After hearing of Hattin, Henry II, Richard the Lionheart and Philip took the cross – the latter in January 1188. War between them prevented any crusade until after Henry's death in 1189. Then Richard and Philip agreed to settle their differences and crusade. Richard was to marry Philip's sister Alice. No women were to go with the crusaders, except laundresses of good reputation (if such existed). Preparations caused delays. Money had to be raised, provisions and transport organized. Philip issued his Testament to cope with government in his absence. Queen Adela and William Whitehands archbishop of Reims were to deputize. The citizens were to have a role in the governance of Paris. Philip arranged an assembly at Vézelay in January 1190, but it was twice postponed. Philip received the scrip, staff and oriflamme at St-Denis on 24 June 1190 but did not reach Acre until the summer of 1191. Richard was even later.

The assembly at Vézelay finally met on 2 July 1190. The two kings set out separately, Philip two days after the meeting. He headed for Genoa where he arranged for sea transport and provisions. He reached Sicily on 16 September, Richard six days later. Philip was welcomed but Richard antagonized the locals by demanding levies. He took Bagnara and an island off Messina, torturing monks who resisted. He stole a falcon and when its owner tried to recover it, beat the man to death with the flat of his sword. He built the siege tower called Mategriffon (Stop the Greeks) outside Messina and erected a gallows to deal with opponents. After a quarrel involving his men he attacked and sacked Messina. Then one of Philip's vassals, William des Barres, opposed Richard in a 'friendly' tournament arranged to pass the time, using canes for weapons. When William bested Richard and broke his cane, the latter was furious and told William to go home and never appear before him again. Philip tried to intercede but Richard would not relent and William departed. He did later go to the Holy Land where his valour earned Richard's pardon. Another cause of trouble between the kings was the festering problem over Richard's agreed marriage to Alice. On his way to crusade Richard decided to marry Berengaria of Navarre, who travelled on with him. He told Philip that Alice had been seduced by Henry II, who had a son by her. Philip accepted that nothing could be done but to recover the dowry and his sister.

Philip left Sicily on 30 March 1191 and made his way to Tyre, reaching Acre on 20 April. Richard sailed on 10 April but meandered via Crete, Rhodes and Cyprus, where he married Berengaria. The Byzantine pretender to Cyprus, Isaac Dukas Comnenus, did homage to Richard but then fled from fear. He surrendered on condition he would not be put in irons. Richard agreed and put him in silver fetters. Isaac died in prison in 1195. Richard took control of Cyprus and finally went on to Acre.

Acre was a great port at the north end of a bay, with good fortifications and a harbour chained against attack from the sea. It had been taken by the Muslims after Hattin. King Guy after his release tried to recover it by siege, but made little progress until the crusaders joined him. Philip rode around the town to look for weak points in the defence. He ordered the building of belfries and engines including the trebuchet called 'God's Own Sling'. He began to mine the walls, and made sure the whole circuit of walls was surrounded. Philip did not immediately attack, waiting for Richard's delayed arrival. Guy went to Cyprus to see Richard so Philip was clearly in charge of the besieging force.

Richard arrived on 8 June and was not keen on an immediate storming. Philip was suspicious of Richard's private dealings with Saladin's brother, Safadin. Philip's paid troops received the reasonable pay of three gold pieces a month; Richard sought to tempt them to join him by offering four pieces. Richard had been ill during his journey, and was ill again now. Philip decided they could delay no longer and ordered the attack to begin. Three days later there was a second assault. Richard refused to take part. On 3 July Acre came within an ace of falling, without any aid from Richard. Then Philip fell ill, though he recovered before Richard. Some died from the disease, including the count of Flanders. Philip refused to let his illness halt the attack and was carried out under a shelter to shoot a crossbow against the Turks. Richard later did the same thing.

The French mined the outer wall and plans were made for a new all-out assault. They gained the walls but were pushed back. The French marshal, Aubrey Clément declared, 'This day I shall perish or, if it please God, I shall enter the city of Acre.'[13] Seemingly it did not please God. Aubrey mounted the wall by a ladder that broke under the weight of those following and left him stranded on the wall. He fought bravely but was killed. Next day the city offered to surrender on terms but Richard and Saladin were both opposed. Saladin had come to relieve the city but could not enter and camped outside. The fighting continued and at last the Plantagenets joined in. The French used their engine, the Evil Neighbour, against the Accursed Tower; after mining it collapsed.

On 12 July surrender on terms was finally agreed. The defenders were allowed to live in return for handing over the True Cross captured at Hattin, the release of Frankish prisoners, and a payment of 200,000 dinars within 40 days. When Saladin heard the terms he sent a messenger to order refusal. The man had to swim to enter but was too late; Frankish banners were already fluttering from the walls. Saladin reluctantly accepted the agreement though he failed to fulfil some of the terms.

Richard continued his abrasive ways. One of the surviving German contingent, Leopold of Austria, placed his standard on the wall of Acre. Leopold also found better accommodation than Richard. Richard had the standard thrown in the mud and trampled upon it. He would later have cause to regret this show of temper. The victors shared the spoils, including prisoners and ransoms. Most crusaders preferred Conrad of Montferrat to be king of Jerusalem, but Richard prevailed in restoring Guy of Lusignan – with Conrad promised the northern part of the Kingdom and the succession.

Philip has been much maligned for returning home from the crusade but succumbed to a worse bout of the illness – a disease called leonardie or arnoldia, thought to be trench-mouth or Vincent's disease, possibly scurvy. Philip fell into a fever that left him trembling. His hair and teeth fell out, and his body became swollen, with sore lips and peeling skin – some suspected poison. Philip also heard that his son, Louis, was ill in Paris. Given recent problems over heirs and succession, it is not surprising that Philip was deeply concerned. It was claimed that Richard may have been responsible for a malicious rumour that Louis had died – though it is difficult to believe.[14] Relations between Richard and Philip had not been good and argument over arrangements for the Kingdom was another factor. There were rumours that Richard intended harm to Philip. These became credible after the suspicious death of Philip's candidate for the kingship. Conrad of Montferrat became king after Philip's departure but was murdered by Assassins sent by the Old Man of the Mountain, leader of the sect, which believed in murder for political ends. Richard was said to have negotiated with them. Philip, before his departure, received a letter warning him that he was an intended victim. The (unsuspicious) death of the count of Flanders also meant that there was urgent need to settle affairs. It is no surprise that Philip decided to return home.

By his return Philip benefited from the settlement in Flanders. He confirmed his hold of Artois, the Amiénois, Vermandois and much of Beauvaisis. The winning of Acre was a reasonable success for the crusade – more than Louis VII had achieved on the Second Crusade. Richard made his reputation by continuing to fight the Muslims and winning the battle of Arsuf (in which the duke of Burgundy was co-commander), but the taking of Acre was the main gain of the Third Crusade, and England suffered from Richard's prolonged absence. Philip left a large French contingent in the Holy Land, and a large amount of cash, to aid the future effort of the crusade. Richard continued his career of hasty acts and provocations. When Saladin was slow to fulfil the agreement after Acre, Richard slaughtered 2,700 Muslim prisoners – losing all hope of co-operation or ransom. He then quarrelled with the duke of Burgundy, who complained of Richard's 'foul and gratuitous aspersions'.[15] This led to the departure of most of the French and left little hope of further gains. In the end, after two marches towards the city, Richard turned back and abandoned his main aim of retaking Jerusalem.

Philip left Acre on 31 July 1191 for Tyre, sailing in August. They were hit by a storm but survived. He sailed via Tripoli, Antioch, Crete, Rhodes and Corfu to Italy. In Rome he was welcomed by Celestine III and continued home, reaching Paris on 27 December 1191. He prostrated himself before relics at St-Denis in thanks for his safe return. New relics were added to the collection from the crusade, including two teeth of the prophet Amos and the finger of John the Baptist!

The crusade provided one more opportunity for Philip. Richard made an agreement in 1192 that allowed Christian access to Jerusalem. During his return he was shipwrecked and continued overland through the lands of the duke of Austria, whom he had insulted at Acre. He was captured in disguise and handed to the emperor, Henry VI, who demanded an enormous ransom. Richard's brother, John, despite pressure from Philip, paid up. After a year's imprisonment Richard was released and returned to the west, where he had to cope with problems caused by his absence.

Philip did not crusade again but he was involved in organizing the Fourth Crusade, a northern French effort by the counts of Flanders, Blois, Perche and Champagne. Philip had little control over the expedition which attacked Christian Zara and then Constantinople. The result was the election of one of Philip's vassals, Baldwin IX of Flanders, as new Latin Emperor in 1204, and French colonization of Byzantine lands in Greece and elsewhere. The Burgundian Odo de la Roche became duke of Athens and Thebes, Louis of Blois duke of Nicaea, and Geoffrey de Villehardouin prince of Achaea. Pope Honorius III called the former Byzantine Empire 'a new France'.[16] The departure of many leading nobles also allowed Philip to increase his authority in Flanders and elsewhere. The Fourth Crusade has been seen as 'a catastrophe from which Flanders never recovered'.[17] France also gained what were seen as valuable acquisitions, several notable relics sent back by Emperor Baldwin, including (it was said) a piece of the True Cross, a thorn from the crown of thorns, and a fragment of Christ's clothing.

Philip played a part in the development of the Albigensian Crusade, the attack on Cathar heretics in southern France. Heresy had appeared in France in the 12th century, both in the north and the south. A Cathar bishopric emerged at Agen. Innocent III set his mind on eliminating heresy and sent agents to persuade Philip to act. Philip took no part but his son Louis was active. The papal legate, Peter de Castelnau, was murdered in 1208 when investigating Cathar heretics. Raymond VI count of Toulouse was blamed. A crusade was organized mainly from France and Germany. Raymond VI submitted, himself taking the cross. Others accused of protecting heretics, such as Roger Trencavel, were attacked. Simon de Montfort, a noble from the Île-de-France, became the leader. Southern bases of heresy were besieged and taken, including Termes and Minerve in 1210.

Raymond VI was soon at odds with the crusade, and was again excommunicated in 1211. His lands were declared forfeit and the crusaders took what they could – though Toulouse held out; the siege in 1211 failed. The southerners, with reason, saw the crusade as a northern conquest. They found an ally in Pedro of Aragon, victor at Las Navas de Tolosa against the Moors. Raymond VI was his brother-in-law. At Muret on 12 September 1213 the southern allies were defeated by the crusaders, and Pedro was killed. Raymond VI and his son fled to England for refuge. King John had been as worried as Aragon over growing Capetian power in the south. Simon de Montfort benefited, taking much of Raymond's land and becoming count of Toulouse, giving homage to Prince Louis. Reluctantly Innocent III accepted the change in 1215.

Thereafter the fortunes of the Toulouse family recovered gradually. Toulouse was re-occupied and when Simon de Montfort besieged it again, he was killed. Simon's son Amaury took over but never gained the same success. The crusade suffered military defeats and several lords returned to Raymond. Raymond VI died in 1222 and his son succeeded to the reduced county as Raymond VII. Prince Louis took command of the crusade. Amaury yielded his southern lands to him. Raymond VII in his turn was excommunicated. This was how matters stood at the death of Philip Augustus. The heresy was virtually suppressed in the end, or at least driven underground. The crusade subordinated large areas of southern France to northern and royal control.

THE CONFLICT WITH THE PLANTAGENETS

Henry II gave support and friendship to the young French king but Philip was responsible for the weakening of that peace. He encouraged the sons against Henry and returned to war over his French lands. Henry II came to that unhappy end, forced into a humiliating peace by the alliance of his sons with Philip. After Henry's death in 1189 Philip's relations with Richard I did not stay cordial for long. Philip expected reward for the former alliance, but Richard was not eager to supply it. His brothers, Young Henry and Geoffrey had died and Henry II's plans to divide the Angevin Empire had not come to fruition. There remained the youngest brother, John, who was ambitious. Richard granted him the county of Mortain in Normandy and six English counties, but this did not satisfy him.

The Third Crusade soured relations further. Philip made promises to Richard over disputed lands and the church forbade attack on the lands of a crusader. Philip took advantage of Richard's absence, only at first to recover lands to which he had a legal claim – such as those promised by Richard at Messina as the returned dowry of Alice and not covered by crusading. But once Richard had been captured by Leopold of Austria he considered him no longer on crusade. The Angevins had lost a natural ally with the death of Philip count of Flanders on the crusade. Philip played on the friction between Richard and his likely heir, John. In 1193 Philip recognized John as heir to the Plantagenet lands, for which he did homage in Paris.

There was rebellion against the Plantagenets in Poitou and Philip invaded Normandy, taking Lyons-la-Forêt, Neaufles and Gisors. Many Norman lords, uncertain if Richard would return, submitted to Philip. Philip took Aumale, Eu, Gournay, Meulan, Perche, Châteauneuf, Verneuil and Le Vaudreuil. He overran the Vexin and reached Dieppe. Évreux was taken and given to John. Philip's major strategic aim was to attack Rouen but the earl of Leicester resisted and Philip abandoned his siege. Philip did take Pacy and Ivry and made progress in Aquitaine and Touraine. Much of this gain was reversed after Richard's release, but the episode demonstrated how rapidly Philip could advance, and was a useful rehearsal for the fight with John.

Richard was released on 4 February 1194. It is possible that Philip and John conspired to oppose it. Henry VI showed Richard letters from the two offering pay in return for his continued captivity. If this were true it is odd that John nevertheless paid the large ransom for Richard's release. Richard reached England on 13 March 1194 and made for London. John's rebellion collapsed and he begged forgiveness, now joining Richard against Philip. Richard set out to recover the lands lost during his imprisonment, and war followed from 1194 to 1199. Richard made steady headway with a series of sieges. Philip suffered humiliation at Fréteval in 1194 during a skirmish when he lost his baggage, including the royal seal and archives, though he managed to escape. In 1195 Richard released Alice, who was promptly married to the count of Ponthieu. Late in 1195 Philip sacked Dieppe, using Greek Fire. By the end of 1195 Richard had recovered two-thirds of the losses.

In 1196 there was rebellion in Brittany and a possible heir to the English throne in Richard's nephew, Arthur of Brittany, came to Philip's court for protection. At Aumale there was another skirmish when Richard was unhorsed but managed to remount and escape. At Gaillon Richard was wounded in the knee by a crossbow bolt and then his horse fell on him. He was carried to safety but needed time to recover. Richard began to build his great castle of Château-Gaillard at Les

Andelys probably as a defence for Normandy rather than, as is usually claimed, a threat to France. Richard's first aim was to restore his position in Aquitaine. In 1196 he established a new alliance with Raymond VI count of Toulouse. Richard now moved beyond his own territories. In 1197 John captured the bishop of Beauvais, Philip of Dreux, who was imprisoned in Rouen where he remained until after Richard's death. In 1197 Richard won over Baldwin of Flanders by a trade threat. Philip got the worst of another skirmish when heading for Gisors. It was not a major battle as some have inferred, nor a great victory; the French force of 200 knights merely withdrew. Philip got the better of similar skirmishes at Le Vaudreuil, Arques and Aumale – though these are usually ignored. However, heading into Gisors, the bridge broke and 18 knights were drowned while Philip 'drank the water'.[18] He was safely retrieved and Richard failed to take Gisors. Most of the lands lost during Richard's absence were recovered by 1198, though not all. It cost Richard dearly in cash and brought no new gains. In 1199 the two kings faced each other over the Epte but could not agree terms. They made a temporary truce, though Philip was able to reach separate terms with the count of Flanders.

There then occurred one of those events that change history. Philip encouraged the count of Angoulême to rebel against Richard. Their ally was the viscount of Limoges, whose castle Richard besieged. Making a reconnaissance without a helmet, Richard was hit by a crossbow bolt between shoulder and neck. He mounted and returned to camp but the bolt proved difficult to extract and the surgeon made a mess of the job. Richard's health deteriorated fast. His mother, Eleanor, came to him and on 6 April 1199 he died in her arms. Philip heard the news and headed for Évreux, which he took.

John succeeded to the English throne and the continental possessions, but he lacked Richard's experience in continental government and in warfare. John had been active in England and Normandy but was not known in Aquitaine or most of the French lands. Eleanor gave him support, but whereas 14 Poitevin castellans had supported Richard, only five declared for John. He also had a rival for the succession in his nephew, Arthur of Brittany – son of the older brother Geoffrey, and once named by Richard as his heir. Philip accepted Arthur's homage for most of the French lands. Maine, Anjou and Touraine declared for Arthur. English nobles showed opposition to further continental action. Richard's taxes had been heavy and the links between the nobility and the Angevin Empire had weakened. There was opposition to further taxation and military operations in France.

Perhaps inspired by Henry II's attitude on his own accession, Philip showed John he was willing for peace. They met on 15 January 1200 to negotiate the treaty of Le Goulet, issued in May. The English king, now 'our dearly beloved and faithful John', did homage and paid a relief of 20,000 marks.[19] Philip received much of eastern Normandy including the Vexin, and parts of Berry. Philip's heir Louis was to marry John's niece, Blanche of Castile – celebrated the next day by the archbishop of Bordeaux. In return Philip restored Angoulême and

Right: 1. Equestrian statuette of Emperor Charlemagne (742–814). Detail of the emperor's torso, 9th century (bronze). (*The Bridgeman Art Gallery*)

Below: 2. King Louis VI (1080–1137). Watching the Construction of a Church (vellum). (*The Bridgeman Art Gallery*)

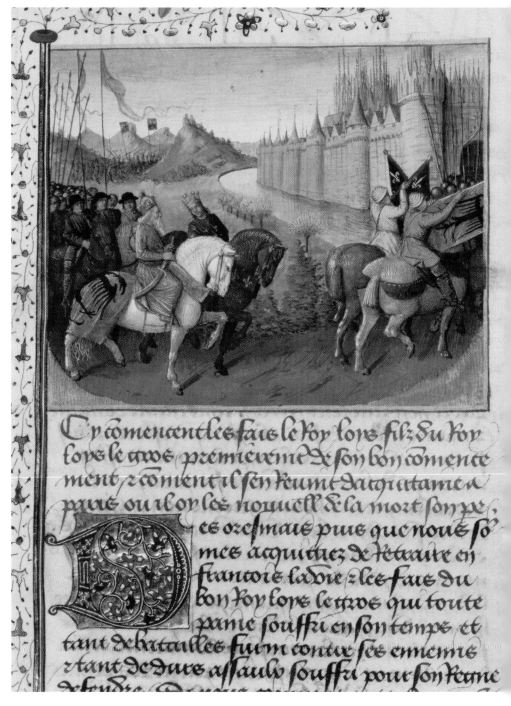

3. Entry of Louis VII into Constantinople with Emperor Conrad III during the Crusade 1147–9 (vellum). (*The Bridgeman Art Gallery*)

King Philip II (1165–1223) of France, from the *Chronique de Saint-Denis*, late 13th century (Vellum). (*The Bridgeman Art Gallery*)

5. Burial of Philippe Le Bel (1268–1314) at St Denis by French School (14th century). (*The Bridgeman Art Gallery*)

6. The gallery of kings at Notre-Dame, Paris. (*Photograph by the author*)

7. Figures on Notre-Dame, Paris including the beheaded St Denis.
(*Photograph by the author*)

8. and 9. The portal of Notre-Dame, Paris. (*Photographs by the author*)

10. The portal of St-Denis, Paris. (*Photograph by the author*)

11. The portal, north door of St-André, Bordeaux, where Louis VII married Eleanor of Aquitaine. (*Photograph by the author*)

12. The head of St Louis (Louis IX) from the statue in the Quinze-Vingts, Paris.
(*Photograph by the author*)

Limoges to John. John then made a disastrous error, though not all historians have seen it as such. He decided to repudiate his wife, Isabelle of Gloucester, to marry Isabelle of Angoulême. He had met her in the summer when she was 12 and he 35. They married on 24 August 1200 despite her betrothal to Hugh de Lusignan. John thus antagonized that powerful family which had been allied to Richard but now switched to Philip. They also gave Philip a pretext for invading the Plantagenet territories.

Philip improved his power against John. He won back the support of Baldwin of Flanders in 1200 through the treaty of Péronne. In 1201 he made terms with Renaud of Boulogne, whose daughter married Philip's illegitimate son Philip Hurepel. He granted Renaud the county of Mortain, formerly held by John. Philip knighted Arthur of Brittany in 1202 and encouraged him to oppose John in Aquitaine. It was planned that Arthur should marry Philip's daughter Marie.

Philip demanded homage from John for the lands of his new wife, which John ignored. Philip used the well-tried ploy of his ancestors, using legal method before turning to force. With the greater power that the monarchy now possessed the method had even more success. Philip claimed jurisdiction over all his vassals but John refused the summons to court. In 1202 the royal court declared John's lands in Aquitaine and Poitou forfeit. After reconnaissance in 1201, Philip invaded Normandy in 1202, heading for Gournay and then Arques. His gains included Eu, Aumale, Driencourt, Lyons-la-Forêt and Mortemer. In 1201 he had concentrated south of the Seine, now he moved north – the first sign of a new aggressive intent. He besieged Gournay which surrendered. In July 1202 he pushed north-west against Arques. He was no longer fighting a border war, he was set on conquest. At this point Philip met a setback and abandoned the campaign. While in Normandy, his ally Arthur of Brittany attacked and took Mirebeau in Poitou. Eleanor of Aquitaine was trapped in the keep, which continued to resist. John set out to rescue her, covering 80 miles in two days, 'quicker than is to be believed', to make a surprise dawn attack.[20] Eleanor was saved and Arthur was captured and taken to Falaise. He disappeared and no one can be certain what happened. Probably John had him put to death. William the Breton says John killed him in person with a sword.[21] A number of Breton and southern lords left John for Philip at this point.

In 1203 Philip resumed the conquest of Normandy. He aimed against the new castle at Château-Gaillard built by Richard at Les Andelys. Philip began his siege in August 1203. He took a number of strongholds around Les Andelys, isolating it. The imposing castle was built on a rock over the river. Approach was difficult from its position, and Richard had made it harder with a series of three enclosures through which one had to pass to reach the keep. The defence was led by Roger de Lacy. Philip blockaded the castle. John sent relief overland and along the Seine. The two forces failed to attack in unison as the water force was held up by tides. The land force attacked at night and was beaten off before the second force arrived at dawn. Archers shot at them and weights were dropped from the bridge. Two ships were sunk, two captured, and the rest retreated. The relief had failed and John did not try again. He raided Brittany in September, attempting to divert Philip's attention. In December John left France, sailing from Barfleur. He never returned to Normandy.

In February 1204 the French took the castle's outer bailey. Philip in helmet and armour encouraged the attack. They forced the middle bailey when Philip's men found a way in by climbing a garderobe chute into a building. They opened the gate and released the drawbridge so that others could break in; the middle bailey was reduced to ashes. The one fault in the construction of the castle was that the bridge to the inner bailey, the final enclosure, was of solid rock and could not be destroyed by the defenders. It offered an entry and gave cover to the attackers mining the wall. The castle surrendered on 6 March 1204. Twenty knights and 120 men-at-arms were led away.

With the fall of Château-Gaillard, Plantagenet control of Normandy disintegrated. Stronghold after stronghold surrendered. Central Normandy and then western Normandy fell into Philip's hands. Caen surrendered without a fight. Philip isolated Rouen, capturing every other major base except Arques. He arrived outside Rouen in May 1204. The citizens destroyed the bridge to deny access but on 1 June they agreed to surrender within a month if no help was forthcoming. They surrendered on 24 June even before the time was up. Philip was master of Normandy.

Eleanor of Aquitaine died on 1 April 1204 putting at risk John's precarious hold on the southern Plantagenet lands. Many of his vassals switched allegiance to Philip who did not rest after the success in Normandy. In 1203 he moved along the Loire and captured Saumur. Maine, Touraine and Poitou abandoned John. In August Philip took Poitiers, then besieged and took the old Angevin strongholds of Chinon and Loches. Southern gains came more from voluntary surrender than military action. Meanwhile Prince Louis led an expedition to Brittany, resulting in further loss to John.

Philip then began to rein in his activities, realizing the need to consolidate. Alfonso VIII of Castile had interests in Plantagenet Gascony and Philip was content to keep out of it. John had problems getting support from his English barons but returned to La Rochelle and his reduced continental lands in 1206. Some Poitevin lords returned to him. On 26 October 1206 a truce was agreed for two years. John retained Gascony and part of Poitou but the rest of the Angevin Empire was lost – in effect it no longer existed. The English king still held some continental lands but not the founding principalities of the Angevin Empire – not Normandy, and not Anjou. Philip was not satisfied with military conquest. He set about establishing royal administration in the newly won areas. He sought to win over urban populations by granting privileges. He built new fortifications and improved old ones as citadels within many towns, including Rouen and Chinon.

Philip developed the first real French royal navy. There was no navy to speak of when he came to the throne. With Ponthieu he gained a new outlet to the sea, and the Plantagenet lands gave him a long coast to defend and use. In the later reign there were plans to invade England and Philip raised a fleet. In 1213 new ships were built until he possessed 1,500 vessels, at least three of them of 30 tons. In 1215 he was able to transport 7,000 men by sea. In 1217 more large ships were constructed. His commander, Eustace the Monk, built a wooden castle for his own ship 'so large that all regarded it as a marvel'.[22]

When John submitted to the papacy 'because he dreaded the arrival of the French king', Innocent III forbade the invasion and it was abandoned.[23] Philip used his fleet against Flanders but suffered disaster at Damme where 400 ships were lost and others fired to prevent capture. A new fleet was assembled in 1217 by Prince Louis under Eustace the Monk but it suffered defeat by the English. Philip's naval efforts were not exactly successful, but the building of the first French naval force remains important. The invasion of England did occur, even though in the end that too would be abandoned.

THE NON-PLANTAGENET PRINCIPALITIES

Philip was intent on imposing royal authority over all the principalities, as demonstrated by his charters, and by insistence on homage. In the areas at issue between French and imperial suzerainty, Philip was ready to take homage from minor lords as well as great – as Bertran de la Tour, Pons de Montlaur and Hélias de Périgord. Philip welcomed homage by lesser lords in return for his protection, as from Hugh de Bergé and Gossuin de Warin. Philip's victories were followed by asserting lordship over defeated nobles. When Philip of Flanders submitted to the king at Boves, his vassal Robert de Boves became a king's man, saying, 'lord count, I was your man, but now, God willing, because of your deeds I have to swear in the court of the lord king'.[24] Under Philip regular assemblies with a national composition emerged to deal with regional measures, a step towards the Estates-General. Such assemblies met at Chinon in 1205, Soissons 1213 and Melun 1216.

Philip was related to the house of Champagne through his mother Adela, an excuse to intervene in the county. He insisted on homage from Theobald III in 1198. Theobald died in 1201 leaving a daughter and a pregnant widow but no son. Philip made the widow, Blanche, agree not to remarry without his consent, and to bring up her children under royal supervision. Adela gave birth to a boy who became Theobald IV of Champagne and king of Navarre. In 1214 he did homage to Philip. The young Theobald reached his majority in 1222 by which time the king had increased the royal hold on Champagne. A similar situation occurred in Burgundy after Duke Odo III died in 1218, leaving a widow Alice and the minor Hugh IV. Alice agreed not to remarry without royal consent and Philip played a significant role in the duchy. Geoffrey of Brittany died in 1186, while the Angevin Empire still survived. Philip demanded wardship of his daughter and posthumous son, Arthur. Philip guaranteed to support Arthur's succession provided he remained loyal, so the fate of his lands would depend 'upon the lawful judgement of his court'.[25]

When Philip of Alsace, count of Flanders, died in 1191, the king made an agreement with his widow, Elizabeth. In return for royal protection she recognized certain lands as the king's, and others would go to him on her death. Philip demanded a relief from the successor, Baldwin VIII, of 5,000 marks. The position there altered with the Fourth Crusade when Baldwin IX participated in the crusade and was elected Latin Emperor of Byzantium in 1204. Baldwin had acknowledged royal overlordship. The king continued to influence affairs in Flanders and was instrumental in choosing Ferrand of Portugal to succeed as count in 1212, taking homage from him. The subsequent desertion by Ferrand we shall examine later.

Philip was equally insistent on royal suzerainty in the south. The Albigensian Crusade led to forces loyal to the king fighting southern lords. Philip took little personal part, though his son Louis did later. Philip benefited indirectly by imposing his authority over northern lords who made gains in the south. Thus when Simon de Montfort seized the county of Toulouse in 1215 along with the duchy of Narbonne and the viscounties of Béziers and Carcassonne, Philip demanded and obtained homage, greatly increasing royal power in the south.

PHILIP AUGUSTUS AND THE CHURCH

Philip II has been seen as a cold and calculating king but he shared the religious passion of his family and seems genuinely pious. There was at his death an (unsuccessful) effort to have him made a saint. In an exemplum (an item for a sermon), recorded by Stephen of Bourbon, Philip's soul was presented to demons to send to hell. They decided, however, that it should go to purgatory because he had honoured the saints, respected church festivals and defended churches, priests and religion. Philip's main motive for crusading seems to have been repentance for former acts, and a desire to visit the Holy Places, rather than to engage in war. He insisted on proper behaviour at court and forbade swearing – 20 sous or a ducking were the penalties. Gerald of Wales wrote that unlike the Plantagenets, Philip was proper in his language. He tried to clean up Parisian morals and removed prostitutes from the re-development site of the Cemetery of the Innocents. He also supported the new house of St-Antoine in Paris for reformed prostitutes. His acts against the Jews and usury were in line with church policy. Philip also supported the church's attitude against tournaments, not a common lay attitude. At the knighting ceremony, he made his son Louis swear not to take part in or attend tournaments.

Philip's grants and almsgiving demonstrate personal attitudes. Many grants were to lepers, as giving privileges for the use of wood in forests. He was a benefactor of the Cistercians. He favoured several smaller and stricter new orders, as the Carthusians, Fontevraud and Grandmont. To commemorate Bouvines he founded Notre-Dame de la Victoire in Senlis for the new Victorine canons and left the house money in his will. He was a frequent benefactor of the genuinely poor. One charter protected a house of charity for 13 poor people in Orléans.

In his will he left money to the poor, orphans and lepers, for the correction of abuses, and for the promotion of crusading. He also supported the crusading orders, the Hospitallers and the Templars.

Like several Capetians before him, Philip came into conflict with the church over his marriages. Philip count of Flanders arranged Philip's first marriage, with his niece Isabelle of Hainault. They married at Bapaume on 28 April 1180 when she was only 10. Despite one attempt by Philip to end the marriage, Isabelle produced a son, Louis, on 5 September 1187, who eventually succeeded to the throne. He was Philip's only undisputedly legitimate offspring. In 1190 Isabelle died bearing twins, who did not survive.

Philip's second wife was the princess, Ingeborg, daughter of Waldemar I of Denmark who died in 1182. Her brothers, Cnut VI and Waldemar II, succeeded in turn. Denmark was a useful ally against the empire. Since Philip now had a claim to the English throne via Cnut the Great, the planned invasion of England may have been behind his choice of wife, but Rigord claimed she had long been the object of his desire. The bishop of Röskilde brought Ingeborg to Philip at Amiens on 14 August 1193 where they married. She was 18, beautiful, tall and blonde. She knew Latin but not French. They were crowned by the archbishop of Reims. In the middle of the ceremony Philip turned white and began to tremble violently. Immediately afterwards he sent her away; she was never his wife except in name. We cannot know the reason for this dramatic event. Innocent III suggested that Philip had acted on bad advice, but it hardly explains his physical reaction. The political reasons for the marriage vanished and the alliance with Denmark became less useful – but that does not explain Philip's action either. Philip sought divorce on the grounds of consanguinity – they were fourth cousins, but that was no more than an excuse. Presumably Philip had been overcome by an overwhelming and sudden physical distaste for the unfortunate young woman.

Ingeborg was not prepared to give in so quickly. Like Isabelle, but in a different way, she sought to remain queen. The French church was prepared to accept Philip's reasons for divorce but the papacy was not, and leading French prelates were persuaded to oppose the separation. Philip claimed the marriage had not been consummated and the church usually accepted this, but not this time. Ingeborg claimed they did have sexual intercourse, though it is hard to see how and when. Philip could not get his way and the unfortunate Ingeborg spent 20 years in virtual imprisonment – in castles, hunting lodges and convents. She wrote 'I am shut in a house and forbidden to go out'.[26] She was treated meanly, having to sell clothes and jewellery to pay for her keep, and denied access to priests and doctors.

Philip's reason was not revulsion for women in general, since he soon found a new partner in Agnes of Méran, a relationship that the papacy refused to countenance – claiming it was bigamous, adulterous and incestuous. Some suggested that Agnes was a sorceress and responsible for Philip's reaction. There are also hints of a relationship with Philip before the marriage to Ingeborg. Agnes was the daughter of Berthold IV count of Méran in the Rhineland, an imperial family. Her father was related to Philip of Swabia and supported the Hohenstaufen. Philip acted as though his divorce was finalized and married Agnes in June 1196. She was treated as queen at court and gave Philip two children, Marie and Philip Hurepel (the shock-headed), though their legitimacy was questioned. The papacy insisted that Ingeborg be restored but Philip refused and an interdict was put on the demesne lands, though Philip harassed the clergy who tried to impose it. Philip eventually reached agreement with the papacy, promising reconciliation to Ingeborg. The interdict was raised in 1200 but Philip's promise proved empty. Ingeborg remained shut up and Agnes remained at court. When a church council investigated the matter and questioned Ingeborg, Philip arrived and seized her, ending the inquiry. He again declared that she would be restored but did nothing to remove Agnes. The situation only eased with the death of Agnes in 1201. She was buried with royal honours at Mantes. Philip continued to heap favours on Agnes' children. Philip Hurepel was given lands and married to the heiress of Boulogne. Marie married the marquis of Namur and, after his death, the duke of Brabant. With Agnes' death reconciliation proved possible. Her two children were declared legitimate. Ingeborg had a slightly easier existence, and later was restored at court, though Philip turned elsewhere for sexual satisfaction. He had an illegitimate son, Peter Charlot, by a 'damoiselle' of Arras.[27]

The pope who dominated this era was Innocent III (1198–1216), born in c.1160 and relatively young for a pope then. He was vigorous, strong-minded, hard-working and conscientious, with legal training and a sharp intellect. Relations with Philip were not bad compared to other secular rulers. In 1198 Innocent wrote to Philip as, 'a very special son of the Roman Church', [to whom] 'we send our first letter'.[28] Innocent had studied in Paris and shown interest in its developing university. A problem for Philip was Innocent's intervention in secular affairs, often in business that Philip thought not of papal concern. Philip declared, 'it is not in the power of Rome to pass judgement on the king or kingdom of France for taking arms to punish rebellious subjects'.[29]

The Capetian tradition and reputation for cooperation with the papacy helped Philip, as opposed to Innocent's dealings with England or the empire. Philip's policies often had papal support, as his attack on heresy and support of crusades. Philip's plan to invade England had papal backing until John submitted to Innocent, after which Philip dropped his plans on papal request. Philip's alliance at Bouvines had papal backing because it opposed the emperor, Otto IV. Philip also frequently won papal approval in his conflict against the Plantagenets.

Philip's relations with Innocent III were aided by the consistent loyalty of the French church. Most bishops did not impose the papal interdict. Philip encouraged reform and the new monasticism while opposing heresy; he made grants and gifts to the church. The role of protector of churches against lay threats was probably more effectively executed by Philip than any of his predecessors, since his power was considerably greater and wider. Philip now operated, for example, in Cahors, Limoges and Clermont and after conquest more effectively in the former Plantagenet lands.

Royal administration depended on clerical staff in chancery, finance, justice or the archives, as diplomats or messengers. They were the educated and literate section of the populace. Some prelates played a major role, not least Philip's uncle, William archbishop of Reims, his 'right hand man'.[30] Another vital ecclesiastical ally was the king's cousin, Philip of Dreux, bishop of Beauvais. A number of counsellors and their relatives gained bishoprics. The sons of William the Chamberlain became bishops of Noyon, Paris and Meaux. The king's counsellor, Guérin the Hospitaller, became bishop of Senlis. William the Breton, who wrote a major work on the reign, was a royal chaplain. Many able ecclesiastics were in royal service, not least Peter the Chanter as a royal judge.

Philip maintained his father's attitude to church appointments, allowing free election but retaining considerable influence. There were few disputes in the demesne. Stephen of Gallardon recorded a conversation when Peter the Chanter recommended the papal line on reform, opposing lay participation in elections. Philip asked why in the past so many bishops had been saints but nowadays none were. When Peter said 'foolishness always arrived unbidden', Philip gave him short shrift, asking what that had to do with the question. Peter answered that in these days kings influenced elections and got the kind of bishops they deserved.[31] The election of leading abbots had a similar history. There is a contemporary description of when an election was about to take place at St-Denis. Philip was just passing by (hmmm), and came in 'as if entering his own chamber'. The monks asked the king for the right to elect their abbot. Philip agreed and they returned to their chapter. The prior, Hugh, was elected, apparently satisfactory to all concerned, and Philip confirmed the election. Nevertheless Philip's manner was acceptable to the church. There is little question that elections in Normandy after the conquest were freer than under the Plantagenets. Over the election at Winchester Henry II had declared 'we order you to hold a free election, but we forbid you to elect anyone except Richard my clerk'.[32] Philip was more respectful and circumspect than that.

The schools of Paris became a fully constituted university under Philip II, in cooperation with the papacy, which desired a concentration on the study of theology. There were problems in the birth pangs. In 1200 the students rioted and a number were killed. The servant of a German student just elected bishop of Liège who went to buy wine in a tavern was attacked and beaten up by some locals. A group of enraged German students came to the tavern and fighting broke out, spreading to wider violence between students and citizens. A gang of citizens under the prévôt attacked the German student quarter. The elected bishop and other students were killed. When the university sought Philip's aid, he antagonized the citizens by supporting the students and imprisoning the prévôt, who later died in a fall when trying to escape. Philip granted privileges to the students, offering the protection normally given to clerics. A college system emerged from the end of the 12th century. Innocent III recognized the university by a bull in 1210. The papal legate issued rules for the university in 1215, as that every student must be attached to a master. Most could not afford expensive accommodation. Stephen Langton described his student lodgings with a simple bed of straw. By 1222 arts students were organized in nations. The university became the leading intellectual centre in Europe. A second university appeared in France, at Montpellier, where the main study was medicine, receiving a charter in 1181 and statutes in 1210.

Heresy became a major problem under Philip. The Catholic Church expected conformity with its dogma. The catholic west had broken with the Orthodox Church of Byzantium. There had always been some who questioned accepted views, whether Catholic or Orthodox. Heretical ideas were persecuted throughout Europe. They were dangerous to hold so that by and large heresy was an underground movement, avoiding publicity and hopefully punishment. Heretical works if found were destroyed, so it is not surprising our knowledge is limited and uncertain. Dualist belief had emerged in early times, accepting an evil being as opposed and equal to God. Dualist belief emerged in the Balkans and spread west. In this period the eastern heretics, usually called Bogomils, sent missions to the west. The major western areas where heresy took root were northern Italy and southern France, often where secular power was weak. Neither the duke of Aquitaine, nor local counts, nor the king, had great authority in southern France in 1180. Another factor was disrespect for the church, despite its attempt to solve the problem of order through the Peace movement. Prelates were rarely respected, clerical abuse was rife, and ecclesiastics lacked authority.

The papacy condemned heretical ideas without reserve and sought support from secular powers to suppress them. A decree of Innocent III in 1199 brought heretics under the law for treason and led to an increasingly vicious response from secular states. Philip was cooperative but not especially active. A few groups of heretics appeared in northern France and were dealt with fairly easily. A few were burned at Arras in 1182. In 1210 the Parisian master Amaury de Bène and his followers were condemned by church councils and handed to the secular authorities for punishment – 10 were burned.

The southern heretics, who were probably dualist, are usually called either Cathars or Albigenses. They established an organization with heretical bishoprics. Their moral leaders were the Perfects (*perfecti*), the pure ones, who dressed in black and contrasted with the local Catholic clergy by living in poverty, going barefoot, preaching and ministering. The heresy also offered women a greater role than the Catholic Church. William the Breton said that the heretics were against marriage and refused to eat meat.[33] A number of southern towns became centres of heresy. Raymond V of Toulouse said it 'had penetrated everywhere' In 1163 the council of Tours condemned 'a new heresy which has recently appeared in the region of Toulouse, spreading like a cancer'. Many lesser nobles were either heretics or ready to protect them. In 1204 the papacy sought Philip's cooperation, suggesting that in return the church would approve the confiscation of their lands. Philip did not leap at the chance, answering that the lands were not the church's to distribute. Nor, at first, was he prepared to attack Raymond VI, count of Toulouse, seen as the main protector of heretics, though he was probably

Catholic. Philip refused to confiscate his lands unless the church first condemned Raymond as a heretic.

In January 1208 two papal legates on a mission against heresy were murdered at St-Gilles near Arles. Raymond VI of Toulouse was blamed for protecting the killers. His lands were placed under interdict and he was excommunicated a second time. Philip still ignored papal requests to lead an army against the heretics, but a force assembled in 1209 under Simon de Montfort. Raymond VI submitted to the papacy and took an oath to expel heretics. He made public penitence, naked to the waist, pulled by the neck and flogged with a birch. He was absolved and joined the crusade. The Albigensian Crusade was never simply a Catholic attack on heretics. To the south it was an invasion by the north, with heresy as the excuse for seizing southern lands. Not all the crusaders saw conquest as the aim, and many fought briefly before returning north, but a hard core fought on under Simon de Montfort, a leader with military ability and territorial ambitions.

The major battle that resulted was not simply between Catholics and heretics. The southerners received support from Pedro II king of Aragon who challenged the Capetians in the region. Aragon allied with the south against the crusaders in the battle of Muret in 1213. The crusaders won a great victory and Pedro was killed. The papacy however became less enthusiastic about the crusade, beginning to see other motives involved, and sought to divert attention to the Holy Land. Simon de Montfort was recognized as count of Toulouse and did homage to Philip Augustus. De Montfort died in 1218 and was succeeded by his son Amaury. The authority of the northern nobility declined but Prince Louis now took over. Amaury placed his county in Louis' hands. Raymond VI's son received a reduced inheritance as Raymond VII count of Toulouse. The result of this phase of the Albigensian Crusade was not the complete destruction of heresy, which continued over the following decades, but an increase in royal authority, never to be relinquished.

GOVERNMENT AND ADMINISTRATION

Philip II's reign has been re-assessed recently through the study of administrative records. Baldwin sees the first decade as a time when Philip relied on existing systems, with major change only after the Third Crusade. However, it could be argued that important changes also occurred in the early period. Evidence comes from Philip's Testament – his arrangements for government during his absence on crusade. Paris was now the home of a permanent administration, though some officials continued to travel with the king. Philip made the importance of Paris clear by regular visits and the amount of business conducted there. The new Louvre meant a better royal and bureaucratic residence. The archives were kept there while a permanent treasury was established at the Temple.

Some of Philip's close officials and counsellors were men already used by his father. A few great lords held major offices, but more came from lesser nobility of the demesne, and a few from obscure origins. Ability rather than background was the necessary qualification. Brother Guérin de Glapion was the king's 'special counsellor, because of his wisdom in the royal hall and his incomparable gift of advising'.[34] Guérin, a Hospitaller, was active in chancery and became the dominant official. His origins were so obscure as to be unknown. He belonged to the inner circle who advised Philip on the invasion of England; 'lesser men, the only people to whom the king was accustomed on all occasions to open his soul and reveal his secret thoughts'.[35] He was also named among those to execute the king's will.

During the early years Philip's government already depended on prévôts and baillis, the latter introduced in the first decade of his reign. Baillis were not tied to locations as prévôts were, though they had their own geographical areas of competence. They represented the king, checking other officials and aspects of government. They operated in pairs and their function compared to that of Plantagenet itinerant justices. They held monthly assizes and responded to complaints about officials. Three times a year they reported to the central government in Paris. Philip developed a group of counsellors of his own choice. The Testament shows that the base for the royal treasury was already in the Temple. The Testament demonstrated the new significance of citizen control in towns – Parisians were to play a major part in the government of their own city. The use of lesser figures to staff the chancery was not new, already employed by Philip in the early reign.

The military conquests led to a geographical extension of royal government with an increase in royal bureaucratic activity and a need for more agents. In 1190 there were 52 prévôtés, by 1203 there were 62. The extension brought an increase in income from taxation. Philip achieved this without making excessive demands in the new regions, often less than his predecessors, thus averting resentment. In Hesdin and Auchy rents were reduced 'for the good will of his new subjects'.[36] With a closer check on all income, leading to more efficient collection, Philip had a greater income than any previous Capetian king. He left £600,000 in his will.

Government records were captured at Fréteval in 1194 and lost. Nevertheless this inspired a new organization of records and the period is important for surviving records. Royal charters were collected from the 1190s, and Philip ordered the collection of inquest records in 1220. The new edition of Philip's registers reveals details of how government worked. The registers contain, for example, a long list of 'securities' or 'cautions', a means of keeping a hold over various subjects. Jews on the demesne had to swear to stay there. Leading administrators and nobles had to give guarantees of fidelity, sometimes against the threat of losing their lands. The registers are the first documents of the kind to survive in France. It is unclear if earlier ones had existed and were lost, or if this was a novel development. One possibility is that they began in an attempt to restore records lost at Fréteval. To Bautier they are 'without doubt the documentary source of the greatest importance which we have from this period'.[37] They are a selection of royal acts, often in the form of lists. They recorded important royal decisions and information valuable to the government – such as how much towns owed in dues. Twice the registers were reorganized. They are now labelled A to E, which is misleading in that B is simply a later copy of A, and D is a copy of C. A, C and E are the original registers. Register A was begun in c.1204. Additions were made over eight years until it consisted of 96 folios and 255 acts. Most likely it was an innovation, a new kind of survey of what could be obtained from the demesne, especially military service. In 1212 the material was reorganized as Register C, after the expansion of the demesne with the conquests. The divisions were clarified under ten headings such as 'alms' or 'communes'. This register was added to until 1220, incorporating 178 new acts. Then Stephen Gallardon began a new reorganization for Brother Guérin, Register E. It had 14 section headings and was added to until 1247, recording 243 new acts. About a quarter of the acts in the registers are not known from other sources. They included charters, peace agreements, judicial decisions and all kinds of useful information such as genealogical connections. It provided a kind of encyclopedia for royal bureaucrats.

Financial information for Philip's government is also better, despite the loss of records at Fréteval and later losses in the 1737 fire. Accounts were presented in Paris thrice a year. Transactions were recorded and records stored in the Temple in locked chests. The earliest surviving accounts are from 1202–3, transactions by prévôts and baillis. The prévôts produced regular income (about 30%), from the demesne, justice, and the towns; the baillis produced extraordinary income (about 70%), such as reliefs on succession to principalities or from the attack on the Jews. The accounts were checked by a small group of Parisian citizens. The chamber dealt with the administration of finance. The citizen role was taken over by the Templars, and a permanent treasury was established at the Temple. The exact meaning of the comments on royal income by Conon of Béthune is uncertain, but we can accept his conclusion that under Philip royal income increased 'beyond what can be believed'. It also increased progressively through the reign. Rigord thought this was due to Philip's moderation and modest expenses.[38] Expenditure was similarly divided between regular needs, and occasional demands such as for crusades, war against the Plantagenets, or the Bouvines campaign.

Philip was modest, admitting 'I am but a man, as you are, but I am king of France'.[39] He knew his role but he knew he was ordinary. The royal lineage was stressed, and descent from Charlemagne, once denied, was now acknowledged. The sword of Charlemagne was brandished at Philip's coronation. Innocent III declared 'it is common knowledge that the king of France is descended from the lineage of Charlemagne'.[40] The name Augustus may have been given from his birth month, but Rigord saw imperial connotations. The same notion was behind using an eagle on the royal seal. Philip's sister married two Byzantine emperors. A Parisian master summed up: 'the king is emperor in his realm'.[41]

There is an improvement in the information on royal justice. Royal officials functioned as judges. The royal entourage was staffed by an ever greater proportion of trained legal experts – notaries and lawyers. Royal acts recorded judicial decisions, often agreements or concords. The royal court was a judicial court where significant decisions were made, as those against King John, and Renaud of Boulogne. Trial by ordeal was now questioned; Peter the Chanter derided those who believed God gave decisions in this manner. He quoted the case of a priest found guilty of murder by ordeal and hanged for it, only for the 'victim' to turn up alive and well. Peter also ridiculed the methods – if ordeal by water worked, why did it only work on lesser folk? Or if judgement in trial by combat was by God, why employ the best warrior they could find? Philip's policy was to replace ordeal by the use of courts.

URBAN DEVELOPMENT UNDER PHILIP AUGUSTUS

Philip II showed interest in urban development, particularly over financial benefit for the crown and political gain by alliance with urban elites. There is a distinction to be made between the treatment of towns in the demesne and those outside it. Philip, like his predecessors, was prepared to make wider grants of privilege to towns outside the demesne so as to appear as their protector.

Paris was now unquestionably the capital of the Capetian realm and a major European city. Its schools became a university in this period, attracting leading intellectuals and scholars, and many students. Philip built a covered market at Les Halles for the merchants and paved the main streets. He built a new wall and the castle of the Louvre, defending Paris from the west. Recent excavations beneath the modern art gallery and its courtyard have shown the true dimensions and strength of Philip's fortifications. The Louvre enclosed a space of 78 metres by 72. The new walls were four metres thick, studded with ten towers, and protected by a moat filled from the Seine. The central keep, the Grosse-Tour, was cylindrical and 31 metres high, protected by a circular dry ditch six metres deep. Ferrand of Flanders was imprisoned there after Bouvines. The Louvre had two gates, a drawbridge to the eastern gate to the town, and a southern gate with access to the river.

Philip added defences to other French towns. His first register noted work on Laon, Compiègne, St-Mard and Melun. Curtain walls, towers, gates and ditches were built. A major new tower was built at Bourges in 1190. Instructions were sent to Garnier the mason and Gilbert the ditcher. By the end of Philip's reign every major town in the demesne had a fortress and wall. Philip's castles were massive. The tower at Villeneuve-sur-Yonne was over 27 metres high with a ditch 13 metres wide. They also have architectural interest with the emphasis on round towers – as in the Louvre. The records mention at least 18 new cylindrical towers. Dun-le-Roi in Berry used the Louvre as a model. The tower at Issoudun was cylindrical; the added spur an early example of an *en bec* tower. Philip's last major castle was at Dourdan with the keep in one corner, concentrating on the walls rather than the interior – the direction in which castle planning would go. Philip II was one of the greatest of medieval castle-builders, on a level with Edward I.

Philip gave protection to fairs and markets throughout the realm, as for

Compiègne in 1185, when merchants going to the fair were guaranteed royal protection. In 1209 the Champagne fairs were promised similar protection. It was part of Philip's bid for support from merchants, and brought additional revenue. Register A recorded demesne rights in 32 towns. Royal towns were more freely able to recruit new citizens from serfs admitted to them. Communes prospered under Philip. They welcomed the new independence in administration, justice and financial arrangements. They raised and trained their own militias and were loyal supporters of the crown. Philip was sympathetic to communes, making grants of the status to Chaumont in 1182, Amiens 1185 and Pontoise 1188. He was more cautious over towns in the demesne, though granted them privileges. Commune status was a means of winning support in newly conquered areas, as at Les Andelys and Nonancourt after the conquest of Normandy. Beauvais valued its new commune charter: 'in no event will it [the charter] be taken outside the city'.[42] Citizens knew the value of royal support. Walter Tirel granted a commune to Foix, but the citizens still wanted royal approval – going to Philip in Paris for a charter. The value to the king was also considerable. The *tailles* collected by the baillis from demesne towns were very profitable – £2,995 from Paris, £1,500 each from Étampes and Orléans. Possibly as much as 15% of royal income came from Paris but less pressure for payment was put on newly acquired towns. The period saw economic advance and prosperity for France. William the Breton noted the fertile fields and vines of his native Brittany, the salmon and eels caught from fishing, and the flourishing of trade.[43]

BOUVINES

The battle of Bouvines was the key event of Philip II's reign. Much that he had achieved might have been lost with this battle. His opponents included princes of France, notably the count of Flanders, and his greatest secular rivals, the German emperor and the English king. John was not there but he was in the opposing alliance and English forces were present. At risk were Philip's conquests, his increased revenue, his control of the northern principalities, his dominance in western Europe, and his life.

By 1214 Philip was an experienced commander. He had been on the Third Crusade and fought a long war against the Plantagenets. He had planned an invasion of England though it had proved abortive. He used the forces raised against Flanders. Count Philip had been powerful in the early reign but the king had thrown off his control. Philip then outmanoeuvred Baldwin IX, who had gone on the Fourth Crusade and became Latin emperor of Byzantium. Baldwin was captured at Adrianople and died in captivity. The king then dominated his brother, Philip of Namur, who became regent for Baldwin's daughters, Joan and Margaret. They became royal wards and were taken to Paris in 1208. Philip of Namur married the king's daughter Marie in 1211 but died the following year.

John of England sought an alliance with discontented elements in Flanders but was not greatly successful. Philip countered by buying support and building a pro-French party. He influenced the election as count of Flanders of Ferrand of Portugal, son of King Sancho I. Through Philip, Ferrand married Joan the heiress to Flanders in 1212. Philip knighted Ferrand, who did homage for the county. Ferrand had little support in Flanders. His position was made worse by the actions of Prince Louis, who seized Aire and St-Omer, claiming them as his mother's dowry. Ferrand had to accept the loss, which diminished his authority in the county. Some called him the 'serf' of the king and demanded that he go home.[44] Ferrand made an unwise move, seeking greater popularity at the expense of his alliance with Philip. He turned to the empire and England, to Otto of Brunswick and King John. To gain their favour he expelled pro-French knights from Flanders. John sent cash, and Flemish towns enjoyed a revival of trade with England. When Philip decided to invade England in 1213, Ferrand refused to participate or contribute. On 10 May Philip embarked at Boulogne. John then yielded to papal demands and the papacy forbade the French invasion.

Philip called off the invasion but used his forces against Ferrand and Flanders. He took Tournai, Cassel, Lille, Bruges and Ghent. Ferrand fled to Zeeland. The French did much damage but then their fleet was attacked and destroyed at Damme by Flemings in alliance with the count of Boulogne and England. Philip's mercenary captain, Cadoc, was probably killed in the attack. Some ships were taken and the French burned the rest to avoid capture. Philip's gains in Flanders had to be abandoned. Ferrand had beaten Philip and won over the Flemish. He was openly allied with John and visited England in December 1213. John was planning an expedition to Poitou to recover his continental lands. The Flemish war continued into the spring of 1214. John's expedition was slow to prepare through trouble raising the necessary funds. Philip had to divide his attention between Flanders and the empire in the north, and John in the south. He chose to deal personally with the northern coalition, sending Prince Louis against John.

One of the key figures in the northern coalition was Renaud de Dammartin, count of Boulogne, formerly favoured by Philip. Renaud betrayed him, organizing the coalition. He joined Theobald count of Bar and various nobles from Flanders and Hainault. Another renegade was Hugh de Boves, who had fled from France after killing a prévôt. He joined the English at Bouvines under William earl of Salisbury, John's half brother. The emperor Otto IV was the senior figure among the allies, but his position in Germany was not secure. When Henry VI died in 1198 Otto had to fight Philip of Swabia, Henry's brother. Philip II had favoured his namesake, while the Plantagenets supported Otto. Philip of Swabia was crowned in 1205 but assassinated in 1208, when Otto recovered the crown. Philip II then favoured Henry VI's young son, Frederick of Hohenstaufen. Otto did not help his cause by invading Italy in 1210, after which he was excommunicated by Innocent III.

King John may have planned to join the allies but was opposed by Prince Louis. John sailed from Portsmouth in February 1214 to La Rochelle. He wrote home that 26 strongholds immediately surrendered. He had an easy passage through

Saintonge, Poitou and Angloulême to the Limousin. Many local lords submitted. Brittany was less welcoming but John took Nantes. He moved on to former Plantagenet territory and entered Angers. He attacked the castle at La Roche-au-Moine which held out for two weeks until Prince Louis came to its relief. His force was smaller than John's and he hesitated over battle. Philip ordered his son to save La Roche-au-Moine and Louis advanced, only for John to retreat. He left his baggage and hastily crossed the Loire, in which many of his men drowned. Louis pursued him to Thouars. There was no battle. John returned to La Rochelle. Whatever happened in the north would be without further aid from him. John made his peace with Philip and returned to face the music in England.

Meanwhile dramatic events unfolded on the border between the royal lands and Flanders. Otto IV assembled his forces at Aachen in March but it was July before he reached Nivelles near Brussels. He was joined by the counts of Flanders, Boulogne, and Boves, and the earl of Salisbury. Philip marched north, reaching Tournai on 25 July. Both armies manoeuvred and passed each other without realizing it, so that when they met the French were coming from north to south. Philip was in danger of being cut off from his own lands. The allies with a larger force were confident of victory. Count Ferrand issued ropes for tying up the prisoners they would take. Otto told his men they had three times as many knights, waving his sword to proclaim they did not like it up 'em – or words to that effect.

Philip reached the River Marcq and secured his crossing by the bridge near the village of Bouvines. Philip widened the bridge so more could cross at a time. He took lunch on a hilltop from which he could see the enemy, removing his armour in a shady spot under an ash tree where he consumed lumps of bread soaked in wine. Otto approached from the rear, believing the French to be in a panic retreat – which proved false. Philip had intended to retreat but his army was in good order. Guérin's scouts spotted the enemy, with 'shields like stars at night, their helmed heads reflecting the sun'.[45] He sought out the king under the ash. Philip entered the nearby church of St Peter's to offer a prayer, then he armed and ordered the army to prepare for battle, leaping on his horse and shouting 'Allons!' The van, which had crossed the bridge, returned. Philip made a speech calling his opponents enemies of the Church, several being excommunicate, and all of them choosing to fight on a Sunday.

Philip, 'a tall figure on a tall horse', formed his army in three.[46] The right was under the duke of Burgundy and Guérin. Philip commanded the centre with his household knights, Galon de Montigny carrying the royal banner with the fleur de lys (the oriflamme was still returning over the bridge). The left was under the royal relatives, Philip bishop of Beauvais, and Robert of Dreux. The returning men were mostly ready before battle commenced. Once they had returned Philip ordered the bridge to be broken so there could be no panic flight over it. The enemy were also in three divisions, with Ferrand of Flanders on the left; Otto IV in the centre; and Salisbury, Renaud of Dammartin and Hugh de Boves, on the right.

The battle was fought on the afternoon of 27 July 1214. The armies faced each other an arrow shot apart. Silence fell. Philip made a speech and embraced those around him, saying 'In God is all our hope'. The clerics behind Philip including William the Breton chanted psalms and prayers. Guérin gave the order for a cavalry charge from the right. One man fell headfirst and his head was buried in the mud. Bodies accumulated. Loose horses ran about. Burgundy was unhorsed but saved. The French left eventually achieved success and Ferrand was unhorsed and captured. Otto IV ordered his central force to attack. Philip countered to find himself in a dangerously isolated position. He was unhorsed and fell to the ground with a halberd hanging from his mail. The household knight, Peter Tristan, stood over him and saved his life then gave the king his own horse. The allied right moved towards the centre but was blocked, the bishop of Beauvais who 'happened by chance to have a mace in his hand' intervening.[47] He clubbed Salisbury and broke his helmet. The earl was taken prisoner and Hugh de Boves fled.

The battle petered out but Renaud de Dammartin's small group fought to the end. Otto IV fled and escaped; his wagon with standards was broken up and the imperial eagle captured, its wings broken off. Renaud formed his small force of pikemen into a circle, two ranks deep. With his cavalry he was safe inside this circle, and from it issued in sudden charges, returning inside for a rest. The numbers against them proved too great and the little force was whittled down until only half a dozen knights remained. A sergeant got under Renaud's horse, wounding it so that it fell on top of its rider who was trapped. He surrendered to Guérin.

The battle lasted three hours. Philip ordered that pursuit be limited to two miles, as he did not want to risk dispersing his army. He spent the night on the battlefield. The dead were buried in the local abbey of Cysoing. Booty, armour and weapons were taken up by the victors. The prisoners, including five counts and an earl, would bring valuable ransoms. Philip gave thanks in the nearby chapel for the victory. He returned to France in triumph, bells ringing along the way, branches and flowers scattered before him. Peasants in the fields shouldered their tools and came to watch. In Paris the citizens came out to cheer, and revels continued for a week – night becoming day from the brightness of torches, with singing, dancing and feasting.

Otto IV never recovered from Bouvines. He had alienated the pope, who now supported his rival, Frederick of Hohenstaufen. The broken remains of the imperial standard were sent by Philip to the young Frederick, who was crowned at Aachen in 1215. Otto returned to Brunswick, broken, reduced to living in a mean house. He died from an overdose of medicine in 1218. Ferrand count of Flanders was taken from the battle chained in a cart. He was imprisoned for the rest of Philip's reign and only released in 1227, no longer a man of consequence. He had contracted an illness that killed him six years later. Renaud de Dammartin count of Boulogne was also imprisoned, chained to a log that allowed him to move only half a pace. It had to be lifted and carried every time he wanted to relieve himself. Boulogne was granted to Philip's illegitimate son, Philip Hurepel.

In the end when it became clear he would never be released, Renaud committed suicide. Hugh de Boves escaped and planned to go to England, but drowned on the way in a storm off Calais. His body washed ashore at Yarmouth. William earl of Salisbury was captured but Philip released him in exchange for the son of the count of Dreux. The earl died on crusade. King John had not been at Bouvines but suffered in its wake. His coalition against Philip was destroyed; his hopes of recovering continental lands dashed. Bouvines inspired the baronial opposition to John in England. Prince Louis was encouraged to renew plans to invade England. The year after Bouvines John was forced to accept Magna Carta. He made efforts to recover but died the following year, leaving a divided land harassed by French invaders.

THE LATER YEARS OF PHILIP AUGUSTUS

Philip reigned for nine years after Bouvines. The defeat of so many enemies at a blow meant these years were relatively peaceful. Prince Louis emerged to play a greater role, engaging in two aggressive campaigns, the first being the invasion of England. Philip recognized that papal approval was unlikely and kept a low profile, leaving it to his son. Louis was encouraged by some of the English nobility offering alliance and the English throne. Some came to France and accompanied Louis to England, including Robert fitz Walter and Eustace de Vesci. They had the backing of Stephen Langton. Louis claimed the English throne through his marriage to Blanche of Castile, grand-daughter of Henry II. He declared John deposed for murdering Arthur of Brittany. An assembly at Melun in 1216 declared that 'the throne of England is vacant, since King John has been condemned in our court'.[48] The papal legate denied the French claim. Philip told Louis that he refused his consent, 'not wishing to offend the pope'.[49] Louis exploded in his father's face, 'it is not up to you to decide matters concerning England ... I fight for the inheritance of my wife'.[50] Plans for invasion went ahead and Louis was excommunicated.

In 1215 Louis sent ahead a force including 140 knights to join his English allies. Louis sailed on the evening of 20 May 1216. The weather was stormy and only some (including Louis) arrived at the intended destination. The eastern half of England declared for him as did London, where he was welcomed as king. Rochester fell and Winchester surrendered. Before long the prince held Orford, Norwich, Cambridge, Colchester, Guildford, Farnham, Odiham, Marlborough and Worcester. Resistance came from royal castles, including Windsor, Lincoln and Dover. 1200 knights, four counts and leading French nobles such as William des Barres and Enguerrand de Coucy crossed with Louis. He also had support from Scotland, Wales and Ireland. Alexander II king of Scots came to Canterbury and performed homage to Louis. Four English earls deserted John for Louis, including William of Salisbury – it was said because John took liberties with his wife while the earl was in captivity after Bouvines.[51]

Having gained a hold in England, Louis returned to France for reinforcements.

Philip refused to speak to his son. The prince sailed to England on 23 April 1217. It was during this lull that Louis began to lose support and English barons rallied around the young king, Henry III. King John died on 19 October 1216 – some said from indigestion after eating peaches and drinking new cider – though it was probably a heart attack. His son Henry, nine at the time, was crowned. Barons with personal vendettas against John had less reason to oppose his son. Among those who returned to the fold was the earl of Salisbury. Louis' support declined and he began to look like a foreign invader.

An English force under William the Marshal set out to relieve Lincoln. Louis had taken the town in 1216 but the castle held out. On 20 May 1217 the Marshal broke through and entered the castle, then made a sortie against the French who were 'killed like pigs'.[52] Lincoln was saved. Reinforcements for Louis from France crossed the channel under Eustace the Monk. Eustace was a former monk who became a mercenary for King John and then for Louis. The English fleet, under Hubert de Burgh and Richard of Chilham, trapped Eustace off Sandwich. Henry III with the Marshal watched from the cliff top. The English threw lime into the wind so that it blew into the faces of the French and blinded them. French ships were boarded and Eustace was captured. He offered money in return for his life but was beheaded on the spot, his head placed on a pike and paraded through Canterbury.

Prince Louis realized his hope of success had gone. Lincoln and Sandwich confirmed the change of heart and strength. He abandoned the siege of Dover and agreed to peace talks in London. An agreement was sealed on a Thames island near Kingston. The English demanded that the prince appear in his underwear as a humiliation but in the end he was allowed to wear a mantle. Peace was confirmed in the treaty of Lambeth. Louis received 10,000 marks to abandon his claim to the English throne. He agreed to persuade his father to return lost Angevin possessions but of course Philip paid no heed.

After Bouvines Flanders was isolated and dominated by Philip. Count Ferrand was in prison. His wife Joan tried to get him released, but without success. More Flemish nobles were in French prisons than free. The ransoms for those released helped to impoverish the Flemish nobility yet further. Castles and strongholds were put under pro-French nobles or Frenchmen. Philip imposed the treaty of Paris which gave France control of Flanders. He tried to get Joan to divorce Ferrand and marry Peter Mauclerc of Brittany, but she resisted. Her younger sister, Margaret, married Bouchard d'Avesnes from Hainault, who hoped to become count of Flanders. Bouchard rebelled against Joan but was captured in 1219, remaining a prisoner until 1221. He was then forced to annul his marriage, and Margaret wed William de Dampierre. The papacy refused to recognize this despite Margaret producing a son by William, and in the end she returned to Bouchard. Flanders never became wholly French but parts of it were taken over permanently, including Artois, the Amiénois, Valois and Vermandois.

Bouvines also confirmed Philip's gains from the Plantagenets. The 'French' principalities had been the main threat but from this point no single principality

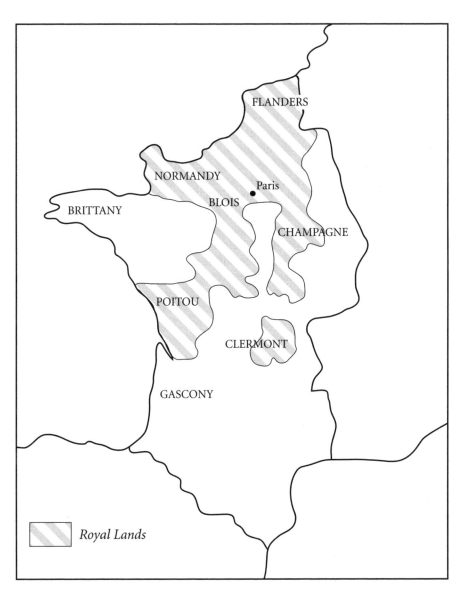

France at the death of Philip Augustus, 1223

could match the power of the crown. Normandy was ruled directly and most former Plantagenet principalities were no longer in hostile hands.

We have mentioned that Prince Louis made two aggressive campaigns during his father's later years. The first was to invade England; the second was in the Albigensian Crusade. The initial stage of the crusade was commanded by northern French nobles, notably Simon de Montfort. Prince Louis took the crusading vow but Philip forbade him to go. Bouvines in 1214 meant that Philip could afford more involvement in the south and he relented over his son's role – perhaps preferring it to the invasion of England. In 1215 Louis entered Toulouse. De Montfort was killed at the siege of Toulouse in 1218. His son, Amaury, succeeded but surrendered his position to the king.

In 1219, after the failure in England, Louis led a second expedition south. He treated his opponents with brutality. Even though Marmande surrendered, 5,000 citizens were put to death. Louis besieged Toulouse but after six weeks abandoned the attempt. Only in 1222 did Philip personally intervene, sending a force including 200 knights under the count of La Marche. Catharism survived for decades but heresy was not the only motive behind this crusade, which seems more of a political conquest of the south by the north, now headed by the royal family.

Philip Augustus became ill in September 1222. He made a will at St-Germain-en-Laye, leaving money for the crusades in the East, and for the Hospitallers and Templars. He made gifts to St-Denis, the poor, orphans, widows and lepers. £5,000 was bequeathed to his long-suffering wife, Ingeborg, who lived on comfortably until 1236. In July 1223 Philip felt worse when at Pacy-sur-Eure. He sent for Louis and summoned a council, telling his son to fear God and protect the poor and giving advice to his young grandson, Louis, later to become St Louis. The king's fever increased as the weather became warmer. He thought he was better and went on to Paris, against doctor's advice. He reached Mantes on 14 July but felt worse again. There at the age of 58 the great king died after a reign of 43 years. The body was carried to Paris on a bier and taken in procession to St-Denis. Philip was buried in full regalia with crown and sceptre. St Louis later erected a tomb for Philip covered in gold and silver.

THE REIGN OF LOUIS VIII (1223–26)

Philip II's son succeeded without question in 1223 as Louis VIII. He had experience in authority and in war, having led an invasion of England and two expeditions in the Albigensian Crusade. He is not much remembered, mainly because his reign proved so short, yet it was not without achievement.

A problem emerged in Flanders when a man declared himself to be Baldwin IX (former Byzantine emperor, 1204–6). 'Baldwin' said he had survived imprisonment after his capture in the east. There was uncertainty about the truth and Louis questioned him at Péronne. There was popular support for the claimant, leading to rebellion in Flanders. Evidence was produced from some who had known

Baldwin and it became clear 'Baldwin' was an impostor. He was executed at Lille in 1225. Louis used force to restore order. With Flanders at peace Louis decided he could safely release Count Ferrand. However the king died before the release was carried out – it was carried through by Queen Blanche.

The south had been Louis' main scene of success as a prince and his interest continued as king. He had campaigned against the Cathars and pressured Amaury de Montfort to stand down in his favour. In 1224 Louis led a new force aimed for the south. He besieged and took Niort, and St-Jean-d'Angely surrendered. He besieged and took La Rochelle after three weeks. Poitou (formerly Plantagenet) was now safely Capetian and became an apanage for Louis' son Alphonse. Louis had begun to take over Gascony, but his early death prevented further progress. As for the Albigensian Crusade, Louis supported action by Amaury de Montfort and made a new expedition himself. Louis sanctioned a decree to burn heretics to death. He marched south but was opposed at Avignon, then seen as imperial. He besieged the city but food ran short and the army was plagued by dysentery and black flies. The count of St-Pol was killed by a stone from an engine. Theobald of Champagne abandoned the expedition and returned home. Avignon surrendered but had delayed the expedition. Louis moved on to Carcassonne, which surrendered, but became ill and turned for home. On arriving at Montpensier he collapsed with dysentery and died on 8 November 1226. The royal position in the south had been improved by the Albigensian Crusade and by Louis' efforts. The count of Toulouse survived but with lands diminished and no longer a match for royal power. Catharism was not destroyed but it had suffered. Further efforts after Louis' death drove it underground. It no longer posed any great threat to French society or the Catholic Church.

8

King and Saint, Louis IX, 1226–70

INTRODUCTION

St Louis loved God with his whole heart and it was on Him that he modelled his actions ... In eating he was so temperate that never once in my life did I hear him order any dish for his table, as many rich men do. He was content to eat what his cook prepared for him and what was set before him. In his speech he was restrained. Never in my life did I hear him speak ill of any man, nor name the devil ... He mixed his wine with water ... Often in the summer he went after mass to the wood of Vincennes, sat down with his back against an oak tree, and made us sit all around him. Everyone who had an affair to settle could come and speak to him without the interference of any usher or other official.[1]

Thus wrote Jean de Joinville, St Louis' friend and biographer.

Jacques Le Goff has called St Louis 'the most central of the great figures of Christianity of the 13th century'.[2] It is often uncertain, when reading accounts of St Louis, whether religion or rule is the main topic. It is hardly our task to judge his saintliness, yet Louis' belief imbued his whole outlook on life and the nature of his kingship. He saw himself as a Christian first and a king second. Any account of Louis' career has one great bonus and one important omission. The bonus is the narrative of Jean de Joinville, a personal account by a layman close to the king with few equals in the Middle Ages. The negative, at present, is the lack of a modern edition of the acts of Louis IX.

THE MINORITY

St Louis was the second son of Louis VIII and Blanche of Castile, born at Poissy on 25 April, probably in 1214. He liked to be called Louis of Poissy, because he was baptized there.[3] His father ascended the throne in 1223 but died in 1226. St Louis' older brother, Philip, died in 1218 so Louis IX succeeded at the age of 12, with his mother at the head of government. Blanche was the daughter of Alfonso VIII of Castile and Eleanor of England. She married in 1200, as part of a peace agreement. The elderly counsellors of Louis VIII wanted her to head the government though she was not called regent, except in modern accounts. Dark haired, fiery tempered, pious, she treated the task as a mission. The regency continued until 1235. Louis remembered his grandfather and referred to things Philip Augustus said to him which he clearly took to heart.

The minority was expected to be disastrous, a weak moment for the monarchy – 'unhappy is the land whose king is a child' – and this was to be a lengthy minority.[4] In the 14th century the age of majority would be set at 14. Both Philip I and Philip II took over government at 14. The length of St Louis' minority was exceptional. It was not due to incapacity but the domination of his mother. She proved a capable ruler and helped make his reign a success. Minority was a tricky time, often marked by rebellion and disturbance. Louis respected his mother and made no overt effort to displace her. The minority also benefited from the experience of his early officials, including Guérin, Bartholomew de Roye and Jean de Nesle – who had all worked for Philip Augustus.

Louis did not simply yield to his mother's or anyone else's demands. There was no doubt that he was the king. He was crowned at Reims – though the ceremony was conducted by the bishop of Soissons during a vacancy at Reims. There were notable absentees, including the counts of La Marche, St-Pol and Brittany. The count of Champagne set out but was kept away by Blanche. Louis was consecrated in 1226 and received homage from his vassals in 1227. Coronation was a religious rite that included anointment with the sacred oil from St-Remy. No king made more effort to keep his coronation promises: to protect the church, to give peace and justice and to defend the Catholic faith. The consecration contained a degree of mysticism, endowing the king with powers verging on the magical. He was believed to have the power to cure by touch, notably scrofula.

Artistic works show Blanche and the king together, but it is Louis who holds the symbols of kingship. Even in the minority he sometimes asserted his will. No one could overrule his religious policy, not his mother, the pope, or the nobles. We must ignore the over-simple view of Louis as under his mother's thumb. The truth is rather that he respected her, with some reason, and began gradually to work with her before taking over himself. The minority regime has reasonably been called 'co-royalty'.[5] Acts were noted under the two royals together. Louis married at 20 in 1234 and gradually became the senior partner in royal rule. Blanche was never altogether sidelined by her son, who appointed her to control government during his first crusade.

The chronicler Salimbene described Louis as slim with the face of an angel and the eyes of a dove. He was brought up strictly, beaten if necessary. He could read Latin and befriended scholars. His upbringing had a strong religious element that affected his whole character and life. The main source is the *Life of St Louis* by Jean de Joinville, born in c.1224 which began 'Je, Jehan, Sire de Joinville' and vowed that his account was true whenever he wrote about things he had seen.[6] Jean was a descendant of the counts of Joigny, hereditary seneschals of Champagne. His ancestor Stephen built the castle of Joinville on a hill over the town. Geoffrey III went to Palestine with the count of Champagne and became seneschal of Champagne. Geoffrey IV fought, died, and was buried at Acre. Geoffrey V, Jean's uncle, won the respect of Richard the Lionheart, and died crusading in Syria. Jean brought home his uncle's shield. His father Simon inherited the lordship on Geoffrey V's death. Jean was related to the Brienne family, including John de Brienne king of Jerusalem defeated in Egypt in 1219, and Walter de Brienne captured at Gaza in 1244 to die in prison. Jean married Alice of Grandpré in c.1239. He lived through the reigns of six kings to the great age of 92, dying on Christmas Eve 1317. His tomb in the chapel at Joinville was destroyed during the Revolution in 1793; neither castle nor chapel survives.

Jean de Joinville first saw the king when they were both young men, the king some 10 years older. Joinville was 17 and squire to Theobald IV of Champagne. He attended the knighting of Alphonse of Poitou at Saumur, when Louis wore a dark blue satin tunic and a cotton cap more suited to an old man. Joinville became Louis' companion on crusade, a councillor and a friend. He told of the king sitting so close that their robes touched. When Joinville ran out of money in the Holy Land and was in desperate straits, the king rescued him with a money fief in return for homage. The chronicle is more intimate than the average medieval account. It is highly supportive of the king and must be balanced by other opinions, but it gives a valuable personal view. Joinville became seneschal of Champagne. He opted out of Louis' final crusade to Tunis. After the king's death Queen Joan of Navarre, wife of Philip IV, asked Jean to write his account of Louis, though she died before it was completed. He proved to be 'an exceptional witness'.[7] As a layman, a knight, and one who fought alongside Louis, he was a close eyewitness. The novelty of the account becomes clear when one considers the rarity of literate laymen until this time. Jean was also a man of sensibility and occasionally waxes poetic, as when describing the musicians of the prince of Antioch blowing their curved horns like 'the song of swans rising from the lake'.[8] He began writing in the Holy Land but was in his 80s before completing the work in 1309.

By all accounts the women in St Louis' life had a strong influence on him. Some believe that he was dominated by his mother. It is rather the case that Louis was a strong character who respected his mother. He grew up under her wing but was never entirely dominated. They reigned together in amity. Having taken over the reins of government, Louis chose his mother to exercise regency during his absence on crusade. It is suggested that Blanche delayed Louis' marriage in order to retain power, which is possible but conjectural. Blanche arranged the marriage to Margaret of Provence that caused difference between mother and son.

Louis' marriage was celebrated at Sens on 27 May 1234. Payments were made for six trumpeters and a minstrel. It was a late date for the king to marry, considering the importance of producing an heir. Margaret was in many ways a good choice, the eldest daughter of Raymond Berengar V count of Provence. At the time of the marriage she was 12. Raymond had produced two sons but both died. He had four surviving daughters. The significance of their possible inheritance was clear. All four became queens, two marrying French husbands and two English. Margaret's sisters were Eleanor who married Henry III and became queen of England, Sanchia who married Henry's brother Richard of Cornwall and became Queen of the Romans, and Beatrice who married Louis' brother Charles of Anjou and became Queen of Naples and Sicily. Louis' marriage

proved a success in broad terms, though it led to coolness between mother and
wife. Joinville described the extraordinary situation between the three. The young
couple favoured the palace at Pontoise because Louis' room was above his wife's
and they could meet on the communicating spiral staircase, or go unseen to each
other's room. When Blanche approached, servants were instructed to knock with
rods so she would not find them together![9]

The marriage made a restrained start. Louis refrained from sexual relations
for three nights to emulate the three nights of Tobias in the apocryphal *Book of
Tobias*. During the first six years, so far as we know, the marriage was childless.[10]
There were rumours that Margaret was barren but between 1240 and 1260 the
couple produced 11 children. On the birth of his first child, the bishop of Paris
consoled Louis on having a girl rather than a son and heir. Seven of the children
survived Louis, four of them sons. The main point of the marriage was achieved
and the succession secured. The link with the family of Raymond-Berengar had
other significance for the Capetians. It added to their direct interest in the south
following the Albigensian Crusade, with royal lands on the Mediterranean for the
first time – 'a new frontier' – making 'a fundamental transformation'.[11]

Louis' outlook was fashioned by his age, when the new mendicant orders
appeared, and Christians came to believe they must examine their consciences
and make confession. From 1215 the papacy declared annual confession to
be obligatory – Louis insisted on weekly confession for himself. A new form
of individualism appeared – a new concept of human personality. Louis was
strongly influenced by those around him and his character was formed during the
minority. His religious interests were soon apparent. He was devout and pious,
in line with paternal and maternal family traditions. He took up his father's wish
to found an abbey. The Capetians had always favoured monastic orders. Philip I
had been buried at Fleury-sur-Loire and Louis VII at Barbeaux. Louis IX acquired
land at Cuimont and built the house of Royaumont, himself carrying stones to
assist the builders and encouraging his knights to do likewise. It became a house
of the new Cistercian order with which Louis formed a strong link.

During the minority St-Denis lost its relic of the Holy Nail, supposedly one
of the nails that pinned Christ to the cross. According to William de Nangis, a
monk of St-Denis, the nail was kept in a vase and brought out for pilgrims to
kiss. On February 28 1232 it went missing. The chronicler said it had fallen out
but it may have been stolen. What is interesting is Louis' reaction. He said he
would rather have his best city destroyed than lose the nail and advertised the
loss in Paris with criers in the streets. He offered a reward of 100 *livres*. The nail
was recovered through a miracle, so we are told.

Another relic story concerned the nephew of Baldwin I of Constantinople,
shortly to become Baldwin II, who came to France in 1237 seeking aid for
Byzantium. News arrived that the impoverished barons of Constantinople
planned to sell the 'original' crown of thorns for which Venice put in an offer.
Louis was most interested and made his own bid. He pressured the barons of
the Latin Kingdom and the merchants of Venice to give way, which the latter did

on condition the crown pass through Venice. Louis had it brought by sea and went to receive it at Villeneuve l'Archevêque in 1239. He and his brother Robert, barefoot in shirts, carried the relic in its container accompanied by knights and onlookers. The crown rested overnight in the cathedral at Sens and was taken to Paris by boat. The brothers went with it, bringing it into the city. Louis developed a craze for collecting relics. The most coveted examples came from Constantinople, including part of the True Cross, the Holy Sponge and the head of the Holy Lance. Louis had the royal chapel rebuilt as the Ste-Chapelle which was completed and consecrated in 1248 to house his growing collection of relics.

St Louis' reign has been seen as a golden age in French history. There was economic prosperity and the development of new technology, such as the mills at Bazacle on the Garonne.[12] Some recent historians have questioned an over-optimistic attitude to the period. Duby suggests it is a case of 'memory deceived', that life was fine for some but also a time of epidemics, famines and 'the impoverishment of the lower classes'.[13] In the later reign one sees the beginning of a decline that would strike home fully in the 14th century.

Louis' minority was problematic for the monarchy but Blanche proved equal to the challenge. The major threat came from a coalition of nobles unhappy with the foreign queen. A novel method of criticism appeared in a pamphlet campaign against her. The dissidents included Philip Hurepel, Philip II's illegitimate son. He had been fairly treated by his father and his half-brother Louis VIII, given a good marriage and made count of Boulogne. The papacy recognized his legitimacy and in the minority he received further lands. His motives for opposition are not clear but probably included ambition and jealousy stoked up by those preferring an adult king.

Other dissident nobles were Peter Mauclerc, Raymond of Toulouse and Hugh of Lusignan. Peter Mauclerc was count of Brittany, a strongly independent principality. Raymond VII of Toulouse had lost lands and power in the Albigensian Crusade. Hugh de Lusignan was count of La Marche, his loyalty divided between France and England. Potentially the most dangerous opponent was Theobald IV count of Champagne whose family held lands either side of the demesne. Theobald had deserted Louis VIII at the siege of Avignon, claiming his 40-day service had been completed. Now in the minority he became a royal ally, some suggest because he was having a love affair with Blanche. We shall never know the truth. Blanche brought him back into the royal fold but whether for personal or other motives we cannot know. The rumour made a good topic for contemporary poets and scandalmongers. An unreliable tale told by the Minstrel of Reims was that Blanche, to prove she was not pregnant by Theobald, appeared before an assembly of barons and bishops. She removed her mantle and stood before them naked, saying 'look at me everyone, who can say I am with child?' while showing herself before and behind.[14] It is a tale told too often about women to accept as true.

Blanche's success in winning over Theobald was a blow to the dissidents. Theobald's former allies were annoyed and attacked him in a private war. Blanche organized a rescue operation and the hostile nobles submitted. It was her greatest success in the minority. Her son never forgot her achievement, or the support she received from the citizens of Paris. The death of Philip Hurepel in 1234 lessened the threat. The inheritance of the kingdom of Navarre from his uncle by Theobald also reduced problems. To keep Navarre, Theobald gave up the counties of Blois, Chartres and Sancerre. Jordan has suggested that one reason for Theobald's change of heart was that to protect his new kingdom he needed Louis as an ally against England. Henry III of England also posed a threat to Louis. The loss of most of the Angevin Empire was still resented, and hopes of reversing the defeat persisted. Henry had aggressive intents but not the military capacity to go with them. His first invasion of 1231–32 was easily fended off.

By 1235 Louis IX moved smoothly into the position warmed for him by his mother Blanche. He was noted for his piety and seemed 'an ideal sovereign'.[15] The role of Blanche is stressed during the minority but most historians agree that Louis was more than a figurehead. His ability to control affairs while remaining in the background had been demonstrated.

THE ESTABLISHMENT OF ROYAL POWER BEFORE THE CRUSADE

The Capetian dynasty by the 13th century was a major power in Europe. The conquests of Philip Augustus and Louis VIII brought new territories under royal control and increased resources. The Angevin Empire had been diminished, its territories in France reduced to Gascony. The powerful northern county of Flanders had been brought under royal supervision. Burgundy was held by Capetian relatives. Kings who had been little more than princes with a demesne around Paris and Orléans, now rivalled the foremost rulers of Christendom.

There had been little time to assimilate this expansion. Louis VIII's reign was unexpectedly brief. The problems of a minority made assimilation difficult. Perhaps Louis' greatest achievement was to achieve this by the end of his reign. We may agree that 'for the first time in the Capetian period the king's power was felt throughout the realm'.[16]

There was a serious problem to resolve in Flanders where Countess Joan, widow of Count Ferrand, died in 1244. She left Flanders to her younger sister Margaret, whose first husband was Bouchard d'Avesnes, the *bailli* of Hainault. Joan had the marriage annulled in 1216, though they had two sons, John and Baldwin. In 1223 she married William of Dampierre, a cadet of the house of Champagne, producing three further sons, whom she favoured over her earlier offspring. The sons of the second marriage claimed to be the only legitimate offspring, those of the first marriage that they were the eldest. Louis tried to settle the problem by dividing the lands between the two families. In 1246, with the approval of the papal legate, Louis ruled that Hainault should go to the Avesnes, and Flanders (the greater inheritance) to the Dampierres. Margaret favoured the latter and so did Louis. The decision meant that less than a third of the lands went to the Avesnes, and they had reason to feel discontented. Margaret recognized William of Dampierre as count of Flanders and he went on the Sixth Crusade, returning in 1250. He died in a tournament in 1251. Margaret then, keeping to Louis' decision, recognized William's younger brother Guy as count of Flanders.

An added difficulty came from Hainault being imperial territory and needing imperial agreement to the arrangements. Frederick II recognized the claims of the Avesnes brothers. In 1249 the papacy complicated the situation by recognizing the Avesnes as legitimate. Margaret confused it further by refusing to recognize John d'Avesnes as count of Hainault. The attempt of Guy of Dampierre with the aid of his brother John to enforce this led to his defeat at Walcheren in 1253. The brothers were imprisoned by the count of Holland.

With Louis in the Holy Land, Margaret appealed to his brother, Charles of Anjou, for help – promising *him* Hainault (though it was hardly hers to give) in return for his defence of the Dampierre claim to Flanders. Charles, the royal *'enfant terrible'*, rushed in wherever there were territories to gain.[17] At this critical point Louis returned from crusade, summoned his brother to Paris and issued the *Dit* of Péronne in 1256. He repeated his former decision that Hainault should be held by the Avesnes and Flanders by the Dampierres. Margaret sold Hainault and used the money to ransom the Dampierre brothers. Baldwin now held Hainault and made peace with Margaret. Louis pressed her to compensate Charles of Anjou for his losses. The contenders all swore permanent peace but there remained much resentment to France in Flanders despite Louis' efforts to sort out an awkward situation.

Royal control of the south followed in the wake of the Albigensian Crusade. Louis VIII had completed the northern conquest of the south. Royal rights and claims were enforced. Raymond VII of Toulouse believed himself the victim of the crusade and rebelled during the minority. In 1229 an agreement was reached, the crown taking some lands from Toulouse, but leaving Raymond with considerable territory. He remained dissatisfied and the invasion of France by Henry III provoked a new rebellion.

Louis IX finally crushed the Cathar heresy. After the murder of two royal inquisitors at Avignonet in 1242, Louis ordered action. Montségur was a stronghold in the Pyrenees, 12 miles east of Foix. Raymond VII besieged it in 1241 but abandoned the attempt. It became the last refuge of the Cathars, though the garrison troops were not heretics. When Louis intervened, Raymond VII submitted to the king. In May 1243 Hugh d'Arcis, seneschal of Carcassonne, besieged Montségur for Louis. The defenders resisted energetically, women operating stone-throwing engines. Against them the bishop of Albi took charge of a trebuchet. A traitor let in the attackers and Basque troops scaled the difficult approach to knife the guards. They captured a tower but it was several weeks before the garrison surrendered, on 2 March. The heretics were faced with the option of recanting or execution. On 16 March 200 Cathars were burned on a great pyre at the foot of the castle hill.

In the subsequent agreement, Raymond vowed to go on crusade. He died in 1249, when embarking for the East. Louis' brother Alphonse married Raymond's daughter Joan, who inherited Toulouse. Louis IX became the first Capetian with lands on the Mediterranean coast as well as real power in the Midi. The influence of the counts of Toulouse had been diminished and never fully recovered. Alphonse, through his marriage, took over the county of Poitou. On the death of Alphonse and his wife in 1271, the county became royal demesne.

The counterpoint of royal advance was a diminution of baronial power. Only a century before, the dukes of Normandy and Aquitaine, the counts of Flanders, Toulouse, Anjou, Poitou and Champagne had been virtually independent lords with almost sovereign power. Now no prince could match the king. Normandy had become royal demesne. The remaining princes were more closely bound to the king, giving homage, their sphere of action much restricted. Louis exercised authority over the whole kingdom. *The Book of Justice* maintained 'all things are in the king's hands'. Local customs were defined in royal favour, with allodial land as well as feudal fiefs subject to the king.

A major benefit from the increase in royal power was an improvement in law and order throughout the realm. Louis sought to end private war – in general he opposed war between Christians. He demanded a 40-day cooling off period before any baronial conflict and made himself the arbiter of disputes, as over Flanders. Louis also commanded there should be no tournaments for three years or baronial conflicts for four years.

Louis IX stressed fair government and sought to give justice. This clearly came from personal belief. On one occasion he might have benefited from a dubious charter granting the county of Dammartin to Renaud de Trie.[18] The seal was broken and incomplete. Louis, with more care than the average ruler, asked to see an old seal to check that what remained was correct. The royal legs remained and matched. He decided that it had been a genuine document and allowed it to stand – against royal interest.

Louis tried to correct royal administration by righting wrongs committed by his agents, and much needed correction. Royal officials had become entrenched in their localities, making office hereditary and abusing their powers. In 1247 Louis set up an investigation to uncover wrongs and provide redress. His enquêteurs were friars and clerics who treated the task seriously. Some wrongs were minor, such as officials who purloined kitchen utensils for their wives, but there were more important cases too. No longer would royal agents be easily able to get away with corruption.

Louis' intentions were underlined by an incident as he journeyed south for the crusade. He followed the Rhône to La Roche-de-Glun whose castellan, Roger de Clérieu, was acting like a brigand, charging toll on all travellers, threatening to kill anyone who refused. Louis, as a pilgrim, refused to pay the toll, so Roger seized some of his men as hostages. The king besieged the castle, which was taken and demolished. Possibly Roger had a right to exact some payment but Louis believed that pilgrims and crusaders were exempt. His action against a recalcitrant subject was firm and effective.

Louis failed to find many allies for the crusade outside of France. Most

European rulers, including Frederick II and the kings of Aragon and Castile, were engaged in their own concerns. Only a few English knights gave any military support. Nevertheless Louis raised a large force from France. He set off in a novel manner, from a new base on the south coast. Louis bought land on the shore and constructed a new port at Aigues-Mortes, 'one of the most remarkable urban achievements of medieval France'.[19] For speed the ramparts were built of wood, and only the Tour de Constance in stone. Louis built up a fleet, including ships bought from Italian cities and Marseille. His demands for wood led to the stripping of some regions. A few years later at Alès the young men could not find enough wood for torches for traditional wedding night ceremonies. Louis organized supplies of food, wine, and other necessities. His financial arrangements with Templars and Italians later allowed the crusade to extricate itself from a desperate position.

THE SIXTH CRUSADE AND LOUIS' STAY IN THE HOLY LAND

Louis' devotion to Christ and the church made him a fervent crusader. In 1244 he was seriously ill at Pontoise Abbey and his death was anticipated – the women wanted to cover his face, believing him dead. While ill Louis had a vision: 'my spirit has long been over the sea and if God wishes it my body will follow and conquer the land from the Saracens'.[20] He made a vow to crusade if he recovered. It was not a popular decision; many believed a king's first priority should be the government of his realm. The fears over sea journeys, health, and the dangers of a long absence, were arguments used against Louis. His beloved mother opposed him, as did his counsellors, suggesting that a vow made when ill need not be observed. Even the papacy was not keen on the crusade. Innocent IV wanted Louis in the west to counter Frederick. Despite the pressure, Louis' determination never wavered.

Louis also had to consider the failures and dangers of crusading. Louis VII's Second Crusade ended in humiliation and disaster at Damascus. Philip Augustus had been at the taking of Acre on the Third Crusade but had become ill. Louis VIII had died pursuing the Albigensian Crusade. These precedents only determined Louis to do better. He respected his grandfather and wanted to revive the reputation of the French monarchy on crusading. In 1248 Louis made preparations for his crusade, including arrangements for government in his absence under his mother, Blanche. Louis took the cross with his three brothers and many nobles, including Jean de Joinville. On 12 June 1248 Louis went to St-Denis to receive the oriflamme. He was also handed a pilgrim's scrip and staff. Louis' mother said if he went she would be 'as miserable as if she had seen him dead'.[21] Blanche had consistently opposed the crusade and fainted when Louis bade her farewell.

Louis' preparations were careful and detailed. Supplies, arms and armour, transport, bases for the journey, money – all were worked out in detail. There was enthusiasm as well as criticism for the venture. Many crusaders were volunteers, including Jean de Joinville. Louis may have put pressure on his brothers but they shared some of his enthusiasm – Robert, Alphonse and Charles all took the vow. Louis did pressure some barons to go, notably those who might cause trouble in his absence, including Raymond Trencavel and Peter of Brittany. In the event fewer rebels went than Louis had intended, partly because some died first. Some went on crusade to fulfil penalties placed upon them by the church. The only aid from outside France came from a few English, Scots and Italians. Although Louis' army was almost entirely French in composition, its size was considerable, with 2,500 knights and 15,000 in total – even if Peter Mauclerc thought them 'rabble'.[22] They were actually well equipped. Alphonse of Poitiers' force included archers and crossbowmen. Joinville described his sadness at leaving behind two children and his 'lovely castle'.[23] He took 10 knights, and there were 1,000 from his region (Champagne).

Louis set out from Aigues-Mortes. Previous kings had to rely on ports not under their own control. The building of a new port made Louis more independent. Embarkation and sailing was planned more effectively. The land for the new port was purchased from Psalmodi Abbey. By 1239 the construction of the port was sufficiently advanced for the Barons' Crusade to depart from there, including Theobald IV and Hugh of Burgundy. In 1248 Aigues-Mortes was the main port for Louis' departure. It was not ideal as it tended to silt up but it proved useful since Narbonne and Montpellier were unsafe assembly points thanks to the attitudes of the count of Toulouse and the king of Aragon. Some of Louis' men left from Marseille and Genoa, but Aigues-Mortes was his own choice.

The Sixth Crusade showed a change in crusading aims. To dominate the Holy Land it was necessary to deal with powerful neighbouring Muslim states. The rulers of the Kingdom of Jerusalem saw Egyptian sultans as the main threat. Christians derived hope from the emergence of the Mongols, whose expansion altered the political pattern of the region. There were also fears of Mongol advance to the west. In 1241 they invaded Poland, returning in 1259. Louis told his mother, 'if they attack us, we shall repulse them'.[24] On the other hand Louis shared hopes of alliance with the Mongols against the Muslims, and of their conversion to Christianity. These hopes would be dashed but in 1248 they were alive.

The 13th century saw a modification of Christian ideas about how to relate to other religions, moving away from crusades and destruction towards peaceable relations, missionary expeditions, and conversion. There were efforts to build a relationship with the Far East. In 1267 Charles of Anjou and James I of Aragon sent ambassadors to the Mongols and Louis sent two embassies to the Great Khan, exchanging letters, presents and views. Louis assumed the mantle of the leading Christian ruler in the west. From William de Rubrouk, who reached Khan Mongka in Mongolia, we gain some idea of the initial impact: 'I had the impression that I was entering another world.' He described the life of the khan with his 26 wives, each owning a great house. He described Karakorum and its palace and met a woman from the west called Pascha who had been captured in Hungary and was now married and settled in the east. During the crusade, hopes of conversion diminished. While returning from crusade, Louis learned that the khan expected Christian allies to be his subjects, which Louis could not accept. He returned to France a wiser and sadder king.

Louis aimed his first crusade against Egypt. In 1244 the Khwarismian Turks and the Egyptians defeated the Franks and their allies and kept Jerusalem. Louis assembled 25,000 men and departed from Aigues-Mortes. He embarked on 25 August; his fleet landed in Cyprus on 17 September. Joinville was amazed at the barrels of wine and hills of wheat piled in the fields by the sea. He remembered the sea covered with sails. Fears of sailing through the winter led to a long stay on the island. Louis did not leave until 30 May 1249. After suffering a storm, only half the fleet reached Egypt, to be shot at by archers so only smaller boats could beach. The knight Plonquet jumped into a longboat but missed and drowned. Louis was angered by the attacks on his men and in his armour leapt into the sea. He waded ashore crying 'Montjoie' (the name of his ship), leaving others to follow. The French fixed their shields point down in the sand and resisted charges by Turks shooting shortbows from horseback 'to the rear as well as to the front'.[25]

In June Louis besieged Damietta. The Muslims used Greek Fire and fire-bolts like 'stars falling out of heaven'. Damietta fell on 5 June but attacks continued on the French camp. There was a lengthy delay before Alphonse of Poitiers arrived. Louis finally moved towards Cairo on 20 November. He claimed victory in the Nile delta on 9 February 1250 but it was a Pyrrhic victory. He camped between two branches of the Nile with the enemy on the other side of the Thaneos. Louis in a gold helmet flourished his German sword. The crusaders were full of hope, spirit and chivalrous bluster. The count of Soissons told Joinville, 'by God's bonnet you and I shall yet talk in ladies' chambers of this day's work'.[26] Louis tried to build a causeway over the river but the enemy dug holes at the far end so that no progress was made. Walter d'Ecurey suggested they should pray on hands and knees, which they did. Joinville described flying dragons – Greek Fire thrown in containers like vinegar barrels, leaving a tail the length of a spear and sounding like thunder.[27]

The causeway was abandoned. A Bedouin was brought in by Hubert of Beaujeu and, for pay, showed them a ford. The first part was deep and the horses had to swim. They waded to the far bank and beat off a force of waiting Turks. Louis' brother Robert of Artois ignored the plan and, despite protests, rushed into Mansurah where he was captured and killed – the whole enterprise undermined. Louis fought hard to hold his ground. Joinville was unhorsed, knocked flat and ridden over. He found a padded Saracen jerkin to protect himself and says he was wounded only five times by arrows![28] Although the king and Joinville were among those who acquitted themselves well, it was not true of all the crusaders. Joinville refused to name men who shamefully fled over the bridge. The Christian camp came under attack and Joinville was woken at night by the cry 'to arms!' The Master of the Temple, who had lost an eye in the earlier fighting, now lost his other eye and died. In March the French retreated and were defeated at Fariskur by 'overpowering numbers'. Many were killed and Louis was captured. Joinville described the terrible sense that death could come at any moment as the Saracens chose to kill or leave alive at a whim.[29]

Louis, like many others, became seriously ill. Joinville described the river filled with corpses, men with dry skin, black and brown spots, gums rotting (a fatal sign), and nosebleeds. Later dead flesh had to be cut away from the gums causing screams of pain 'like women in the pains of childbirth'. Joinville blamed it on eating eels from the river, but it was probably scurvy.[30] Louis suffered from chronic diarrhoea and a slit had to be made in his breeches. He probably had scurvy and dysentery, his teeth fell out and he became white and frail. Louis promised a large sum to ransom his men and agreed to surrender Damietta. The sultan demanded the king as a hostage. He was advised to return to Damietta by galley, as Joinville did, but though ill said 'he would never abandon his people'. They carried Louis into a house and laid his head in the lap of a Parisian woman. The surviving crusaders, mostly ill, surrendered.

Joinville, badly wounded, was captured trying to reach Damietta by water. His crew converted to Islam to save their lives. Joinville was offered a choice between conversion and beheading. He refused to convert but was spared. During his captivity Louis was offered freedom at the cost of conversion and was threatened with torture by the 'bernicles' and death. This instrument consisted of two planks with teeth between which the victim's legs were placed while someone sat on the top, driving in the teeth and breaking the legs in several places. This was repeated after three days.[31] Louis refused to convert but the threat was not carried out. Eventually terms were agreed.

Louis' captivity did not last long. His wife escaped and heard of his capture three days before the birth of another child, John-Tristan. An 80-year-old knight held her hand through the birth and promised to cut off her head rather than let her be captured. She recovered and raised the ransom of 500,000 *livres tournois*. The first instalment of 200,000 *livres* was paid and on 6 May the king was freed. The crusade had been a disaster, arguably greater than that of Louis VII. It was followed by the abandonment of Damietta, the crusade's only gain. The cost of the expedition is reckoned at 1,537,540 *livres*, mostly paid by the clergy and towns of France.[32]

Many crusaders returned home, including the king's brothers. Louis said he ordered them to leave but others said he was annoyed at their departure.[33] Joinville was one of the few who stayed on. The agreement was not entirely kept. Some sick Christians were killed. On the way to Damietta the galleys were attacked and Joinville was locked in the hold, but again survived. Louis had trouble raising the ransom and Joinville made up the difference by seizing the amount required from the Templars – as a 'loan'. Some of Louis' men tried to cheat the enemy of 10,000 *livres*, though the king protested. Joinville stood on the foot of the man who admitted cheating and made him say it was a joke. Seemingly the Saracens *were* cheated out of the full amount.

Louis' most positive contribution came from his decision to stay in the Holy Land after his release in 1250. Most crusaders returned home but Louis was absent from France for six years, a long gap in any reign. He wanted to improve the defences of the Holy Land and joined in the building by carrying baskets of earth. He spent much on the fortifications of key strongholds at Acre, Caesarea, Jaffa and Sidon – spending a further 100,000 *livres*. This work entailed holding off Saracen attacks.

It was news of his mother Blanche's death that decided Louis to return home. She died on 27 November 1252 but Louis only learned of it the following spring at Sidon. He spoke to no one for two days. He finally embarked at Acre and sailed on 25 April 1254. The journey was eventful. His ship hit a sandbank off Cyprus when four fathoms of keel were carried away. Louis refused to leave the ship and abandon 800 men. The storm required five anchors to secure the ship. Joinville warned against being in mortal sin in a ship as you might wake at any time at the bottom of the sea. He described the religious processions on board to ask God's mercy. Louis wanted to go to Aigues-Mortes but was persuaded to land at Salins d'Hyères in Provence on 3 July. He travelled back via Aix-en-Provence, Clermont and Vincennes, returning the oriflamme to St-Denis on 7 September 1254. He was greeted warmly but the crusade had taken its toll. It was a sombre and determined king who set about governing his realm.

LOUIS' REFORMS AFTER THE SIXTH CRUSADE

Many historians have seen the crusade as a turning point in Louis' life and career. Jordan believes the crusade 'produced a profound crisis in his life'.[34] Louis had always been pious but now he was penitential, blaming the failures on himself and his government. He believed that 'all Christendom has been covered in confusion for my fault'.[35] Joinville suggests a move to an even more devout life after the crusade.[36] Louis told him he had found crusaders debauching in his tent (given Louis' attitudes this may have been relatively harmless activity) on which he blamed the failure of the crusade. Louis took even more note of mendicant counsel and initiated reforms with a strongly moral flavour. Evil must be rooted out, whether in the actions of his agents or in the conduct of his people. He set an example as an austere king who never wore flamboyant clothes.

Blanche had carried out her task of government well during Louis' long absence, though there had been problems, some yet unresolved – such as Charles of Anjou's involvement in Flanders. At Westkapelle on Walcheren in 1253 the Dampierres were defeated by their rivals and their leaders ended in captivity. Their champion, Margaret, appealed to Charles of Anjou, offering Hainault for his assistance. Blanche showed sympathy to the Pastoureaux movement (the shepherds' crusade) but when it turned to violence she allowed its suppression. They intended another People's Crusade and Blanche gave them supplies. With the emergence of the Master of Hungary as leader they became more hostile to stay-at-home nobles. Instead of crusading they went on the rampage – killing clerks and Jews. They attacked Bruges whose people fought back and scattered them. Some turned up on the beach at Shoreham where the locals killed them. After this violence the pastoureaux were repressed and the Master of Hungary was hanged.

The greatest difficulty, almost anarchy, came after Blanche's death in 1252. Alphonse of Poitiers was nominally in charge but was ill. Joinville wrote that in the king's absence France's 'condition grew constantly worse'.[37] Government was in the hands of a group of churchmen – the archbishop of Bourges and the bishops of Senlis, Évreux, Paris and Orléans. Their pro-papal activities provoked opposition. Royal revenue fell and Louis did not receive his usual income in 1253, causing difficulties. The need for his return was not so much to mourn his mother's death as to deal with the crisis caused by it.

Louis made reforms in administration but they were badly needed with local administration 'very inadequate'.[38] The main reforms were incorporated into the Great Ordinance, a series of ordinances issued over a period of time and collected in coherent form. On his return Louis began a series of tours, to appoint new officials and settle disputes. Some officials had become too entrenched in their locality despite earlier attempts to prevent it. Louis began in the south in 1254 and in the following years toured through the north, Normandy, the Loire and Flanders. Many petitions were received for justice, including wrongs against widows. These were dealt with and about 90% of the cases were decided in favour of the petitioner.[39] Louis spent the last six months of 1254 formulating this work. He extended the main orders to the whole kingdom, the first ordinance for the whole realm dating from his minority. The second made inquisitions by *enquêteurs* to check abuses, a permanent part of the system. Louis appointed new *enquêteurs* in the south, where about half were mendicants, and then followed the same practice in the north.

Several measures made for one region were extended to the realm. The most obvious point of this was that the conquests from the Plantagenets and the gains in the south were integrated into a united realm. In 1240 the southern rebel Raymond Trencavel was defeated. With the defeat of Henry III's invasion, Louis was able to settle Toulouse through the Peace of Lorris in 1243. The Cathars were crushed. Louis ruled through ordinance, and was 'to a degree the first Capetian legislator king'. Louis' measures covered the south as well as the north, making him 'the first king of all France'.[40]

Royal officials were expected to set an example. They must not blaspheme, resort to brothels, or enter taverns unless on journeys! They must treat the accused as innocent until proved guilty. They must not sell offices, accept gifts above a trifling amount, or take property without good cause. The Jews were penalized and usury was treated as a crime. Town centres were cleaned up and prostitutes not allowed to ply their trade near churches or cemeteries. Taverns were to be used only by travellers, not for drunken evenings. Gambling, including at chess, was prohibited.

As Louis toured France he made new appointments, notably of *baillis*. Average length in office was reduced. The inquisitions became regular along with other checks. Each new appointee was expected to check for abuse by his predecessor. Louis made efforts to enforce these measures – with some success.[41] *Baillis* could expect checks on their activities by their successors, by the enquêteurs, by regular audits and by the king on tour. Louis increased wage earning for officials, giving greater royal control. Hereditary succession among higher officials was virtually abolished. However the reforms were not 100% successful, especially among lower officials – such as sergeants, the target of most complaints.

The significance of Parliament grew because Louis wanted a government that provided final judicial decisions in a fair manner. Parliament was the king's court making judicial judgements. A major innovation was introduced in 1254 with the recording of acts of Parliament, the archive known as the *Olim* because it opened '*Olim homines de Baiona*'. These registers began in 1254, the year of Louis' return, the year of the Great Ordinance. The work of recording was begun in the 1260s and depended largely on the work of the *curia judicialis*. The records looked back to 1254 from an important decision of that year and their quality quickly improved.

National administration was provided through three major departments dealing with finance, documents, and justice. Royal counsellors – ecclesiastics, nobles, and professional administrators – headed the departments. Beneath them operated a new structure of local government through royal agents. Paris became the permanent centre for all aspects of government. Louis reorganized the administration in Paris. Royal authority in the city was challenged by other authorities, notably the bishop of Paris. The city controlled its own trade and crafts. The papacy claimed powers over the University of Paris, even dictating in 1219 that Roman or civil law could not be taught. But Louis kept a royal authority over all these aspects. The bishop remained nearly always a royal candidate or one acceptable to the king. The trades and the university realized the importance of royal protection and were nearly always loyal to the king.

From 1264 Louis intervened more in the control of Paris. Previously the city had no *prévôt*, now Louis appointed Stephen Boileau, a royal official, salaried by the king. He had experience as prévôt of Orléans and went on Louis' Egyptian crusade. He proved a good choice and a successful administrator. Taxes upon the citizens were reviewed and some abolished. Paris prospered. By 1250 its population stood at about 160,000, including 5,000 students.[42] Boileau's appointment brought Paris into the national pattern of administration. In all but title he was a *bailli* with broad control of the city's government – for the king. He was given a home in the Châtelet on the right bank of the Seine. The policing of Paris was also reformed; the existing forces (royal and mercantile) were brought under royal control and became more effective.

Louis took care over the quality of his officials. He inherited a weak position in local administration. The major local officials, about 20 in all, were too attached to their localities. Rebellions and difficulties distracted the monarchy from maintaining control. Louis sought to recover and improve royal authority. He revived the local inquests of Philip Augustus. Replacement of individuals, whether at fault or not, was an important means of restoring control and limiting agents' power.

Apart from restrictions upon local agents (*baillis*, seneschals, and *prévôts*), Louis appointed new counsellors – the clerks of chancery, the great officers of the household, the members of Parliament, and of his council. Louis wanted only suitable men. He issued regulations for their conduct, both in their public work and their personal conduct. He rooted out unsuitable men, organizing inquiries into his agents' work, and ordering major reshuffles in 1254–56 and 1264–66. *Baillis* were the main royal agents in the regions. They supervised the *prévôts*. The latter presented their accounts for audit in Paris and had to list gifts received, expenses on king's works, and wages paid by the king. The *baillis* were also checked, supervised by royal *enquêteurs* from 1247. Mendicants were often chosen for this work, touring the country to check corruption and inefficiency.

The king brought tighter control over taxation, not welcomed by all. There was criticism of the humble origins of some of his agents – 'sons of serfs' who 'judge free men and the fiefs of free men according to their own law'. For all Louis' efforts it must be accepted that his system did not always succeed. Joinville thought that during the Sixth Crusade the royal agents impoverished the people on his estates – a reason for not joining Louis' final crusade. The bishop of Lodève in 1255 claimed that royal agents were encroaching on church rights. There is little doubt that some of the criticism was aimed against the king and his increasingly centralized government. One of Louis' problems were the limitations of royal power. He was no absolute monarch. In all areas outside the demesne there were serious restrictions on what he could do; he had to rely on co-operation. The nearly independent apanages were a possible source of trouble though in practice the royal relatives co-operated with the king. The great principalities proved more of a threat. Louis insisted on many greater princes accompanying the Egyptian crusade to remove a threat at home during his absence.

Louis sought advice from a few personal acquaintances, including Simon Monpris de Brie a mendicant adviser who became keeper of the seal and later Pope Martin IV, Robert de Sorbon canon of Notre-Dame and founder of the famous college, Guy Foulcois later Pope Clement IV, and Louis' biographer Jean de Joinville. The Dominican Geoffrey de Beaulieu was Louis' confessor; the Franciscan St Bonaventure preached 19 sermons before the king in Paris; the Franciscan Odo Rigaud preached before Louis and conducted royal ceremonies. The king was attracted to the monastic life and mendicants were welcomed at court and used on embassies.

Louis gave France a more centralized administration, integrating the extended demesne – the basis of an increased and stable income. Normandy contributed a third of royal demesne income – the main source of royal income. There was a parallel increase from the extension of royal justice. The Templars played a part in guarding royal treasure and The Temple in Paris was the royal treasury. Louis introduced a recoinage in 1266, with new symbolic gold coins, and a new large *sol tournois* (silver shilling). He reduced the coinage to two main types of *livres*, the parisis and the tournois. He emphasized the dominance of royal coinage, allowing baronial minting to continue but restricting distribution to its own region. He tried to exclude from France the English sterling. He prohibited the copying of royal coins and introduced the écu in 1266, the first Capetian gold coin, modelled on eastern types. Louis stressed royalty and Christianity on his coins with the symbols of the fleur-de-lys and the cross, as well as a Christian inscription. His main achievement was to promote a national coinage at the expense of local and seigneurial competition.

A financial measure inspired as much by Louis' beliefs as by economic causes were the ordinances against usury of 1257–58. These followed the Ordinance of Melun which penalized Jewish usurers. It was in line with papal policy and that of Philip Augustus. One of the few royal duties Louis did not follow was that of protecting Jews. He shared the prejudices of his Christian contemporaries. The prohibition of usury was a measure against Jews because some of them profited from a practice supposedly forbidden to Christians, though commerce was practically impossible without loans and credit. Louis himself borrowed 100,000 *livres* from Italians in 1253. He saw usury as sinful and his ordinances condemned the Italian moneylenders, usually called Lombards. The expulsion of Jews for usury was extended to Lombards and Cahorsins in 1269. It should be noted that the definition of usury was more limited than historians usually realize and that, for example, a bill of exchange was not treated as usury. The Church recognized the right of lenders to cover their costs and it was accepted that penalties could be imposed for late repayment of loans.[43]

France prospered under Louis, though how far he was responsible is debatable – perhaps largely by maintaining peace and stability. He repeated earlier measures to keep the peace and renewed the prohibition of private war. He reserved the right to decide if war was justified. Apart from the crusades, Louis did not initiate war as an aggressor. There was continuous peace in the realm and on its frontiers from 1254, when he returned from the Holy Land, until his death in 1270 (and indeed until 1284). There is no doubt the country prospered economically as a result of peaceful times.

JUSTICE

Louis' attitude is summed up in his own aim to 'do justice to all men'. Joinville portrayed the king sitting under a great oak at Vincennes to give judgement to even the most humble of his subjects. After mass Louis would sit under the tree and invite his familiars to sit around. Then each person with a cause to be heard was led before him in turn. Duby has called this a 'fictitious image', yet it would be hard to find a better witness than Joinville. Joinville referred to appeals for Louis' personal judgements as 'pleadings at the gate'.[44] Louis ordered an enquiry into the judicial system in 1254 when corruption was investigated, leading to a purge of the judiciary.

Louis sought to modernize the judicial system. He wanted traditional 'judgements of God' to end, prohibiting ordeal by fire or water and trial by combat. In ending ordeal he followed the Fourth Lateran Council. Louis' ordinance of 1261 replaced it by an inquest requiring proof by witnesses, ordaining harsh penalties for false witnesses to make the new system work. Louis wished to end private war, believing that only just wars were permissible. He saw himself as the arbiter for France of what made a just war. In 1259 he ordered that his representatives in the south should temper justice with mercy and instructed them to treat accused persons as innocent until proved guilty. Louis believed that royal justice should protect the poor. In a dispute between a rich man and a poor man, the latter should have the benefit of doubt until the truth emerged. He tried to protect the weak, including women and the church, against nobles. He was too late to save the lives of three youths who crossed the path of Enguerrand de Coucy, but the crime was not ignored. Three young nobles from Flanders came to learn French under the abbot of St-Nicolas. In their spare time they hunted rabbits with bows but on De Coucy land. The baron had them hanged without trial. The abbot was among those who appealed to the king. Louis investigated and condemned De Coucy for acting without recourse to law. De Coucy claimed the right to be judged by his peers but Louis found that the land was not part of the barony. He wanted to imprison De Coucy in the Louvre but, after taking advice, imposed a large fine, extracted a promise to build chapels where the souls of the boys could be prayed for, and demanded a commitment to crusade for three years (which was not kept). Louis intervened to make Hugh duke of Burgundy deal with Anseri lord of Montréal-en-Auxois for exposing a priest to attack by bees. Another example was a case between an ordinary knight in Vendôme and Louis' brother, Charles of Anjou, who had imprisoned him. Louis investigated and decided in favour of the knight.[45]

Louis advised his agents to act with tolerance but he was not tolerant of those who ignored Christ's way. He hated any form of swearing. A guilty goldsmith in Caesarea was pilloried in shirt and drawers with pig's entrails around his neck. In 1255, against advice, Louis insisted on a severe punishment for a citizen who used the Lord's name in vain, having him branded with a hot iron on the lips. In another instance he showed no mercy to a noble adulteress who had encouraged her lover to kill her husband. She repented and others suggested Louis show mercy, but he had her burned to death in public.

Louis gave judgements around the realm as an itinerant king but justice in the shape of Parliament gained a permanent home in Paris. It met as the royal high court in the Palais de la Cité and made final decisions in judicial matters. The *Olim* records began under Louis – the first judicial archive. From the 1240s the royal archives were kept in the Ste-Chapelle. Local customs were now written down, for example by Pierre des Fontaines, and Philip de Beaumanoir – both with lawyers who were also *baillis*. Roman law, known better in the south and emerging from the law schools at Orléans, began to influence the north. Some of Louis' reforms stemmed from this, including inquisitions and the right of appeal.

TOWNS

Louis IX followed Capetian practice in allying with citizens against the nobility. The 'good' towns were wealthier than ever and powerful. Louis sought to ensure royal control over them as well as over his lords. Paris had become a great European capital of some 200,000 citizens. It was the home of government and possessed a university whose fame was increasing. Scholars were attracted to Paris from far afield and many noted Englishmen, for example, were educated and taught there.

Louis had close relations with two masters of the university. Robert de Sorbon was a clerk of humble origins from the Ardennes who was master of theology at the university. He was a familiar at Louis' court, a confessor to the king. Together they founded the college for poor students called the Sorbonne. Vincent de Beauvais joined the Dominican priory of St-Jacques in Paris and became subprior at Beauvais. Louis commissioned him to compile an encyclopedia of everything a good man needed to know. Its three main sections were on nature, science and history. Vincent's work was not original in content; he simply collected current knowledge – perhaps slightly old-fashioned knowledge – but the development of encyclopedias was a new genre and an achievement of the age. The production of works in French rather than Latin was another development. *Chansons* and *romans* blossomed, while French became the cultural tongue of Europe in the 13th century.

Paris witnessed much building and re-building, becoming an architectural model for other towns. It was the heart of Louis' building programme. The Sainte-Chapelle was built and Notre Dame rebuilt. The Ste-Chapelle was consecrated in 1248. St-Denis became the royal necropolis with royal tombs rearranged in a newly built home. St-Denis had been the burial place for most Merovingians but a gap occurred under the Carolingians. With the division of the Carolingian Empire, Paris became again the necropolis of the West Frankish kings and of the Capetians. Of the latter, only Philip I and Louis VII were buried elsewhere. Louis made clear that St-Denis was reserved for crowned kings and queens. Other royals, beloved as they might be, were buried elsewhere. Louis emphasized the point by creating effigies for the tombs. Sixteen statues were arranged in lines on either side of the enlarged transept, on one side the Carolingians, on the other the Capetians – underlining the continuity from one to the other. The tombs of his father and grandfather were particularly impressive. Louis added the Ste-Chapelle to the royal palace as well as homes for his library and the archives. To the north he built the '*salle sur l'eau*', which survived until 1865. Here was the small palace with the Bonbec Tower, the only surviving part of Louis' palace. Under Louis' new prévôt, Stephen Boileau, the administration of Paris came more clearly under royal supervision. From 1261–67 the *Livre des métiers* was drawn up, recording statutes of the Parisian gilds. The first part contained the statutes and customs. The second part dealt with trade and listed royal rights in the city.

The Capetians made good use of their alliance with the developing towns, recognizing communal aspirations in return for support. Louis referred to his 'bonnes villes' (by which he seems to have meant the major towns), which 'aided me against the barons when I was newly crowned'. The crown gained financially and militarily from the alliance. With the church the towns were the main source of finance for Louis' crusades. The communal movement was losing momentum and Louis sought rather to increase royal control directly. In 1260 he commanded that town accounts be submitted to royal audit, and in 1262 that town councils be renewed every year.

THE CHURCH

Louis has been said to exercise kingship 'like a priest'. He was canonized early, in 1297 – ironically by Boniface VIII who was to clash with his grandson. Most historians have supposed that the Sixth Crusade affected Louis greatly. On return from the Holy Land Louis was even more strongly influenced by friars, including the Spiritual Franciscan and 'madman of God' Hugh of Digne, who accepted the ideas of Joachim of Fiore. This was dangerous ground since the papacy condemned Joachimite ideas in 1256.

Le Goff however sees the later reign as simply a continuation of the early reign. Louis had always been pious. The crusade had some effect; it certainly affected his health, it undermined a rosy view of his place in God's plan – why had God permitted his failure in Egypt? There was no sudden conversion; if anything Louis' attitudes were confirmed and strengthened. He moved into the abbey of Royaumont for long periods, living a semi-monastic existence. He ate simply, drank sparingly and dressed in worn, drab clothes. He rarely smiled but gave much time to helping the poor and tending lepers. He fed 120 poor every day, welcoming 13 into his chamber and three to his table – where they were possibly disappointed at the basic fare.

Louis sought to translate his religious views into government policy, not always with success. He wanted to reform institutions and the ethos within which they operated. He ordered monks to 'destroy sin' and sought to reform the kingdom. He prohibited usury, ordering the expulsion of Italians as well as Jews. He banned games of chance and ordered that prostitutes be confined to ghettos. In his household he enforced punishments for swearing. He stopped his own brother, Charles of Anjou, from gambling at backgammon on board ship, scooping up the board and dice and throwing them into the sea. He banned the manufacture of dice. He attacked heresy, agreeing the massacre of Cathars at Montségur. Louis is presented as a merciful and kindly king but he was also a pious fanatic who believed in the severest punishments for sinners and heretics.

Louis respected the papacy but was not subservient, a contrast with his contemporary Henry III of England. A few examples will suffice to demonstrate Louis' attitude. He refused to act against Frederick II, despite papal encouragement and would not allow the papacy to interfere with royal rights over the church in France. In 1235, despite threats of excommunication, he maintained his position over the bishopric of Beauvais, enlisting support at St-Denis for a letter stating his position. He claimed that episcopal temporalities were under lay not ecclesiastical jurisdiction. Louis took the baronial rather than the papal view on the church role in secular jurisdiction. His response was sharp enough to be known as *The Protest of St Louis*. His ambassador proclaimed 'we are not children of bondwomen but of the free'.[46] He threatened to seize church wealth in France – albeit for the crusade. In general Louis defended his kingdom against papal interference, complaining about benefices going to absentees, and protesting at certain financial exactions. His bishops complained that those who died while excommunicated did not suffer financially, claiming their goods should be confiscated. Louis agreed on condition that he could be given proof of guilt. The bishops refused because they saw this would give the king jurisdiction – as Louis had clearly realized.

Louis was fortunate in living when the papacy was weak and French influence strong. The papacy needed support against Frederick II. Louis kept on good terms with individual popes. Innocent IV proved less co-operative but was followed by two French popes, Urban IV and Clement IV. Under Urban three of Louis' counsellors were made cardinals, one of whom became Clement IV. Louis' policy of defending the rights of the Gallican Church met with less opposition than would otherwise have been the case.

Louis was sincere, his belief powerful. When residing in abbeys he lived as a monk. Joinville described how he lived and introduced similar conduct in his own household. Louis once asked Joinville whether he would prefer to be a leper or in mortal sin. Joinville gave the wrong answer and the next day the king told him 'there is no leprosy as ugly as being in mortal sin'.[47] Yet Louis was more practical in his Christian conduct than Henry III of England. On one visit Henry accompanied Louis to the French Parliament. Every time they met a priest, Henry insisted on hearing mass, making them late. Next time they set out Louis ordered the priests to keep out of the way. On the positive side of Louis' Christian rule was his aid to the poor and needy. He encouraged, funded, and supported numerous institutions for the poor, disadvantaged, and ill, including a hospital for the blind and a House of the Daughters of God for former prostitutes.

Louis was a supporter of the religious orders, the Cistercians and mendicants in particular. He built and funded houses and frequently visited them. He trusted the mendicants to act for him whenever possible. They formed a majority of his *enquêteurs*, who investigated and corrected faults in local government. Mendicants acted on embassies and missions, often the most sensitive, such as to the Mongols. Mendicants became his confessors and featured prominently at court. A less praiseworthy role for them was as inquisitors. From 1233 the papacy set up the Inquisition in France. Louis gave it wholehearted support and employed mendicants for its activities. His hope was probably to convert heretics but the Inquisition became increasingly punitive. Its activities in the south led to the final drama of the Cathars, when the killing of inquisitors at Avignonet was followed by the slaughter at Montségur. From 1256, through Alexander IV, torture of the accused was permitted.

Louis supported various religious projects including church and monastic building. He financed some and encouraged others to do the same. He instituted a royal library, inspired by that of the sultan in Egypt, a collection of religious and philosophic works; he also studied the works in his collection. This was a great age in French architecture – and paralleled a golden age in the arts – poetry, literature, music, and art. The new Gothic script in handwriting accompanied the new architecture. Where the largest funds were available the most impressive structures could be built, with Louis a major patron. New houses such as Royaumont, new churches such as the Ste-Chapelle, belong to this age when new Gothic flourished, spreading from the Île-de-France. It produced structures of great beauty – higher, lighter, with flying buttresses and crossed ogives supporting magnificent vaults. It provided greater space for windows and allowed more use of stained glass. This was another art that reached its height now, as in the Ste-Chapelle, or at Chartres.

This was a great age for church building. The early interior Gothic work at St-Denis was in place by 1231. Notre-Dame in Paris was largely completed in 1245. The west front of Reims was built from 1244–50, Chartres was consecrated in 1260, Amiens in 1264. By about 1260 the new Gothic style was established and dominated architecture for a century. Many older buildings were renewed or extended. The new religious orders spread rapidly during Louis' reign and needed new buildings to accommodate them. By Louis' death there were 100 Dominican priories and twice as many Franciscan, 'the missionaries of French art'.[48] Louis financed various charitable buildings – for the poor, the ill, the blind and lepers. The Quinze-Vingts in Paris was for the blind. Louis attended the opening of the maison-Dieu at Compiègne and helped carry in the first impoverished sick patient. Louis' reign was important for military architecture, with work at Coucy, Angers, Boulogne, Provins and Aigues-Mortes. France also financed defences in the Holy Land, at Acre, Caesarea, Sidon, Krak des Chevaliers and Jaffa, as well as in Greece and Cyprus.

FOREIGN POLICY

It might be argued from crusading evidence that Louis lacked a good grasp of policy for remoter areas, though his relations with European powers were more successful. The generous agreements with England and Aragon were criticized by his fellow countrymen, but they brought peace for a generation and completed the formation of France as we know it.

Louis explained his policy in biblical terms as 'blessed are the peacemakers'; war was an evil to be avoided unless 'just' in the papal sense, and only then undertaken as a last resort. He tried to end private war in the realm and sought peace with his neighbours. He was, according to Jean Richard, 'a born arbiter', 'the greatest peacemaker that the 13th century had known'.[49] Louis was seen as the natural arbiter of international disputes. The major threat to France came from the Plantagenet Henry III, who still held Gascony and Guyenne. Henry sought to regain lost lands and twice invaded France. His first expedition came during the minority in 1231. Blanche's efforts added to the incompetence and ill health of Henry resulted in the latter's defeat and a truce in 1234. Louis was involved in the military campaign. Henry's main hope came from the dissident French nobles, Pierre Mauclerc and Hugh de Lusignan, but the alliance soon crumbled. The second invasion occurred in 1241 and seemed a greater threat. Henry allied with the king of Aragon and dissident French nobles. The major clashes occurred during 1242–43. Louis led the defence of his realm and attacked strongholds of Henry's allies, taking Moncontour and, after a 15-day siege, Fontenay-le-Comte in Saintonge. The English retreated to Taillebourg but failed to hold the bridge over the Charente, and Taillebourg surrendered. Henry retreated in panic to Saintes where Louis caught and defeated him. Henry blamed his allies for lack of support and fled at night to Bordeaux and Saintes surrendered. A new truce was agreed. Hugh de Lusignan sought pardon, given in return for certain major castles.

Louis had fended off the English invasions. Henry returned to Bordeaux in 1253 because of rebellion in Gascony, but with little hope of success against Louis. He accepted the French king's invitation to Paris for Christmas 1254, when the four sisters from Provence were reunited – Margaret and Beatrice married to Louis and his brother Charles; Eleanor and Sanchia married to Henry III and his brother Richard of Cornwall. The two pious kings got along quite well. Louis accompanied Henry to Boulogne and later sent him an elephant acquired from the sultan of Egypt. Louis now supported Richard of Cornwall's election as king of the Romans in 1257. From a position of friendship and strength Louis negotiated the treaty of Paris in 1259 which recognized the *status quo*. Henry accepted the loss of Anjou, Maine, Touraine, Poitou and Normandy but retained Gascony. Louis granted him lands in Limoges, Cahors and Périgueux. On the death of Alphonse of Poitiers Henry would receive part of Saintonge, and the Agenais and Quercy in Poitou if Alphonse's wife Joan died without children.

Louis' council complained that he was 'throwing away the territory'. Viewed from a distance one can see that recognition of the conquest of most of the Angevin Empire was worth a few grants. Henry also agreed to do homage for the lands he retained, recognizing the overlordship of the king of France. Louis claimed 'the great honour of having him as my vassal, which he was not before'.[50] In 1259 Henry performed homage in the garden of the royal palace in Paris. English hopes of recovering lost lands were not dead, and would be revived by Edward I and Henry V, but Louis had brought peace that lasted until 1293. Later rulers lacked his generosity and statesmanship.

A parallel agreement was reached with the king of Aragon in the 1258 treaty of Corbeil. The Spanish kingdom had claimed lands north of the Pyrenees, including Carcassonne and Foix. The king of Aragon, James I the Conqueror (1213–76), was born north of the Pyrenees at Montpellier. The French from the time of Charlemagne claimed lands south of the Pyrenees, establishing the Spanish March around Barcelona. In 1162 the count of Barcelona became king of Aragon. At the end of the 12th century Aragon gained the county of

Provence. These developments threatened the Capetian position in the south. The Albigensian Crusade and victory at Muret in 1213 restored French authority. Spanish rights north of the Pyrenees were now denied. As with England, Louis dealt from a position of strength but sought a fair settlement. After negotiation, the treaty of Corbeil was signed in 1258. Each agreed to make the mountains the frontier and hand over lands on the other side. An exception, not unlike the arrangement made with Henry III, was that James would keep Montpellier in return for homage. The fate of Montpellier and Roussillon was not finally settled until 1659. Marriage was agreed for Louis' son Philip to James' daughter Isabella, and took place in 1262. The similarity between the treaties of Paris and Corbeil suggests that Louis was pursuing a deliberate policy of allowing certain territories to be held by neighbouring powers in return for recognition of his overlordship and his possession of vital territories. The major consequence (and presumably aim) was a peace that was likely to last and more permanent boundaries with the Plantagenets and Aragon.

These treaties show Louis as a statesman, a view held then and now. Contemporary respect is shown by the occasions when his arbitration was sought in disputes. In 1246 Louis arbitrated a settlement between Flanders and Hainault. In 1264 he was asked to decide between the claims of king and barons in England. His response, the Mise of Amiens, favoured Henry III and condemned the baronial reform provisions. It has been said that Louis could not support baronial rebellion against a king though this may undervalue Louis' sense of justice. However, the barons ignored the ruling and civil war ensued, leading to Henry's defeat at Lewes. Louis continued to seek peace in England and supported the case for the return of Simon de Montfort's son to England, without success.

Louis' other major foreign involvement was in southern Italy. Normans had intervened there in the 11th century, becoming rulers of a new kingdom of Sicily in the 12th century. That kingdom fell to the German imperial family through marriage but Frederick II's descendants found control difficult. The papacy sought more co-operative rulers and wanted to end the combination of imperial power in northern and southern Italy. Louis took a position that threatened the Hohenstaufen, contrary to his normal moderate approach. He accepted the papal offer of Sicily for his brother. Charles of Anjou was crowned king of Sicily in Rome in 1265. In 1266 he led a crusade against Frederick II's descendants. Manfred was beaten and killed at Viterbo in 1266. After defeat at Tagliacozzo in 1268, Conradin was captured and executed. Charles assumed his position as king with papal approval. French control endured through Louis IX's reign. It is true that in 1282 the Sicilian Vespers ended French control but the episode demonstrated another side to Louis' foreign policy. Possibly one motive was to use Sicily as a base for crusade voyages.

Relations with the Holy Roman Empire were vital. Frederick II owed his throne to French support. He made things easier for Louis by devoting his energies to the conflict with the papacy and in Italy. For both rulers peace on their mutual frontier was desirable. Louis had opportunities to go to war with

Frederick; the papacy constantly sought his aid against the emperor. Louis equally consistently refused, and remained neutral. Louis' reward was the emperor treacherously informing the sultan of Egypt about Louis's preparations for the Sixth Crusade.

LOUIS THE KING

Let us sum up Louis' achievements and failures as a king. There was a significant increase in royal activity in France. This is true geographically, the king now ruling practically all the area we call France. Louis began to legislate for the realm rather than for regions, centralizing government. In judicial terms this is reflected in the development of Parliament, established in Paris. That city's significance increased as a capital and base for government. The great princes of the realm – for example Alphonse of Poitiers, Theobald V and Hugh of Burgundy – now needed a residence in the capital. Louis spent much time in Paris and added to its royal and ecclesiastical buildings. His local agents submitted their accounts in Paris.

It is fair to conclude with Richard that under Louis royal power 'assumed new dimensions'.[51] Jordan's comment that Louis' rule was essentially personal government is equally true. The delegations and representations were extensions of the king's views, attitudes and policies. Government by legislation was developing but the ordinance or *établissement* was still a royal command. The balance between royal and baronial power continued to move in favour of the king. Territorial control by royal relatives was important. The creation of apanages, a system sustained by Louis, had the possible dangerous consequence of overmighty barons and division of the realm, but in practice the loyalty of younger sons remained strong. Through marriages the whole kingdom came under family rule. Louis' brothers held great principalities at Anjou, Poitiers and Artois. Louis' children also made significant marriages – his son Louis to Yolande becoming count of Nevers, his daughter Isabelle to Theobald V king of Navarre.

Louis' reign soon seemed a golden age from the misfortunes that followed. The 14th century saw economic decline, serious epidemics whose climax was the Black Death, and the onset of the Hundred Years' War. How far was the golden age due to Louis? France was prosperous, partly because of royal financial policy and peacekeeping. Louis was a great diplomat who made vital frontier settlements with England and Aragon. His wisdom was recognized beyond France by the frequency with which he was asked to arbitrate. His success rate was not 100% but it was impressive. He also avoided involvement in the papal-imperial conflict, refusing to back either side entirely. He refused to provoke Frederick II despite papal encouragement, and despite his respect for the church.

There is however a need to balance Louis' achievements with his failures and incomplete successes. In the view of Jordan, Louis' sanctification has meant that commentators 'have exaggerated his achievements to the detriment of the earlier Capetians'.[52] Hagiographical works and those presenting him as a saint gloss over faults. Joinville was fond of Louis but mentions a few blemishes, notably lack of attention to his wife and children. In five years after leaving France Louis did not once talk to Joinville about his family – 'I do not think it was kindly so to be a stranger to his wife and children'. The chronicler noted the king's anger when asked for gifts – as when Joinville asked that a confiscated horse go to a poor knight and was refused.[53] Louis was authoritarian with his wife and others. He made the Master of the Temple renege on an agreement with an emir because Louis had not been consulted first – though his right to demand this is unclear. The Templar was forced to leave the Holy Land.

We note also that Louis' financial demands were considerable and had damaging effects. The crusade demands for armies and supplies were expensive, so were his own and others' ransoms. There were complaints from the church and towns over levies – other countries contributed little. Louis' expenditure in the Holy Land placed great pressure on the regency government. The problem was perhaps more political than financial but by 1253 Louis was not receiving what he needed. Joinville quoted Louis' comment that the treasury was 'drained to the dregs'.[54] Jordan suggests that Louis did make hitherto unrecognized efforts to restrict expenses at home to compensate for crusade costs. His building programme was slowed and projects were suspended. Less not more was spent in payments to officials. It is impossible to know if these economies balanced the cost of the crusade – it is unlikely they did – but it was a statesmanlike and businesslike attempt.

Louis made efforts to reform local government but did not altogether succeed. The records show the extent of corruption and abuse that continued. His attack on the Jews led to their decline with the expulsion of many from France and a severe problem for trade and commerce where loans were essential. His foreign policy brought peace with England but his critics felt he had been too generous. It became clear that England had not abandoned its old claims, and what Louis allowed England to retain became the base for the Hundred Years' War.

Medieval kings needed to be military leaders and Louis' achievement in this respect was modest. His chief success was against the inept Henry III and hardly establishes a great reputation. The main field for military activity were his two crusades. The second gave him little opportunity since he died before much could be done. The Egyptian crusade however is worth a summary. He did well in the planning and preparations. Aigues-Mortes was not a perfect departure point – with its tendency to attract storms, its silting harbour and its lack of good communications but it gave Louis a better royal base and port than his predecessors had possessed. He raised an estimable force and supplied it. The failure came in the action. One can defend Louis' strategy in attacking Egypt – success would have had beneficial effects for the Kingdom of Jerusalem, but Louis was over-ambitious and not aware of all the problems. Illness was bad luck but the campaign is hard to defend. Damietta was taken but Louis became isolated. Too much blame for failure has fallen on the rash attack by Robert of Artois. Louis failed to find a suitable target and failed to defeat the enemy. Defeat and capture was a disaster. Louis was fortunate to escape with his life and regain his freedom.

The final crusade to Tunis gave Louis little opportunity to fight but allows criticism of his strategy, possibly from inadequate geographical knowledge and poor intelligence. It proved another disaster with less to commend it than the attack on Egypt. Success at Tunis would have incurred considerable expense and not guaranteed aid for the Holy Land. One notes how quickly Charles of Anjou abandoned the project.

In short Louis deserved to be made a saint but a saintly king is not necessarily a great king. Louis gave enormous support to the church. He made tremendous efforts to fulfil his Christian commitments. There were benefits for France but also losses.

LOUIS THE MAN

Thanks largely to Jean de Joinville we may see Louis as a man. Most surviving sources were written to show the king's saintliness. Pope Boniface called him a 'superman' (*superhomo*) but other works remind us he was human.[55] Several were by men who knew him, including his confessor for 20 years, the Dominican Geoffrey de Beaulieu, William de Chartres a Dominican chaplain on the crusade, and Queen Margaret's Franciscan confessor William de St-Pathus. One could, however, hardly claim that most works were much more than hagiographies. He was often compared to biblical kings, to David the good king, to Solomon for wisdom, to Josiah for removing prostitutes from the Temple and fighting pharaoh. The faults were generally omitted.

William de Nangis wrote a universal chronicle in which Louis figured and a life of Louis, but he came from St-Denis which depended on Louis' patronage. He had not met the king and his material was borrowed. Joinville was an admirer but he also knew Louis as a companion and warrior. Joinville's work is in French and he quotes the king directly – 'the first king in the history of France who really speaks'.[56] Joinville described an incident when he was looking out of a window. Someone came up behind and placed hands on his head. Joinville muttered, 'Leave me in peace', believing it to be Philip de Nemours. Then he spotted the king's emerald ring. Louis had come to tell Joinville he would accept his advice to stay in the Holy Land.

Louis showed faults of character, though Joinville usually put a kindly construction upon them. He could lose his temper, mostly over unchristian behaviour, as his brother's gambling. He could be impatient, as when rebuking an old servant Ponce for being slow to bring his pony. Joinville reminded the king of the servant's age; he had served the king's father and grandfather. Louis turned on Joinville, 'Seneschal, he has not served us. We have served him by allowing him to stay with us in spite of his bad habits. My grandfather, King Philip, told me that in rewarding your servants you should give one more and one less according to their service.'[57] Louis also lost his temper with six young men on the Sixth Crusade who went ashore and were late back. They landed on the Saracen island of Pantellaria to look for fruit but were holding up the fleet. When he discovered their trivial excuse, Louis put them in the boat (for murderers and robbers) that trailed behind the ship as they continued through rough seas, endangering their lives.

There are other informative works on Louis. Salimbene of Parma was an Italian Franciscan who came to France in the 1240s and met Louis at Sens in 1248. He described the king as graceful and angelic. Salimbene was impressed by his humility, walking rather than riding, kneeling to pray, offering the best food to the friars and sharing his meals with them. At Vézelay Louis chose to sit on the ground with the brothers rather than take an offered chair. Salimbene also saw Louis' remains transported through Reggio in 1271. Matthew Paris was an English monk at St Albans who acted as a messenger for Henry III to Louis. His view altered from hostility to respect for 'the king of earthly kings', in contrast to his own master.[58]

Another source of information about Louis was the work of his own hand, written by him rather than dictated. He wrote works of instruction in French (the *Enseignements*, on how to behave), to his son Philip (III) and his daughter Isabelle. He advised his son to refrain from criticism of the church. 'When I think of the honour that Our Lord has done me, I prefer to put up with a hurt rather cause a breach between myself and the church.' Further advice was to 'uphold the poor rather then the rich until you know the truth; when the truth is known, do justice'.[59]

We do not have a realistic portrait of Louis, though we have written descriptions. Realistic portraits only appear from c.1300. Louis is only shown in conventional images, such as a Bible illustration from c.1235 at the age of about 20 with his mother. Louis is on a throne, holding sceptre and orb. Another picture comes from a fresco in the Ste-Chapelle, but is only a late copy. An early 14th-century picture at Cordelières shows the bearded king washing the feet of the poor. The statute at Mainneville, once thought to be Louis, is now identified as Philip IV. The figure of Louis on the tomb at St-Denis is beardless. We do best to rely on word descriptions by those who saw him. He was tall, blond, blue-eyed, rosy complexioned, with a delicate nose and a small mouth. He seemed angelic, with the eyes of a dove, a shining face and hair that turned prematurely white. The idealized portraits may have something of the king in them, but he was also an athletic warrior trained in arms, able to ride well and swim.

Louis received a good education with a strong religious emphasis. He learned Latin, philosophy and theology and joined in learned discussions. He was an avid listener to scholars and a reader, collecting his own library. When reading a Latin manuscript, if a familiar who lacked Latin was near, Louis would translate into French.[60] Louis helped to educate his own children, telling them bedtime stories of good kings and evil men to stress morality in rulers. Nevertheless Louis' mind was of his time. He was not greatly interested in recent intellectual views, more in the practical application of religion than ideas.

Louis had traditional views on other religions. It was widely believed by Christians that Jews, frequently referred to as scorpions, were responsible for the ritual murder of Christian children. The Jews to Louis were responsible for the crucifixion and he persecuted them. Louis once said laymen should defend their religion against Jews by giving them 'a good thrust in the belly, as far as the sword will go'.[61] There were perhaps 100,000 Jews in France, some 7,500 in Paris. Louis' persecution, following papal encouragement, included prohibition of the *Talmud*. Copies were seized and in one conflagration 22 cartloads were destroyed. As a result only one French medieval *Talmud* survives. Following papal recommendations, Jews were treated as serfs for whom, in an age when many serfs were enfranchised, there could be no freedom. Their goods were subject to arbitrary taxation, the *captio*, and to confiscation. Royal agents were forbidden to aid Jews in recovering debts. Gregory IX had to remind Louis that, as king, he should protect Jews. Jews complained that persecution in France led to their impoverishment. Louis' final ruling on usury was that it must either stop or the Jews responsible must be expelled, and many went into exile. The crippling of the Jewish community and the attack on usury had unforeseen results on the economy. The growth of business and trade brought a need for credit. The destruction of the most obvious source of loans had unfortunate effects. In France the Jews were made to wear distinguishing yellow discs on their chest and back. Louis made efforts to convert Jews, especially after the Egyptian crusade. They were made to attend Christian sermons and he encouraged conversion by offering royal protection for converts, allowing them to reside anywhere, and paying them a pension. He sought fairness by his own lights, ordering inquiry into illegal confiscation of Jewish property and allowing restricted worship. Action was taken against two agitators responsible for the only pogrom in France under him. However we can agree that 'for the Jews, Louis IX was not Saint Louis'.[62]

Louis' knowledge of the Old Testament gave him a certain respect for the Jewish faith. He could find no such respect for Islam, though he showed sympathy for certain individual Muslims, such as the Sultan of Egypt during his captivity. Louis sought the conversion of Muslims as preferable to war. He said 'if the whole visible world were mine, I would give it all in return for the salvation of souls', and added 'I would not even want to return to my realm of France provided that I gained for God your [the sultan's] soul and that of other infidels'. He could only see Mohammed as a magician and enchanter, the *Koran* as literally 'full of shit'.[63]

St Louis was a family man. He respected his ancestors, as witness the rearrangement of the St-Denis mausoleum, demonstrating continuity from Merovingian to Carolingian to Capetian. He particularly respected his grandfather, Philip Augustus, seemingly the first French king 'to have known his grandfather'.[64] He often quoted Philip as an example. He was also respectful of his father, Louis VIII, who died while Louis was still young. The tombs of father and grandfather were emphasized at St-Denis. Louis loved and almost worshipped his mother,

Blanche, a powerful woman, called 'a perfect virago'.[65] She coped with the difficult minority as few mothers could have done. Some view him as a mummy's boy, tied to her apron strings after his marriage – a situation that caused grief to his wife, Margaret. There was certainly friction between mother and wife. Blanche was angry when he wanted to go off to his wife's room. Yet Louis maintained a balance. He respected his mother, twice giving her the regency in his absence and he grieved tremendously at her death. Yet he went on crusade against her wishes and sustained his marriage. Joinville says that after Blanche's death he found Margaret in tears and asked why she mourned for the woman she most hated, who had treated her 'with great harshness'.[66] Margaret replied that the tears were not for Blanche but for her husband in his grief. Joinville hints that Louis neglected his wife on occasion, yet affection survived between them, and they produced 11 children. One reason for Blanche's opposition to Louis' crusading was that Margaret went with him. Three of their children (John-Tristan, Peter and Blanche) were born during that time.

There is no question that Louis treated Margaret in a domineering manner, quite unlike the picture we usually receive of him. He would not let her make decisions without consulting him – as she confided to Joinville. Louis' attitude to wife and children was 'authoritarian'.[67] In 1242 Margaret had to swear she would abide by royal policy whatever her own interests – she was not trusted as Blanche was. Louis expected to be obeyed by wife and children though his attitude was caring, as evidence the *Enseignements* to son and daughter. At times he ignored his wife and children, to the point where Joinville felt the need to comment. Louis' constant religious devotions must have strained family relations, on his knees five times every evening for example. During the return from crusade in a storm Margaret wanted to undertake a pilgrimage in thanks for her safety, but Louis was 'so difficult' she dared not make the vow without his prior permission.[68] In 1263 Pope Urban IV, on Louis' request, released his son Philip from an oath to Queen Margaret to stay under her tutelage until he was 30, to ignore advice hostile to her, not to make any agreement with Charles of Anjou, to ignore rumours hostile to his mother, and to keep the oath secret. It seems to be Margaret's revenge for the oath forced on her in 1242. At the very least it hints that all was not calm and light in the royal household. It also suggests that Margaret saw herself as a second Blanche. Louis's wishes were sometimes thwarted; he wanted three of his children to enter religion but none of them fulfilled his wish; all married.

Louis kept his father's promises to his own brothers, confirming their apanages and arranging good marriages. Robert of Artois, next in age, was probably closest to Louis. The king was distressed by Robert's death on crusade, seeing it as martyrdom. Louis was upset by the failure of Alphonse and Charles to visit him after their release from imprisonment during the Egyptian Crusade, and by their early return to France, but neither suffered as a result. He might have been more upset had he discovered that they ignored his views and continued to play dice. Alphonse of Poitiers gained enormous territories from his apanage, and from marriage to the heiress Joan of Toulouse, becoming the greatest magnate in the realm. After his return from crusade, Alphonse suffered a stroke. He recovered sufficiently to go on the Tunis Crusade, but he and his wife died on their way home. They were childless and Alphonse's possessions reverted to the crown.

The youngest brother, Charles of Anjou, was potentially the most difficult but Louis kept good relations despite the backgammon incident, the problems caused by Charles' ambitions in Flanders and Sicily, and those during the Tunis crusade. Louis helped his brothers acquire lands, though he had to restrain Charles over Flanders and gave him little aid in Italy, none at all over the Byzantine Empire. Charles' victories in Italy established him as king of Sicily though his gains were lost after Louis' death. Louis provided for the future of his children, arranging good marriages for his daughters and on the eve of his final crusade setting up apanages for his sons.

All the sources agree on the sincerity of Louis' belief. The major efforts of his reign sprang from it – the crusades, the administrative reforms and the desire to make peace. He was attracted to the monastic life, torn between desire for a private life in religion and to do good in the world. In his daily life he maintained the religious hours and throughout the year kept all the Christian festivals. He attached great significance to relics and often visited pilgrimage centres. He encouraged the building of churches and abbeys, the founding of the Sorbonne, the collection of a royal religious library, the making of beautiful illuminated manuscripts, and various literary works. He financed hospices and houses for the poor, the ill and the deprived. In Paris he built the Quinze-Vingts for 300 blind persons.

Louis lived his whole life on the Christian model. Uniquely among medieval French kings, Louis never hunted, probably following the ideas of Gilbert of Tournai. He read other works that condemned hunting, for example St Augustine and St Jerome ('I have never seen a hunter who was also a saint').[69] Nor are there any stories of affairs or mistresses. Louis dressed drably and ate simply – though once Joinville mentions him wearing a hat of white peacock feathers.[70] He put more water in his wine than anyone else – one quarter wine to three-quarters water. Once he asked Joinville why he did not water his wine. Joinville replied on doctor's orders as he had a large head and a cold stomach. Louis said this was rubbish and he would suffer from gout and disease of the stomach if he carried on, adding that it was sad to see a good man drunk.[71] Louis even put water in his gravy to weaken that. He only drank beer because he did not like it. His eating and drinking were always moderate.

Louis strove to live like a monk. At table he liked religious persons to guide the conversation. In abbeys he served meals to the monks and washed their feet. At Royaumont he watched preparations for the meal through a serving hatch, and then took up the plates to serve the monks. When a dish was too hot to handle he used his cloak to protect his hands. When the abbot pointed out that he was making a mess of his cloak, Louis replied, 'it is not important, I have others'. Louis often washed the feet of the poor. He once asked Joinville to do the same but the latter replied 'God forbid, sir. I shall not wash the feet of those brutes', and Louis rebuked him.[72] The king often gave his own food to others, especially the poor and the sick. Once he fed by hand a man too ill to feed himself, dipping a piece of fish in sauce to put in the man's mouth. He tended lepers in person and ate with them from the same plate. Once he peeled a pear and placed pieces in a leper's mouth with the result that blood and pus from the man ran over his hand – but he continued with the task. His almsgiving went beyond the usual practice. Distributing alms one Good Friday he was nearly knocked over by the hopeful poor. His men wanted to push them off but Louis held them back. Early one morning he found some poor people outside the palace while everyone else was asleep. He came out with a servant to distribute coins. A cleric saw him from a window and asked what he was doing. Louis was embarrassed and invented a white lie that he was paying salaries that were owed.

Louis was not always private. His people were able to see him as a Christian king. He often toured the northern and demesne areas of his realm, constantly distributing alms. On other journeys, for example south for the crusades, he visited practically every holy site on the way and again distributed alms. He was keen to visit pilgrimage centres especially those connected with the Virgin Mary. He never took a holiday from his devotions, whether riding on horseback around France, at sea on the crusading voyages, in distant parts, or a prisoner of the Muslims – Louis maintained his daily, weekly and yearly routine of worship.

There was an ascetic element to Louis' conduct. He ate sparingly and dressed modestly. At times he wore a hair-shirt. After confession he insisted that his confessor flagellate him. He carried around with him secretly an instrument made of five small iron chains with small ivory boxes at the ends, for flagellation. Another account described a similar scourge of three thin knotted cords, a foot and a half long. He made presents of such instruments to members of his family and friends – one can only speculate on their response! Geoffrey de Beaulieu wrote that sometimes the confessor hit too hard and wounded the king's flesh. However if the confessor did not flog strongly enough Louis would order him to strike harder.

As a result of his Christian life Louis was canonized and the sources after his death stressed his saintliness. We need to balance this. Louis was a sincere Christian king but was he a great king? His Christian attitude had some commendable results, including the reforms. However his achievements have probably been overestimated. He was not a great conqueror. His father and grand-father achieved far more in that respect. He was not a great military leader. He did defeat Henry III but this hardly required brilliant ability. His two crusades were disasters, military failures. They were also extremely expensive, as was the ransom paid for his release in Egypt and for that of his men. The only saving factor for the Holy Land was his effort at building defences, but they were costly and only prolonged the life of the Kingdom for a few decades. His efforts also meant a six-year absence from his realm. Joinville was circumspect in his comments but decided against going to Tunis because his own previous absence had brought unfortunate consequences for his lands and people.

We can be overwhelmed by the literature supporting Louis' claim to sainthood. Much was written to press for his canonization and after it had occurred. Joinville was a friend, and wrote years after the king's death. There are a few texts that give a different picture. One critic was Rutebeuf, the first great French lyric poet, who expressed a common contemporary view that Louis would have been better employed at home than crusading. Rutebeuf also opposed the prohibition of private war and tournaments. He disliked the king's subservience to clerics and did not agree that Louis gave justice to all. In the poet's view 'the king does neither right nor justice to the knights, but despises them'.[73] Louis' liking for mendicants did not bring universal praise; the woman Sarrete confronted him on the palace stairs to say he was 'only king of the friars minor and friars preacher, of priests and clerks' – though he received her comment modestly. A blunt messenger reckoned the king wore a friar's hood over his arse.[74] In the dispute between seculars and regulars at the University of Paris from 1254–57, Louis supported the papacy and the mendicants, which did not please the seculars who called him 'Brother Louis'. The king followed papal demands in exiling the Parisian master, William de St-Amour, who had written a pamphlet against the mendicants but had been a leading university master. Many resented the king's action; Rutebeuf thought he had been exiled 'without trial'.[75]

Louis' Christian conduct was extreme. The pope made annual confession obligatory, but Louis insisted on weekly confession and kept a confessor on hand (in shifts day and night) in case he committed a mortal sin and needed to confess immediately. At one time he supported Robert the Bugger's efforts against heresy. Robert had been a heretic who went with a heretic woman to Milan and became a sect leader. He returned to France and Catholicism, joining the Dominicans and was active in the Inquisition, ruthlessly ordering executions by burning. Three archbishops complained about his conduct to the pope. Gregory IX suspended him in 1234 but he remained active. He was finally stopped in 1241 but Louis must take some blame for allowing him to operate. The fall of Robert did not halt the ruthless and persistent activities of the Inquisition in France.

Louis believed in harsh measures against heretics, non-believers, and blasphemers. Even popes tried to restrain his more extreme actions. How realistic were some of his moralizing acts – to prohibit prostitution or remove it from public view, to stop visits to brothels and taverns, end usury, stop gaming, swearing and bad language? What were the feelings of the sailors forced to attend his numerous services on board ship because they were men who rarely heard the word of God? No doubt those at court watched their tongues but any wider impact is doubtful. How many followed his three-day abstention from sex at marriage? He suffered from his lusts and would get out of bed to walk around his room until desire subsided. Louis' severe punishments for sins rather than crimes have been praised but how just were they? At times the barons resented his decisions against individuals. It is clear that counsellors had to tone down his original intentions. Even the pope asked that he moderate his punishments for bad language, suggesting that mutilation or death were not appropriate penalties.

Louis might seem a fanatic, a zealot, over harsh against sinners, blasphemers, heretics and non-Christians – his character less appealing than it was to contemporaries. Yet somehow through the records, even discounting their wish to present him as a saint, shines an attractive personality. The virtues – sincerity, humility, sympathy for others, sociability – outweigh the faults. We know that Louis suffered poor health, yet he maintained a cheerful face. Only when mourning for family and friends was he depressed. He suffered from erysipelas but tried to hide it from others. His right leg came out in regular painful rashes three or four times a year. For three days he could neither eat nor drink, followed by painful inflammation. Louis had his clothes put out but always dressed himself – to hide the disease and the fact that he wore a hairshirt. He also had special shoes made without soles so that he could walk barefoot without observers being aware of it. He insisted on sleeping on a hard wooden bed that was carried around with him, and slept on cinders. These acts of self-denial must have aggravated his ill health. He probably suffered from malaria. He had dysentery after the campaign against Henry III in 1242 and again in Egypt, where he also contracted scurvy. He was often ill, for example when he was thought dead and made his first crusading vow, at Fontainebleau in 1259, and again just before he set out on the final crusade. In Tunis the probable cause of his death was typhus.

THE TUNIS CRUSADE

The failure of the Egyptian crusade hit Louis hard but did not discourage him from further efforts. In the wake of his first crusade he spent years trying to bolster the defences of the Kingdom of Jerusalem and was reluctant to return to France. In 1267 he declared his intent to take the cross again, a decision probably made the previous year. It was no surprise that Louis contemplated a new crusade but there is debate over why he chose Tunis. There were other possible targets. The Kingdom was much reduced from its peak and weakened by internal divisions – Venetians against Genoese, Templars against Hospitallers, the prince of Antioch against the lord of Gibelet. The Kingdom was facing its final onslaught as, in rapid succession, the remaining strongholds fell to the Muslims – Nazareth, Caesarea, Haifa, Arsuf, Safed, Toron, Jaffa, Beaufort, Antioch, Acre, Krak des Chevaliers, Montfort – only a few coastal towns remained. Byzantium had been lost again to the Latin West. Egypt remained as significant as it had been in 1248.

Despite all the possible targets, Louis chose remote Tunis. This may have been a late decision rather than the original plan. He heard that the emir of Tunis was ready to convert to Christianity, though on what grounds is unclear. There has been debate over the role of Charles of Anjou, but no clear conclusion. It is not certain that Charles wanted to go to Tunis, let alone that he was responsible for persuading his brother. Charles had Mediterranean interests from the acquisition of Naples, but they were targeted at Byzantium rather than Africa. Recent historians have doubted that Charles was behind the choice of Tunis.[76] Another suggestion is that the west was not very good at geography and Louis, like others, thought Tunis would be a good base against Egypt, believing it closer than it was. No one is certain about Louis' motives. Probably he expected Tunis to become Christian and a base against Egypt.

Louis made preparations for government in his absence. He renewed several moral measures. Jews were to wear distinctive clothing; measures against blasphemers, prostitutes and criminals were hardened. A new seal was put in the care of the abbot of St-Denis and Simon de Nesle. Queen Margaret did not accompany her husband and was not given regency powers. Religious affairs were left to the bishop of Paris. Louis drew up a will and left advice for his eldest son and daughter, Philip and Isabelle. Louis obtained little support from other rulers. James I of Aragon set out for the Holy Land in 1269 but abandoned the effort because of bad weather. Edward I of England, who had borrowed from Louis in order to crusade, went to the Holy Land later. Joinville doubted the value of the new crusade and chose to stay home. He summed up the crusade curtly, saying it 'achieved little' and thanking God he was not there.[77]

Louis took the oriflamme and pilgrim symbols on 14 March 1270. He walked barefoot to Notre-Dame. At Vincennes he bid farewell to Queen Margaret. He again left from Aigues-Mortes, this time with a French admiral, Florent de Verennes. They sailed on 2 July to Sardinia where the forces assembled, and landed at La Goulette near Tunis on 17 July. Louis' plans came to nought. The only success was the taking of Carthage on 24 July. The emir showed no sign of converting or of allying with Louis. The army suffered in the heat. An epidemic of dysentery or typhus struck, and many, including Louis, became ill. The king's younger son, John-Tristan, died on 3 August. For four days Louis could not speak, though still joining his hands and raising them to heaven. On a bed covered with ashes he crossed his arms on his breast. His final expressions were religious, including 'O Jerusalem! O Jerusalem!' On his last day he begged for God's mercy to his people. His final words, in Latin, were to trust his spirit to God. He breathed his last at Carthage on 25 August at three o'clock in the afternoon. It was a sad and pathetic end to a long career. Charles of Anjou captured the Muslim camp and made terms. The last French crusade was over.

The bodies of Louis and John-Tristan were boiled. There was a dispute over the disposal of the king's remains. Philip, now Philip III, wanted his father's body brought to Paris; Charles of Anjou wanted to take the body to Sicily. As a compromise the entrails went to Sicily, the bones to Paris. The fate of the heart is uncertain, but it probably went to France. The body reached Sicily and travelled through Italy on the backs of two horses, reaching Paris on 21 May 1271. It was claimed that the entrails performed miracles in Sicily and the bones achieved similar results on the journey and at their resting-place. Boniface VIII canonized Louis in 1297, with a ceremony at St-Denis the following year. His saint's day was 25 August. The bones were not allowed to remain in peace. Philip IV wanted the body moved to the Ste-Chapelle, where the skull was taken in 1306. A rib went to Notre-Dame; other bones to Norwich, Sweden, Prague and Bavaria. What remained was irretrievably disturbed in the Revolution in 1793. Similar travels troubled the entrails which were transferred to Monreale in Sicily in 1860 and then pursued by Garibaldi to Gaeta. They reached an Austrian castle and came to rest in Carthage. For canonization the miracles had to belong to the period after death. Writers claimed countless miracles on the journey of the remains, at the tombs, and with the relics. Sixty-five miracles were authenticated, including raising two people from the dead (one a child), but most were about healing illness and disability – giving hearing to the deaf and sight to the blind.

9

The Bold and the Fair, 1270–1314

PHILIP III, THE BOLD (1270–85)

Two Philips were the last major Capetian kings: Philip III the Bold, and Philip IV the Fair. The son and successor of St Louis was Philip III, 1270–85. His tomb at St-Denis was the first to display a genuine portrait of a Capetian king. His health was poor and he has been called 'an insignificant man', 'of small intelligence'.[1] Hallam thought on the other hand he was 'not a nonentity' though his achievements did not compare with his father's (Louis IX) or son's (Philip IV). His policies were quite distinct from those of his father and his courage in implementing them led to him being called 'the Bold'. It is arguable that his son and successor, Philip IV, followed his father's example early in his reign and modified them later.

Philip III was the oldest son of St Louis, originally allotted the Orléanais. His faults included accumulating debts that caused problems for the monarchy. In 1278 he was accused of unnatural practices but there is no other evidence to support the charge. He produced sons, the eldest being Louis of Bourbon, and his male heirs continued in line until 1589. One cannot help but feel that his main fault was to die young.

Apanages by the late 13th century had become 'a royal institution'.[2] Two of Philip's brothers, Peter and John-Tristan, were granted apanages but died young without heirs so their territories returned to the demesne. Philip's only surviving brother, Robert of Clermont, 'the skeleton in the Capetian closet', held another apanage. He was injured in a tournament in 1278, which affected his brain. He offered no challenge to Philip as heir. The apanage system was formerly condemned by historians for breaking up the state and weakening the monarchy, but is now widely accepted as placating younger sons with large estates, preventing these lands from going out of the family, and ensuring that if the line died out they would return to the demesne. We have referred to it as a system but it was more of an organic development, gradually becoming more defined. The practice of reversion to the crown was usual but not inevitable, until in 1284 Parliament made it 'the custom of France'.[3] Female succession was excluded by the terms of apanage grants.

Philip was 25 at his succession when his father and John-Tristan died on the Tunis Crusade. The ministers in Paris summoned the young king home. He made arrangements for his father's corpse and then left Africa in a storm with waves like mountains. His pregnant wife, Isabella of Aragon, was thrown from her horse while travelling through Italy and died soon afterwards; the child was stillborn. Philip's uncle Alphonse of Poitiers and his wife also died on the way home.

Philip III had the pious reputation of the dynasty. He read good works and wore a hair shirt.[4] In 1274 he married again to Marie of Brabant – 'beautiful, wise and full of good deeds', but accused of dabbling too much in affairs of state.[5] Peter de la Broce, formerly St Louis' chamberlain, was favoured by Philip III and led the Capetian intervention in Brabant but the new queen became the centre of court opposition to him. When Philip's son and heir, Louis, died in 1276 his stepmother Marie was accused (almost certainly falsely) of poisoning him, and Broce was one of the accusers. In 1277 the minister was in turn (probably with false evidence) accused of treachery, arrested, tried, and hanged at Montfaucon in 1278. Marie had gained her revenge.

An early problem for Philip was the succession in Poitou after the death of his uncle without heir. Alphonse of Poitiers and his wife Joan had died when returning from crusade. The succession was not clear. Henry III of England made a claim based on the treaty of Paris, but it was ignored. Philip took over the county of Foix by force in 1272 and in the same year the English king died while his son Edward was on crusade. Philip repossessed Alphonse's apanage. On his return Edward I did homage for his French lands and was granted the Agenais by the treaty of Amiens.

In 1274 Henry III of Navarre died leaving as heiress a three-year-old daughter Joan. The English sought marriage with her but Philip outmanoeuvred them and arranged a match with his son Philip. The seneschal of Toulouse ruled Navarre for Joan and acted harshly, causing revolt in 1276 which was crushed ruthlessly. Another problem arose over the succession to Castile. Philip III took more interest in affairs south of the Pyrenees than was common with the Capetians. He has been called 'less wise' than St Louis but his premature death makes it difficult to judge.[6] Fernand, the eldest son of the king of Castile, died in 1275 leaving two sons by Blanche (Philip III's sister). The sons therefore, known as the *infantes* of La Cerda, were Philip's nephews but Alfonso of Castile recognized his other son, Sancho, rather than the *infantes* – a snub to France, which he increased by sending Blanche home. Philip supported the claim of the *infantes* which led to war, a reckless war in the view of Fawtier.[7] In 1276 he invaded Navarre and Castile but with little chance to fulfil his hopes.

France became more engaged in Spanish and southern affairs. When there was revolt in Navarre, France allied with Aragon against Castile. This policy was at odds with the wishes and interests of his Angevin relations in Italy. Philip and Pedro III of Aragon met in 1281 at Toulouse. Charles of Anjou, Philip's uncle, was opposed to the alliance. His interests in Italy and elsewhere were threatened by Aragon. Charles had married Margaret, daughter of Charles II of Sicily, which brought him Anjou and Sicily. However in 1282 the Sicilian Vespers led to his defeat, and the loss of Sicily to Pedro III of Aragon. The old kingdom was now divided between the Angevins on the mainland and Pedro in the island.

The new French pope Martin IV declared Pedro III of Aragon deposed and there were plans for Charles of Anjou to succeed in Aragon. Louis IX had avoided such direct intervention but Philip III accepted the papal offer and sought the throne for Charles. The pope declared a crusade against Pedro and in Paris the crowns of Aragon and Valencia were accepted for Charles. Martin IV died in 1285 but the 'crusade' went ahead, one of the few wars of conquest outside France instigated by the Capetians and a disaster. The French took Gerona but were then besieged within the city. The French fleet was destroyed at Las Formiguas by Roger de Loria. Philip III became ill and ordered his troops to withdraw. When Philip died at Perpignan the French garrison at Gerona surrendered. The war had cost 1,229,000 *livres tournois* and gained absolutely nothing.[8] Philip III reversed St Louis' policies with aggressive expeditions to Spain, though with little success. His Angevin relatives lost Sicily and their position in Italy was weakened. Charles of Anjou died in 1285 and his son, Charles II was captured in Naples. Charles of Anjou had been desperate for some acquisition. He and Philip took an interest in the vacancy for the king of the Germans in 1272, but that also came to nothing and Rudolf of Habsburg was elected.

Philip III did follow St Louis in home policies, and the continuity, pursued also by Philip IV, is important. Philip III furthered growing links to the south. Commissions were sent to Toulouse and Carcassonne, and appeals to royal justice from these areas were encouraged. Philip continued to allot apanages to younger sons. Thus Valois was granted to Charles and Beaumont-sur-Oise to Louis. These were enlarged by grants by their older brother when he became Philip IV. Philip III ceded the Venaissin to Gregory X in 1274, though Gregory died two years later. This proved a vital step towards the Avignon residence, and stronger French influence over the papacy through the 14th century. Philip III died at Perpignan on 5 October 1285. His son, who now became Philip IV, was just 17.

INTRODUCTION TO THE REIGN OF PHILIP THE FAIR

The reign of Philip the Fair (le Bel – beautiful, handsome – generally translated as 'the Fair'), as well as his character, was a mix of foul and fair. Even Elizabeth Brown, who has done much work on the reign, feels that his personality has 'eluded historians'.[9] He has been denounced and praised in equal measure – both to some extent deservedly. Some emphasize the positive side. A Spanish contemporary saw him as 'ruler, emperor, pope and king rolled into one'.[10] A chronicler thought him 'liberal, munificent, gracious and good', winning the hearts of all in the south.[11] In modern times Douglas thought the French monarchy was never stronger than under Philip and he has been called 'one of the greatest kings and one of the noblest characters in history', 'a great king'.[12] Favier lists reasons for Philip being seen as significant, 'a champion of French nationalism', 'a precursor of laicism' – he wrote his book to investigate such clichés. He saw Philip as 'the last of the great Capetians' and credited him with genuine belief, a 'deep faith', that inspired works of piety, religious foundations and pilgrimages.[13] Philip was to exit with 'an impressively pious death'.[14]

There is little doubt that Philip had respect for his grandfather, Louis IX. He arranged Louis' canonization in 1297 and built a convent at Poissy where Louis had been born. Philip's oldest son, Robert, was buried there and Philip ordered that his own heart should also go there. He sought to have Louis IX's remains moved to the Ste-Chapelle, which Philip turned into a monument to his grandfather. There was opposition from St-Denis but twice Philip persuaded the pope to agree to his plans. He ordered the making of a reliquary for the purpose. Eventually most of Louis' head was moved to the Ste-Chapelle and a rib went to Notre-Dame. In a compromise certain bones remained at St-Denis, including the chin, teeth and lower jaw.[15] Not everyone was placated and one source reckoned that a leg injury Philip received when hunting was a deserved punishment. Philip reorganized the royal tombs at St-Denis, ordering that his own should be next to St Louis'. Like St Louis he wore a hair shirt. He went on pilgrimages – twice to Mont-Saint-Michel, three times to Notre-Dame at Boulogne, and made lengthy stays in religious houses at Maubuisson, Longpont and Poissy. Yet as Strayer (who admitted that his own wife had to live with Philip for 40 years) puts it, Philip was not another St Louis. Strayer did think the reign marked 'the culmination of the medieval French monarchy'. His assessment of the king's belief as a 'narrow piety' hits the mark.[16]

There is however much criticism of Philip IV, by contemporaries and historians. Some of Philip's officials wrote glowing reports but others were less admiring. Bishop Bernard Saisset, who had reason to feel hostile, called Philip 'a statue'. Others thought him silent and aloof. When Count Guy of Flanders came to kneel before Philip, the king looked but 'did not speak a word'.[17] The bishop of Pamiers referred to Philip as 'not a man but a beast', who gave no answer – all he could do was pass wind. The bishop saw him as reserved and remote, 'like an owl, the most beautiful of birds that is worth absolutely nothing … he can do nothing except stare at men'.[18] Philip listened and rarely spoke, leaving it to ministers to speak for him. He is accused of letting officials do the work and giving way to their demands. Some though have seen him as more manipulative, cynical, ready to down opponents by any means available while letting his officials take the blame. He has been attacked for destroying the order of the Temple and hounding Pope Boniface VIII to his death.

Philip was the last Capetian with a claim to greatness, so that our story ends with a climax and an enigma. If one had to choose someone to represent *all* the Capetians it would be hard to find a better example. St Louis may have been the ideal monarch but Philip represents all that was best and all that was worst at the same time. He was intelligent and educated, a reader of Boethius, yet narrow-minded. He was pious and cynical; a son of the Church and grandson of St Louis yet reputed the enemy of Rome and the killer of a pope; he was badly defeated at Courtrai but victorious at Mons-en-Pévèle. His reign coincided with a turning point of French and European history. He appeared when the Capetian monarchy was at its height, master of the nobility, ruling almost the whole of France, the most powerful kingdom in the west. Bureaucratic administration developed apace with increasingly professional officials. France was the most intellectually advanced and economically prosperous country in the west. Yet all was in the balance. Shortly ahead loomed the collapse of the dynasty, the Hundred Years' War, the Black Death, and economic disaster.

However one assesses Philip IV's contribution, there is no doubt that his reign was of major importance. He followed in his ancestors' footsteps, presenting a pious image. We cannot know the private thoughts of Philip but he demonstrated piety. He made grants and gifts to churches. Like St Louis he ordered his confessor to beat him with chains as penance. Philip seems genuine in his belief but it was a belief that persuaded him of the rectitude of all he did. He made a pilgrimage to Mont-Saint-Michel and went into religious retreat at Poissy. He venerated St Louis and was keen to crusade. In old age he lived a life of personal self-denial. Duby believes this is his true character, and that historians have misrepresented him. He has a point, but it could be argued that most historians have seen only one side of Philip – either the fair or the foul, and that the real Philip was both at once. Part of the problem is that evidence about him as an individual is slight; there is no Joinville for Philip IV.

Philip had advantages from his upbringing, including an excellent education. His teachers included the reputable scholars Egidius Romanus and William d'Ercuis. He is said to be of only average intelligence yet he could appreciate readings of Boethius. He was physically attractive hence 'le Bel'. The statue at Mainneville of a slim, handsome, innocent-looking man, now thought to be of Philip IV, was long taken to be St Louis. Philip had fair hair and was a *pulcher homo*.[19] An anonymous source described him as 'golden-blond, ruddy, fair, and seemly, he stood erect and was so tall that he was immediately noticed in a crowd'.[20] Some thought him rather fat, a feature of several later Capetians. He lacked the depth of religious spirituality of St Louis but he looked the part. Unlike Louis he liked the popular sports of his day and was a keen huntsman.

Philip may have appeared like a statue – cold, unmoving, not speaking – but he took in what he heard and he directed affairs. Strayer has pointed out that ministers were 'picked by the king, not foisted on him'. Flote, Nogaret, Marigny and others spoke for him in public, but they could not act without his direction and approval. There is a tone, a character, an attitude, a cunning that runs through the reign which cannot be associated only with individual ministers. They were intelligent men who advised and participated in affairs, but Philip pulled the strings. Strayer has detected a personal style – sarcastic, biting, legalistic – in Philip's letters, that matches his policies.[21] Brown concurs that Philip was in control: he 'determined the policies which his ministers carried out'. Nor was Philip always aloof. He was accused of letting ordinary folk, 'low-lifes', chat to him. Perhaps Philip was following the advice of Giles of Rome, whom he commissioned to write on the conduct of princes. Giles recommended avoiding familiarity and appearing 'graver' than other men. Some who knew Philip saw another side and believed him to be chaste, humble and modest.[22]

Philip was born at Fontainebleau in 1268, second son of Philip III and Isabella of Aragon. His nurse, Héloise, was rewarded with clothing and paid two shillings a day. Philip was two when Louis IX went on his fatal crusade. His mother died while he was a child and his father Philip III remarried to Marie of Brabant in 1274. Philip was knighted at 16 in 1284. Shortly afterwards he married Joan of Navarre, who was aged only 11; they had been betrothed since 1276. The liaison brought Navarre and Champagne to the crown. Philip became heir to the throne on the death of his brother Louis in 1276, and the first king of both France and Navarre. His wife Joan died in 1305 aged only 32 and Philip did not remarry. He seems to have been genuinely fond of her, often making grants that she desired. She shared his admiration of St Louis and had urged Joinville to write his life of that king. She often travelled around with Philip. In 1294 he showed his trust by declaring that she should be regent if he died. Philip was also close to his daughter Isabelle and kept contact with her after she became Queen of England in 1308. Philip had four sons – Louis, Philip, Charles and Robert.

France by 1285 was the most powerful European state, with a population of about 20,000,000 'the largest state in Europe'.[23] This was 'the apogee of royal power'.[24] The Holy Roman Empire sank into decline after the death of Frederick II, damaged by civil wars, divided elections and internal problems. The papacy had previously needed to accommodate the emperor, now it was the king of France whose co-operation mattered most. French clerics were promoted within the church. Conditions in Rome and Italy made it difficult for the popes to remain there. With Philip IV the papacy became more French in its nature, with more French cardinals, several French popes, and a base outside Italy – established at Avignon.

FRANCE IN THE EARLY 14TH CENTURY

Under Philip IV the enlarged demesne was consolidated and royal administration tightened its grip over both demesne and realm. Champagne was added to the demesne through Philip's marriage to Joan of Navarre. He made further acquisitions by purchase, including Beaugency and the county of Bigorre. The only great fiefs not now in Capetian hands were Brittany, Burgundy, Flanders and Aquitaine, and the last two came temporarily under Philip. The balance between king and dukes or counts weighed heavily in the king's favour and would never be restored. Magnates could not compete with royal power and wealth.

The apanages granted to younger sons proved less damaging to royal power, control and wealth than some anticipated. Apanages looked like feudal principalities but had significant features of their own. Wood concluded that apanages formed 'a basically non feudal institution that was clothed in feudal forms'.[25] Most of those previously established returned to the crown under Philip III. Apanages proved beneficial to the monarchy, a system that kept younger sons satisfied with large and valuable territories, and powers beyond those of normal fief-holders. The ruler of an apanage was a king within his territory. Apanage holders performed homage only to the king. The apanage retained practices used in the royal demesne, could refuse entry to royal agents and hold their own assemblies. The system proved to be a useful 'training ground' for officials, many of whom moved on to a career in royal administration.[26] On the whole the arrangement worked well and Capetian younger sons were more loyal than in almost any other contemporary state. It was an arrangement that was unlikely to harm the monarchy in the long run with the built-in limitation of succession so that they were likely to return to royal hands. Philip IV initiated the policy of making apanage princes peers of the realm. He also clarified succession practice that possession could only continue to direct male heirs. He insisted on reversion to the crown. He ruled that if his son Philip the Long died without a male heir, the apanage would 'be rejoined to the demesne of the kingdom'.[27]

Philip extended the demesne in key areas. Quercy was added in 1289; Bigorre was acquired from the bishop of Puy for a rent. This was the age of acquisition by pariage – sharing control with an existing landholder. Philip was prepared to pay for some territories, such as Beaugency in 1291, or Maguellone and part of Montpellier in 1293. In 1301 his authority over the county of Burgundy was recognized. There was resistance from the empire but Philip IV maintained control and administered the county, the later Franche-Comté. French control was not maintained for long and the county was returned to the empire by Philip V. In 1302 Philip the Fair gained the counties of La Marche and Angoulême as well as the lordship of Forges. In 1313 he confiscated Montagne and Tournai.

The concept of 'France' was strengthening and with it the idea of a king who ruled the whole. Territorially Philip concentrated his policy on strengthening the frontiers. He did not seek to extend the boundaries under direct rule but rather to extend recognition of his suzerainty. He was prepared to acknowledge the rights of others over disputed territories in return for recognition of that suzerainty – even in his greatest conflicts in Aquitaine and Flanders.

Under Philip Paris was truly the capital, now with a population of 200,000 the largest city in western Europe.[28] Building continued and the nave of St-Denis was completed. Paris was a magnet for men of ambition – lawyers, administrators, clerics, students, lecturers, merchants and financiers. Nobles needed a base there. The duke of Burgundy spent more time in Paris than in his duchy. Government was concentrated in the city with new permanent homes for several departments. It was the common meeting place for the royal council and the new Estates-General.

The University of Paris continued to expand. New colleges were founded, including that by Joan of Navarre. Philip needed the university's support, especially in his quarrel with Boniface VIII. It was a leading intellectual centre, especially for the arts and theology, 'the greatest of all the European universities'.[29] It attracted many great figures, including Roger Bacon and Aquinas, and hordes of students.

The reign of Philip IV was the close of a period of economic expansion. Now the Champagne Fairs fell into decline. The growing significance of the cloth trade in Europe highlighted the lack of such industry in France. Flanders and Italy led the way, not France. Rising costs hit the monarchy as well as the nation. Philip's greatest problem was to raise enough money to finance his projects.

GOVERNMENT AND ADMINISTRATION

Philip's immediate entourage was both political and personal. He had need of services that one would call administrative, such as keeper of the seal and financial officers. He also needed groups to look after worship, dining, clothing and hunting. Philip's household contained some 200 men at the start of the reign, nearer 300 by its close. They had to be fed but Philip, private man that he was, usually dined with a few chosen companions. Unlike St Louis, Philip indulged in rich food including swan, heron and exotic fruit, as well as good wines. He liked to dine off silver plate with ivory-handled cutlery. The larger household required additional accommodation and Philip extended St Louis' palace.

Philip IV retained a large degree of personal control. Advice from counsellors, chosen by the king, accepted or rejected by the king, played an important part in central rule. It has been said the council was simply 'the political entourage'.[30] Members of the royal household or *curia* formed a permanent council, chosen by the king. Advice could be sought for specific problems; over Saisset, for example, from prelates. The council consisted of men related to the king, useful to the king, of high social standing and low. When he was present, Philip's brother Charles of Valois had considerable weight and was usually first to speak. He was the king's closest political relative but was often absent. Philip, though fond of him, made little effort to aid Charles in his broader ambitions. Philip was also fond of his wife but allowed her little part in decision making. Nor did Philip's youngest brother, Louis of Évreux, have much influence on policy. Philip's sons played an increasing role consistent with their growing maturity and importance, but always under the guidance of Philip's counsellors. Some great nobles attended council, including Robert II of Artois and Robert duke of Burgundy. Some held offices, thus the duke of Burgundy was Chamberlain of France, but magnates did not dominate the council.

Most active administrators were lesser men who took their place in council, including chamberlains like Hugh de Bonville or Peter de Chambly. Some were favoured advisers and held office as chamberlains, or keepers of the seal who ran the chancery. Philip's advisers were loyal and he treated them well. At first he used his father's officials. His first new choices included the Italian financiers known in France as Biche and Mouche. Latilly, Flote and Nogaret were also early appointments – all to play a significant role. It is notable that those associated with the war against England included Flote, Nogaret, Biche and Mouche – all promoted by the king. After 1300 Philip mostly relied on existing officials. Enguerrand de Marigny was Philip's last leading minister and he was appointed first as a simple chamberlain.

The keeper of the seal was probably the chief office, held by a string of Philip's greater ministers including Flote, Mornay, Belleperche, Nogaret, Ascelin and Latilly. A degree of specialization developed among the leading advisers, for example Philip le Convers dealt with forest matters, though Nogaret and Marigny had a more general role. Many officials came from the demesne though a few were from further afield – Flote, Nogaret and Aycelin from the south; the Guidi brothers from Italy. Several ministers came to notice through a relative, often a prelate, as did Flote, Nogaret and Marigny.

The leading advisers attended the council, including Peter Flote, William Nogaret, Enguerrand de Marigny, Peter de Latilly and Philip le Convers. They did not form a body with defined functions but simply an 'inner group'.[31] Councillors were not paid enormous amounts but most acquired lands and gifts. A few became wealthy but most received a moderate living and a pension. Flote came from a noble family in the Dauphiné and received a castle and lordship. His son William acquired considerable wealth. Royal service brought status and some power – though this could vanish on the king's death. Some of Philip's advisers were resented for gaining wealth from office, including Marigny 'who from a state of poverty had soon risen to riches'.[32] Le Convers was a convert from Judaism to Christianity who acted as an *enquêteur* and acquired lands to the value of 1,000 *livres* in Normandy.

An important feature of Philip's advisers was the number of lawyers. This was partly because of the development of legal education, including canon law at Paris and Roman civil law at Orléans. It also reflected the growing importance of a legal approach to business. Many of Philip's advisers had legal training and it showed in how they approached the clash with Boniface VIII and the trial of the Templars, as well as in formulating legislation. Lawyers were essential for some of the newer tasks, not least to overlook the inquests as enquêteurs. Several of Philip's lawyers came from the lesser nobility, including Flote, Aycelin, Mornay and Belleperche. Flote was a trained lawyer who acted as judge in the parliament at Toulouse and a diplomat in England, the empire, the Vatican and Flanders. He died fighting for Philip at Courtrai. Nogaret was a teacher of law at Montpellier who was a judge at Beaucaire. Peter de Belleperche was a master of law at Orléans who became keeper of the seal and bishop of Auxerre. William de Plaisians was a pupil of Nogaret who became a judge. Raoul de Presles, an advocate for the king, was an expert on Roman law. Latilly, who served as a tax collector, ambassador and bishop, was Philip's last keeper of the seal and a leading lawyer.

The council became a more prominent institution under Philip. Its members often proclaimed royal policy in public and represented the king at assemblies and diplomatic meetings. Some historians have argued that Philip was little more than a cypher, more interested in hunting and chess than government, his policy determined by Marigny and Nogaret. Recent work has modified this and we see Philip as the power behind the councillors, proclaiming his views rather than theirs. The continuity and unity of views through the reign support this, as does a closer study of Philip's involvement behind the scenes. Letters of command sent from court are instructive. Of 939 that survive no less than 440 were personal orders from the king.[33] When the council was divided over how to act against Saisset, Philip made the final decision. As Elizabeth Brown argues, Philip had little to gain politically from his treatment of either Saisset or Guichard of Troyes.[34] On policy over the Val d'Aran (land on the French side of the Pyrenees claimed by Aragon), having listened to council discussion, Philip accepted the view of a lesser councillor over that of Nogaret. In his inflation policy Philip chose to ignore the advice of Biche and Mouche.

It was useful to have policy approved by assemblies and declared by councillors, making it more difficult for the pope or other rulers to criticize Philip. Even within France it was useful to lay the blame on ministers for unpopular policies. The council was not a regulated body, only those the king wished to consult on affairs of state or a personal matter. The king set the agenda. We may believe the councillors offered intelligent advice, to which the king listened and then decided whether or not to use. Occasionally we know the council acted under its own steam, as in Paris when Aycelin, Belleperche and Mornay were present during the absence of Philip on the Courtrai campaign. In 1307–8 Charles of Valois, Nogaret and Marigny attended councils held during Philip's absence, though any decisions made remained subject to royal approval. It shows the trust Philip put in his favoured advisers. He certainly consulted his council. In 1313 he shut himself away for four days with a few councillors at Poissy.[35] There is no question that at times there was genuine debate in council, as over the Templars, when Philip and a majority wanted a new order, but Charles of Valois and Marigny opposed. In this case Philip abandoned his position.

The very number of prominent councillors argues against any one of them having overwhelming influence over the king, though some contemporaries claimed that officials held the reins. The papacy blamed Flote for the clash up to 1302, and Nogaret for worsening matters before the death of Boniface. Even Clement V was not quick to forgive the latter. Marigny was said to be the minister 'who knows all the secrets of the king' and whom Favier suggests had more power than any other councillor. Loudéac called him 'a body without a soul, who cares nothing about anyone's rights but only wants to increase the wealth of the king of France'.[36] Strayer feels that Philip made an error in delegating control to Marigny, who had too much power.[37] Jean de Condé wrote of Marigny, 'the king did nothing without him'. In an anonymous work, Marigny was the fox with red hair who governed in place of the lion (king). The continuator of William de Nangis saw Marigny as a new mayor of the palace, and a foreign diplomat thought him the 'second king in France'.[38] Possibly the more moderate financial policy of the later years reflected Marigny's caution. We can however maintain that Philip was the decision-maker. On his deathbed he declared that if he received bad advice it was because he asked for it! This is not to say his decisions were always correct. Strayer has suggested that Philip's 'will was stronger than his intelligence'.[39] Like many another political leader, he always thought he was right and lacked the ability to see an opposing point of view.

Ministers were attacked partly because it was less dangerous to criticize them than the king. It was at times useful for Philip to blame policy on his council, or postpone a decision by saying that his council must debate the matter. Once he avoided giving a foreign ambassador the hoped-for response because 'his council would not consent'.[40] There are other examples of Philip rejecting council advice. The relation between Philip and his councillors was close and good; he trusted them and they were loyal. Through a long reign there was no serious clash. Philip did not dismiss ministers and defended them against criticism. Councillors might take the blame for policies but they were not removed or disgraced.

Philip's reign saw the beginnings of the Estates-General, which first met at Notre-Dame in Paris in 1302 to support Philip against the papacy. This was an assembly of delegates and at least partly representative of the nation. General assemblies (*parlements*) met in 1302 and 1303 over Boniface VIII, in 1308 about the Templars, and 1314 over the subsidy for Flanders. Philip saw the value of demonstrable public support for his acts. He used *parlement*, council, and local assemblies to back his policies, especially the more controversial ones.

Parliament was defined by an ordinance of 1307. As Favier has said, over Boniface and the Templars, Parliament provided 'a sort of national consent to a delicate operation'.[41] A contemporary chronicle referred to 'a Parliament of nobles and non-nobles of all the realm'.[42] It was primarily a judicial assembly, 'the *curia* acting in its judicial capacity'.[43] Its functions were judicial and financial but not legislative. Its classic composition was of clergy, nobility and commons – the three estates. The chief organ of Parliament was the Chamber for Pleas or Great Chamber, dealing with pleas and ordering arrests. The Chamber of Requests emerged at the end of the 13th century. From 1307 the Chamber of Inquests appeared. Parliament operated from the royal palace in Paris, rebuilt by Philip IV with a Great Hall. Parliament had little chance of independent action. It was only called when the king needed its support. Then his ministers expressed the royal view. Speeches were made at critical moments by Flote, Nogaret, Plaisians and Marigny. Consent was expected. The king could in any case by a letter of remission reverse any decision made in parliament.

Local assemblies also developed, with which Philip made efforts to co-operate. They first appeared in Languedoc in the 12th century. Representation commonly was based on urban communities. They were prepared to attack abuse by royal officials in the localities. At times the crown was forced to give way and dismiss or punish officials but local assemblies were manipulated by the crown to back up treaties, as over Flanders, or to agree to taxation. Philip found little difficulty in getting wide support in his clashes with the papacy.

The reign of Philip IV saw the extension of royal power within the localities. Sometimes this was used for national defence, as with the building of *bastides* in Plantagenet border areas. These were virtually new towns, fortified as refuges. Philip increased the royal role by controlling local lords. This happened in many ways. In 1296 he placed a ban on private wars, duels and tournaments – in line with the policies of Louis IX. In 1306, to conciliate baronial opposition, Philip allowed the judicial duel to be revived. The introduction of national taxation increased involvement in the localities. Philip's care to explain his taxation, to seek approval by council and assemblies, to claim he was taxing only in case of need, and even to return money when that need ended, encouraged popular acceptance of national taxation, though there was still resistance. Philip in the war with England claimed support 'for the defence of the realm'.[44]

Philip's reign saw a re-organization of central administration. The administrative departments were separated from the court and found a home in the palace on the Île-de-la-Cité – the Chambre aux Deniers for the treasury, the Chambre des Comptes for accounts in a new building in the Ste-Chapelle, the Hôtel du Roi for the writing office to the north of the chapel, the archives in a small building behind that. Parliament in Paris met in the great rooms of the royal palace. From Philip's reign the records of the Trésor des Chartes, or administrative archives, began to be kept regularly. A compilation had begun under Philip II but it was Nogaret who ordered new copies, one for the chancery and one for the archives. Peter d'Étampes, the first specialist archivist, was appointed by Philip.

The first known Master of the financial Chamber appeared in 1286. The Keeper of the Seal was a major figure, often a leading minister such as Marigny, and often acting virtually as chancellor. More professional officials were employed, including foreigners. Philip needed advice on policy outside his kingdom, having never travelled further beyond it than a brief visit to Catalonia in 1285. He valued foreign advice on finance, where Italians stood supreme. Accounts were presented thrice a year to the Trésor, or Treasury. At the beginning of the reign sessions were held at the Temple in Paris, as they had been since the 12th century. From 1295 the commissioners met at the Louvre rather than the Temple. The Lombards Biche and Mouche were named as treasurers and saw the Templars as rivals, one cause for the attack on that order. In 1299 the treasure was moved to the Louvre. The Chambre des Comptes emerged, between 1300 and 1310 – when the term first appeared. The move to the new palace occurred at the same time and royal officials took over from the Templars. In the late reign finance was under the care of Enguerrand de Marigny, which helps to explain his unpopularity.

The household or Hôtel travelled with the king, visiting palaces and bases in the demesne, occasionally going further afield. Much of the itinerary was to suit Philip's love of hunting – six hunting expeditions in 1287. The household's most common base was Paris, where it spent on average three months each year in the palace opposite Notre-Dame. It contained many lawyers including the 'knights at law' with university education from Montpellier and elsewhere. Some were civil lawyers, including William de Nogaret, trained in Roman law. The emphasis in training though was still on feudal rather than civil law, as one can see in the work of Philip de Beaumanoir of c.1285, on customs in the Beauvaisis. De Beaumanoir was a knight and *bailli* who emphasized the importance of keeping order through lordship, claiming that every man had a lord, and 'all lay justice is held from the king'. For Philip recourse to the courts prevented private war. Philip enforced the use of his officials outside the demesne, expanding royal authority and judicial profits, though not without local complaint.

Local administration for the king was under *baillis* and seneschals. The traditional methods in north and south were retained. The old demesne came under nine *bailliages* – Paris, Senlis, Vermandois, Amiens, Sens, Orléans, Bourges, Mâcon and Tours. Five additional *bailliages* covered Normandy. Seneschals had the same function in the south. The administrative circuits had their own systems of subdivision: *prévôtés* in the old demesne, *vicomtés* in Normandy, and *vigueries*, *bailes* and *jugeries* in the south. The *juge-mage* became the head of the seneschal's court in the south. But compatibility increased and local administration became 'more structured'.[45] The northern *baillis* and southern seneschals carried out largely the same work. They were royal representatives who held assizes, carried out justice and policing, collected taxes, maintained royal rights in finance and raised troops. The leading *baillis* and seneschals were not generally allowed to establish a strong local link and on average were moved to a different region after three years to avoid corruption and ensure a stronger link to the king than to the region. However, frequent transfer was more common in the north than the south. Leading officials had to attend court regularly to make reports and receive instructions. Nevertheless royal administration was not universal. The four surviving principalities retained their own systems.

Under the major officials were *prévôts* in the north and *bayles* in the south. From 1300 every *bailliage* had an advocate or procurator for causes with a royal interest. Thus *baillis* were given trained legal assistance. Officials were assisted by royal sergeants to enforce decisions, undertake arrests and deal with opposition. Two hundred sergeants were employed by the *prévôt*'s court at the Châtelet in Paris. The zeal of officials throughout the kingdom (sergeants, agents, collectors, clerks and notaries), especially of sergeants, provoked complaints, as at Laurac in 1297 when goods were seized in lieu of payment. Even after a compromise, women and children were left weeping in the street.[46] Philip continued efforts to prevent local officials becoming too entrenched in their district. Nearly all *baillis* and seneschals were moved from 1286–87. Like St Louis, Philip used inquisitions to check his officials, and sometimes ordered redress, but usually the officials were supported. Philip issued an ordinance in 1303 to reform local officials, aimed at preventing the official from having a personal interest in his region, and stressing the need to respect local custom.

Inquisitions under *enquêteurs* begun by Louis IX became a permanent part of government. Some *enquêteurs* were major royal officials, others were 'respectable clergymen and worthy knights', mostly rising younger men.[47] It was a good career move, several clerics going on to gain bishoprics. Some 70 enquêteurs have been identified under Philip, half based in Paris. They checked royal administration in the localities and had power to make amends when necessary. They were the king's 'eyes and ears'. As Philip put it, 'we cannot be everywhere'.[48] The king expected written reports and acted upon them. They worked on a circuit in pairs, one cleric and one knight, commonly one a local and one from the court. Under Philip *enquêteurs* were more involved in local affairs than under St Louis, dealing with royal business and investigating local government, as over property and taxation. As a result they could become unpopular and some were accused of corruption. Charges were made against them, often difficult to prove one way or the other, of high-handed activity such as torturing awkward customers. One was accused of killing a man who had criticized him by stuffing excrement in his mouth.[49] There is no doubt that some of Philip's efforts in the localities were unpopular, notably the levying of taxes. There were several outbreaks of violent opposition, as in 1296 at Puy when tax collectors were blinded and killed.

Philip IV encouraged appeal to royal justice, and with success. The judicial system became more uniform. Appeal was encouraged from ecclesiastical and seigneurial courts to royal justice, initially to the local official such as the *bailli*, and then to Parliament. Philip eventually had to halt direct recourse to Parliament because appeals became too numerous. Sometimes the local lord or abbot opposed such appeals, usually without success. Sometimes the royal case was enforced by sending sergeants, 40 on one occasion to Gascony.[50] It was in the interest of royal justice to be fair, attracting more custom. Nevertheless constant checks on officials, care for the rights of poorer subjects, just decisions and fair punishments were a considerable achievement for the time.

Philip moved towards administering justice evenly throughout the realm. The group that provided most opposition to royal authority was the clergy, especially in the clash between Philip and Boniface VIII. For all his power and success against the church, Philip had to admit that it held a special position, for example, over questions of marriage and legitimacy that could have widespread social repercussions. Individuals could claim benefit of clergy, which still had some impact. Two men imprisoned in the Châtelet tonsured themselves so they could claim benefit of clergy. The core of the clash was over jurisdiction. Philip sought royal authority over all secular justice; some prelates and the pope opposed this view.

FINANCE

Philip IV's major administrative problem was finding sufficient money for his needs, a problem exacerbated by economic trends over which he had little control. It may be that the French economy was stagnating.[51] Royal income and expenditure was reasonably predictable until c.1290; thereafter expenses rose and fluctuated alarmingly. Philip could raise considerable sums from the demesne, with traditional demands such as *cens*, rents and *corvée*. Money came from justice, tolls, mills, markets and fairs. There was income from land, including the sale of produce, of wine, of wood. Philip profited from every possible source of income, including feudal aids – for knighting his son or marrying his daughter. He collected all available levies, such as crusading taxes and money in lieu of military service. The demesne had expanded but the king could no longer live off his own landed income. Costs rose too fast, exacerbated by the expense of war. A medieval king could rarely avoid war entirely. Philip only once engaged in an avoidable war when he first took on Edward I. Otherwise he tried to avoid war, to use it as a last resort. He quickly pulled out of the Aragon conflict initiated by his father. He was prepared to negotiate and compromise, but the cost of war in the crisis years was about 2 million *livres per annum*.[52] Even when war was avoided, there were costs for garrison troops and defence. Philip did raise money by commuting military service, charging those who did not appear – whether summoned or not.

One of Philip's most original financial solutions was to demand general taxation for the first time in France – a hundredth, and three fiftieths – levied between 1295 and 1301 for the war with England, and again later. The English war cost 3 million *livres tournois*.[53] Taxes were imposed on all non-noble subjects. The nobility often received a share from the tax, which helped to win their acceptance but meant it fell more heavily on ordinary folk and aroused opposition. The war in Flanders made Philip extend his demands to the nobility, but opposition meant he did not repeat the experiment. The levy of 1304 raised more than any tax from the previous 50 years. In the end general taxation was the direction royal finance had to go, though Philip's efforts were little more than a failed experiment. Subsidies for war in Flanders were demanded twice at the end of the reign but dropped because of opposition after truces were agreed.

There was other contemporary criticism of Philip's financial efforts. The first came from their impact on the currency. The monarchy had always made a small profit from coining but Philip IV tried to make more, abandoning the policy of St Louis and risking the loss of respect for the currency. Philip revalued the coinage, changing the value of the *gros* against the *denier*. This was followed by debasement of the metal content of coins. In 1295, 1303 and 1311, the coinage was revalued, which brought short-term profit but meant the coinage lost its reputation. Financial stability suffered and Philip was dubbed 'the false coiner' by Dante among others.[54] This was a distortion since Philip was no forger and devaluation was hardly a novelty – for three centuries there had been gradual devaluation. The 13th century saw a monetary revolution. Italian cities minted heavier and better alloy coins. In 1266 St Louis produced the silver *gros tournois*. Silver money was good but there was too little silver and too few coins. In 1295 Philip introduced his 'black' coinage, using less fine silver. He also introduced the new 'double'. Money no longer held its intrinsic value. Black money became the main coinage simply because there was not enough of any other kind.

Devaluation was used in the central period of the reign, from 1295 to 1306, a policy used from 1303 for the Flemish war. By 1303 the coinage lost three times its value against gold. The devaluation in 1303 affected the value of the silver *gros* for the first time. From 1309 gold rose in value and the balance became more unstable. Peter Dubois expressed a common complaint, that the value of his revenue decreased annually by 500 *livres*.[55] The use of two standards, gold and silver, bi-metallism, probably caused more instability than devaluation. The changing value of silver against gold was alarmingly erratic, gold rising by up to 40% against silver. The lack of silver resulted in its diminishing use in the coinage, hence the 'black' coins. In effect there were never enough coins to meet need. The constant change in the monetary system, six times in 15 years, created even more instability. The good faith of Philip's government was brought into question. Philip did gain, doubling his profit from manipulating the difference between the real and the devalued value, but at great cost in popularity.

Partly this was caused by the increasing need for money. Philip began his reign with debt from Philip III's war against Aragon. The problem was increased by wars against England and Flanders late in the reign. Strayer labels these engagements 'a mistake'. Peter Dubois at the time suggested that Philip was 'poorly advised' and was making the situation worse by extravagance, paying more to troops than was necessary – even those who owed military service. There was organized opposition and Philip was forced to promise a return to the good money of St Louis. He finally kept this promise in 1306 but only provoked new resentment from those possessing the new money that now lost its value. Before his promise became effective, political resentment boiled over. At Châlons-sur-Marne in 1306 a crowd attacked the mint. Prisoners were freed and there were marches at night to music by the light of torches. There was a rising in Paris in 1307, crowds assembling under the royal windows, after which many were imprisoned and 28 hanged. One positive move to set against this damage was the production of a new coin. In 1290 the gold *royal* appeared, worth ten *sous tournois* or 120 *deniers*. The *petit royal* was lighter than ancient coinage but of pure gold and appreciated. In 1311, the gold *agnel* or angel was minted but suffered from the unstable relation between silver and gold.

Further complaint arose from Philip's desperate search for new methods of raising money. The reign saw the introduction of indirect taxation in 1292, a tax on sales called the *maltôte* (evil levy) raised at a *denier* in the *livre*. Like much in this reign, necessity bred invention, and ways of raising money that became important later were introduced, even if they failed – the new tax proved costly to collect. Too many were exempt, too little came in, and it fell heavily on the ordinary population. It brought large and unpopular profits for certain officials and after five years was dropped. Collection of unpaid tax was another problem. In 1297–98 officials virtually raided Toulouse to collect what was owed, seizing goods and evicting debtors. The result was complaint, resentment, and penalties cancelled. Philip gained less from his innovations than was believed by his subjects – itself a major problem, bringing unpopularity without the income sought. Geoffrey de Paris wrote:

> You have had the hundredth,
> And after that the fiftieth,
> And then such aids …
> From the Templars in silver and gold
> Which must be in your treasury,
> From the Jews and usurers
> And the Lombards, many pennies.[56]

Philip's subjects could see that his ministers profited. Marigny made a fortune, raking in over 15,000 *livres per annum*.

The other main difficulty was that Philip provoked hostility by taking taxation the church claimed for itself. The financial argument was part of a growing conflict with the papacy. Philip forbade the export of precious metal to deprive the papacy of income from France. The papacy was not mentioned in his orders but suffered because payments to Rome were halted. The king ordered customs posts to be built on the border with Italy to stop gold bullion going from France to Rome. This led to papal complaints, which contributed to the clash with Boniface VIII. Nevertheless Philip received considerable amounts from taxes on the church, much of it with papal consent. A tenth was levied on the French clergy in 1295 and, though not taken every year, continued to the end of the reign. In 1312 Clement V granted a crusade tenth for six years.

Probably Philip's least successful financial efforts were what Strayer termed 'one-shot operations', that could only be used once or only once with effect. Attempted gain from the treatment of Jews, Lombards and Templars are of this kind. Because of the prominence given to the Templars, it is sometimes forgotten that Philip IV pursued the anti-Jewish policies of his grandfather, Louis IX. Such short-term projects occurred in the years after 1304, when the last large general tax was imposed. Philip tried to present a more moderate face to his subjects – halting major taxation, restoring good money (in 1306), and not collecting the full tenth allowed by Benedict XI. Any chance to fill the gap was welcome and unpopular minority groups were targeted.

Philip's acts concerning the Jews probably stemmed from a Christian contempt for those held responsible for the killing of Christ, and hope of gain from their supposed wealth. In 1295 the Jews of Beaucaire were arrested and the richest held as hostages. They had to hand over their wealth before being released. In 1306 all Jews were arrested and their goods seized and sold off. Later they were allowed to return from exile on certain conditions. They found fewer defenders than the Templars and the matter was less of a public issue. As with Louis IX the measures harmed the French economy for relatively small gain. Favier compared squeezing money from Jews and Lombards to the pressing of fruit, at first there is plenty of juice, but the more one presses the less there is to come.[57]

Philip tried to defend his demands. Local assemblies and the council were frequently consulted and their agreement broadcast. Philip paid heed to the growing belief, developed by the church, that extraordinary taxation should only be levied in case of necessity. The Aristotelian maxim of *cessante causa, cessare debet effectus* ('when the cause ceases, the effect also ceases') had been popularized in the 12th century.[58] Peter of Auvergne applied it to royal taxation and Peter Dubois in the early 13th century suggested it was immoral to collect or keep more tax than was needed. Perhaps surprisingly, Philip was the first French king to take the idea seriously. (St Louis believed all his taxation was just and there was no need to halt or repay it.) Philip instructed his officials to act carefully, 'to speak to the people with gentle words'.[59] At times he halted war tax when truce or peace was established. In 1313 he ordered the repayment of money collected when peace was made with Flanders. He did much the same in 1314 the year of his death. His will showed remorse over taxation and a desire to make amends. On the day before his death he cancelled the tax for a war that had not developed.

As with St Louis, there was a royal move against Italian moneylenders. In 1291 the order against the 'Lombards' was repeated. In 1311 a royal ordinance expelled all Italians and their goods were seized. Ironically, Philip placed much trust in Italian moneylenders from whom he borrowed, in particular the Florentine brothers 'Biche and Mouche', royal advisers who arranged hefty loans for the king. They were Albizzo and Musciatto Guidi dei Franzesi, who came to France under Philip III. Philip's leading ministers, like Flote and Nogaret, were not financial specialists, perhaps a reason for the unsuccessful financial policies. Towards the end of the reign Marigny took over finance with a better grasp of the subject and advised moderation, but by that stage, given the economic trends, he had less success than one might have expected.

Philip's attempts to raise more tax with broad acceptance fell apart at the end of the reign. He received assent from national and local assemblies and expressed his reasons for taxation, accepting limits on it, in particular to halt tax if the cause ended. One problem was that in seeking greater efficiency he caused greater resentment. Thus in 1287–98 two senior, experienced officials, Peter of Latilly and Ralph of Breuilly, led a commission into Toulouse and Albi.[60] They negotiated amounts of tax and collected what was owed, investigating local officials. They planned to reform local corruption but collected a considerable sum and provoked complaints. Some royal agents acted harshly. At Laurac in 1297, to collect what was owed, two lesser agents backed by 24 sergeants seized property and locked people out of their homes. A bishop called such agents 'officials of hell'.[61] The number of such 'reforming' missions increased and so inevitably did resentment. There was also opposition to new forms of tax and experiments with the coinage. Philip survived the financial crisis of 1302–5. He did note criticism and in 1303 assessments were reduced.

Philip dropped major taxation in the latter part of his reign until the final year. In 1314 war with Flanders demanded a new major levy – but it had to be dropped. In 1314 local communities banded together to oppose the growing burden of tax. Philip was accused of breaking his coronation oath and raising new taxes. Leagues were formed for example in Burgundy, bringing together nobles, commons and clergy. They elected representatives to bring complaints before the king. Only certain regions participated and it never became quite a national movement, but the assemblies posed a serious threat to methods of government. Local leagues planned a more general confederation with representatives from each – for example one assembly for Vermandois, Beauvais, Ponthieu and Arras, another for Champagne, Burgundy and Forez. Philip's death left the solution of this crisis to his son, Louis X.

FOREIGN POLICY

Like St Louis, Philip IV's foreign relations were mainly concerned with France's neighbours, border disputes rather than foreign policy. Philip avoided involvement in foreign adventures – in Italy, Spain, the Holy Land and Germany. The two main concerns in his reign were Flanders and Aquitaine, which inevitably meant conflict with England. Disputes in Flanders also involved the empire, as did the southern border with the Iberian powers, notably Aragon.

It is unlikely that the views of Peter Dubois had much effect on policy but they reflect a contemporary opinion. Dubois was a Norman who studied in Paris and became an advocate in Coutances. He was patriotic and thought France deserved to be the most powerful nation. He wrote pamphlets condemning Boniface VIII and the Templars. He offered himself for royal service but was not employed, possibly because of his forceful ideas. He believed France should lead a new crusade to recover the Holy Land, a common contemporary view for which Philip expressed some support. In 1313 he took the cross but showed little sign of actually going. Dubois also supported every possibility of the expansion of France – in Tuscany, Sicily, Aragon, Castile, Hungary and Byzantium, as well as against England and the empire. The pope should reside in France and to Dubois the future was universal sovereignty for the Capetians. Although these matters were debated at the time, Dubois' views were too facile and unrealistic, and not shared by Philip's chosen advisers.[62]

ENGLAND

Philip was a cautious king who avoided war when truce or compromise was possible. He learned a lesson early in his reign from the conflict with England when he pressed a dispute to the point of war – though some historians have attached blame to Edward. Strayer argues that Edward did not desire war and tried to avoid it while Philip was the aggressor.[63] There were coastal attacks by both sides, by France against Dover, and by England against the Île-de-Rhé. The English under the Earl of Lincoln were beaten at Bonnegarde. Between 1291 and 1296 the French overran Guyenne under Charles of Valois and Robert of Artois. England and Flanders allied but were beaten at Furnes and a truce was made followed by peace despite a brief rising in Bordeaux. Edward wanted to evade personal submission and sent as proxy his brother Edmund of Lancaster, married to Joan of Navarre's mother Blanche. Edward was prepared to hand over officials from Gascony who had caused offence, and to surrender six strongholds. The conditions were tough but Edmund accepted them. Edward offered to come before Philip if given a safe-conduct but it was refused and he declared Guyenne forfeit because Edward did not appear. Each accused the other of breaking the agreement. The war proved demanding and costly. Peace was agreed in 1299, cemented by marriage alliances. Edward I was to marry Philip's sister Margaret, and Edward's son Edward was to marry Philip's daughter Isabelle (as happened in 1308). Guyenne was then restored. Philip did not generally seek confiscation of lands and was content with recognition of his overlordship. What he discovered was that this outcome could be reached without the expense of a dangerous war.

The other main problem area between Philip and England was Aquitaine. The stress on far north and then far south suggests that Capetian authority was firmly established in the heart of France. At first Edward I was prepared to conciliate France and concentrate on Britain. He did homage to Philip for his French lands, ceding Limoges, Cahors and Périgueux to receive them back as fiefs, a move he later regretted. Philip refused to return the territories and in 1295 attacked surviving English-held territories. Guyenne was conquered by Charles of Valois and Robert of Artois. English troops in Gascony were massacred and allies of England persecuted, 50 of them hanged. Philip claimed he was countering English raids but modern historians see Philip as the aggressor.[64] He 'wanted a war – and he got it'.[65] Aquitaine was handed to Ralph de Nesle and Philip prepared to invade England. He had, however, miscalculated the reaction of Edward who now invested resources in a war with Philip, the costliest of Edward's several costly wars.

One possibility for Edward was to seek allies on the continent. Many lords on the borders of France and the empire were ready to listen, including Adolf of Nassau, the duke of Brabant and the counts of Bar, Savoy and Jülich. Philip sought his own allies there, and on Edward's Scottish border. With Philip engaged in Flanders, a rising occurred in Bordeaux, provoked by unpopular taxation. Finally in 1303 Philip compromised. Aquitaine was returned to Edward on condition that he abandon his intervention in Flanders. Peace was consolidated in 1308 with the marriage between Edward (II) and Isabelle. Philip usually avoided war where he could. The only example of uncalled for conflict was that initial clash with Edward.

FLANDERS

The dispute in Flanders was halted by St Louis' compromise, but not resolved. The interests of the empire, France and England remained likely causes of conflict. The rivalry between the claimant families of Dampierre and D'Avesnes remained. Louis had favoured the Dampierres, while the D'Avesnes who received Hainault were allied with the empire. A dispute in 1291 led to a new French invasion under Charles of Valois, and the submission of the count of Hainault. Edward I of England sought alliance with Flanders, offering money and the continuation of the wool export from England. Count Guy could hardly refuse and became embroiled in war against Philip. When Charles of Valois invaded Flanders for Philip in 1297 no one came to the count's aid. The French took Lille and Cassel, while Courtrai and Bruges surrendered. The French occupied all western Flanders except for Ypres and Douai. Edward I made a separate peace, breaking his promise to Count Guy, who was isolated. Boniface VIII offered no encouragement against Philip, and Robert of Béthune took over in Flanders for Philip.

Flanders remained unsettled and hostile to France. Charles of Valois invaded again in 1300 and occupied most of the Flemish towns. Guy submitted and this time he and his sons were imprisoned. Guy was taken to Paris and then Compiègne. A relation of Queen Joan, Jacques de Châtillon, was made governor of Flanders. He proved a poor choice and unpopular, acting harshly and favouring the patricians. Bourgeois discontent was increased by the need of English wool for the cloth industry. Philip never found a satisfactory policy in Flanders. At times he tried to reverse previous policy and ally with the towns against the count and the nobility, but the pro-French Flemish were the patrician *gens des lys* or *leliaerts*. In 1301 Philip and Joan were actually given a warm welcome in several major Flemish towns but although divide and rule worked well elsewhere, it did not pay dividends in Flanders, partly because of inconsistency. The wars with England damaged Flemish commerce. The truce imposed an enormous burden on Flemish towns and could not be fully enforced. Philip's attempts to return to alliance with the pro-French patricians were ruined by the unpopular truce.

Ghent did not share in the early welcome given to Philip and resented the tax. The people in Ghent attacked the patricians, and captured or killed their officials, the *échevins*. It was the start of a war that lasted until 1305. In 1302 there was a rising against the French governor of Flanders, Jacques de Châtillon, known as the Friday or Matins of Bruges. The *bailli* of Bruges arrested some ringleaders but others broke into the prison and released them. The governor removed liberties from Bruges and restored the tax in Ghent. In Ghent the patricians were besieged in the fortress. On the fatal Friday the citizens slaughtered the patricians of Bruges and the French garrison. The governor entered with troops and, thinking the danger over, went to bed. In the morning rebels arrived at his gate to find the French guards asleep. The rebels took over the town and killed any they saw as enemies. The governor and Peter Flote escaped to Courtrai. Bruges was joined by the towns of western Flanders. Leaders emerged in Peter de Coninck a clothier from Bruges, and William of Jülich the exiled nephew of the count. The count's son Guy also returned. The rebellion was not popular with all; its leaders were seen as extremists and, after initially wide support, the rising began to lose its grip.

Philip sent in a French army under his brother Robert of Artois, which suffered a major disaster at Courtrai on 11 July 1302. The French tried to recover Bruges and relieve the citadel at Courtrai. The Flemings assembled under Guy of Namur, William of Jülich and Jean de Renesse. The Flemish urban militia was mainly infantry armed with pikes, knives, crossbows and *goedendags*. When the armies faced each other the Flemish dug ditches against the cavalry. The French charged but were held. The French garrison from the castle sortied against the Flemish rear but was beaten off. Robert of Artois made a final bid with the rearguard but his horse was wounded, dragged to the ground and killed. Peter Flote, Jacques de Châtillon and 1,000 French knights were among the dead. Courtrai was called the battle of the Golden Spurs from the 700 pairs removed from French corpses. It was the first infantry force 'to defeat a great knightly army since Roman times'.[66]

This was 'the great crisis of Philip's reign'.[67] The defeat in Flanders coincided with the climax of his dispute with Boniface VIII, and with financial crisis. Flemish rebels now invaded Artois. Philip IV, however, was nothing if not dogged. He made efforts to restore his authority. A truce was agreed in 1303. Count Guy was released in a bid to regain French control and, although this failed, Philip recovered in Flanders within two years. A sea battle was won off Zierikzee in Zeeland in 1304 by a French fleet under its Genoese commander Rainier Grimaldi. The Flemish leader, Guy of Namur, was captured. Three sons of the old count became prisoners of the French and Flanders was again isolated. Philip gained his revenge. He invaded Flanders but was retreating when his route was blocked at Mons-en-Pévèle between Douai and Lille. Both sides hesitated before the Flemings took the offensive. It was a hot day and men on both sides died of sunstroke. The count of Boulogne, for Philip, set up balistas and began a barrage. Philip ordered cavalry attacks on the flanks, plus an infantry attack on the enemy rear. The Flemish had some success with crossbows, and reached the French baggage train. Philip was unhorsed but handed an axe to defend himself. The knight who gave Philip his horse was decapitated. Philip's new horse bolted but the king came to no harm. He led the vital charge, crying 'Montjoie St-Denis'. William of Jülich was killed and his head brought on a pike to Philip. The Flemings retreated and Philip entered Lille.

Negotiations followed in Paris, though with Flemish knights rather than citizens. Count Guy died at Compiègne and Philip released Robert of Béthune to be installed as count in 1305. Peace was agreed by the treaty of Athis-sur-Orge. Lille, Douai and Béthune were ceded to Philip but passed to the new count. Robert agreed to pay an indemnity of 400,000 *livres* over four years, and other charges were levied on the defeated towns that could have paralysed economic life. Bruges was set to pay heavily for the massacre of the Matins. Flemish patricians recovered their property. Defences and citadels of major towns were to be razed. Three hundred offenders from Bruges had to undertake pilgrimages as penance. The Flemish towns had to accept this 'peace of misery' though they resisted its terms and remained resentful, blaming the count as much as the French.[68] Robert and his two brothers were to be imprisoned if the 'impossible' treaty was not carried out.[69]

The divisions in Flanders reappeared. Count Robert had nowhere to hide. Siding with France made him unpopular in Flanders; it meant yielding practically all power. In 1311 he failed to attend a conference at Tournai. A document was read to the assembly reminding it of the fate of disloyal counts. Enguerrand de Marigny was probably responsible for a mellowing of the French attitude over the treaty.[70] The fine for Bruges was lowered. In 1309 all the towns except Bruges attended the making of the treaty of Paris, a modified agreement. Bruges finally submitted though resentment still simmered. By 1311 Marigny was pressing for Count Robert to abdicate in favour of his son, Louis of Nevers. Marigny sought various solutions through marriage alliances, which did not work. He angered Charles of Valois, who felt that his own interests were being neglected. Count

Robert and his son distrusted Marigny and refused to enter Tournai even under a safe-conduct. When Philip summoned them to Paris, Louis went but Robert did not – wisely. Accusations were levelled against Louis, who was imprisoned. On the way to Montlhéry the guards got drunk and, wrongly believing Louis to be in the same condition, allowed him to escape. Robert fled to imperial Flanders seeking aid which he failed to get. In 1312 he had to submit again. Philip raised an army but had no need to use it. By the treaty of Pontoise Philip reduced his financial demands and returned Cassel to the count, while Robert ceded Lille, Douai and Béthune. Philip had gained his ends. The count of Flanders had submitted and he gained three valuable towns. At the council of Arras in 1313 Count Robert swore to keep the peace, offered Courtrai to Philip, and his son Robert of Cassel as hostage.

There was a further threat in 1314 when Robert again broke his promises while accusing Philip of bad faith and various crimes – including the murder of his father Count Guy in prison. The French were forced out of Courtrai, and French garrisons in Flanders were attacked. Only Ypres kept out of the rebellion. Again Philip prepared to use force but an advance into Flanders was enough to break the revolt. A new agreement returned to Philip all the lands held at the outbreak of trouble, including Courtrai, and 13 castellanies. Philip's death marked the end of a chapter but a new one was bound to begin. Count Robert did homage to the new king, Louis X, but the Flemish problem had not found a final settlement. Nevertheless from this time onwards Walloon Flanders remained French.

THE HOLY ROMAN EMPIRE

Philip's relations with the empire were delicate but mainly peaceful. Problems arose from mutual interest in several regions, not least Flanders. In the south lands that had formerly been imperial became papal and increasingly French, including the county of Burgundy (as opposed to the duchy), later known as the Franche-Comté. When Count Otto IV became embroiled in conflict with the emperor in 1289 it was natural that he should turn to France for aid. Philip sought to increase French involvement in the region.

At times the empire threatened alliance with England and Flanders but Philip always found allies among the divided princes of Germany. Philip's interest lay in areas that bordered the empire and might be won over, notably French-speaking areas and territories west of the Saône – Vivarais, Lyon and the county of Burgundy. Philip acted ruthlessly over Lyon, knowing that the citizens favoured his authority over their archbishop. He appointed a seneschal and annexed it to the demesne. However, dispute followed, and Louis of Navarre had to enter Lyon in force in 1310 to capture the archbishop, Peter of Savoy, who ceded jurisdiction in 1312. Lyon then remained part of France.

Philip took opportunities as they arose. At every vacancy for king of the Germans a French candidate was named, though hope of election was never high and never realized. Philip also sought marriage alliances. After the death of

Frederick II the empire suffered chronic instability. With the election of Adolf of Nassau came a new period of conflict. Adolf supported Jean d'Avesnes against the Capetians but in 1296 was forced to make peace with Philip in order to conciliate the papacy. Adolf was defeated and killed in conflict with Albert of Austria in 1298. Though Albert opposed the peace between Philip and Adolf, he now found himself in a similar position, needing support against Boniface VIII. Terms were agreed in 1299. It was arranged that Albert's son Rudolf should marry Philip's sister Blanche. Boniface sought to break the alliance with offers and promises to Albert, but the pope's death removed most of the problems. However, the settlement with Albert was ended when he was assassinated in 1308.

In the elective empire there was no certainty over the succession and policies constantly changed. France intervened in every election during the period, often putting up a candidate. On Albert's death, Philip's brother Charles of Valois was named. Philip made half-hearted efforts on his behalf but was not greatly distressed when Henry of Luxembourg was elected. Henry was a pro-French prince who had been at Philip III's court and done homage to Philip IV, who knighted him and paid him a pension. Philip's main aim was to find a co-operative candidate and Henry VII seemed perfect. He sided with Philip against Boniface VIII and attended the coronation of Clement V. Henry died in 1313 and this time the French candidate was Philip's son Philip the Long, count of Poitiers. Philip IV's interest was only prompted by the unwelcome candidacy of Louis of Nevers. Philip's councillor, Marigny, was against involvement because of the expense and probable failure. Lewis of Bavaria was elected and caused no serious problem for Philip.

Although the Holy Roman Empire was not Philip's main problem, this was the turning point of their relative positions in Europe. St Louis had stressed that the king of France was under no one but God and that idea was worked out more fully by Philip IV. Boniface VIII provoked Philip by declaring in 1302 that the empire had supremacy over the king. In 1312 Henry VII repeated the claim. Philip protested and his supporters claimed 'Rex est imperator in regno suo' (the king is emperor in his own realm).[71] In terms of their relative position as states France was stronger than the empire through the rest of the Middle Ages.

SPAIN AND ITALY

Philip made peace with the Spanish powers. At his accession France was committed to a crusade against Aragon undertaken by his father. Philip was the son of Isabella of Aragon and maintained a friendly attitude to his Spanish relatives, notably his uncle Pedro III. During the war in his father's reign Philip had been in secret contact with his uncle. As king he withdrew from the crusade and made peace. Philip IV's brother, Charles of Valois, had hoped for gains in the conflict and was compensated. The dispute over the Val d'Aran was settled later. Charles abandoned his hopes in Spain, diverted by other ambitions. He was granted lands in Italy as well as the counties of Maine and

Anjou, and chased possible crowns in Italy and Byzantium. In 1296 he married Catherine de Courtenay the granddaughter and heiress of the Latin Emperor Baldwin II.

In Italy the main possible source of conflict was over rival claims of the French Angevins and Aragon. After the loss of the island of Sicily, Philip's Angevin relations sought his aid to recover the island but received little help. In the end the old kingdom was divided between the Angevin kingdom of Naples on the mainland and the insular Aragonese kingdom of Trinacria. Charles of Valois' marriage to Catherine was approved by the papacy, although they were cousins, on condition that Charles oppose the Spanish in Italy. Charles made the mistake of allying with the Blacks against the Whites in Florence in 1301, and was blamed for their atrocities on entering the city – for which Dante placed him in Purgatory in *The Divine Comedy*. In 1302 Charles left Naples to recover Sicily. Boniface withdrew support as the clash with Philip developed so Charles failed in Tuscany and then in Sicily. Villani, who hoped Charles would aid his side in Tuscany, expressed bitter disappointment: Charles had 'come to Tuscany to make peace and left it at war'; he had 'gone to war in Sicily and made a shameful peace'.[72]

Charles of Valois was the loose cannon in the Capetian family abroad. He had high ambitions that were constantly thwarted. His marriages brought various involvements, notably through Margaret of Sicily in Italy, and Catherine de Courtenay in Byzantium. Philip was fond of Charles and made him promises, but in the end gave little real aid. It was said of Charles that though son, brother and father of a king, he never won a kingdom for himself. The failures must however be balanced by the knowledge that his son founded the Valois dynasty in France.

THE CHURCH

Philip IV is generally best remembered for his conflict with the church, or more precisely with the papacy. This is ironic in that Philip aimed to follow his saintly grandfather, Louis IX. Philip wanted to appear pious and devout. He worried about life after death. The enigma is partly answered by noting that Philip did give much support to the church in France, and the French church regularly supported him in the clashes with the papacy.

It might be argued that clashes with the Church have featured overmuch in reviews of the reign. There were dramatic clashes with certain bishops, with Boniface VIII, and with the Templars, but Philip's reign also saw close co-operation with the papacy under Clement V, and during the move of the papacy to Avignon. Philip made gifts to religious foundations. He had ecclesiastical councillors and often heeded their advice. He restored taxes on the maxim of *causa cessante* – as the church recommended. He attacked heresy, Jews, and usurers in line with church policy. It was in Philip's interest to co-operate with the papacy, since he needed assent to tax the French clergy. Until the 19th century Philip was not viewed as an enemy of the church. He was on good terms with the papacy for all but five years of his long reign and was almost always on good terms with his own bishops and clergy.

HERESY AND BISHOPS

Philip IV made efforts to follow Louis IX, to favour the church and to eradicate heresy. He found difficulty in pursuing such aims when at odds with the papacy. Early in the reign he tried compromise, as with Nicholas IV over jurisdiction in Chartres and Poitiers. Ironically the future Boniface VIII helped to make the peace and Philip promised to aid the papacy in Sicily.

Philip was torn between politics and religion in southern France where Capetian power had increased but was not secure. Philip found that by taking sides in local disputes he endangered his overall position. The king had influence over the operation of the Inquisition in France; Bernard Guy, inquisitor for Toulouse, was allowed annual expenses from the royal budget. The inquisitors became increasingly unpopular in the aftermath of the Albigensian Crusade. They acted on rumour and anonymous denunciations, and from 1250 used torture. Sympathy for opponents of the Inquisition began to look like support for heresy. After a period of dabbling in hostility to the Inquisition, Philip settled for a more traditional royal view.

The central incident concerned Bernard Délicieux, a young Franciscan from Carcassonne, who was born at Montpellier and travelled in France and Italy. He was an eloquent preacher who inflamed local feeling with criticism of the Dominican Inquisition. He claimed that the bishops of Albi and Toulouse used it for political ends and became a spokesman for the local people who felt oppressed. He came to court to put their case. Philip listened in his customary silence, prepared to take action against the bishop of Albi. Nogaret, who may have been the grandson of a Cathar, encouraged Philip against the Inquisition. Its agents used powers that Philip thought should be reserved for royal officials. Joan of Navarre was addressed by a citizen of Albi as 'our hope'.[73] The royal couple travelled south where Philip received a welcome from the supporters of Élie Patrice the 'little king of Carcassonne' who opposed the Inquisition. Philip soon saw the danger of associating too closely with the popular movement and backed off. He was worried by the radicalism of Délicieux, who suggested that even Peter and Paul would have been unable to clear themselves before the Inquisition. Increasing disorder spurred Philip to action. When Patrice tried to make a speech before him, Philip ordered the sergeants to remove him. Presents from the citizens of Carcassonne were returned. Philip made his peace with the papacy and recognized papal authority over the Inquisition. Patrice and Délicieux were disillusioned and turned to the prince of Mallorca for support. Philip's fears were confirmed when they began to consider an independent Languedoc. Benedict XI ordered the arrest of Délicieux in 1304. Bernard went to Paris seeking Philip's support but was refused an audience, arrested, and sent to Rome. Philip now saw it as a problem for the papacy to resolve.

The radical Patrice was arrested by Philip's seneschal of Carcassonne. With church and noble assent, Patrice and 15 others were hanged. Bernard was returned to the care of Philip and finally released in 1308. It is thought that this lenient treatment was due to Joan of Navarre. Bernard entered the Franciscan priory at Béziers in 1315. When he went to the pope at Avignon he was arrested again in 1318. He was accused of opposing the Inquisition, of treachery against Philip, and of poisoning Benedict XI. He was sentenced to life imprisonment and died two years later.

The second clerical confrontation was with Guichard, bishop of Troyes. Guichard was abbot of Mortier-la-Celle and close to Queen Blanche of Navarre and her daughter Joan. He was short and fat, ruddy complexioned, ugly and bad-tempered. His rapid rise ended in a sudden fall. A suspected fraudster, Jean de Calais, was put under his care. When Jean fled, Guichard was accused of conniving at his escape. It seems likely that the accusations were made by a jealous rival, Simon Festu. Guichard was also accused of irregularities over Blanche of Navarre's finances. After her death in 1302, Joan continued to hound the disgraced bishop, who was accused of poisoning Blanche. Guichard finally agreed to repay 40,000 *livres*. In 1305 Joan died but the royal persecution continued, despite support for Guichard from Clement V. It was said that the bishop travelled at night in company of a sorcerer, and had planned to poison Charles of Valois. Philip pressured the papacy into an investigation. Guichard was imprisoned at Sens and then in the Louvre. The accusations were elaborated by spin into unlikely charges against a declared enemy. He was accused of sodomy, having a child by a nun that he later killed, sorcery, making and piercing wax images, homage to the devil, spitting on the cross, usury, killing Queen Joan, making poison from scorpions, toads and spiders – which he denied. When his valet declared that he had not even gone out at night, the unfortunate servant was suspended naked by four limbs. Nogaret further embroidered the charges – claiming Guichard had a mistress who was a butcher's wife, had killed a priest, poisoned his own prior, was a usurer, a sodomite, a forger, an alchemist, and had beaten his concubine in public. Nogaret declared the bishop was not a man but an incubus.[74]

There are those historians who accept that Philip and his ministers believed what they said. Strayer thought Philip 'was inclined to believe the worst of everyone'.[75] Elizabeth Brown suggests that contemporaries did think Philip rather credulous.[76] Can one in all honesty accept as even credible the sort of drivel that was produced against Guichard? When one multiplies the number of times such charges were made against enemies of Philip IV, one must conclude that charges were exaggerated and invented as a cynical propaganda exercise. In the event this was not a major case, and Guichard did not suffer long or hard. Several contemporaries doubted his guilt. Noffo Dei, who as a royal agent had made charges against the bishop, dropped the accusations when facing his own execution – declaring the bishop innocent. He had little to gain by lying and one is inclined to believe him. For some time Guichard was kept in prison at Avignon, and then quietly appointed to a job in remote Croatia as bishop of Diakovar, though he may never have gone there. He died in 1317.

THE CLASH WITH BONIFACE VIII

As France became the most powerful monarchy in the west, so relations with the church deteriorated. One result of a more powerful Capetian monarchy was opposition to papal intervention in France. There was a hostile reaction to papal efforts at increasing control in secular states. The French king had been the papacy's best friend, frequently giving refuge to popes in retreat from imperial power and secular opposition in Rome. The power of the empire was in decline and France became the main threat to papal monarchy. St Louis upheld the position and rights of the church in France against the papacy but managed it without a major conflict. With Philip IV came the first serious clash between church and state in France.

The clash came with Boniface VIII (1294–1303), formerly Cardinal Benedict Gaetani. There is a story about his election, probably untrue, which reflects contemporary views on him. The previous pope, Celestine V, was a peasant who became a Benedictine abbot and then retired as a hermit on Mount Majella before his election. He was over 80 and a weak pontiff though on good terms with France. Of the 12 cardinals he appointed, five were French, one Provençal and one Angevin. Celestine was contemplating resignation when Boniface introduced a secret speaking tube into his chamber through which, acting as the voice of God, he whispered 'Resign! Resign!' Celestine believed it and resigned. The tale sounds far fetched, and probably Celestine abdicated for his own reasons, but Boniface did shut him up in the castle of Fumore in Campania, where he died 18 months later.

Boniface was from a powerful Italian family, nephew of Alexander IV. He was a confident and assured pope, already suffering from the stone, though still active. He was an experienced jurist and diplomat and one of the most powerful late medieval popes. Boniface called the 1300 Jubilee celebrations in Rome, which proved a great success, bringing thousands to the city. He had considerable experience of the French court, having been the papal representative in Paris for some years from 1290. Perhaps he did not set out to antagonize the French king. He canonized Louis IX in 1297, though it has been suggested that Boniface was slyly criticizing Philip by contrasting him with his saintly predecessor.[77] It is not hard to see the pope's phrases as ironic when he praised Louis' good rule and 'happy reign' as that of a king who did 'neither wrong nor injury'. Boniface's move, if aimed against Philip, backfired. Once his grandfather had been made a saint, Philip played on it for all it was worth – as a symbol of kingship and royal superiority. According to one of Philip's lawyers, 'before there were priests there were kings'.[78]

There were several clashes between Boniface VIII and Philip IV, part of the rival claims to authority between church and state. Philip stated his position under Pope Nicholas IV (d.1292) – declaring there is no territory in the realm 'exempt from our jurisdiction'.[79] The first conflict with the pope was over taxation on the French clergy. The papacy authorized additional imposts for the crusades. The money was used for war against Aragon (declared a crusade) and England. Philip was inclined to raise money on his own decision. Some French clergy appealed against this. In 1296 Boniface issued the bull *Clericis laicos*, claiming that the king could not raise extraordinary taxation from the clergy without papal permission. The pope guaranteed the liberties of the church. Threats were issued against clergy who co-operated with the state, including excommunication and deposition. They were forbidden to acquiesce 'without having obtained the agreement or permission of the apostolic see'.[80]

Two bishops brought the details to Philip who listened in silence. He thanked them and left without a word but he was not planning to sit back. His view was 'Render unto Caesar that which is Caesar's'. He called an assembly, which supported him, and sent bishops to represent his views to the pope. Philip found support within France, where growing anti-clericalism was reflected in pamphlet literature, including the *Dialogue between a Clerk and a Knight*.[81] It was claimed the clergy were not supporting national defence, asked 'was Christ raised from the dead only for clerks?', and stated that 'the church is in the state, the clerks in the nation'.[82]

The king responded to Boniface's attack by forbidding the export of precious metal which halted the payment of French taxes to the papacy. Boniface backed down in 1297, agreed that the king could tax the clergy in an emergency, and canonized Louis IX. Increasingly the pope needed French support for his clash with the Colonna family, powerful in the area between Rome and Naples. They broached the idea of removing Boniface from office because his election was illicit, a suggestion that would be taken up by Philip.

The second major dispute between Philip and Boniface was over the bishop of Pamiers in the Languedoc. Pamiers was a bishopric created by Boniface in 1295 to strengthen the papacy in the Cathar heartland. Bernard Saisset, abbot of St-Antonin in Pamiers, had represented the pope in Sicily and was made bishop of Pamiers. Not surprisingly he proved a loyal supporter of Boniface. The new bishop was soon at odds with his neighbours, the bishop of Toulouse, and the count of Foix. He was outspoken and careless with his comments, over-fond of his drink. He opposed the count's alliance with the crown, which gave the count control of Pamiers. Saisset was critical of Philip IV and expressed himself in somewhat provocative language, suggesting that St Louis should be in hell while Philip was a bastard and false moneyer! Philip had a cool, cold personality but once roused he could stoke up an almost unquenchable anger. Saisset was summoned to Senlis in 1301 and confronted with the accusations, including treason, heresy and voicing obscenities. The archbishop of Narbonne, Gilles Aycelin, could not support the king's position and said that only the pope could judge Saisset, who appealed to Boniface. The pope in December 1301 demanded Saisset's release and sent papal bulls defending him, claiming that his throat had become dry from voicing so many complaints against the king. The accusations against Saisset were sent on to Rome and now included his supposed declaration that fornication was not a sin for priests. Philip did not release Saisset until 1308 and he died in 1311.

When Boniface ordered Saisset's release, he issued the bull *Salvator Mundi* to revoke any subsidy granted to the French king. He called an assembly of French bishops to Rome. Philip called his own assembly and won more support from the bishops than did Boniface. The 30 bulls issued by the Lateran in 1301 were little short of a 'declaration of war'.[83] In Paris the bull *Ausculta fili* was read out before an assembly. Philip maintained his usual cool but his brother Robert of Artois did not. Robert seized the offending document and threw it on the fire. Philip called an assembly in Paris of nobles, clerks and commons to meet in Notre-Dame on 10 April 1302 – widely seen as the first meeting of the Estates-General. Flote made a speech reflecting Philip's response to *Ausculta fili*. He claimed to be the defender of the church against an unworthy pope. No person on earth was superior to the king in temporal affairs. Flote proposed the reform of the Gallican church as a separate entity. Boniface saw this as a threat to church unity, responding that what God had joined no man could separate. He accused Flote of heresy, as 'one possessed by the devil'.[84] He correctly claimed that his own bull had been distorted before its presentation in France. He was perhaps the first to note what had become Philip the Fair's practice of spin on events and views. Boniface in consistory in June 1302 came to an extreme conclusion before the cardinals: 'Let me remind you, my brethren, that our predecessors deposed three kings of France'. Since Philip had committed the same offences as his predecessors, 'we shall cast him down'.[85]

The defeat of the French at Courtrai in 1302, this 'judgement of God', seemed to offer Boniface his chance.[86] He blamed the clash with France on Flote who was among those killed at Courtrai, proof of divine justice. The final clash underlined the principle behind the conflict – the question of final jurisdiction over the church in France. In 1302 Boniface issued the bull *Unam Sanctam*, 'the most absolute proclamation of the theocratic doctrine formulated in the Middle Ages'.[87] He suggested a new definition of the relations between church and state in the old metaphor of the two swords representing the powers. Both swords, he claimed: 'are in the power of the church, the spiritual sword and the material … none can control the spiritual power save God alone'. The church had only one head, the spiritual head, not 'two heads like a monster'. This re-opened the question of investiture, resolved by the compromise of recognizing spiritual authority for the church, and secular authority for the state. An obvious corollary was that a bishop could only be judged by the pope and not by a secular ruler. Events proved what was probably already obvious, that the church was claiming greater authority over secular states in an age when there was little hope of enforcing such a position against powerful nations such as France. Boniface sent a cardinal to France with the bull. Philip made a conciliatory reply but his attitude soon changed. He was probably playing for time after Courtrai. With the death of

Flote, William de Nogaret took over as Philip's main representative. From early 1303 the French pronouncements became markedly more hostile. Jean de Paris was one who defended Philip's position, claiming that royal power did not come from the pope but depended on God.

A notable element in this clash between church and state was Philip's approach. He took refuge behind advice that he sought from ministers and representative bodies, making papal criticism more difficult. Often it seemed that the anti-papal measures came not from the king but from representative groups in France – the council, the assembly, the Estates-General – or from individual ministers acting on their own initiative, such as Peter Flote, William de Nogaret, or Enguerrand de Marigny. These ministers rose through their abilities, winning the respect and trust of the king. They were loyal and he supported them. Flote was a leading lawyer. Marigny had been a squire in Normandy and served Queen Joan before being taken on by the king. Nogaret was from near Toulouse, a respected professor of law who became a royal judge.

In effect Philip put up a smokescreen to blur his own actions. Boniface was forced to direct his hostility against the officials. He accused the king of being 'led by deceiving and spiteful counsel'.[88] Boniface disliked the one-eyed chancellor Flote, whom he called 'half-blind in body and completely blind in spirit'.[89] The pope rejoiced in his death at Courtrai, little realizing that Flote would be replaced by the even more dangerous Nogaret, already with eight years' experience as a royal councillor. Philip launched a propaganda attack on Boniface who was accused of usurping the papal throne, of simony, and heresy. The king suggested a council of cardinals to consider deposing the pope. An assembly called by the king met at the Louvre in 1303 and the accusations were repeated with additions that included buggery, sodomy, idolatry by raising silver statues of himself in Rome, and nepotism for choosing his nephews as cardinals. Nogaret issued accusations against Boniface as a thief who had stolen the papacy, and a simoniac. Nogaret declared 'he is not pope'. 'Nogaret's right arm', William de Plaisians, accused Boniface of sodomy and of defending fornication. The abbot of Cîteaux and the bishop of Autun dared to oppose the attack on the pope; both were arrested and deposed. Few others voiced opposition; the foreign Franciscans at the Cordeliers in Paris did, and were expelled. Two knights were sent to Rome to demand a general council. Others went to foreign princes.

In 1303 the king sent William de Nogaret to Italy 'to secure the peace and unity of the church'. Boniface was about to excommunicate Philip IV, and the king meant to bring him to heel before it was proclaimed. He could count on the support of the Colonna family. Boniface was said to have opposed Charles of Anjou in Sicily and sent an assassin against Philip.[90] Nogaret stayed near Siena in a castle belonging to Mouche. Boniface left Rome for the Gaetani palace in Anagni; in effect he was on holiday and the papal court dispersed. Nogaret heard that the bull *Semper Petri solio*, hostile to Philip, was about to be published and decided to act. He reached Anagni with Sciarra Colonna and 300 men. Colonna attacked and ransacked the Gaetani palace. The troops entered the town before dawn, crying 'Long live the king of France, long live Colonna'.[91] Sciarra had once been captured by pirates and been a galley slave for four years until rescued by the French. He had spent time in France. The Colonnas were long-time enemies of Boniface's family. Historians have argued over the degree of Nogaret's responsibility for what happened but he cannot be cleared completely. The soldiers fired the doors of Anagni cathedral and overran the papal palace. Nogaret made a speech in the town square. Boniface stayed in bed, grasping a reliquary of the True Cross and prepared for martyrdom. Colonna struck him and the pope reacted much as Thomas Becket had done – offering himself for martyrdom: 'Here is my neck, here is my head.' The citizens came out to support Boniface, declaring 'long live the pope, death to foreigners'. They threw things from their windows at the troops. Colonna wanted to execute Boniface but Nogaret had the pope escorted to Rome. Nogaret denied any part in a personal attack on the pope and arranged for his removal south. Nevertheless there is no doubt that Nogaret and the Colonnas were responsible for the disgraceful treatment of a pope. Boniface was moved to safety but he was a bewildered and broken man of 86. Within a month, on 11 October 1303, he died in the Vatican. The Dominican cardinal, Nicholas Boccasini, was elected as Benedict XI. Christendom was scandalized. The new pope cleared Philip over the treatment of Boniface, and all except Nogaret and Colonna. Nogaret was excommunicated and not pardoned for seven years. Benedict XI was honest but timid and died the following year – it was said from eating poisoned figs. Philip's attitude is clear from the fact that he rewarded Nogaret.

On the death of Benedict XI a conflict of views among the cardinals led to a year's vacancy before Bertrand de Got, the Gascon archbishop of Bordeaux, was elected as Clement V. He had studied civil and canon law, and participated in negotiations between France and England. Boniface made him bishop and then archbishop. In 1305 Bertrand seemed a neutral figure but he proved to be one of the most pro-French popes in history and it has been said that no later medieval pope was 'more subservient to a king'.[92]

Clement was amenable to Philip's demands. The papacy deserted Italy and in 1305 settled at Avignon, not French territory but under French influence. Clement never returned to Italy. By the bull *Rex gloriae* Philip was absolved over Boniface, his 'good and just zeal' praised. Langlois blames the church rather than the king for some of the events of the reign because it did not sufficiently resist the 'sacrilege' of Nogaret, the attack on Boniface, and the assault on the Templars. He was thinking of the French church as well as the papacy, and noted that Philip appointed royal clerks and household familiars to bishoprics.[93] Apart from Boniface VIII, the popes were agreeable to Philip's demands for tenths imposed on the clergy.

There was a disaster at Clement V's coronation when a wall collapsed and some were killed. Clement was thrown to the ground and a jewel fell from his tiara. Charles of Valois was injured. It was hardly a promising omen. Clement's election was good news for France but perhaps not so good for the papacy. One of his first acts was to name 12 new cardinals of whom nine were French. *Clericis laicos* was revoked and all the bulls of Boniface hostile to France. Nogaret was pardoned on condition he undertook a pilgrimage – which he never did. Clement was a serious and well-meaning pope but without the backbone to withstand Philip IV. Boniface would never have agreed to the destruction of the ancient and honourable order of the Knights of the Temple.

THE TEMPLARS

The clash with Boniface harmed Philip IV's reputation outside France and with historians. Another damaging development was about to occur. This time Philip took the initiative without provocation. In one of the most dramatic and infamous episodes of history, he attacked the military order of the Templars. The order was founded in Jerusalem in 1118 and recognized by the papacy in 1129. Baldwin II king of Jerusalem granted it accommodation in the palace below the Temple. A Grand Master was appointed and a rule was drawn up by St Bernard and approved by the papacy in 1139. It allowed secular knights to live as monks, and to take arms against the enemies of the church. The order's task was to protect pilgrim routes and defend the Holy Land. This remained so until the collapse of the Latin Kingdom in1291. The Templars had acquired wealth and fortifications. They made loans to crusaders, including a large sum to Louis VII during the Second Crusade. Among the fortifications they built or rebuilt were Athlit (the Pilgrim's Castle) and Safed. They played a major role in defending the Kingdom. In battle Jacques de Vitry said they were 'the first to go forward and the last to retreat'.[94] However, they provoked criticism by their independent behaviour, and feuds with the Hospitallers. With the fall of the Kingdom, the order lost its way though retaining 2,000 knights and 10,000 sergeants – mostly in France. Jacques de Molay was elected Grand Master two years after the loss of the Holy Land. The order was still trying to reorganize and find a new place in the world in the wake of that blow.

Perhaps because they combined holiness with military might and had strong stone buildings the Templars were entrusted to guard secular wealth. They became the 'bankers of Christianity', particularly in France.[95] The order lost its *raison d'être*, and its popularity among ordinary Christians – as was demonstrated by the lack of popular sympathy during the crisis that now developed. Jacques de Vitry condemned brothers who had made a vow of poverty but 'want to have everything'.[96] Many Templars fell away from their ideals. In France 'to drink like a Templar' became a saying; in Germany *Tempelhaus* became the term for a brothel!.[97]

At first Philip approved of the Templars; his sons were educated by them. It was said that in his youth he had wanted to join the order.[98] He protected their privileges and used them to guard the royal treasure. In 1306 Philip was in the Paris Temple when it was besieged by rioters but there was no immediate sign this had turned him against the order. It is difficult to be certain of Philip's motives.

Perhaps the financial system with Templar bankers did not work efficiently during Philip's wars. Before the crisis Philip had experimented by transferring work to other trusted officials. There was criticism of the order in the west and in the French court. There were rumours about Templar conduct, including hints of heresy and occultism. Philip suddenly turned hostile in 1307. Esquieu de Floyran voiced complaints of Templar conduct to James II of Aragon and, receiving little encouragement, went on to Philip IV. Either Philip suddenly saw possibilities of gain from an attack on the Templars, or he genuinely believed the accusations – perhaps both. He pressured the amenable Clement V to investigate. The pope made acquiescent noises, showing no enthusiasm for action.

The accusations sound distorted and exaggerated and are hard to believe in their entirety. They were formulated first, and the confessions to confirm them extracted afterwards. Templars were accused of spitting on the cross, sodomy, sexual perversion, sacrifice to idols including some with human and feline heads. This last was linked to the idea that such heads had special powers and were the offspring resulting from sex with a dead woman – like several of the tales this was borrowed from the east. Kingdoms outside France were approached but none showed the same hostility. Many were sceptical of the charges and confessions. Edward II of England declared them 'more than it is possible to believe', and wrote to other rulers to defend the order. In Aragon it was suggested the French motive was 'to have their money'.[99] Aragon, as we have seen, ignored the initial accusation. The bishop of Valencia considered it unjust for the order to be punished for the faults of individuals. Defenders of the order said that such confessions were only obtained in France and no one else would talk of the order in such a way: 'it is clear enough why they [these lies] have been spoken in the kingdom of France'.[100] Forty-three Templars were questioned in London but none made confessions – though a few did later after torture. Such action as was taken came only after it was virtually forced by papal decisions. The pope seemed unconvinced and only succumbed after prolonged French pressure. Philip employed personal confrontations, sought support from assemblies and propaganda pamphlets, and made threats against the pope.

Questioning was done by senior royal officials – prelates, knights, baillis and seneschals. Templars were sent to a prison from which 'no one comes out'. Evidence in the form of confessions was extorted under torture.[101] Methods included the rack, flames applied to the soles of feet, the dislocation of wrists and ankles, and the *strappado* (dropping by rope from a beam with weights attached to feet or testicles). Thirty-six Templars died of torture in Paris. Not surprisingly most yielded and confessed to whatever was demanded – 134 of the 138 questioned in Paris. The whole business may be viewed as a cynical act motivated by gain. Some suggest Philip believed the accusations to be true.[102] A problem for the Templars was that much of their business was conducted in secret; chapter meetings were often held at night in a guarded room. The ordinary sins of some Templars were easy to exaggerate. Accusations were voiced of orgies, idolatry and debauchery. The confessions followed a pattern set by the questioners – of heresy, sodomy, worship of idols, orders to spit on the cross, obscene initiation ceremonies, and so on. They are clearly forced confessions, or given under threat, but remain fascinating nonetheless. One Templar confessed he had been received into the order by kissing on the body but did not know if it was the usual practice. He was taken away and when he returned said he had been mistaken and everyone in the order was guilty of the same thing! One brother confessed to homosexual relations with the Grand Master – three times in one night. The confessions included details of heads brought out to worship – of various kinds. An elderly Templar who had only joined recently said he was told to spit on the cross, but refused and was let off because he was old. Jacques de Saci later reported seeing 25 Templars die under questioning. One brother claimed he had been tortured, hands tied behind his back in a ditch.[103] Even under torture some protested their innocence, including Brother Jean who was 80, and Lambert de Toisy who said he had observed the customs of the order as he had promised. Given hope by the papacy some were prepared to defend the order in Paris. Many did make confessions – of adding obscene words to psalms in services, and all the crimes claimed. One terrified Templar declared on his knees 'I have confessed certain articles because of the tortures inflicted upon me'. He had been tortured by two royal knights.[104] No doubt there were faults in the order, and some committed homosexual acts, some who were not ordained overstepped the mark of their rank or function, but it is hard to believe all the accusations and confessions.

The admissions and retractions of the Grand Master Jacques de Molay are of interest. He has been called weak, but he was not a coward, and went to a brave death.[105] In 1307 he confessed to faults in the order. In 1308 he denied that his confession was true. Later that year he confessed again. In 1309 he denied the confession. So far as we know De Molay was not tortured as others were, but he was pressured by Philip and his agents. He was at times given hope by the pope and his cardinals. The swings from confessions to retractions reflect his reaction to threats from royal agents against hope of papal support. Philip IV launched a series of vicious accusations against the Templars, of corruption and heresy involving demonic ceremonies. His initial intention may have been to reform the order, and possibly replace it with a new French order. He finally decided to destroy the Templars and put into operation his usual spin, embroidering real and imagined faults.

We are asked to accept that Philip and his ministers believed the accusations. We are told that if we question their sincerity we do not understand the medieval mind. In fact, however, not all contemporaries did believe the charges. One saw it as 'a fable invented by Nogaret'.[106] Villani, Compagni, Boccaccio and Dante were among Italians who expressed doubts. Clement V found it hard to accept the charges and was not keen to act against the Templars even under pressure. In the end Philip acted without papal approval, believing the pope would not resist.

On 14 September 1307 Philip issued secret orders to *baillis* and seneschals. On 22 September 1307 the arrest of all Templars in France was ordered. On

13 October Jacques de Molay was arrested for heresy in the name of the Inquisition. The day before, unaware of the royal intentions, he had attended the funeral of Catherine de Courtenay, wife of Charles of Valois. Only about 20 brothers avoided arrest. Accusations were read aloud to an assembly in the garden of the royal palace in Paris. The prisoners were given only bread and water. Many were tortured and, on the basis of their confessions, Philip demanded the order's dissolution. Those who confessed to idolatry and heresy were absolved if they repented.

Only the papacy offered hope for Jacques de Molay and his men. In 1308 Clement V suspended proceedings against the order but in 1309 agreed to Philip's demands for an inquiry. When papal intervention seemed most likely, many knights retracted their confessions. In 1310 a delegation of nine Templars offered to defend the order. Soon 573 brethren were ready to witness to the order's innocence under oath – claiming their confessions had been given under torture. Peter of Bologna, imprisoned in Paris, declared that the accusations were 'lies, false, indeed most false', fabricated and invented by 'lying enemies'.[107] Those who retracted their confessions found themselves in trouble, treated as perjurers and relapsed heretics.

Clement was not best pleased at the arrest, done in his name but without his consent. He complained but Philip pressed on with the attack. Individual brothers were examined by local provincial commissions. The king acknowledged ecclesiastical rights over the Templars and their goods, but kept control of the whole business. Lists of questions were drawn up. Templar guilt was assumed. It was asked how innocent brothers should be treated. The response was that it was almost impossible for a Templar to be innocent. The brothers in Philip's care were questioned and either threatened with torture or actually tortured – whatever was necessary to extract the confession. They were kept in prison, often fed only on bread and water. Those who confessed were treated more leniently than those who refused – not unlike our modern British system where those who confess to their crimes are released before those who might be innocent but refuse to admit their guilt. Many were chained up for months or even years. After three months of torture in Paris, Jean de Furnes became 'infirm of reason'.[108] Jacques de Cormeilles under torture lost four teeth. It is hardly surprising that many brothers broke and confessed. Later, in the hope that their case would come before the pope, many said their confessions were false. Jean de Furnes said he had only confessed to sodomy out of fear. One unfortunate after torture was simply declared unable to give further witness, but hundreds were prepared to defend their order.

Philip used the tactics employed against Boniface VIII, seeking to gain popular support. The University of Paris was asked to consider the matter. An assembly was called at Melun for representatives from the regions. The accusations were presented and generally accepted. The unpopularity of the Templars was their undoing. Nogaret led a campaign against Clement V – who was accused of simony and protecting the Templars. Clement weakened, but declared that the order could not be dealt with in the same way as individual brothers. He advocated a General Council at Vienne for 1310. Clement allowed action against individual Templars but reserved decisions on the whole order and its leaders. Philip set about dealing with individual brothers. Seventy-two knights were taken to prisons in Paris and tortured.

The process against the order began on 8 August 1309 at Ste-Geneviève in Paris. On 26 November Jacques de Molay was brought before the commission and declared he would defend the order, protesting that he could not do it properly as a prisoner. After a short delay he was questioned again and replied, 'I am just a poor, illiterate knight' and asked to be brought before the pope. He listed the order's achievements including fighting at Mansurah. He declared his belief in 'one God, one faith, one Church'.[109]

There were able and brave Templars who tried to defend the order. Some with legal knowledge presented a case, pinning their hopes on papal justice. Royal actions were criticized. At this point, in 1310, the most cynical card of all was played. Philip IV was tiring of growing Templar resistance with many brothers prepared to defend the order. He decided to act. The archbishop of Sens, Philip de Marigny, brother of Philip's minister Enguerrand, was prepared to use the papal permission for provincial action. Questions halted and executions began, mainly of those who had denied their original confessions. Fifty-four brothers were burned alive on the edge of the wood of Vincennes. Other burnings quickly followed. Some of those executed had been preparing to voice defence. Most who had expressed a willingness to defend the order became paralysed with fear and decided they no longer wished to go ahead. The outspoken Peter of Bologna disappeared. The commission examining the order halted. The burnings were clearly ordered by the state and not by the pope. They marked the end of any attempt to defend the order. It was a cruel, cynical, and effective move.

The Council at Vienne opened in 1311. The evidence collected from confessions was presented. Philip IV appeared with a considerable force and sat beside the pope during the hearings. Prelates defended the order, but not those from France. According to the English chronicler Walter of Hemingborough the French prelates acted 'on account of fear of the king of France'.[110] Perhaps after Anagni, or perhaps because he was at Avignon, Clement V saw no escape from French pressure and agreed to Philip's demands. The council re-opened in 1312 with the pope presiding and Philip at his right hand. The suppression of the Templar order was announced, and the process concluded with the reading of the bull Vox in excelso – without the council's consent. A new crusade was announced in which Philip promised to participate – he never did.

In Spain, Templar possessions were used against Islam. Elsewhere they mostly passed to the Hospitallers. Possessions in France were seized by the crown. Philip had tentative plans for transforming the Templars, of a merger with other orders. Both Charles of Valois and Marigny favoured merging the Templars with the Hospitallers. Philip also had schemes for the possible formation of a new French order that could take over Templar possessions in France, linked with the idea of a recovery crusade, and even of Philip abdicating to become king in the recovered Holy Land. In the end all these schemes were abandoned. Most of what the Templars owned was handed to the Hospitallers, though Villani claimed that after deductions, blocked assets, and compensations, the Hospitallers were worse off than they had been before![111]

The surviving leaders of the order had been promised freedom but were sentenced to life imprisonment. The pope declared that he had the right to judge them and nominated three cardinals to act for him. One of them announced the sentence of life imprisonment. A royal council in Paris declared that judgement belonged to the king. There was an attempt to make the Grand Master issue a public confession but he claimed that the accusations were absurd, a conclusion with which one is inclined to agree. He bravely refused to admit guilt, retracting his former confession, and was sentenced to death by the council. In 1314 De Molay and De Charnay were brought out wearing only their shirts. De Molay was in his 70s and had been in prison for seven years. He declared 'God will avenge our death'. The two insisted on facing east and were burned to death in the evening on the Île-des-Javiaux in the Seine. The Florentine Giovanni Villani called it the death of martyrs, though a poet who witnessed the event thought they treated the Grand Master 'like a dog'.[112]

An obvious answer to why Philip destroyed the Templars was for money. Certainly many at the time thought so and Philip's financial position was difficult. Villani commented Philip was 'moved by his avarice'.[113] On the other hand, Philip did not gain very much. Crown debts to the order were cancelled and Templar property did produce some immediate profit – but it was scant compensation for the effort required. The pope said that Philip was not acting from avarice, as he did not claim benefits from the event. But, given Clement's general submissiveness, it was probably said in the hope of persuading Philip to abandon his plans. The pope may have swayed Philip to give up some anticipated profit. He had to make promises to the papacy to obtain support against the order. In fact he kept more Templar wealth than he had promised, claiming expenses – but it came nowhere near to solving his financial problems. Another possible motive was the wish to form a French military order for future crusading. These plans disintegrated as it proved impossible to transfer Templar possessions in that manner. The other possibility is that Philip believed the accusations against the order, in particular heresy, and thought the order deserved to be destroyed. These motives do not necessarily exclude each other. We are unlikely to get closer to Philip's actual thoughts, and may conclude that the answer lies somewhere between these three suggestions.

It remains difficult to condone Philip's action against the Templars. Provocation was minimal, the motives either greed or credulousness, the treatment harsh and probably cynical. The blot left on Philip's character and career seems deserved. Duby seems too tolerant in his conclusions. Philip emerges as an able but harsh and narrow king, who helped to create the first serious clash between the French monarchy and the papacy.

THE SCANDAL OF THE TOUR DE NESLE

The end of Philip IV's reign was marred by a personal affair, a family scandal that broke in 1314. We shall examine the detail of this episode in the following chapter because of its ramifications in the period after Philip's death. But we need now to consider briefly Philip's role and its immediate effect. The truth of the scandal is hard to establish now. One cannot be sure if Philip genuinely believed the reasons given for his actions.

The scandal of the Tour de Nesle suggests that Philip could indeed believe in the unlikely and act ruthlessly upon his beliefs. It is difficult to see a cynical explanation for his actions in this family matter. He may have been led to his conclusions by accusations against the girls made by his daughter Isabelle, whose own career was not that of a model of probity. At the same time the affair suggests a cold disregard for the feelings of his sons. If we suppose the scandal to be real, the adulteries to have occurred, then they could still have been dealt with more discreetly. For the sake of the royal family's reputation Philip could have swept the business quietly under the carpet. Instead he broke the marriages of two of his sons and deeply embarrassed all three.

Philip ordered the arrest of his three daughters-in-law and their supposed lovers in 1314. Margaret was imprisoned until death. Blanche's marriage was annulled and she was released from prison 10 years later to become a nun, dying in 1326. Joan was cleared of personal involvement and was taken back by her husband, Philip the Long. The accused lovers, the D'Aulnay brothers, were judged guilty, castrated, flayed alive, and burned at Pontoise. The affair damaged the reputation of the crown and the prospects of royal offspring for Philip's sons. It leaves another stain on the assessment of Philip IV through his harsh and brutal action – whatever the provocation.

THE DEATH OF PHILIP IV

Philip IV made three wills, in 1288, 1297 and 1311. They suggest a genuine religious belief in attempts to compensate for his mistakes and sins, and concern for his own salvation. There were gifts to religious establishments, especially the Cistercians, and money for a crusade – after failing to keep his promise to participate. Philip's first will was made at Maubuisson when he was only 20. He wanted his debts and 'illicit exactions' repaid. Twenty thousand *livres* were bequeathed to churches and charity. The second will of 1297 was made at Royaumont. It suggested concern for his father's memory, and interest in the Dominicans. It ordered compensation to those who had suffered from his coinage policy. The final will of 1311, in French, was also made at Maubuisson. It showed respect for St Louis, whose heart was to be buried at Poissy. Some beneficiaries in the earlier wills were to receive more. Philip was still making additions to his will on the day before his death. A foreigner in France said Philip told his heir that he would be blessed if he carried out the will, but would die early if he failed to do so! The young Philip found it impossible to carry out all the extravagant bequests – and died two years later.[114]

Philip was a healthy 46-year-old in 1314 when he fell from his horse near Port-Sainte-Maxence. He broke a leg and the wound became infected. He was taken to Poissy, the Dominican priory he had founded. He contracted a fever and suffered stomach pains. He tried to control events after his death, with a vain attempt to protect Marigny. Philip died on 26 November 1314 at Fontainebleau where he had been carried, and where he had been born. The corpse was taken along the Seine to Paris and embalmed. The heart was returned to Poissy. In the same year Clement V and William de Nogaret died. A number of Philip's unpopular leading officials were now removed from office and some executed.

10

The end of the line, 1314–28

THE SCANDAL OF THE TOUR DE NESLE AND THE SUCCESSION IN 1314

In 1314, at the end of the reign of Philip IV, the scandal of the Tour de Nesle broke. Without warning the wives of all three of Philip's sons were arrested: Margaret of Burgundy the wife of Louis (X) king of Navarre, Blanche of Burgundy the wife of Charles (IV) count of La Marche, and Joan of Burgundy the wife of Philip (V) count of Poitiers. Margaret and Blanche were accused of adultery with two royal knights, the D'Aulnay brothers, Philip and Walter. The person who revealed the affair was said to be Isabelle, daughter of Philip IV and wife of Edward II of England – given her own career, hardly of lily-white character. She was said to be jealous of her sisters-in-law. Under torture one of the D'Aulnay brothers admitted the affair had lasted for three years. The brothers were judged guilty, castrated, flayed alive, and burnt to death in the Place du Martrai in Pontoise. Their private parts were thrown to dogs and the bodies dragged through the streets and left to hang on a public gibbet. Their possessions were confiscated. A Franciscan, accused of aiding the brothers, was imprisoned in Paris.

Joan was later released, but Margaret and Blanche remained in prison, accused of taking the D'Aulnay brothers as lovers. Margaret was the daughter of Robert II duke of Burgundy and had married Louis le Hutin king of Navarre in 1305. She was imprisoned at Château-Gaillard, treated harshly, given no decent clothes to wear and shut in a high tower open to the winter winds. She died after catching a cold. Blanche of Artois was the daughter of Otto IV, count of Burgundy. She married Charles count of La Marche and Angoulême. Blanche was also imprisoned at Château-Gaillard and her marriage annulled in 1322. She survived and was released after 10 years to become a nun at Maubuisson, where she died in 1326. Joan of Artois was Blanche's sister and had married Philip the Long count of Poitiers. She was only accused of not revealing the other girls' adultery but was taken off in a black wagon to the castle of Dourdan. Parliament cleared her of involvement and she was restored to her husband.

There must be a doubt over the charges against these royal princesses. Evidence under torture cannot be trusted. Isabelle was said to have denounced her sisters-in-law but her history does not encourage trust. Her relationship with Edward II had embittered her and she expected more standing at the French court. Afterwards she had an affair with the English lord, Roger Mortimer, with whom she invaded England and seized the throne from her husband who was probably put to death. Her hopes were for the succession of her son, who became Edward III. He was to claim the French throne, a possibility no doubt present in her mind. It was said that when in France on the earlier occasion, Isabelle had presented purses to her sisters-in-law, Margaret and Blanche, and then noted them in possession of the knights – hardly damning proof. There was a suggestion of hatred between the women and it is possible she invented or exaggerated the charges, but there is no way we can know.

1328 was the end of an era. Philip IV left three adult sons, but the Capetian dynasty died with them. Each inherited the throne in turn and died within a fairly short space of time. Louis X died in 1316 after a two-year reign. Louis' son John I lived only a few days. Philip V died in 1322, leaving four daughters and a son, Philip Louis, but the latter died as an infant. Charles IV died in 1328. His disgraced first wife had borne a daughter who died as an infant.

Female succession to the throne had been ruled out, which helped to end the dynasty, since the female offspring were excluded. Philip IV's daughter Isabelle married Edward II and passed a claim (by the English system) to the French throne to Edward III, a cause of the Hundred Years' War. Louis' daughter, Joan, became queen of Navarre but was excluded from the French throne. By 1328 there was no direct male heir in the main line of the Capetian family. The throne passed to Philip IV's nephew Philip of Valois who became Philip VI. He was the son of Philip IV's brother Charles of Valois but this is another story.

THE REIGN OF LOUIS X (1314–16)

Louis was known as 'le Hutin', variously translated by historians as the Turbulent, the Quarrelsome, or the Stubborn – which all catch something of his character. He and his brothers were knighted in Paris in 1313. He became king of Navarre. His wife, Margaret of Burgundy, whom he married in 1305, was imprisoned after the Tour de Nesle scandal, leaving a daughter Joan. On his deathbed Philip IV called Louis before him and said 'for my part, I love you above all others'.[1] He told his son to rule with moderation, to take heed of the advice of his uncles, and to think about 'what it is to be king of France'. Louis married a second time to Clementia, daughter of the king of Hungary. Philip IV died in November 1314 and Louis was crowned the following year.

Louis' uncle, Charles of Valois, emerged as the dominant figure. He was aggressive and forthright and keen to continue the military advance against the English in France. He tried to remove potential rivals and any opposed to him under Philip IV. The most prominent of the latter was Enguerrand de Marigny. Charles forced him out of office, despite Louis X's attempt to save him. Marigny was tried for treason and hanged at Montfaucon in Paris. Louis X actually left money for Marigny's wife and family in his will. Other officials of Philip IV were removed. Ralph de Presles was accused of witchcraft and tortured. Peter de Latilly was imprisoned; Nogaret was ruined. Stephen de Mornay, a favoured clerk of Charles of Valois, received the royal seals.

Another major political force under the young king was that of the provincial leagues, able to flex their muscles once Philip IV was dead. In 1314 and 1315 a series of regional and inter-regional alliances was formed between groups of nobles, inspired by opposition to the tax for Flanders. Champagne and Burgundy played a leading role. Regional leagues of nobles now became more numerous, as for example in Forez, Auxerre and Tonnerre. Various inter-league alliances were formed, as between Burgundy and Forez, Forez and Champagne and Champagne and Burgundy (sounds rather alcoholic). They pressed Louis to negotiate and grant charters of liberty in return for agreement to tax. The generally reasonable response of the Capetian kings to the leagues in this period reflected some weakness, but also a degree of common sense. The leagues were loyal rather than anti-royal – negotiation was frequent, and they provided a means of co-operation and understanding between king and subjects.

The regional assemblies possessed an element of representation, though it was not organized or uniform. The king arranged to meet assemblies that he summoned, sending messages to towns to select representatives. Louis X hoped to get support for coinage reform and war against Flanders from assemblies summoned in 1315 to meet in 1316. Toulouse, for example, elected six leading citizens to represent them in the coming assembly.[2]

Louis faced problems in Flanders, where rebellion had broken out before the start of his reign. The French had been driven from Courtrai and Lille was attacked. Philip IV had raised tax for a campaign, but then cancelled it the day before he died. Louis X was faced with demands for repayment. The idea under Philip IV that if the need for a tax was removed then the tax should not be paid had come from a philosophical argument based on the idea 'cessante causa'. In 1315 Louis ordered that the money raised be returned if collected after the cause ceased. This did not satisfy the lords in the Languedoc. To raise money for his intended campaign, Louis had to agree to follow that maxim and promised the Languedoc assembly that it need not pay the subsidy 'if the occasion for the subsidy had ceased'.[3] The repetition of a military crisis, followed by summoning the army, and then by a peace – meant a constant expectation that subsidies would be returned. Yet the raising of forces, even if not employed in fighting, was not without expense. The problem would return.

Trouble arose again in Flanders when Count Robert of Béthune (1305–22) refused homage and ejected the French garrison from Courtrai. Louis was backed by the court of peers, which ruled that Robert's lands were forfeit. Louis allied with William count of Hainault and a force was assembled but the expedition was a disaster, thanks to heavy rain and flooding in Flanders. A peace was agreed in the treaty of Paris of 1316. Floods saved Flanders but Flanders, like other regions, suffered from the bad weather accompanied by poor harvests, famine and plague. Grain prices rose as much as 24 times. Jan Boendale called them the three disasters – rain, price rise and plague. It is reckoned that a third of the population of Flanders died; 'dancing, games, song, all revels were done away with in those days'.[4]

Louis X died at Bois de Vincennes on 5 June 1316. The cause of death is not clear, variously suggested as a mystery illness, overheating while playing tennis, a chill from consuming a cold drink, or poison (Matilda of Artois was later accused – and cleared). It was probably a sudden infection. His body was taken to Notre-Dame and on to St-Denis. It is perhaps appropriate that one of the most interesting things about the reigns of the last Capetians is their funerals. Louis X had two funerals, 'the only double funeral ever held for any French king'.[5] In fact eventually there were three funerals. The first was held two days after his death, with the usual pomp and expense so there hardly seemed need for a further ceremony. The probable reason for a second funeral was Philip the Long's absence from the first – it was the practice for the successor to be present but Philip was at Lyon on royal business over the papal election. There was a delay before he returned to Paris. The second funeral emphasized his presence and position as heir but was a simpler and less expensive ceremony. Louis X's bones, along with others, were exhumed in 1793 and thrown into a ditch. With the restoration of Louis XVIII a third funeral was ordered in 1817 for a mass re-burial of the disturbed royal bones, including Louis X's. He left behind a daughter, Joan, by his first marriage to Margaret of Burgundy, and a pregnant wife Clementia of Hungary.

THE REIGN OF PHILIP V (1316–22)

Louis X's oldest surviving brother was Philip, known as 'le Long' (the Tall or the Long) for the obvious reason that he was of considerable height. Philip IV had been tall, but Philip V was even taller, made more noticeable by his thin figure. Philip the Long had been count of Poitiers and married Joan of Burgundy in 1307. She had been arrested in the Tour de Nesle scandal but only accused of keeping silent about her fellow princesses' behaviour. Her mother, Matilda, supported her and she was released after the death of Philip IV. Philip the Long was not under the same pressure as his brothers and his marriage survived. The couple produced four daughters and then in 1316 the hoped-for son, also named Philip and known as Philip Louis.

The death of Louis X left a quandary over the succession. His daughter by Margaret of Burgundy, Joan, was born in 1312. Her mother Margaret died in 1315. Joan was accepted by Louis as his daughter, but being born after the scandal there was a question over her legitimacy – real or imagined. She did receive support from her mother's family, notably from her uncle, the duke of Burgundy. When Louis died his wife, Clementia of Hungary, was several months pregnant. The assembly of barons declared against female succession to the throne, a move that was repeated in 1322, and established a rule for France that became particularly contentious when challenged by Edward III, son of Philip IV's daughter Isabelle. It was later known as the Salic Law, though its antiquity is dubious.

There followed a period of uncertainty. A council of 24 barons was formed. The powerful uncles, Charles of Valois brother of Philip IV, and Louis of Évreux half-brother of Philip IV, sought control. The oldest of Louis X's surviving brothers, Philip, held back. At the time of Louis' death he was in Lyon, acting on his brother's behalf to pressure the cardinals over the papal election. He did not immediately leave for Paris to assert a claim, though he did when the situation became more critical. The subsequent election of Pope John XXII pleased the French. Philip arrived in Paris on 11 July to counter the pretensions of Charles of Valois in collaboration with the leagues. Philip's arrival gave him the initiative and he arranged the second funeral.

Philip the Long acted as regent, taking the title for the first time in France. The situation seemed to be resolved when Louis X's widow gave birth to a son who was named king, as John I, but tragedy followed. The widow had been ill during her pregnancy and died giving birth. John I was born on the night on 13 November 1316 and lived only five days. The infant corpse was taken to St-Denis for burial. Philip the Long then assumed the throne with no great opposition and was crowned at Reims on 9 January 1317. Charles of Valois remained a powerful figure. He sought to control affairs but did aid the king against rivals.

Philip pressed for homage from Edward II for his continental lands. There were negotiations and delays and eventually homage was done for Aquitaine and Ponthieu, by proxy in 1319, and in person in 1320. There was some opposition to Philip around support for Joan, the daughter of Louis X, including from the duke of Burgundy. However, an agreement was reached. Joan was given a pension of £15,000 and given lands in Champagne and Brie as well as her kingdom of Navarre. Those of her supporters who remained in arms were defeated by Charles of Valois.

Philip V took up where his brother had left off in Flanders. Further problems emerged. The new king supported Louis of Nevers, the oldest son of the count, for the succession to Flanders. After the latter's death in 1318, Philip supported his son Louis II of Nevers, who married the king's daughter. Count Robert's younger son, Robert of Cassel, felt his claim had been ignored and Count Robert himself broke the peace agreement. He prepared an attack on Lille, but held back when Ghent refused to assist. The king raised a force against Flanders in 1319 and the league in Artois gave way. The problem recurred of tax for a campaign that did not happen. Philip V repaid money in 1316 but sought new subsidies in 1318 and 1319. Negotiation meant that war was avoided and a compromise was reached in a new treaty of Paris in 1320. It seemed reasonable to Philip that he must cover expenses and he repaid only half the subsidy.

Another problem for Philip V was caused by Béraud VII of Mercoeur, constable of Champagne, who possessed lands in Champagne and the Auvergne, and was married to the count of Forez's sister. He acted as an agent for Philip in Toulouse, the Rouergue and the Auvergne. He was an aggressive individual who had caused trouble under Philip's father, and who now engaged in private war with Hugh of Chalon, lord of Arlay in the county of Burgundy. The pope imposed a truce but Béraud broke it and was excommunicated. Philip V stepped in and confiscated Béraud's lands. Béraud made his peace with the pope and asked for protection against the king! The value of regional assemblies was then demonstrated. Philip called an assembly at Bourges and the local nobles supported him against Béraud, and promised aid against Flanders. Béraud submitted in 1319.

Philip V tried to keep on good terms with the towns. Once crowned, he set off on a tour of major towns to establish his position. He received support from an assembly in Paris in March 1317, and from an assembly at Bourges. Despite the problems over tax, Philip obtained fair support from regional assemblies. In 1319 at separate meetings he received promises of a fifteenth from the nobles of the Auvergne, and those of Berry – in return for confirming privileges. In 1321 an assembly that turned down his plans for reform was apologetic for its 'petit conseil'.[6]

Despite the brevity of the reign there were attempts at some important reforms, referred to as Philip's 'Grand Design'.[7] The national militia was put on a new footing. New regulations were suggested for weights and measures, seeking uniformity. Philip also sought to introduce a uniform coinage. These ideas were put before assemblies in Poitiers and Paris. There was some support from the clergy, but the call to cover the cost of the reforms, and new tax demands in 1321, provoked opposition. It became clear that his 'tax-weary' subjects would only agree to a subsidy for military emergency, and Philip yielded – the reforms were dropped.[8] Nevertheless it had been an interesting attempt to raise money through agreement with assemblies to carry through major reforms rather than just military expeditions.

Although there were problems over subsidies, Philip made some gains from them, and kept at least a proportion. He also took other measures to raise money, including another act against the Jews, though it was later rescinded – after Philip had profited. There were rumours of a plot between Jews and lepers with strange accusations against them, including pollution of water with bags of blood mixed with urine and consecrated wafers. Such talk led to riots. Philip succeeded in some of his efforts. Areas of demesne land alienated by his predecessors were recovered. Although his major proposal was withdrawn, he made a start on coinage reform through private agreements, seizing non-royal coins that were declared unsound, and taking over their production in return for a lump sum. Philip was prepared to take this step even against his powerful uncle, Charles of Valois. The count of Clermont was another prepared to sell to the king his right to coin.

Philip had taken the cross in 1313 and, as king, made plans for a crusade though he failed to raise the money for it, and died before it could take place. Crusading fervour was stirred up, and in 1320 led to the Pastoureaux rising, when poor folk under an unfrocked priest marched on Paris. A prévôt was thrown down the steps of the Châtelet. The 'crusaders' marched on Toulouse where the authorities broke them up. They were hanged in groups of 20 and 30. Other plans also proved abortive. One reason was his early death; another was the half-hearted support he received from towns and nobles. A third reason was the economic difficulty of the period. The years 1315–17 saw heavy rains, poor harvests, famine and plague. In such circumstances new taxation was not likely to be welcomed.

Philip became ill after a visit to his brother Charles of La Marche at Crécy-en-Brie. He returned to Paris in a hot summer. When he reached Bois de Vincennes he was suffering from dysentery and fever. He made a new will, wishing to be buried at St-Denis, while his heart should go to the Cordeliers' church in Paris – where his wife and son were also buried. He wanted his entrails to go to the Dominican church of the Jacobins in Paris. Philip V died at the convent in Longchamp where his daughter Blanche had taken her vows in 1322. He had been poorly throughout his reign; his coronation had been postponed because of ill health. He was buried at St-Denis on 7 January 1322, his heart and entrails elsewhere as requested. After his death his wife Joan lived on at the place where the scandal had occurred. In her will she ordered that proceeds from the sale of the Tour de Nesle should go to found the college of Burgundy as part of the University of Paris. She died in 1329. The early death of Philip V was perhaps the worst of the tragedies that befell the dynasty in this last period. He was the most promising of the sons of Philip IV, and in a brief reign showed the potential to be a great reforming monarch, 'the most inventive and imaginative of the sons of Philip the Fair'.[9]

THE REIGN OF CHARLES IV (1322–28)

Charles had been made count of La Marche by his father. His first wife, Blanche of Burgundy, whom he had married in 1308, was imprisoned after the Tour de Nesle scandal. Charles repudiated her on the grounds of affinity rather than adultery. She entered the convent at Maubuisson, where her daughter had been buried, taking her vows in 1325, and dying the following year. Charles' second wife was Mary of Luxembourg, daughter of the Holy Roman Emperor, Henry VII. On Philip V's death there was no great opposition to the succession of the third brother.

Charles IV did not take up Philip V's reforms. Rather than reform the coinage there was another debasement. A new attack was made on the Jews. Probably because of the sensitive relationship with England, Charles was wise enough not to get involved elsewhere. Pope John XXII suggested that he should seek the imperial crown, but Charles ignored the idea. He did ally with Louis of Nevers in Flanders against rebellion there in 1325 but agreed the peace of Arques in 1326. Charles IV brought in new advisers to replace the men around his brother. Henry de Sully was removed and Charles of Valois became even more powerful. His military efforts against England increased antagonism between the nations. England was in difficulties as Edward II's authority crumbled through the unpopularity of Gaveston, and then of the Despensers, together with humiliating defeat by the Scots at Bannockburn.

An odd episode occurred concerning Jordan de Litte, lord of Casaubon. He was accused of no fewer than 18 crimes, but was pardoned by the king probably because he was the pope's nephew. Jordan was, however, summoned to Paris. He killed the royal official who brought the summons and marched into Paris with men from Aquitaine. He was captured, tried, sentenced and executed – dragged by a horse and hanged.

Charles IV had again to face the perennial problem of Flanders, unsolved by his brothers. Since the death of Philip IV trouble had continued, fluctuating between war and truce. Charles imposed a new peace between Flanders and Hainault in 1323. The accession to Flanders of Louis II of Nevers eased the position, since he was an ally of the crown. However Louis' dependence on France made him unpopular in Flanders. The towns were discontented and rebellion broke out in maritime Flanders in 1323, followed by five years of civil war. Count Louis was captured and imprisoned, released and captured again. The situation in Flanders became a class war between the nobles and the bourgeois. Charles IV stopped trade with Flanders. The peace of Arques was agreed in 1326 when France destroyed rebel forts and imposed fines – but the war did not end. Count Louis escaped and fled to Paris. His fate would be decided under the Valois.

France became a refuge for the enemies of Edward II. Queen Isabelle had turned against her husband, alienated by his homosexual relationship with Gaveston. She equally detested Edward's new favourites, the Despensers, father and son, and turned to her country of birth for refuge and aid. In 1322 the French Parliament authorized the building of a *bastide* at St-Sardos in former English territory in the Agenais. This antagonized Edward's seneschal for Gascony, Ralph Basset, as well as the local Gascon lord, Raymond-Bernard of Montpezat. When the French arrived to commandeer the site, Raymond-Bernard came with a force and burned what he found. He hanged the leading French official from the stake marking the French claim to the site. Edward II declared he had no part in this and recalled Basset. The latter excused himself on the grounds of illness, but was later removed from office. Roger Mortimer escaped from imprisonment in the Tower of London and joined Isabelle in France. Charles IV demanded homage from Edward II for his French lands. The English king procrastinated and Charles seemed set on war against England. He attacked the Agenais. It was said the earl of Kent had abducted a young girl from Agen, though the truth is impossible to disentangle. The fact or the propaganda helped Charles of Valois to take over Agen. He also captured a series of fortified strongholds, including Marmande, and besieged the earl of Kent in La Réole for five weeks. It looked as if the English position in France might collapse under a king in great trouble at home – as King John had been. The English did manage to keep Bordeaux and Bayonne, but there were riots in Bordeaux. Edward was slow to raise a fleet, which did not arrive in Bordeaux until 1325. The supply of cash was a major problem for him. Edward eventually agreed to do homage but fell ill on his way to Beauvais. His son Edward performed the ceremony in his place, at Vincennes.

Queen Isabelle had gone with an embassy to France to treat with her brother. She had no wish to act for Edward and the mission was another mistake by him. She was on good terms with her brother Philip, but it was overly optimistic to expect she would seek to benefit her husband. Apart from her reaction to Gaveston and the Despensers, who advised the king to seek divorce, Isabelle had

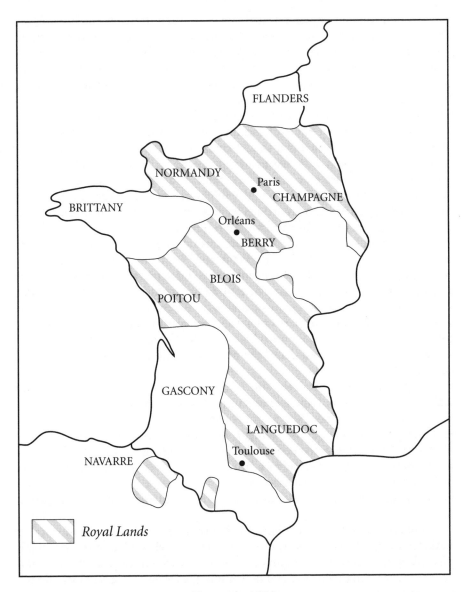

France in 1328

been treated badly in England. Lands had been taken from her and her servants removed. She came to France in 1325. The 'negotiations' with her brother Charles IV were one-sided. Charles simply dictated his terms, including his right to nominate the seneschal of Agenais, and a new demand for homage from Edward, who again prevaricated claiming illness. The homage was eventually performed by Edward's son, Edward (III) on 24 September 1325.

In England fears grew of impending French invasion. Enemies of Edward II came to join Isabelle in France, including Roger Mortimer, who now became her lover. Edward II demanded that she return home with their son but she refused unless the Despensers were banned from court. In the meantime Charles of Valois invaded English territory in Aquitaine and was active in matching the young Edward to Philippa, daughter of William count of Hainault. Charles of Valois died in 1325 but the marriage went ahead. Isabelle went to Hainault in 1326, making it her base for the invasion of England.

The invasion fleet, composed of Dutch fishing ships, sailed from Dordrecht in Holland carrying 1,500 troops including 700 from Hainault. The count of Hainault accompanied Isabelle but young Edward remained for a time in France. Edward II ordered the seizure of all Frenchmen in his lands and their goods. Charles IV responded with a similar order regarding Englishmen in France. Edward planned to counter the invasion by raiding Normandy but found difficulty in raising support. Many deserted him to join Isabelle at Orwell in Suffolk. She was offered overnight accommodation in the castle of the earl of Norfolk.

Edward II abandoned London and went west via High Wycombe to Gloucester, heading for Wales with Isabelle in pursuit. He left Chepstow by sea as his queen closed in. At Bristol Hugh Despenser the Elder, earl of Winchester, was taken and executed. Hugh Despenser the Younger was captured with the king and taken to Hereford. There he was stripped and his arms reversed, a crown of nettles placed on his head. He was drawn by four horses and hanged from a 50-foot gallows, taken down still alive, his genitals were cut off and burned in front of him before he was decapitated. There was disorder throughout the country with rioting in London.

An illicit assembly deposed Edward II with little opposition. He was kept in Berkeley Castle. His real end is obscure. The later legend had a red hot poker pushed up his anus, but contemporary accounts are not clear. Historians have generally accepted that he was put to death in the castle. There remains, though, a possibility that he escaped and survived secretly on the continent. It is the sort of story that one normally dismisses, but Natalie Fryde has shown it may be a possibility.[10]

Isabelle meant to rule through her son with the aid of her lover Mortimer. Their regime proved hardly more popular than her husband's and support evaporated. The Hainault troops returned home. The cash the regime had seized was disappearing fast. The Scots raided England under Robert the Bruce. Young Edward III was not easily kept down and was crowned on 1 February 1327.

Mortimer was made earl of March and had the earl of Kent executed for treason. Edward III conspired against his mother and her lover. On 19 October a band of knights entered Nottingham castle by a secret passage and seized Mortimer, who was tried and executed. Isabelle was confined in a convent. Thus began the real reign of Edward III. The difficult times in England took a while to settle.

These troubles eased problems for France during its own difficulties, as the last Capetians died one after the other. Following the death of Philip IV in 1314, Louis X ruled for 18 months, John I for five days, Philip V for 5 years, Charles IV for six years – five kings had died in 14 years. Had Edward III's reign begun a decade earlier who can guess what might have happened? Charles IV, the last of the Capetians, died at Vincennes on 1 February 1328. There was no son or brother to succeed.

11

The achievements and legacy of the Capetian Dynasty

FRANCE

The Capetian contribution to the making of modern France is great and obvious. One only needs to note the contrasts between the situation in 987 and that in 1328. In the 10th century the old structure of Europe was collapsing with the break-up of the Carolingian Empire. The emergence of separate kingdoms was at first uncertain and remained unstable for some time. The take-over of the kingdom by the ruler of a principality condemned the western sector of the old empire to a relatively minor role for many years. The position of Hugh Capet was rather neatly encapsulated in his self description as '*Hugo dux gratia Dei rex*' (Duke Hugh, king by the grace of God).[1] Others in the west accepted Hugh partly because it meant that the new king barely impinged on their own principalities. The Robertians were relatively powerful among the princes but relatively weak among kings and emperors. Yet by 1328 the Capetian king was probably the most powerful ruler in Europe. The Holy Roman Empire was becoming attached to single principalities in turn rather than to one dynasty. Its pretensions in Italy were not being fulfilled. The Byzantine Empire had suffered major loss through attack from the East and then collapse in face of the Fourth Crusade, a catastrophe from which it never entirely recovered. The English kings as rulers of the Angevin Empire had threatened the very structure of France but the triumph of Philip Augustus gave France the upper hand at least for the remaining years of the Capetian dynasty.

It may be true that France was 'still in the making, not yet made' but its outlines were now clear in a way that they were not in the 10th century.[2] Europe could have developed in many different directions. We tend to think too easily that what has actually happened was inevitable. But, for example, given the language and cultural differences there could easily have developed a state of northern France and another of southern France, perhaps around Aquitaine. Or, the Holy Roman Empire might have continued to grow as seemed likely in the 10th century and given Europe a truly new Roman Empire of which France was but a province. Or, the Plantagenets might have continued the successes of Henry II and western France have remained part of an Anglo-French state. There are numerous other possibilities.

The Capetians were prepared to grant away actual or potential demesne, especially to members of the family as in apanages to younger sons. By chance these mostly returned to the crown through deaths and lack of heirs – but it could have gone otherwise. Henry I granted Burgundy to his brother. Philip Hurepel received the county of Boulogne. Louis VIII had 12 children and five sons survived him, of whom Robert was given Artois, John Anjou and Maine (which was transferred after his death to a younger son Charles), and Alphonse Poitou and the Auvergne. Louis VIII had thereby granted away about a third of the demesne. St Louis made lesser apanages for his sons, but still gave Valois to John-Tristan, Alençon and Perche to Peter, and Clermont to Robert. Philip III gave his sons Valois (again), Anjou, Maine, Alençon and Évreux. Philip IV's sons received Navarre, Champagne, Brie, Poitou and La Marche. Chance brought nearly all of these lands back to the crown, in the case of the three sons of Philip IV because they each in turn became king. Nevertheless by chance, policy, purchase, war, or otherwise, the Capetian demesne had increased tremendously, and the realm under Capetian control expanded greatly too. It is calculated that by the end of the Capetian period the royal demesne was greater in extent than all the demesnes of other lords put together.[3]

By 1328 the shape of France was reasonably clear, though the eastern extent was not complete, the fate of Flanders and Brittany not yet certain, the southern boundaries not entirely settled with the Iberian kingdoms of Castile and Aragon. Navarre was an independent though attached kingdom. The eastern border did not extend as far as it eventually would against imperial claims. The French Mediterranean coastline was shorter than it would become. The king's position was now acknowledged broadly in the French principalities, and his right to involvement in their affairs settled. This meant also a more or less national administration that was accepted in the regions.

PARIS

Significant in the move towards unity within France was the development of Paris as a capital. That likelihood had not been clear in 987. The Capetians played a great part in making Paris a great city. Of course much also depended on its own efforts in trade, culture and other respects, but the kings made it their centre. Fawtier suggests this was partly because the area around Paris was a favourite hunting ground for the kings.[4] Paris became the settled base of government even though royalty remained itinerant. The Capetians did much to improve the condition of the capital. Philip II paved the streets, built a great new wall, and constructed the great castle and residence of the Louvre. The kings had a part in the building of the great churches of the city. Paris led the way in various urban improvement schemes. By 1292 it possessed 26 bath-houses; seemingly in Paris these were used properly, whereas those in Germany sound more like massage parlours![5] Paris attracted men of all kinds from scholars to merchants. The right bank was the main urban area, while the left bank attracted the schools. By the end of the Capetian period the city's population was about 80,000, 'the biggest town in northern Europe'.[6]

Royal support was vital in the rise of the great university in the city. Early in our period schooling was concentrated in abbeys but then the cathedral schools grew. France benefited from the growth of leading schools in Chartres, Reims, Laon and Orléans. In Paris the main schools were those at Ste-Geneviève, St-Victor and Notre-Dame. The development of these schools in the 12th century was the beginning of the universities. That at Orléans became a leading law school. Paris may be called a university from c.1160, and received statutes in c.1208, confirmed by the pope in 1215.

The papacy dictated that Paris should concentrate on arts and theology, arts being the necessary prelude to the study of theology. The liberal arts consisted of the Trivium – grammar, rhetoric and logic, and the Quadrivium – arithmetic, geometry, music and astronomy. This derived from Roman education and was the course followed by arts students. In theology the dominant theme came to be how to relate ancient ideas with Christianity, especially those of Aristotle, and particularly his thoughts on logic. Canon law and medicine also developed in the 13th century, but arts remained the largest faculty and theology the most reputable. The arts students were organized in four 'nations' from 1219 – French, Norman, Picard and English (which included German). The French nation was in turn divided intro five tribes, representing the ecclesiastical provinces.

A collegiate system developed to house the students, beginning with the Collège des Dix-Huits in the Hôtel-Dieu. In 1137 a London burgess returned from pilgrimage to Jerusalem and bought a room at the Hôtel-Dieu which he endowed as a dormitory for 18 students.[7] The best known college was the Sorbonne, founded in 1257 by Robert of Sorbon a chaplain to St Louis. Philip IV's wife, Joan, founded the Collège de Navarre in 1304. By the mid-14th century there were 60 colleges.

On more than one occasion the kings supported the university in Paris against local attack, even from the appointed prévôt. Royal policy also helped to suppress or diminish the role of other potential university cities in the realm – as at Toulouse, Orléans and Angers. The kings were well repaid. With Latin as the international language of learning, students came from many countries. William the Breton believed that Paris attracted students because of the 'special privileges which King Philip [II] and his father before him conferred upon the scholars'.[8] Student numbers rapidly expanded until there were some 7,000 in the later Capetian period.[9] Paris attracted major scholars from throughout Europe. They wrote works of vital importance in many fields, including theology and philosophy – and on political matters. Many went on to play important parts in politics or the church. Quite a few became popes, with a natural fondness for their home of learning. Regularly the university supported the kings in disputes with the papacy, and gave intellectual argument to support the royal viewpoint. Scholars who led the way of new thinking most often were to be found at Paris, from the realists to nominalists, from those influenced by the ancient Greeks to those who learned from Islam. The university gave Paris and France a new and deserved reputation for scholarship. It was also a key institution in the development of arguments in favour of the state over the church, despite its concentration on theology. The University of Paris has been called 'the battlefield of all the most significant intellectual conflicts of the age'.[10]

Paris, besides being the intellectual centre, became the literary, artistic and cultural capital. The university attracted leading teachers and many were also authors. The royal court never gained the reputation for cultural achievement that at times belonged to the princely courts of Champagne or Burgundy, yet it played its part. The university probably played a greater part.

CULTURAL ACHIEVEMENT

The future of French culture was far from clear through most of our period. Southern culture seemed more advanced. It was closer to Roman civilization and seemed to benefit from that. The southern courts, notably those of the counts of Poitou and the dukes of Aquitaine, were more noted for patronizing poets and literary figures. The troubadours are probably the best known medieval poets and they were based in the south. One of the greatest was Marcabru, born in Poitou in the early 12th century, and he like others used the southern Provençal tongue.

LITERATURE

Nevertheless, Paris was the base for many intellectuals, which also meant that literary work in the language of the north became prominent and eventually dominant – and the French language what it is today, based on the langue d'oïl rather than the langue d'oc. The royal role in this was not negligible. The langue d'oïl was the language of the Île-de-France and of the kings, the royal court, royal commands and of the proceedings of Parliament.

There was an enormous literary achievement in Capetian France, in both northern and southern tongues, from scholars to jongleurs. The University of Paris was an obvious base for many scholars who wrote significant works on theology. One of the most famed is of course Abelard, though possibly better known now for his personal misfortunes than his theological views. He was a Breton, born at Le Pallet, east of Nantes, the son of a knight. Hugh of St-Victor said he was the son of a Jewish father and an Egyptian mother.[11] He actually gave up his rights as an eldest son to lead a life of scholarship. He studied under Roscelin of Compiègne at Loches and then William des Champeaux at Notre-Dame in Paris. He established himself in Paris as a leading and popular teacher and set up his own school in Melun and then at Corbeil. In 1108 he returned as a teacher to Paris at Ste-Geneviève, and then from 1114 at Notre-Dame. Abelard had connections with Stephen Garlande, who may have helped promote him. Abelard went to live in the house of a canon in the cathedral precinct. The house was next door to the school and the canon was Fulbert. Fulbert was guardian of a niece to whom Abelard agreed to give lessons. The niece was Heloise. The girl's father is unknown, and was possibly Fulbert. Abelard when he was about

50 wrote about his earlier life in his *History of Calamities*. As Abelard confessed, his career was marred because he 'yielded to the lusts of the flesh'.[12] Heloise was a brilliant pupil and became an accomplished Latinist, almost unique for a female in her time. Approaching 40, Abelard was supposed to instruct the young Heloise (some years younger than him) but, he confessed, 'my hands strayed more often to her breasts than to the pages', and his nights became sleepless with making love.[13] Apparently he beat her or pretended to beat her in order to cover her cries of pleasure.[14] He was a brilliant and admired teacher, noted for his light-hearted approach and use of jokes. He also wrote poetry and composed songs which were said to attract women. He may have forced himself on her – she later said she had not consented. However Heloise fell deeply in love and recalled, 'what married woman, what young girl, did not desire you in absence'.[15] Their affair was probably real rather than fictional, as was its consequence. Sent to his home in Brittany, she bore a son named Astrolabe. She was reluctant to marry him or damage his career, but they married in secret. Her relatives attacked Abelard. He wrote, 'I was deprived of those organs with which I practised it [his lust]'.[16] Two of the men who had attacked Abelard were caught and punished – blinded as well as castrated, and Abelard felt no sympathy.

Astrolabe was brought up by Abelard's sister, Heloise became a nun, and Abelard returned to his theology. Heloise became prioress at Argenteuil and then at the Paraclete, founded by Abelard himself in the woods near Provins. Abelard was elected abbot to the remote house of St Gildas in Brittany, 'the last point of land by the horrifying waves of the ocean'.[17] But everywhere he went he stirred up controversy and had to move on. He was accepted in St-Denis, but could not stop himself pointing out that the abbey had combined three individuals in their claims for the work of their saint. They were so enraged that he had to move on. He built himself a hermit hut but students flocked to him. His cutting-edge ideas antagonized various clerics, not least St Bernard, who in the end virtually put an end to Abelard's public career.

Abelard's most controversial ideas involved placing understanding before belief, 'by doubting we are led to inquire, by inquiry we perceive the truth'.[18] St Bernard's slant on this was to damn 'academics who doubt everything and know nothing'.[19] Abelard's *Sic et Non* deliberately put forward contradictory views from the Fathers on 158 theological questions. The trouble was that his open thinking laid him open to charges of heresy. For all this, Abelard's brilliance had given a shine to the reputation of Paris. Abelard was saved from a worse fate through the protection of the great abbot of Cluny, Peter the Venerable. The pope condemned as heretical his work, which was burned in public. Abelard had set out to defend himself but was invited to stay at Cluny where he lived until 1142. His body was taken to the Paraclete for burial by Peter the Venerable who also wrote Heloise a letter of condolence. She lived on until c.1164.

Abelard was only one of the many leading scholars from throughout Europe who learned or taught in Paris. One could mention hundreds of important figures. Some of the greatest names of the medieval period studied or taught at the university, including Anselm, Hugh of St-Victor, John of Salisbury, Innocent III, Roger Bacon, Albert the Great, Peter Lombard, Bonaventure (Giovanni di Fidanza), Thomas Aquinas, Duns Scotus, and Meister Eckhart.

Poetry was another major French achievement, notably the *chansons de geste* mainly from the north, and the works of the troubadours in the south. Epic poems became popular from the 11th century and as *chansons* blossomed in the 12th century. The *Song of Roland* was among the earliest, beginning a major theme on the age of Charlemagne. Another favourite theme emerged around the almost entirely fictional court of King Arthur, which became entwined with tales about the Holy Grail. Perhaps the most famous poet was Chrétien de Troyes (1135–83) who came from Champagne. He popularized the Arthurian stories for Marie countess of Champagne, Eleanor of Aquitaine's daughter by Louis VII. Chrétien made it clear that on occasion he had been encouraged to compose by her, 'since my lady of Champagne wishes me to begin a Romance'.[20] One of the best known works of medieval literature is the *Roman de la Rose*, which stresses the element of love, 'the *Roman de la Rose* it is, and it enfolds/Within its compass all the Art of Love'.[21] Lesser-known poets left interesting works, not least the romances by Jean Renart and Gerbert de Montreuil, both using northern French, sometimes called 'Francien'.[22] These two wrote with contemporary settings. They also dotted their works with lyrics for songs. It is generally thought that the Capetian court took little interest in such works but Gerbert's *Roman de la Violette*, dedicated to Marie countess of Ponthieu, includes an interesting scene of singing and dancing when the royal court was at Pont de l'Arche.[23]

The first surviving troubadour work was that of no less a person than William IX of Aquitaine, grandfather of Eleanor of Aquitaine. The theme of courtly love, *amor*, adulterous love, was especially popular in the south, reflecting the courts where the works were performed – if not the behaviour. Whether true or not, the Englishman William of Malmesbury said the duke built a brothel in the form of a convent (possibly a convent that gained a bad reputation).[24] William shared the erotic approach, 'until I may have my hands under her cloak'.[25] These noble courts patronized the great jongleurs and troubadours. One unexpected fact is that perhaps 20 of the troubadours were women.[26] They also shared the erotic approach. The countess de Dia, wife of the Provençal William of Poitiers, wrote what sounds much like a modern pop song: 'If only I might lie with you one night', and she was requesting this of a lover whom she wished to have 'in place of my husband'.[27] We know of the poems because they were written down, generally at a slightly later period and for the benefit of princes, but this was essentially a performance art, increasingly associated with song. As many as 2,600 troubadour poems survive and some 275 tunes.[28]

The noble courts were the setting for most performances. One of the major achievements of this work was the introduction of the vernacular into leading literature, which occurred from about the end of the 13th century. One of the greatest contributors was the poet Rutebeuf, who lived in Paris from 1245 to 1280. The poetry also inspired treatises on its themes, notably *The Art of Courtly Love* by Andreas Capellanus, chaplain to Marie of Champagne to whom he dedicated. it. The vernacular was also used for scholarship with treatises on astronomy, astrology, birds, beasts, plants, weather and medicine.[29] Science was not ignored and not as mistaken as usually presented. We mentioned earlier that at least some medieval men appreciated that the world was round; similarly the idea of gravity was discussed.

ARCHITECTURE AND ART

It was in the Île-de-France that Gothic architecture first appeared, though influences from elsewhere were involved, as from southern France, Normandy and Iberia. Romanesque style did not disappear overnight. 'Romanesque' is a term that only appeared in the 19th century and is used chiefly to describe architecture in western Europe in the earlier Middle Ages, especially church architecture. It is associated chiefly with rounded arches, barrel vaulting and their accompaniments. The term suggests a continuation of Roman forms into the Middle Ages. It is especially associated with Charlemagne and the Carolingians, who deliberately sought to emulate Roman culture in their new 'Roman' empire. A key example would be Charlemagne's palace at Aachen. In fact Romanesque was nothing like a copy of Roman architecture, owing debts, for example, to barbarian, Byzantine and Islamic work. Fewer churches survive in their original state from this period than later; more buildings were still in wood and most were bound to be altered over time. Good examples though can be seen at St-Sernin in Toulouse, and Ste-Madeleine at Vézelay.[30] The decoration of Romanesque churches used Biblical themes such as the Last Judgement, but ornament often included strange and grotesque figures and animals – what St Bernard lampooned as 'several bodies beneath one head ... several heads upon one body'.[31] At St-Lazare in Autun is an inscription on the tympanum, '*Gislebertus hoc fecit*' (Gilbert made this), though it is debated whether he was the sculptor or the patron.

It is widely suggested that the first major Gothic work was for the abbey church of St-Denis, planned and organized by its great abbot, Suger. Suger wrote about the building of the church and makes it clear that 'wonderful and uninterrupted light' was indeed his aim.[32] The architecture was intended to reflect the spiritual experience, so that 'the dull spirit lifts'.[33] Visiting St-Denis now, one must remember that subsequent alterations have reduced the amount of light that once entered Suger's church. We can agree, 'a new style was born'.[34] Suger had the problem of building on a revered existing church, and incorporated some of its elements. In his *Adminstration* Suger describes the work done, beginning with the western side. The great west door was consecrated in 1140. The eastern side was completed during the following years; its semi-circular plan of radiating chapels was much copied. After Suger's death further work was supervised by 'one of the most remarkable architects' of his day, Peter of Montreuil, in the 13th century, including flying buttresses.[35]

Sadly St-Denis experienced a series of accidents and attacks, suffering from war and vandalism. Even restoration in the 18th and 19th centuries is now seen as further disaster. Crosby considers even the west door 'today is only a poor copy of the original efforts'.[36] The first serious damage was done in the Hundred Years' War when St-Denis was pillaged. The tombs of Philip Augustus, Louis VIII and St Louis were destroyed. In 1771 much of the decoration was removed and replaced. New ornament was added in the 19th century. The French Revolutionaries treated St-Denis as a prime target because of its long association with royalty. Some tombs, including that of Hugh Capet, were destroyed. Royal remains were dumped together in a ditch. Services in the church were stopped and in 1793 it was closed and abandoned. St-Denis was used for meetings, storage and as a military hospital. Gradually the great abbey fell into ruin. Napoleon ordered restoration and had emperors buried there but the abbey suffered still; restoration 'disfigured it more cruelly than the vandalism of the populace'.[37] In 1839 the apostles were given new heads with moustaches and beards. It was noticed that there were now 13 apostles! The 'restorers' had failed to notice that one figure was the Virgin Mary. The architect then ordered one of his men to chip off the beard and moustache from one figure.[38] The north tower was hit by lightning and badly damaged, needing to be rebuilt, which was done – badly. Further harm was done in the succession of wars – in 1871, 1918 and 1945. Nevertheless enough remains to recognize a truly great work of art and architecture – the vaults, the windows including the two great rose windows, many of the sculpted figures – the signs of the zodiac, the work of the months and so on. Finally also St-Denis has found some sympathetic restorers.

Gothic style is seen chiefly as depending on pointed arches or ogives, for windows and structure. They allowed slimmer columns for support and provided greater height. This in turn allowed more light, both as a result of the height and because large spaces could be filled with window rather than supporting walls. Thus we also associate closely with Gothic the emergence of large stained glass windows, such as the magnificent rose windows in many cathedrals.

Sens, where Hugh Capet had been elected king, was rebuilt for archbishop Henry le Sanglier (the Boar) after the earlier building had suffered from a fire. It was the first cathedral in Gothic style and others soon followed. The builder, William of Sens, fell 50 feet from a scaffold during the construction, but survived and continued to direct operations. Flying buttresses were added to Sens after another fire in the later 12th century, an early example of this improvement to Gothic structure.

Chartres was one of the greatest new cathedrals, and retains some of the earliest examples of Gothic sculpture. It was probably the first fully to use flying buttresses to support the structure. The later Gothic work at Chartres, after a fire in 1194, incorporated no less that 173 windows containing 2,500 square metres of glass.[39] The famous great bells of Chartres were sadly melted down at the Revolution to make cannons.

Laon is considered the best preserved of 12th-century French Gothic cathedrals.[40] Here, despite the new style of building, old customs were long preserved – and much criticized by reformers. These included ringing the bells in a thunderstorm to frighten away the devil, clerics dressing up in costumes including as a donkey for festivals, reversing the normal social order on such occasions, and consuming 4250 litres of wine on Christmas Eve.[41] Other great early cathedrals appeared at Senlis, Bourges, Reims and Amiens. Bourges had some interesting sculpted figures, especially the Last Judgement on the west door. Here appear figures of the damned, including a bishop – the only one in clothes![42] In Paris, apart from St-Denis, the great Gothic cathedral of Notre-Dame was rebuilt under Bishop Maurice de Sully from 1163, including the new idea of flying buttresses. The sculpted Tree of Jesse was badly damaged in the Revolution because the citizens wrongly believed the figures were kings and cut off their hands and feet!

Nor must one ignore the magnificent art in the stained glass windows of all the great Gothic churches. St Louis' Ste-Chapelle has been called 'a glass shrine'.[43] Gothic had practical advantages as a style of church building, using the pointed arch, ribbed vaults, flying buttresses, stained glass windows, thus providing greater light within a building, and allowing impressive height. It required mathematical ability and techniques and has been called 'applied geometry'.[44] Medieval architects did not always get it right and the problems and difficulties so often overcome are only underlined by the failure of Beauvais, whose enormously tall spire collapsed in 1284 not long after it was built. It was partly the prestige of royal support for buildings in the new style that assisted its spread. Gothic remains the essential style that we associate with medieval churches and it was fundamentally a French achievement, even referred to by Germans as 'opus Francigenum'.[45] The ornament and colour favoured by Suger and his followers was criticized by some of the more austere clerics, notably St Bernard in his treatise on moderation in building. Cistercian abbeys led the way in a more restrained development of Gothic style.

Artistic achievement was linked to both scholarship and architecture, through manuscript illustration, sculpture, and paintings in churches. In churches there was an element of education and enlightenment involved. The council of Arras in 1025 declared, 'the illiterate contemplate in paintings what they cannot see through writing' – hence the great emphasis of biblical and religious subjects, and on the importance of kings.[46]

MUSIC

The 11th and 12th centuries saw an important development in music. Musical notation was developed and musical treatises were written. Thus we see the appearance of what would be more or less familiar today as the five-line staff, and notes as ut (do)-re-mi. It is true that they were not written in quite the modern fashion, but they are recognizable and can be repeated so that now medieval music can be recreated.

Much of the music we know of was church music, more likely to be recorded than secular work. Notre-Dame was a leader in music with a choir school. The choristers were treated harshly, and beaten with rods for the least offence. Here developed the musical equivalent of Gothic in polyphony, first in two-part and then four-part singing. Polyphony had appeared by the 11th century. The earliest form was *organum*, singing more than one pitch at the same time. Strict *organum* kept the same interval between the two pitches. This was later modified to allow a principal voice for the chant, and a *vox organalis* singing below and not exactly in parallel, though they would end together on exactly the same note.[47] Leading figures in developing polyphony at Notre-Dame included Leonin in the second half of the 12th century, and Perotin in the later 12th and early 13th century. Leonin was referred to by an English student as 'the best composer of *organum*'.[48] Perotin introduced descant using the idea of several individual modes. The 13th century saw the birth of the motet – named from the French for 'word', using Latin text for the upper voice and different words and sometimes a different language for the lower voice.

Music was also part of the art of minstrels and jongleurs – and even some jongleuresses.[49] We can see representations of musical instruments in sculpture and in manuscript illustrations and can identify them as, for example, the trumpet, bagpipe, vielle or viol, the rebec with its gourd shape, the lute, the psaltery, and so on.[50] The 13th century saw the appearance of the *rondellus* or *rondeau*, that is, a round dance where a leader and his group played alternately. The period also saw the beginning of the *Ars nova* in music, explained in contemporary treatises, as by Philip de Vitry. This introduced a more flexible rhythm into music and a more subtle sound. Not everyone liked the new sound, including Pope John XXII, who criticized singers conveying emotion in music 'by their gestures' and 'the great proliferation of little notes'; he preferred 'singing in the old way'.[51]

WAR – DEFENCE AND ADVANCE

It is true that the Capetians in general sought to advance only through legally correct means. They more than any rulers of the time followed the precept of making war for correct reasons, in the view of the church, for defence, for protection of the subject population, and to support Catholic Christianity. In the terms of Fawtier they 'put right before might'.[52] Otherwise much was gained through purchase or by territory that fell to the crown without war, as by marriage or failure of noble heirs.

Of course the Capetian position was threatened at times and there were serious setbacks. The early Capetians had difficult struggles with the lords in their own demesne and even suffered defeats. Louis VII lost Aquitaine with the end of his marriage to Eleanor. The minority of St Louis was a time of danger for the monarchy, though his mother Blanche of Castile held her own.

The emergence of France as we know it owes much to the Capetian kings, partly from military effort – frontiers had to be defended or territory expanded, rebellions must be suppressed and rival princes contained. To quote but one, though probably the chief, of these successes – consider the difference that the battle of Bouvines made. It confirmed Philip II's conquests from the Plantagenets, and it halted pretensions for expansion of the Holy Roman Empire. It also helped to bring eventual dominance over Flanders.

There can be little doubt that the conquests of Philip Augustus at the expense of the Plantagenets in the early 13th century were of vital importance to the growth of modern France. Normandy, Maine, Anjou were conquered. Normandy was added to, and immensely increased, the royal demesne. Of course the Capetians suffered defeats, none perhaps greater than that at Courtrai. That also had important repercussions and delayed royal control over Flanders – but it did not have the same long term effects for the French monarchy as Bouvines.

As we have suggested, war was not the only or perhaps even the major means used by the Capetians. They chose whenever possible to act within legal boundaries, so that they could claim that what they won was by right. Troublemaking enemies were dealt with first by legal means, and the development of royal justice and especially of the great court that met in Paris and was called Parliament, were vital to this process. Almost always an aggressor was tackled first in court and only after condemnation was further action taken. Military force was usually the last rather than the first resort.

PEACE – SOCIETY AND THE ECONOMY

The contrast between 987 and 1328 is as clear in many ways. Social change was enormous. Economic change led to movement of population and greater personal freedom for the individual. As towns became larger and wealthier, so they became more powerful. As a result, control of towns became an important issue. In various ways authority was disputed between rival lords, between lay and clerical lords, between local lords and the king and between groups within the towns. One effect was the growth of organizations within the towns, as well as increasing involvement by the king.

Urban society became increasingly important. Citizens were free and sought to use their freedom. Some became wealthy through trade and business. Social classes developed within the towns, including an urban elite that was usually dominant in town government, and the emergence of the bourgeoisie. The very use of that term underlines the importance of French towns in this development. In the view of Le Goff, towns 'forged a new society'.[53] Documents show the growth of town gilds including some 130 in Paris under Louis IX. The commune movement arose with towns demanding greater rights to govern themselves – often seeking royal protection from local lords in order to do so. The king valued co-operation with towns for economic reasons, and for political and military support, but communes were also much feared and hated, by the nobility and often by the church – to Guibert 'commune' was 'a destestable name'.[54] The idea of a commune carried a whiff of revolution. Wace quoted citizens banding together, swearing common oaths, and declaring against having a lord since 'our enemy is our master'.[55] Kings were less keen on communes within the demesne and did not always support the development but outside the demesne it was often a useful connection to the principalities. In the late Capetian period a personal connection between the king and certain favoured citizens appeared with the appointment of the *bourgeois du roi*, citizens who acted as royal agents and were given the privilege of not being tied to any particular town. These men proved especially loyal to the crown.

Wider organizations emerged in the 14th century, in regional and even national assemblies. The national assemblies did not prove very effective under the Capetians, partly because the principalities were still too different and separate. The regional assemblies within the principalities, however, proved a significant means of giving a form of representation to local communities and a means of bargaining over royal taxation and rights. More worrying for the crown was the emergence in the late period of regional leagues, since these threatened to be independent organizations outside royal control. The threat appeared greater when these leagues began to ally with each other and press for concessions. However the movement never became national, the leagues were bargained with separately, and the movement died down before 1328.

The expansion of France as a nation was a matter of royal effort on the boundaries – the conflicts with the empire, the Plantagenets and the Iberian powers. Only rarely did Capetians venture into more distant affairs, and then with little effect. The major exception to this was crusading, spurred largely by religious motives so far as the monarchy went. Crusading to the Holy Land was fundamentally a French movement, the '*Gesta Dei per Francos*'.[56] The Kingdom of Jerusalem was formed mainly from principalities set up by the French in the Holy Land. Its rulers and lords were chiefly of French extraction. There has been much debate about the value of the crusades, and their failure, but in the process the benefits once seen have been erased. The crusading movement undoubtedly did give Europe a broader view of the world. It was also responsible for the French and western missions to the Mongols and a greater connection to the East. Products from and trade with the Kingdom were not negligible, nor was the increased knowledge gained from Islamic sources.

Economic change must also be noted. The Capetian period was one of great change in Europe, including population growth. The population of France roughly doubled in the period. By 1328 it was about 18 million, and that was probably slightly down on the figure for 1300 following the famine and plague years of 1315–17. One effect of the greater population was to make demands on the economic structure. Food, housing and employment had to be found.

France was a major centre of farming improvements, including the rapid spread of watermills and windmills, the change to horse ploughing, and three-field rotation. Marginal land or land not previously farmed was cleared, including forest areas and marsh. Farming that could operate on less fertile ground developed. Not all peasants could be employed in the same existing farm estates.

There was pressure for greater freedom that would include greater freedom of movement. There was an inevitable transfer of population from rural to urban places. Towns therefore grew, including new towns. The population pressure helped to explain the outward movement of the age, including settlement elsewhere, wars against Muslims in Spain and the East.

The produce of France, which came from both rural and urban areas, expanded greatly. Some areas grew naturally, such as Flanders with its textile production, and part of that came by 1328 under French control. Wine was an important product across much of France, not least in Gascony under threat of English control. But there were other wine regions too, such as Champagne. For export, wine was kept in barrels lined with pitch, the taste of which may have made Peter Damian's mouth itch, but allowed easier export.[57]

There was economic expansion and development. Larger towns in the Capetian era developed markets and fairs to cover their local region, and some had wider links. Paris and Orléans had fairs, including the famous Lendit Fair at St-Denis. The principalities also developed fairs, as at Rouen in Normandy, or at Bordeaux. The great fairs grew and became significant, notably the cycle known as the Champagne Fairs, 'the chief emporium of Western Europe' in the 12th century.[58] Import and export became a major element in royal as well as mercantile wealth, as taxation on these activities emerged. Lords, nobles and the monarchy all stood to gain from the profits of trade, and thus there was great stress upon rights over river transport and roads, over the holding of markets and fairs, over the taking of timber, over mills and fishing, and virtually every other means of producing food and goods – on which the towns depended for their wealth. The king was the greatest of all the beneficiaries. By the end of our period the Capetians had ensured that no other lord in France could compare with the king in income, wealth, and thus of power.

Nevertheless the late Capetian period saw economic decline, due to factors beyond the control of kings – bad weather, poor harvests and population decline. An early sign of what was to come was the food shortage of 1305. The years 1315–17 saw a series of poor harvests together with plague – a foretaste of the Black Death years. Prices became unstable and there were problems with the value of the coinage. The reign of Philip IV was the first with serious trouble of this kind, and eventually he introduced the first major devaluation, though its consequences were not good. The crown tried to solve the problem by borrowing, but there were then problems over repayment, notably to the Italians. There were signs of rural and urban unrest. In 1320 the Pastoureaux episode, otherwise known as the Shepherds' Crusade, caused disturbances in several areas of France and led to noble and royal anxiety.

ADMINISTRATION

Royal power and profits from rights depended on administrative efficiency. The early Capetians relied on Carolingian methods and change was neither rapid nor revolutionary. The position of the early members of the dynasty made it impossible to organize anything on a nation-wide basis. Government was largely a personal and local matter. Those close to the king retained a major role in government throughout our period. The court and those in attendance varied in rank and quality but the king could keep a finger on the pulse of administration. Government was largely carried on through a few great officers – seneschal, chancellor, butler, chamberlain and constable. Gradually the princes faded from court and their tasks were taken over by lesser nobles and then by more professional officials. Inevitably, since most of the work required literacy, the officials tended to have a heavy clerical predominance. The great offices often remained in noble hands but became increasingly honorary.

As the practical work came to be carried out by lesser nobility, the offices fell to certain leading families such as those of Montmorency, Clermont, Dammartin, Beaumont, Rochefort and especially the Garlandes. With this development came a tendency for offices to become hereditary – it was in the interest of the families to hold on. The kings at first went along with this, but when over-powerful families caused problems, they began to restrict family power over office. One way to do this was to leave office vacant before a new appointment. More and more the major officials were able individuals selected by the king and in office only so long as they retained royal favour. This should not give an impression of unstable government. Far from it, Capetian officials proved remarkably loyal and most held office for 20 years or so. Some, in the later period, received social promotion as a reward – thus William de Nogaret was knighted in 1285.

At first Capetian administration followed the king. Since the kings remained itinerant, this element did not altogether disappear but the increasing load of work meant need for detailed records and a permanent base. This base almost naturally was Paris, though the development itself assisted the rise of Paris to prominence. Major officials stayed in Paris and had permanent staffs. The legal high court of Parliament, emerging from the royal court, was held in Paris under the late Capetians. The treasury was established at the Louvre, moved to the Temple, and then returned to the Louvre – but always in Paris. The first mention of the Chambre aux Deniers established in Paris was in 1303. The Chambre des Comptes was separated off in 1304, and organized fully in 1320. The Argenterie appeared in 1315. The royal archives were also kept in Paris.

Local government played a central part in the development of Capetian strength. At first the kings had authority only over a limited area – the royal demesne. The demesne itself gradually grew, as did royal authority beyond it. Royal power expanded into other French regions in the principalities and royal administration followed. In the demesne, as it expanded, there was increasing need for royal agents on the spot, and then for these agents to be checked by central government.

There developed a centrally controlled organization of administration that depended on agents such as baillis and prévôts. The baillis supervised the local prévôts and were expected to bring their accounts to Paris three times a year so that they in turn could be checked centrally. The baillis at first had a broad and not clearly restricted geographical region of action, but gradually this became more clearly defined. They too in the 14th century lost power to the more central Chambre des Comptes in Paris. Within the principalities the king used existing methods and officials and incorporated them into the royal system.

Raising finance was a basic need for the king, and a constant problem, always a major task of royal agents, especially in the demesne. There were many sources of profit, from tax, rights, or the profits of production. The Chambre des Comptes was the climax of Capetian administrative development in this respect. Levies for war were a major source of finance. Defence of the realm was a cause with which few could quarrel. The king had rights of raising troops from feudal sources and the towns offered military aid. Increasingly the king found it more convenient to commute actual service for a money payment.

The reign of Philip the Fair was a key point in the history of royal taxation. Aids previously taken from the nobility were extended downwards through society and demanded from lesser men and towns. The moving force was increased need and a developing economic crisis. Thus it was also Philip IV and his immediate successors who pressed harder on the Jews to take from them ready existing wealth. No less than four tallages were imposed upon them and there followed a series of expulsions. The trouble with thus seizing wealth was that the wealth progressively diminished. There was a similar attack on the Lombards, whose expulsion also prevented the need to pay off debts owed to them. Exports and imports were taxed. The church remained a regular source of income, exploited to the full, and any quarrel with the papacy could result in the king keeping taxes raised for Rome. The idea of a hearth tax roused too much opposition to be established but the Capetians were feeling their way to a more modern tax system and many of their experiments would be tried again later.

From Philip IV there was an attempt to raise subsidies for intended campaigns and for other uses. Subsidies were demanded in 1313, 1314, 1315, 1318, 1319 and 1324. This regularity was one cause of the opposition that arose. Another was the royal attempt to use the system to raise money for reasons other than war. As we have seen, the argument emerged that once the cause for a subsidy ceased there was no right to raise it. It led to refusals to pay, demands for repayment, and the late Capetians had to back down. Nevertheless they had begun to spread taxation demands from the demesne to the realm, and to demand money for general government and reforms.

Another notable development in royal administration was the increasing role and influence of lawyers and legal men. This was partly because so much of Capetian government rested on a legal basis – dealing with the papacy and secular powers, making judgments on all sorts of matters such as land disputes or rights. It was partly also because legal study and training was developing apace in the universities. Bright and able legally trained men became vital to the administration and increased in numbers in the later Capetian period. The significance of law in government was underlined by the emergence and growing power of Parliament in Paris – an entirely judicial court. In the view of Fawtier, making judgements was 'the king's essential function'; his representatives were 'all judges in varying degrees'.[59]

CHRISTIAN MONARCHY AND THE CHURCH

The monarchy stressed its religious aspects. Kings were agents on earth for God. God gave them authority and they carried out God's wishes. They supported His church, and protected the clergy, the poor and the weak. As Le Goff puts it, 'the Church endowed royal power with a sacral character'.[60] The king was God's representative but also a 'sacred person', and even possessed qualities not shared by ordinary humans.[61] There developed the belief that Capetian kings could cure by touch. This claim began with Robert the Pious and was later associated especially with curing scrofula. In a world full of skin diseases this seemed a precious power. Lepers on crutches with their rattles were feared, 'deformed, with shrivelled whitish flesh'.[62] St Louis' and other Capetians' care for such people was brave, and a sign of special powers. Louis VIII left money to 2000 leper hospices. The sacred nature of kingship made difficulties for any secular lord who opposed the ruler. The Capetian stress on legal right stressed that they were doing God's work.

The use of the oriflamme, claimed to be the standard of Charlemagne, had its religious significance. It was kept at the abbey of St-Denis. From Louis VI on, it was handed to the king going on a military expedition, and denoted Christian backing for his efforts. The relation between the Capetian kings and the church was significant throughout the period, and developed into something special. No other major power in Europe had quite the link with the papacy that the French monarchy possessed. This was built up by a series of kings who supported the church, acted with piety, gave gifts, and encouraged new movements. The military orders in the Holy Land and the new monastic orders in the west both owed much in their early development to support from the Capetians. The character and life of Louis IX gave the Capetians greater respect throughout Christendom and eventually their own dynastic saint. St Louis' reputation developed further after his death and enhanced the reputation of the dynasty. On the whole only personal affairs caused trouble, namely royal marriages and liaisons. Even so, there were never the disastrous differences that divided empire and papacy and damaged German development. The papacy also suffered growing problems in the late Capetian period. Italy was an unstable political region, damaged by the papal-imperial struggle. Powerful families in Rome made papal residence in the Holy City almost impossible. At first as a temporary home and then seemingly permanently, the popes settled at Avignon – thus beginning the Avignon residence which did not end until the 15th century. Avignon was not then in French territory but was more under French influence than Rome. For decades prelates born and based in France and pro-French regions, especially from Languedoc, were elected as popes – often with royal pressure applied in their favour. The result was an even closer link between France and the papacy.

The relation between the kings and the bishops of France was also significant. We have seen how the Capetians were careful to allow at least a degree of freedom in episcopal elections. The result was co-operation rather than conflict. At times of difficulty between the papacy and the monarchy, the French prelates by and large supported the crown.

The Capetians had a special place in the crusading movement that throughout its course was dominated by the French. We may question the achievement of any of the crusades – Le Goff thought 'the only benefit brought back from the crusades by the Christians was the apricot'![63] But even if the crusades ended in failure and the collapse of the Latin Kingdom, it was an episode of significance. The crusades brought contact with Byzantine and Near Eastern civilization, and the west learned much from it. The settlement of westerners in the Holy Land, in Greece and other regions, was a sign of European population growth and movement, and a foretaste of 16th-century expansion. It is no coincidence that these crusaders and settlers were called 'Franks'.

The First Crusade was called at Clermont. French lords predominated in the crusade and among those who stayed to colonize the Holy Land. The Second Crusade was called at Vézelay when Louis VII and Conrad III were the first kings to crusade. Philip Augustus and St Louis had also gone on crusades. The Albigensian Crusade was another matter, not concerned with the Holy Land but with the destruction of Catharism in the west. It had led to royal control in southern France. The Fourth Crusade was fundamentally French and led to the defeat and rule of the Byzantine Empire, an event of tremendous consequence, even if the new Latin Empire only survived for just over half a century.

Whatever one's conclusions about crusading and its achievement or failure, one must agree that the French part, largely encouraged by royalty, had been tremendous. Apart from the gains in southern France, crusading brought advantages to the French crown, notably in prestige. Even the failure of Louis VII, the limited success of Philip II, and the failures of St Louis, resulted not in disgrace or even criticism; the main outcome was added prestige to the monarchy for participating. The very last Capetian, Charles IV, was still planning a crusade to Armenia, though he died before anything came of it.

THE KINGS

It was luck as well as judgement that the Capetians produced such a long line of competent kings. It required a certain amount of effort; each king had to marry, choose a suitable wife, and produce an effective heir. One or two Capetians left their marriages a little late but all succeeded in this modest effort. In the Middle Ages producing enough children to ensure an heir was a chancy business; many families failed in a very short space of time. Stillborn children, infant deaths, early deaths, fatal illness, fatal accidents, death in war – the possibilities were many, and survival into mature years by no means certain. Some Capetian kings did not live to have long reigns, but in general their survival rate was good and minorities were rare. The Capetians did their best to protect their heirs but they were also fortunate. The quality of a man that would make a competent king was another matter. Kings could do little about this beyond choosing a capable wife. Again the Capetians were remarkably fortunate. Compared to other dynasties the mental ability, common sense and general competence of the dynasty was evenly spread. There was no King John, Henry III, Edward II, Henry VI or Charles VI. One must recognize through the earlier period the importance attached to succession by the oldest son. The importance of this can be seen by comparing the Merovingian, Carolingian, and imperial practice.

In France kings made a great point of organizing the succession for the oldest son, known as association, and it worked. It was invariable practice by all the Capetians from Hugh Capet, who associated Robert the Pious in the very year that he himself became king. The deed of association meant that the son was made king before his father died, thus validating the future succession. By the time of Philip Augustus it had become so accepted, and the dynasty so well established, that association was no longer necessary.

The endurance of the dynasty was important. Comparison with the Holy Roman Empire makes the point. In the German case families failed to retain the crown and impose sons. The result was 'election' of the new emperor, in practice a move to the strongest candidate from any of the principalities, or just as often the weakest candidate as the only one all the others would accept. The result was a series of disputed successions, lack of continuity and of stability. The relative growth of France as a power and the decline of the Holy Roman Empire through the Middle Ages owed much to the practice of succession.

The family loyalty of the Capetian dynasty was another important factor. Rebellions by one member of the family against another were not unknown but they were rare. The comparison with other dynasties is telling, as the almost constant problems in this respect of the Merovingians and the Carolingians, of the civil wars in Germany or England. The granting of apanages helped this process but there was also a strong family tradition, and nearly all younger brothers and close relatives were loyal and assisted the king of the day. As a result the reputation of the dynasty for good government stood high. Good and competent rulers were the mainstay of the dynasty – men such as Hugh Capet, Robert the Pious, or Louis VI. Philip Augustus and Philip IV were outstanding rulers in their own ways, while St Louis became an icon of medieval kingship throughout Christendom.

THE LEGACY

On 1 February 1328 the last Capetian monarch, Charles IV, died. The only survivors of the dynasty were female. His widow was pregnant and there was a period of uncertain waiting. On 1 April (appropriately?) she gave birth to a daughter. Recent development had excluded female succession, and it was ignored in 1328 – though some compensation was made to the surviving women of the family. The opinion of the nobles of France counted most, and they preferred Philip of Valois as king. He became Philip VI (1328–50) and initiated another long line of kings to 1589. They belonged to the same family as the Capetians but direct succession from father to son or brother had been broken. Philip was the son of Philip IV's brother, Charles of Valois, and grandson of the Capetian Philip III. Philip VI was crowned at Reims on 29 May 1328.

One legacy of the dynasty was this stress upon excluding female succession, practice rather than law. The so-called Salic Law was suddenly discovered resting in the library of St-Denis in the 1350s. The uncertainty resulted in some dispute over the succession. Female members were compensated. Joan of Burgundy received the kingdom of Navarre; her son, by Philip of Évreux, was Charles the Bad of Navarre. Others received considerable cash payments. The female who created the most serious problem was Isabelle, daughter of Philip IV, wife of Edward II of England and mother of Edward III – who in time made a claim to the French throne. It is true that this was only in response to Philip VI claiming the confiscation of Gascony, but its consequences were great – though as an excuse rather than a reason perhaps. It initiated the Hundred Years' War with all its horrors and instability for France. But it seems more a result of the rule of the Valois than a consequence of Capetian failure.

The Valois dynasty makes a contrast to the Capetian. Their defeats were more fundamental, notably in the war with England – at Crécy, Poitiers and Agincourt. No Capetian king had suffered such disastrous losses – King John II was taken prisoner at Poitiers in 1356 and incarcerated in London. A notable point about the Capetians was continuity. One after the other the Capetians were able, competent men. They may not have been great intellectuals but they were mostly pious, hard working, and generally respected. The Valois kings were less fortunate. The unfortunate consequences of the accession of the mentally unstable Charles VI can hardly be exaggerated.

Not all matters Capetian continued to dominate. Perhaps deliberately, the Valois set some new values and changed certain aspects of rule. The Capetians had supported and raised the abbey of St-Denis as the royal abbey, and St Denis as the patron saint of France. The Valois did not exactly attack or destroy this, but they made a change. They placed more emphasis on St Michael, who became the patron saint for their dynasty, and then for France. They also replaced the oriflamme as the royal standard by the banner of St Michael.

The same kind of comment could be made for all the troubles in later medieval France. They were hardly consequences of Capetian rule. Perhaps the greatest problems came from natural disasters. The late Capetian period had seen the beginnings of this trouble with bad weather followed by poor harvests, and plague. These problems increased under the Valois, particularly with the Black Death and its dreadful social and economic results – decline in population and social upheaval. Capetian times began to look like a golden age in French history.

Notes

Notes to Chapter 1: Carolingian Francia

1 Glaber, p. 41.
2 See e.g. Nelson, *Frankish World*, chapters 11, 12, 13.
3 Riché, p. 54, '*in nomine patria et filia*'.
4 Lewis, p. 1.
5 Dhondt, p.vii.
6 Dhondt, p. 1.
7 James, p. 185 sees Louis IV and Lothar as competent; Dhondt, p. 66.
8 Wood, p. 41; *Epistulae Austrasiace*, 2, ed. W. Gundlach, MGH, Epistolae 3, Merowingici et Karolini Aevi 1.
9 Gregory of Tours, p. 379; Nelson, *Frankish World*, p. 195.
10 Riché, p. 13.
11 The battle was fought between Tours and Poitiers and is sometimes called the battle of Poitiers.
12 Riché, p. 50.
13 Collins, p. 276.
14 Sometimes numbered as Stephen II.
15 Riché, p. 68.
16 Riché, p. 63.
17 There is some dispute over the date and some prefer 742 but see Nelson, *Frankish World*, p. 172.
18 Einhard describes Charlemagne in detail, looks and character, pp. 63–71.
19 *Carolus Magnus*, Charles the Great, Charlemagne.
20 *Carolingian Chronicles*, Royal Frankish Annals, 775, p. 51.
21 King, p. 139, *Lorsch Annals*.
22 Riché, p. 126.
23 King, p. 271, Stephen III to Carloman and Charles.
24 Einhard, p. 56.
25 Einhard, p. 56.
26 Kurze, *Annales*, pp. 91, 93.
27 Dhondt, pp. 13–4.
28 Bordonove, p. 23.
29 In general see Godman & Collins.
30 Karl Ferdinand Werner, 'Hludovicus Augustus, Gouverner l'empire chétien – Idées et réalités', in Godman & Collins, pp. 3–123, p. 3–4.
31 Werner in Godman & Collins, p. 65.
32 Barraclough, p. 63.
33 Werner in Godman & Collins, p. 24, who suggests that Hildebrand may have been deliberately taken to the region for the birth.
34 Timothy Reuter, 'The End of Carolingian Military Expansion', in Godman & Collins, pp. 391–405, p. 400.
35 Werner in Godman & Collins, p. 20.
36 Riché, p. 145.
37 Riché, p. 288.
38 Nelson, *Charles the Bald*, p. 73.
39 Barraclough, p. 58.
40 Barraclough, p. 61.
41 Stuart Airlie, 'Bonds of Power and Bonds of Association in the Court Circle of Louis the Pious', in Godman & Collins, pp. 191–204, p. 198.
42 Elizabeth Ward, 'Caesar's Wife, the Career of the Empress Judith, 819–829', in Godman & Collins, pp. 205–27, pp. 207–8.

43 Her first child was the girl, Gisela.
44 Nelson, *Frankish World*, pp. 37, 50.
45 Dhondt, pp. 13–4; Riché, p. 158.
46 Nelson, *Frankish World*, p. 41.
47 Riché, p. 160; Nelson, *Charles the Bald*, p. 105.
48 Nelson, *Frankish World*, p. 41.
49 *Carolingian Chronicles*, p. 154.
50 B. Scneidmüller, 'Constructing identities of medieval France', pp. 15–42, in Bull, p. 18; Bordonove, pp. 25–6; Riché, p. 160.
51 Riché, p. 169.
52 Riché, p. 166.
53 Nelson, *Charles the Bald*, p. 180.
54 Barraclough, p. 70.
55 Dhondt, p. 1.
56 Ward in Godman & Collins, p. 216.
57 Riché, p. 332.
58 Nelson, *Charles the Bald*, pp. 75, 78, 86.
59 Nelson, *Charles the Bald*, p. 13.
60 Nelson, *Charles the Bald*, p. 16.
61 Riché, pp. 143, 205.
62 Nelson, *Charles the Bald*, p. 207.
63 Dhondt, p. 266.
64 Riché, p. 193.
65 Nelson, *TRHS*, p. 21.
66 Koziol in Bull, p. 48.
67 Nelson, *Charles the Bald*, p. 236.
68 Nelson, *Charles the Bald*, p. 263.
69 Nelson, *Frankish World*, p. 231.
70 Barraclough, pp. 68–9.

Notes to Chapter 2: The rise of the Robertians

1   Barraclough, p. 54.
2   M.Schmidt-Chazan, 'Les origins germaniques d'Hugues Capet', in Iogna-Prat & Picard, pp. 231–44.
3   Pognon, p. 70.
4   Nelson, *Charles the Bald*, p. 166.
5   Dudo, p. 21.
6   Nelson, *Charles the Bald*, p. 163.
7   Riché, p. 211.
8   Bordonove, p. 67.
9   MacLean.
10 MacLean, pp. 23, 41.
11 MacLean, p. 25.
12 Barraclough, p. 106.
13 Nelson, *Charles the Bald*, p. 256.
14 Martindale, 'The kingdom of Aquitaine and the "Dissolution of the Carolingian fisc"'.
15 Martindale, p. 155.
16 MacLean, p. 87.
17 MacLean, pp. 14, 19, 41, 81.
18 MacLean, p. 108.
19 Pognon, p. 78.
20 MacLean, p. 37.
21 Martindale, p. 171.
22 MacLean, p. 1.
23 MacLean, pp. 40–1.
24 MacLean, p. 9.
25 Dhondt, p. 45; MacLean, p. 3.
26 Riché, p. 219, MacLean, p. 230.
27 MacLean, p. 233–34.
28 MacLean, p. 116.
29 Riché, p. 220.
30 Dhondt, p. 45.
31 Dhondt, p. 244.
32 Dhondt, p. 245.
33 Dhondt, p. 52.
34 Fliche, p. 19.
35 Glenn, p. 203.
36 Bordonove, p. 65.
37 Bordonove, p. 67.
38 Nelson, *Frankish World*, p. 170.
39 Dhondt, p. 56.
40 Pognon, p. 183.
41 Bordonove, p. 68; Riché, p. 246. Glenn, eg p. 2, prefers to call him Charles the Straightforward.
42 St-Maixent, p. 83, '*Follus*'.
43 Riché, p. 247.
44 M. Sot, 'Les élévations royals de 888 à 987 dans l'historiographie du Xe siècle', pp. 145–50, in Iogna-Prat & Picard, p. 148.
45 J. Dunbabin, 'West Francia: the kingdom', in *CMH*, iii, pp. 372–97, p. 377.
46 Glenn, p. 196
47 Glenn, p. 239.
48 Glenn, p. 210.

49 Bordonove, p. 84.

50 Dhondt, p. 120.

51 Glaber, p. 16.

52 Glenn, p. 230.

53 Riché, p. 254.

54 Riché, p. 256. Louis IV 'd'Outremer' or Latin Ultramarinus, the Foreigner or Exile, sometimes also called 'the Englishman' (l'Anglais)

55 Glaber, p. 16.

56 Sot, in Iogna-Prat & Picard, p. 149.

57 Dunbabin in CMH, iii, p. 382; Dudo, p. 69.

58 Bordonove, p. 90.

59 Dhondt, p. 138; Bull, Introduction, p. 10.

60 Bordonove, p. 13; McKitterick, p. 305.

61 John XII died in 964 in bed with a married woman.

62 Pognon, p. 189.

63 Riché, p. 262.

64 I. Voss, 'La Lotharingie, terres de rencontres Xe-XIe siècles', pp. 267–72, in Iogna-Prat & Picard, p. 268.

65 Pognon, p. 189.

66 Glenn, p. 222.

67 Lewis, p. 13.

68 Dudo, p. 81.

69 Some historians have mistakenly suggested she married Raymond duke of Gothia.

70 Pognon, p. 228–29.

71 Bordonove, p. 159.

72 St-Maixent, p. 97.

73 Bordonove, p. 162.

74 Glaber, p. 25.

75 Bordonove, p. 163.

76 Bordonove, p. 133.

77 St-Maixent, p. 97.

78 Luchaire, p. 146.

79 Bordonove, p. 178.

80 St-Maixent, p. 97.

Notes to Chapter 3: The new principalities, 800–1000

1 Pognon, p. 246, Richer.

2 Hallam, p. 34.

3 Glaber, p. 39.

4 MacLean, p. 87.

5 M. Roblin, L'Époque Franque, pp. 55–69, in Mollat, p. 57.

6 Dhondt, p. 247.

7 Dhondt, pp. 109–14.

8 Jean Dunbabin: 'West Francia: the Kingdom', in CMH pp. 372–97, p. 383.

9 Favier, Principautés, p. 33.

10 Favier, Principautés, p. 34.

11 Dudo, p. 49.

12 Dhondt, p. 116.

13 Pognon, p. 314, Richer.

14 Fliche, p. 318.

15 Dunbabin, p. 69.

16 James, p. 181.

17 Pognon, p. 199, from Richer.

18 Tilley, p. 15.

19 Fliche, p. 318.

20 Bachrach, p. 4.

21 Bachrach, p. 20.

22 Bradbury, Fulk le Réchin.

23 Dhondt, p. 245.

24 Jones, p. 2.

25 Tilley, p. 34.

26 L. Paterson in Bull, 'The south', pp. 102–33, p. 106.

27 Nelson, Charles the Bald, p. 2.

28 Roger Collins, 'Pippin I and the Kingdom of Aquitaine', in Godman & Collins, pp. 363–89.

29 For translations of Plantevelue/ Plantapilosa as Hairypaws, Hairyfeet, Hairysole, Foxy, see eg James, p. 173; Nelson, Charles the Bald, p. 211.

30 James, p. 173.

31 Dhondt, p. 216.

32 Dunbabin, p. 59.

33 Paterson in Bull, p. 103.

34 Dhondt, p. 151.

35 Dunbabin, p. 64.

36 Dhondt, p. 162.

37 Dunbabin, p. 65.

38 Riché, p. 222.

39 King, p. 68.

40 Pognon, p. 212, Richer.

41 Pognon, p. 343.
42 For example Godman and Collins on Louis the Pious, Nelson on Charles the Bald, and MacLean on Charles the Fat.
43 Tilley, p. 47.
44 James, p. 124.
45 Martindale, p. 172.
46 Barraclough, p. 94.
47 Favier, *Principautés*, p. 32.
48 G. Walter in Pognon, pp. 9–58.
49 Pognon, p. 278, Richer.

Notes to Chapter 4: The first Capetian kings, 987–1031

1 Raymond Cazelles, 'La Multiplication des Pouvoirs' in Mollat, pp. 89–109, p. 95.
2 Fliche, p. 317.
3 Barraclough, p. 84, believes that West Francia suffered most.
4 Glenn.
5 Glenn, pp. 115, 119, 242.
6 Glaber, p. 46; Masson, p. 1.
7 E.A.R. Brown, 'The Capetian Genealogy in the Historiography of the Middle Ages', pp. 199–214 in Iogna-Prat & Picard, p. 203.
8 Lewis, p. 21, *socia et particeps nostri regni*.
9 Funck-Brentano, p. 38.
10 Pognon, p. 357–68; Masson, p. 14.
11 M. Schmidt-Chazan, 'Les origines germaniques d'Hugues Capet dans l'historiographie française du Xe au XVIe siècle', pp. 231–44 in Iogna-Prat & Picard, pp. 234–35.
12 P.A. Maccioni, 'Une Note sure Hugues Capet, sa chanson de geste et l'historiographie médiévale anglaise', pp. 227–29 in Iogna-Prat & Picard, p. 228.
13 See F. Suard, 'Hugues Capet dans la chanson de geste au XIVe siècle', pp. 215–25, in Iogna-Prat & Picard.
14 Funck-Brentano, p. 47.

15 Pognon, p. 251.
16 Helgaud, p. 98.
17 Lewis, p. 36.
18 St-Maixent, p. 101.
19 Glenn.
20 Glenn, p. 68.
21 Pognon, p. 169.
22 Schneidmuller in Bull, p. 33.
23 Glenn, p. 95.
24 Glaber, p. 50.
25 Karl Leyser, p. 165.
26 Bordonove, *Capet*, pp. 176, 178.
27 St-Maixent, p. 97.
28 Bordonove, *Capet*, p. 183.
29 Bautier, p. 52.
30 Calmette, pp. 67–8.
31 Hallam, p. 90, Fliche, p. 319.
32 Calmette, pp. 67, 68.
33 Hallam, p. 90, comparing him to Fulk Nerra.
34 De Castries, p. 56; Bordonove, *Capet*, p. 13; Lemarignier, p. 37.
35 Barraclough, p. 84; Lemarignier, pp. 37 quoting F. Lot, 38.
36 Hallam, p. 90: 'little was achieved by Hugh … beyond mere survival'.
37 Glaber, p. 166.
38 Newman, pp. 3, 7–9.
39 Pognon, p. 343.
40 Lewis, p. 39.
41 Luchaire, p. 149.
42 Glenn, p. 124.
43 Glenn, pp. 112–3.
44 Glenn, p. 115.
45 Glenn, p. 101.
46 Bordonove, *Capet*, p. 231, '*interreges*'.
47 Favier, p. 43.
48 Gérard Walter, 'The social and religious infrastructure in the reign of Hugh Capet' in Pognon, pp. 9–58, p. 44–5.
49 Bachrach, *State-Building*, pp. 405–14.
50 Jumièges, ii, p. 32.
51 Jumièges, ii, p. 34.
52 Hallam, p. 28.
53 Lemarignier, p. 38.
54 Pognon, p. 293
55 Glaber, p. 58.

56 Bachrach, p. 44. Richer has Conan killed but in Glaber's account Conan was captured alive and his right hand cut off.

57 Newman, pp. xii, iv.

58 J-P. Evrard, 'Verdun au temps de l'évêque Haymon (988–1024)', pp. 273–78 in Iogna-Prat & Picard, p. 276.

59 Leyser, p. 222.

60 Glenn, p. 122.

61 Pognon, p. 147.

62 St-Maixent, p. 99.

63 Pognon, p. 290.

64 Glenn, p. 104.

65 Pognon, p. 354.

66 Waldman in Iogna-Prat & Picard, p. 193.

67 Pognon, p. 345.

68 Charles Vulliez, 'Les centres de culture de l'Orléanais', pp. 125–32 in Iogna-Prat & Picard, p. 125.

69 Helgaud, p. 84.

70 Luchaire, p. 154.

71 Helgaud, pp. 58–60.

72 Helgaud, p. 62.

73 Theis, p. 151, quotes Gérard of Cambrai.

74 Chartres, p. 146.

75 Helgaud, p. 124.

76 Helgaud, pp. 56, 122.

77 Helgaud, p. 122.

78 Helgaud, p. 116.

79 Theis, p. 157.

80 See the introduction to *Helgaud*.

81 Helgaud, see the introduction by R-H. Bautier and G. Labory.

82 Fawtier, p. 50.

83 Theis, p. 81.

84 Thietmar, p. 340.

85 Helgaud, p. 64.

86 Helgaud, p. 104.

87 Helgaud, pp. 76, 126

88 Helgaud, pp. 92, 94; Theis, p. 131.

89 Helgaud, p. 96.

90 See Penelope An Adair, 'Constance of Arles: a Study in Duty and Frustration', pp. 9–26 in Nolan.

91 Glaber, p. 106.

92 Chartres, p. 192.

93 Glaber, p. 168; Adair in Nolan, pp. 9–10; Theis, p. 141.

94 Theis, p. 141.

95 Thietmar, p. 196.

96 Adair in Nolan, p. 12.

97 Theis, p. 142; Helgaud, pp. 64, 74.

98 De Castries, p. 56; Duby, see Theis, p. 142.

99 Theis, p. 243.

100 Fliche, p. 324.

101 Adair in Nolan, p. 14, quoting Odorannus.

102 Jumièges, i, p. 132: 'rege piisimo'; Chartres, p. 46.

103 Hallam, p. 91.

104 Theis, p. 226.

105 Theis, p. 193.

106 Jumièges, ii, p. 244; Favier, *Principautés*, p. 20.

107 Dunbabin, p. 396.

108 Chartres, p. 50.

109 Glaber, p. 134.

110 Glaber, p. 88.

111 Theis, p. 210.

112 Glaber, p. 138.

113 Luchaire, p. 196.

114 Theis, p. 216.

115 Theis, p. 218.

116 Theis, p. 229.

117 Chartres, p. 178–80.

118 Chartres, p. 230.

119 Helgaud, p. 72.

120 Nolan, pp. 14–5; Helgaud, p. 74.

121 Glaber, p. 104.

122 Bachrach, *Fulk*, p. 63.

123 Theis, p. 129, from the *Annals of St Aubin*.

124 Theis, p. 143.

125 Chartres, p. 26.

126 Chartres, p. 152–54.

127 Jumièges, ii, p. 52.

128 Helgaud, p. 90.

129 Chartres, p. 192.

130 Theis, p. 233.

131 Theis, p. 238.

132 Helgaud, p. 138.

133 Glaber, pp. 128, 132.
134 Theis, p. 152.
135 Jumièges, ii, p. 26.
136 Lewis, p. 43; quotes Lemarignier.
137 Lemarignier, p. 76.
138 Brooke, p. 201; Bull, p. 11.
139 Favier, *Principautés*, p. 8.
140 Favier, *Principautés*, p. 21.
141 Pognon, p. 68.
142 Karl Leyser, p. 165.
143 C. Amalvi, 'L'Historiographie française face à l'avènement d'Hugues Capet et aux terreurs de l'an Mil (1800–1914)', pp. 245–55 in Iogna-Prat & Picard, p. 251.
144 Richard Landes, 'L'accession des Capétiens, une reconsideration selon les sources aquitaines', pp. 151–66 in Iogna-Prat & Picard, p. 163.
145 Helgaud, pp. 102, 104.

Notes to Chapter 5: Successful failures, 1031–1108

1 Bachrach, p. 258; the quote is from the Annals of Vendôme.
2 Hallam, p. 97.
3 De Castries, p. 58.
4 R-H.Bautier, *Recherches sur l'histoire de la France Médiévale, des Mérovingiens aux premiers Capétiens*, Variorum, Hampshire, 1991, X, 'Anne de Kiev, reine de France, et la politique royale au XIe siècle, étude critique de la documentation', pp. 539–64, p. 541.
5 Koziol in Bull, p. 57.
6 J. Dhondt, 'Quelques Aspects du Règne d'Henri Ier Roi de France', pp. 199–208, in Mélanges à Halphen, p. 200.
7 Fliche, p. 326.
8 Petit-Dutaillis, pp. 7, 17, 18, 33.
9 Lemarignier, p. 83.
10 Dunbabin, *Speculum*, p. 963. See also S. Fanning, *Speculum*, p. 114, and Jones, *Brittany*.
11 Dhondt in Halphen, p. 199.
12 Bates, *Normandy*, p. 72, suggests Poitiers and Jumièges 'can cast a false light'.
13 Hariulf, p. 2.
14 *Life of King Edward*, p. 106.
15 Bachrach, p. 207.
16 Jumièges, pp. 54, 56.
17 Nolan, p. 21.
18 Bautier, X, p. 551.
19 Nolan, p. 20.
20 Jumièges, p. 54.
21 Bachrach, p. 225.
22 Luchaire, p. 161.
23 Orderic, ii, p. 196.
24 Crouch, p. 65.
25 Douglas, p. 38.
26 Bates, *Normandy*, p. 73.
27 Bates, *Normandy*, p. 73.
28 Douglas, p. 46.
29 Bates, *Normandy*, p. 176.
30 Wace, p. 6.
31 Jumièges, p. 120.
32 Jumièges, p. 120.
33 Wace, p. 135.
34 Wace, p. 135.
35 Douglas, p. 52.
36 Jumièges, p. 122.
37 Jumièges, p. 122; Guillot, p. 50.
38 Poitiers, pp. 22, 24.
39 On dating, see Bates, pp. 255–57 and Douglas, p. 383–88. We have followed Bates' conclusions, agreeing that certainty is not possible.
40 Guillot, p. 82.
41 Jumièges, p. 124 and n.2; the passage means that the jeer was about funeral preparation of humans, and nothing to do with tanners – as later chroniclers mistakenly said.
42 Luchaire, p. 161.
43 Dhondt, *Revue Belge*, p. 89; Guillot, p. 63.
44 Dhondt, *Revue Belge*, pp. 94–6.
45 Bachrach, p. 226.
46 Dhondt, *Revue Belge*, p. 87.
47 Bachrach, p. 87.
48 Guillot, p. 44.
49 Guillot, p. 50.

50   Crouch, p. 68.
51   Crouch, p. 98.
52   eg Guillot, p. 79.
53   Bates, *Normandy*, p. 77.
54   Orderic, ii, p. 78.
55   Poitiers, p. 62.
56   Jumièges, p. 94.
57   Jumièges, p. 98.
58   Poitiers, p. 64.
59   Guillot, p. 66.
60   Guillot, p. 87.
61   Guillot, p. 83.
62   Poitiers, p. 28.
63   Guillot, p. 77.
64   Wace, p. 129.
65   Wace, p. 129.
66   Orderic, ii, p. 78.
67   Jumièges, p. 104.
68   Jumièges, p. 104.
69   Wace, p. 145–6; Jumièges, p. 144.
70   Benton, p. 69.
71   Benton, p. 69.
72   Poitiers, p. 72.
73   Wace, p. 146.
74   Wace, p. 149.
75   Guillot, p. 81.
76   Bautier, X.
77   Bautier, X, p. 548 and n.2.
78   Bautier, X, p. 546.
79   Bautier, X, p. 547.
80   Bautier, X, p. 564.
81   Bautier, X, p. 41.
82   Roger Bonnaud-Delamare,
     'Fondement des Institutions de Paix
     au XIe siècle', pp. 19–26 in Mélanges à
     Halphen, p. 24.
83   Lemarignier, p. 107.
84   Orderic, ii, p. 88.
85   Hallam, p. 98.
86   Dhondt in Halphen, p. 207.
87   Dunbabin, *Speculum*, p. 951.
88   Dunbabin, p. 956.
89   Fliche, pp. 5–7.
90   Hariulf, p. 234, '*custodiendus*'.
91   Fliche, pp. 8–9.
92   Hariulf, p. 236.
93   Bautier, IX, p. 552.
94   Bautier, X, p. 552.

95   Benton, p. 147; in general see Benton
     for Guibert of Nogent.
96   Benton, p. 18.
97   Benton, p. 87.
98   Hallam, p. 99; Orderic, v, p. 212.
99   Hollister, p. 69.
100 Fawtier, p. 17.
101 Luchaire, *Institutions*, p. 233, Luchaire,
     Premiers Capétiens, p. 169.
102 L. Gallois, I, 'Geography', pp. 1–29 in
     Tilley, p. 51.
103 De Castries, p. 58–9.
104 Luchaire, *Premiers Capétiens*, p. 168.
105 Hallam, pp. 99, 102.
106 Calmette, p. 106.
107 Barlow, *Rufus*, p. 165.
108 Fawtier, p. 17, 19.
109 Barber, p. 253.
110 Lemarignier, p. 141.
111 Luchaire, *Institutions*, p. 228.
112 Luchaire, *Institutions*, p. 229.
113 Hallam, p. 118.
114 Petit-Dutaillis, pp. 7, 86, 92.
115 Fliche, p. 122.
116 Fliche, pp. 31, 269.
117 Fliche, p. 258.
118 Fawtier, p. 63.
119 Wace, p. 150.
120 Bates, *William*, p. 158; 'minimized'
     from D.C. Douglas, p. 233, 'the first
     serious military check that he had
     suffered in France for more than
     twenty years'; 'success', Fliche, p. 273.
121 *ASC*, D. 1076, p. 158.
122 *ASC*, D. 1074, p. 155.
123 On Maine, see Barton.
124 Douglas, p. 235.
125 Bates, *William*, p. 178.
126 Fliche, p. 282.
127 *ASC*, E. 1087, p. 163.
128 *ASC*, E. 1090, p. 168.
129 Orderic, iv, p. 236.
130 Orderic, v, p. 218.
131 On Berry, see Bautier, *Recherches*, IX,
     'La Prise en Charge du Berry par le
     roi Philippe Ier et les Antecedents de
     Cette Politiques de Hugues le Grand à
     Robert le Pieux', pp. 31–60.

132 Bautier, IX, p. 32.
133 Luchaire, *Premiers*, p. 173.
134 Funck-Brentano, p. 90.
135 Bradbury, *Fulk.*
136 Guillot, p. 124.
137 Orderic, iv, p. 260–62.
138 Bradbury, *Fulk*, p. 36.
139 Duby on Guibert of Nogent, p. 154.
140 Duby, p. 155.
141 Luchaire, *Premiers*, p. 173.
142 Duby, p. 17.
143 Duby, p. 14; Orderic, iv, p. 263 and v, p. 10.
144 Fliche, pp. 47–8.
145 Duby, pp. 5–6.
146 Fliche, p. 54.
147 See Bradbury, *Fulk.*
148 Fliche, p. 64.
149 Luchaire, *Institutions*, p. 174.
150 Duby, p. 13.
151 Fliche, pp. 73–4.
152 Orderic, iv, p. 264.
153 Fliche, p. 138.
154 Luchaire, *Institutions*, p. 233.
155 Newman, p.xiii.
156 Bautier, X, p. 556.
157 Bautier, X, p. 560.
158 Bautier, IX, p. 43.
159 Bautier, IX, pp. 43, 54.
160 Bautier, IX, p. 58.
161 Bautier, IX, p. 32.
162 Luchaire, *Institutions*, p. 235.
163 Luchaire, *Premiers*, p. 172.
164 Funck-Brentano, p. 84.
165 Luchaire, *Premiers*, p. 172; Suger, p. 40.
166 Fliche, p. 159.
167 Hariulf, eg p. 235 records an act referring to Walter the son of Hugh the '*pincerna*' of the king.
168 Fliche, pp. 113–14.
169 Fliche, p. 119.
170 Lemarignier, p. 153.
171 Lemarignier, p. 159.
172 Fliche, p. 112.
173 Lemarignier, p. 171.
174 Funck-Brentano, p. 91, quoting William of Malmesbury.

175 T. Reuter, 'Nobles and Others: the Social and Cultural Expression of Power Relations in the Middle Ages', pp. 85–98 in *Nobles and Nobility*, ed. Anne J. Duggan.
176 Fliche, p. 163. In his charters as *Rex Francorum*; once at least as *rex Francorum augustus*; and *Monarchiam regni Francorum tenente Philippo serenissimo rege.*

Notes to Chapter 6: The Fat and the Young, 1108–80

1 Grant, p. 297, in comparison with Henry I of England.
2 Funck-Brentano, p. 130; Deeds, p. 124.
3 Panofsky, p. 7.
4 Grant, pp. xii, 28.
5 Panofsky, p. 29.
6 Panofsky, pp. 80, 122.
7 Panofsky, p. 10.
8 Grant, *Abbot Suger.*
9 Deeds, p. 61.
10 Deeds, p. 2: Dionysius the Areopagite at the time of St Paul; Dionysius the bishop of Paris in the 3rd century; Dionysius the Areopagite from the 6th century. Peter Abelard, a contemporary of Suger, noted the inaccuracy but was called a traitor for pointing it out.
11 Grant, p. 12–3.
12 The work is translated in English as *The Deeds of Louis the Fat*; in French as *Vie de Louis VI le Gros.*
13 Grant, p. 38.
14 Deeds, p. 152.
15 Grant, p. 7.
16 Deeds, p. 64.
17 Luchaire, *Annales*, p.xxxiii.
18 Deeds, p. 135.
19 Deeds, p. 29.
20 Luchaire, p. 312.
21 Luchaire, p. 313.
22 Delperrié, p. 163.
23 Deeds, p. 81.
24 Dunbabin, p. 256.

25 Thalamas, p. 27.
26 Luchaire, p. 311; *Annales*, p. lxvii.
27 Ibid.
28 Gobry, *Louis VI*, pp. 323–25.
29 Bayac, Preface.
30 Hallam, p. 149.
31 Dunbabin, p. 295.
32 Luchaire, *Louis VI*, and Bournazel, *Le Gouvernement Capétien*.
33 Bournazel, p. 94.
34 Bournazel, pp. 10–12.
35 Grant, p. 131.
36 Grant, p. 55. She adds of Stephen, that 'like most old reprobates, he must have had considerable charm'. Perhaps she knows some.
37 Bournazel, p. 151.
38 Funck-Brentano, p. 130.
39 Grant, pp. 124–5.
40 Bournazel, p. 104.
41 Luchaire, *Annales*, p. liv.
42 Bournazel, p. 65.
43 Bournazel, p. 65, quoting Guibert of Nogent on the 'viles personnae' around the king.
44 Dunbabin, p. 260.
45 Newman, p. 49.
46 Newman, p. 46–7.
47 Bournazel, p. 146.
48 Bournazel, p. 138.
49 Luchaire, p. 314.
50 For example Raymond Cazelles, 'La Multiplication des Pouvoirs', pp. 89–109 in Mollat, p. 91.
51 Luchaire, *Annales*, p. xxxix.
52 Deeds, p. 35.
53 Deeds, p. 36.
54 Deeds, pp. 84, 85.
55 Grant, p. 93; Deeds, p. 88.
56 Luchaire, *Annales*, p. lxxxi.
57 Bournazel, p. 45.
58 Deeds, p. 41.
59 Deeds, p. 64.
60 Hallam, p. 152.
61 Deeds, pp. 37, 106.
62 Luchaire, p. 316.
63 Koziol in Bull, p. 56.
64 Koziol in Bull, p. 71.
65 Newman, p. 64.
66 Luchaire, p. 318.
67 Deeds, p. 110.
68 Deeds, p. 133.
69 Dunbabin, p. 257.
70 Bautier, p. 58.
71 T.N. Bisson, 'Princely Nobility in an Age of Ambition (c.1050–115)', pp. 101–13 in Duggan, p. 109.
72 Deeds, p. 141. William of Ypres was a natural son of Philip of Loos, son of Robert of Frisia.
73 Deeds, p. 141.
74 Luchaire, p. 320; Funck-Brentano, p. 138.
75 Luchaire, p. 321.
76 Luchaire, *Annales*, p.c.
77 Deeds, p. 112.
78 Deeds, pp. 112–3; Orderic vi, p. 187.
79 Deeds, p. 114.
80 Deeds, p. 117.
81 Grant, p. 297.
82 Map, pp. 286.
83 Deeds, p. 131.
84 Grant, p. 119.
85 Deeds, p. 128.
86 Deeds, p. 81.
87 Luchaire, *Annales*, p. cxxxiv.
88 Delperrié, pp. 287, 290.
89 Luchaire, p. 327.
90 Funck-Brentano, p. 142.
91 Odo of Deuil, p. 128.
92 Gerald of Wales, viii, p. 132.
93 Luchaire, p. 78.
94 Walter Map, p. 443.
95 Map, p. 459.
96 Map, p. 451.
97 Gobry, *Louis VII*, p. 313.
98 Sassier, p. 7.
99 Ralph Diceto, *Opera Historica*, ed. W. Stubbs, 2 vols, RS no. 68, London, 1876, p. 412.
100 Sassier, p. 263.
101 Sassier, p. 370, 'rex pacificus'.
102 Pacaut, *Louis VII et les Élections Épiscopales*.
103 Pacaut, *Élections*, p. 93.
104 Sassier, p. 354.

105   Pacaut, p. 34.
106   Luchaire, pp. 62–3.
107   Pacaut, *Élections*, pp. 59–63.
108   Pacaut, *Élections*, p. 71.
109   Fawtier, p. 73.
110   Gerald of Wales, viii, p. 160.
111   Sassier, p. 115.
112   Luchaire, p. 60.
113   Odo of Deuil, p. 6.
114   Sassier, p. 145.
115   Sassier, p. 148.
116   Phillips and Hoch, p. 29.
117   Odo of Deuil, p. 64.
118   Odo of Deuil, pp. 58–60.
119   Odo of Deuil, p. 42.
120   Odo of Deuil, p. 54.
121   Odo of Deuil, p. 114.
122   Odo of Deuil, p. 116.
123   Odo of Deuil, p. 134.
124   Sassier, p. 191.
125   Phillips and Hoch, p. 11.
126   Aryeh Grabois, 'The Crusade of King
      Louis VII: a Reconsideration', in
      Edbury, pp. 94–104, p. 94.
127   Robert of Torigny, iv, p. 164.
128   Gervase of Canterbury, I, p. 149.
129   William of Tyre, ii, p. 186.
130   Sassier, p. 231.
131   Luchaire, p. 28, Cartellieri, I, p. 28.
132   Walter Map, p. 475.
133   Fawtier, p. 140 and n.1.
134   Pacaut, p. 192.
135   Gobry, *Louis VII*, p. 219.
136   Gobry, p. 229.
137   Gerald of Wales, viii, p. 165.
138   Ralph of Diceto, I, p. 432.
139   *RHF*, xvi, pp. 69–70
140   Robert of Torigny, p. 127.
141   Luchaire, p. 81; Sassier, p. 427.
142   Suger, Molinier, p. 150.
143   Walter Map, pp. 447–59.
144   Bournazel, pp. 65–6.
145   Bournazel, p. 163; Sassier,
      pp. 415–6.
146   Sassier, p. 425.
147   Sassier, p. 407.
148   Sassier, pp. 406–9.
149   Sassier, p. 409.
150   Hallam, p. 120; Cartellieri, I, p. 2;
      Petit-Dutaillis, p. 180; Tout, p. 285.
151   Owen, p. 41.
152   Duby, p. 189.
153   *Gesta Regis Henri Secundi*, I, pp. 240–3.
154   Sassier, p. 473.

Notes to Chapter 7: Philip the Great

1   Gerald of Wales, viii, pp. 292–93.
2   Hallam, p. 127.
3   William the Breton, Guizot, p. 5.
4   William the Breton, Guizot, p. 81.
5   *Chronique du chanoine de Tours*, p. 304.
6   Bradbury, in *King John*, p. 355.
7   J. Le Goff in Bautier, p. 152.
8   Giselbert of Mons, p. 154.
9   Alice G. Hornaday, 'A Capetian Queen
    as Street Demonstrator: Isabelle of
    Hainaut', in Nolan, pp. 77–97, p. 83.
10 William the Breton, p. 71, l. 169.
11 Giselbert of Mons, p. 131.
12 Rigord, ed. Guizot, p. 47.
13 *Itinerarium*, p. 223.
14 *Estoire*, II, pp. 179–81.
15 *Itinerarium*, p. 395.
16 Godfrey, p. 145.
17 Nicholas, p. 75.
18 Roger of Howden, RS, iv, p. 56.
19 Roger of Howden, IV, p. 148.
20 Wendover, I, 314.
21 William the Breton, pp. 171–74.
22 M. Mollat du Jourdin, 'Philippe
    Auguste et la mer', in Bautier,
    pp. 605–23, p. 618.
23 Wendover, II, p. 69.
24 Giselbert of Mons, p. 185.
25 Roger of Howden, II, p. 511.
26 Luchaire in Lavisse, p. 148.
27 Philip Mouskes, p. 318, l. 20724.
28 From M. Maccarrone, 'La papauté
    et Philippe Auguste', pp. 385–409, in
    Bautier, p. 385.
29 Roger of Wendover, II, p. 72.
30 *Recueil*, I, no.109, p. 137, 1184: 'in
    negociis dextra manus'.
31 Baldwin, *Masters*, p. 171.

32 Warren, *King John*, pp. 159–60.

33 William the Breton, Guizot, p. 21.

34 William the Breton, *Vie*, ed. Delaborde, p. 256.

35 *RHF*, XXIV, pp. 750–75.

36 Duby, p. 227.

37 *Registres*, p. 1.

38 Bautier, p. 23.

39 Mouskes, II, p. 359.

40 Duby, p. 226.

41 P. Ourliac, 'Législation, coutumes et coutumiers au temps de Philippe Auguste', pp. 471–88 in Bautier, p. 476.

42 Carolus-Barré in Bautier, pp. 685, 682.

43 William the Breton, pp. 287–88.

44 Luchaire in Lavisse, p. 172.

45 William the Breton, p. 315.

46 William the Breton, Delaborde, II, p. 316, ll. 836–37.

47 Duby, *Bouvines*, p. 211.

48 Luchaire in Lavisse, p. 255.

49 William the Breton, Delaborde, I, p. 359, l. 304.

50 Luchaire in Lavisse, p. 256.

51 William the Breton, p. 155; B.W.Holden opposes this story in *Haskins* 14, 1995.

52 Roger of Wendover, IV, p. 22.

Notes to Chapter 8: King and Saint, Louis IX, 1226–70

1 Joinville, pp. 27, 37–8.

2 Le Goff, p. 14.

3 Le Goff, p. 763.

4 Le Goff, p. 92.

5 Le Goff, p. 128.

6 Joinville, Hague, p. 23; Le Goff, p. 480.

7 Le Goff, p. 16.

8 Joinville, Hague, p. 158.

9 Joinville, Hague, pp. 179–80.

10 Le Goff, p. 135. Tobias m. the daughter of Raguel, who had been married seven times before, and all her partners had died on the wedding night before consummating the marriage. They had been killed by demons but Tobias found the solution with the aid of the Archangel Raphael. As a result, the Church then recommended three nights of abstention – though one doubts that everyone followed it.

11 Jordan, p. 15; Le Goff p. 174.

12 *Siècle*, p. 38.

13 Duby, *France*, p. 253.

14 Le Goff, p. 378.

15 Fawtier, p. 225.

16 Hallam, p. 337.

17 Le Goff, p. 272.

18 Richard, p. 177.

19 Le Goff, p. 176.

20 Le Goff, p. 159.

21 Joinville, Hague, p. 51.

22 Joinville, Hague, p. 83.

23 Joinville, Hague, p. 54.

24 Siècle, p. 231.

25 Joinville, Hague, p. 123.

26 Joinville, Hague, p. 85.

27 Joinville, Hague, p. 75.

28 Joinville, Hague, p. 84.

29 Joinville, Hague, pp. 250, 83, 86, 88.

30 Joinville, Hague, pp. 100, 97.

31 Joinville, Hague, p. 109.

32 Le Goff, p. 201.

33 Joinville, Hague, p. 253.

34 Jordan, p.xiii.

35 Le Goff, p. 873.

36 Joinville, Hague, p. 196.

37 Joinville, Hague, p. 213.

38 Jordan, p. 45.

39 Jordan, p. 153.

40 Le Goff, pp. 326, 890.

41 Jordan, pp. 160, 158.

42 Le Goff, p. 234.

43 Tan, p. 178.

44 Joinville, Hague, p. 203; Duby, *France*, p. 255.

45 Richard, pp. 212, 214.

46 Jordan, p. 23.

47 Joinville, Hague, p. 28.

48 Siècle, p. 144.

49 Richard, p. 332.

50 Joinville, Hague, pp. 39, 40, 200.

51 Richard, p. ix.

52 Jordan, p. 217.

53   Joinville, Hague, pp. 176, 151, 153.
54   Jordan, p. 104.
55   Le Goff, p. 826.
56   Le Goff, p. 597.
57   Joinville, Hague, pp. 194–95.
58   Le Goff, p. 449.
59   Le Goff, pp. 741, 41; Richard, p. 171.
60   Le Goff, p. 756.
61   Joinville, Hague, p. 36.
62   Jordan, p. 86.
63   Le Goff, pp. 788, 790.
64   Le Goff, p. 706.
65   Le Goff, p. 710.
66   Joinville, Hague, p. 179.
67   Richard, p. 251.
68   Joinville, Hague, p. 186.
69   Le Goff, p. 692.
70   Joinville, Hague, p. 38.
71   Le Goff, pp. 626, 635; Joinville, Hague, p. 27.
72   Le Goff, p. 630; Joinville, Hague, p. 29.
73   Richard, p. 217.
74   Le Goff, pp. 823–24.
75   Richard, p. 234.
76   Richard, p. 321.
77   Joinville, Hague, pp. 212–13.

Notes to Chapter 9: The Bold and the Fair, 1270–1314

1   Bloch, pp. 124, 16; Fawtier, p. 34.
2   Wood, p. 31.
3   Wood, p. 41.
4   *Grandes Chroniques*, p. 41.
5   *Grandes Chroniques*, p. 49.
6   Bloch, p. 29.
7   Fawtier, p. 35.
8   Favier, p. 144. There were two main current valuations of the *livre*, that of Paris and that of Tours. Approximately 4 *livres parisis* equalled 5 *livres tournois*.
9   Brown, *Monarchy*, II, p. 282.
10   Strayer, p. 4.
11   Brown, *Politics*, IV, p. 184.
12   Funck-Brentano, p. 420; Fawtier, p. 35; Douglas, p. 92.
13   Favier, p. 523.
14   Brown, *Monarchy*, IV, p. 8.
15   Brown, *Monarchy*, III, p. 175–77.
16   Strayer, pp. ix, xii, xvi, 83.
17   Favier, pp. i, ii, 1.
18   Strayer, p. 3; Brown, *Monarchy*, V, p. 228 & n. 41.
19   Brown, *Monarchy*, V, p. 221, from Peter Jacob.
20   Brown, *Monarchy*, II, p. 285.
21   Strayer, pp. 16, 20.
22   Brown, *Monarchy*, V, pp. 221, 229, *vilissimi ribaldi*, 232.
23   Duby, p. 261.
24   Hallam & Everard, p. 351.
25   Wood, p. 150.
26   Wood, p. 111.
27   Wood, p. 48.
28   Favier, p. 104.
29   Douglas, p. 83.
30   Favier, p. 13.
31   Strayer, p. 71.
32   Favier, p. 39, from Geoffrey de Paris.
33   Strayer, p. 22.
34   Brown, *Monarchy*, II, p. 290.
35   Favier, p. 46.
36   Strayer, p. 29.
37   Strayer, p. 71.
38   Favier, p. 44–5.
39   Strayer, pp. 34, 35.
40   Favier, p. 46.
41   Favier, p. 71.
42   Favier, p. 66.
43   Strayer, p. 70.
44   Langlois, p. 252.
45   Strayer, p. 137.
46   Favier, pp. 86–9.
47   Strayer, p. 91.
48   Langlois, p. 348; Favier, p. 97.
49   Langlois, p. 351.
50   Favier, p. 94.
51   Strayer, p. 420.
52   Favier, p. 198.
53   Favier, p. 142.
54   Favier, p. 150.
55   Langlois, p. 234.
56   Favier, p. 520.
57   Favier, p. 203.

58 Brown, *Politics*, II, pp. 569, 585.
59 Favier, p. 179.
60 Brown, *Politics*, IV, p. 153.
61 Barber, p. 35.
62 Favier, pp. 402–7.
63 Strayer, p. 318.
64 Favier, p. 211.
65 Strayer, p. 319.
66 Verbruggen, p. 111.
67 Strayer, p. 335.
68 Favier, p. 248.
69 Favier, p. 481.
70 Favier, p. 481.
71 Bloch, p. 32.
72 Favier, p. 314.
73 Favier, p. 335.
74 Langlois, p. 209–10.
75 Strayer, p. 19.
76 Brown, *Monarchy*, II, p. 287
77 Gaposchkin, p. 1.
78 Favier, p. 6.
79 Favier, p. 258.
80 Favier, pp. 274–75.
81 Langlois, p. 133.
82 Favier, p. 281.
83 Favier, p. 344.
84 Favier, p. 356.
85 Fawtier, p. 94.
86 Favier, p. 358.
87 Langlois, p. 153; Favier, p. 360 views it in similar terms.
88 Gaposchkin, p. 19.
89 Strayer, p. 272.
90 Langlois, p. 157–59.
91 Favier, p. 385.
92 Strayer, p. 284 and n. 146, quoting Finke, *Bonifaz VIII*, p. 289.
93 Langlois, p. 240.
94 Barber, p. 10.
95 Langlois, p. 176.
96 Langlois, p. 177.
97 Strayer, p. 172; Langlois, p. 178.
98 Funck-Brentano, p. 409.
99 Barber, pp. 69, 187.
100 Barber, p. 140.
101 Barber, pp. 89, 56-71.
102 Duby, p. 265.
103 Langlois, pp. 184, 191.
104 Langlois, p. 193.
105 Favier, p. 469.
106 Langlois, p. 199.
107 Barber, p. 135.
108 Barber, p. 116.
109 Langlois, p. 189–90.
110 Barber, p. 226.
111 Barber, p. 232.
112 Funck-Brentano, p. 415; Barber, p. 242.
113 Barber, p. 230.
114 Brown, *Monarchy*, IV, pp. 8–17, 28.

Notes to Chapter 10: The end of the line, 1314–28

1 Funck-Brentano, p. 419.
2 Brown, *Politics*, VI, p. 284.
3 Brown, *Politics*, II, p. 580.
4 Nicholas, p. 206.
5 Brown, *Monarchy*, VII, p. 228.
6 Brown, *Politics*, VIII, p. 430.
7 Brown, *Politics*, VIII, p. 399.
8 Brown, *Politics*, VIII, p. 421.
9 Brown, *Politics*, VIII, p. 399.
10 Fryde, pp. 200–6.

Notes to Chapter 11: The achievements and legacy of the Capetian Dynasty

1 Calmette, p. 36.
2 Fawtier, p. 229.
3 Hallam, p. 384.
4 Fawtier, p. 186.
5 Le Goff, p. 355.1
6 Le Goff, p. 293.
7 Evans, p. 130.
8 Evans, p. 128.
9 Heer, p. 254.
10 Heer, p. 240.
11 Heer, p. 105.
12 Abelard & Heloise, p. 23.
13 Abelard & Heloise, p. 25.
14 Clanchy, p. 59.
15 Clanchy, p. 1.
16 Abelard & Heloise, p. 23.
17 Clanchy, p. 29.

18 Evans, p. 106.
19 Clanchy, p. 35.
20 Slocum, p. 302.
21 Slocum, p. 403.
22 Baldwin, *Aristocratic Life*.
23 Baldwin, p. 22.
24 Clanchy, p. 127.
25 Slocum, p. 306.
26 Heer, p. 173.
27 Slocum, p. 307.
28 Slocum, p. 308.
29 Evans, p. 110.
30 Slocum, p. 233.
31 Slocum, p. 245.
32 Heer, p. 397.
33 Crosby, p. 28.
34 Crosby, p. 31.
35 Crosby, p. 60.
36 Crosby, p. 34.
37 Crosby, p. 71.
38 Crosby, p. 36.
39 Dunlop, p. 87.
40 Dunlop, p. 48.
41 Dunlop, p. 55.
42 Dunlop, p. 112.
43 Heer, p. 398.
44 Heer, p. 396.
45 Heer, p. 399.
46 Le Goff, p. 351.
47 Slocum, p. 256.
48 Slocum, p. 397.
49 Slocum, p. 293.
50 Slocum, p. 254–58.
51 Slocum, pp. 422–3.
52 Fawtier, p. 230.
53 Le Goff, p. 74.
54 Le Goff, p. 292.
55 Le Goff, p. 301.
56 Le Goff, p. 172.
57 Le Goff, p. 234.
58 Heer, p. 79.
59 Fawtier, p. 189.
60 Le Goff, p. 272.
61 Bloch, p. 41.
62 Le Goff, p. 316.
63 Le Goff, p. 67.

Bibliography

PRIMARY SOURCES

Abbo, *Le Siège de Paris par les Normands*, trans. and ed. H. Waquet, Paris, 1942

Abelard and Heloise, The Story of His Misfortunes and the Personal Letters, trans. and introduction Betty Radice, London, 1977

Adémar de Chabannes, *Chronique*, ed. Jules Chavanon, Paris, 1897

Akehurst, F.R.P., trans. & intro., *The Coutumes de Beauvaisis of Philippe de Beaumanoir*, Philadelphia, 1992

Akehurst, F.R.P., trans. & intro., *The Etablissements de Saint Louis*, Philadelphia, 1996

Anglo-Saxon Chronicle, The, ed. Dorothy Whitelock, D.C. Douglas & S. I. Tucker, London, 1961

Annales regni Francorum, MGH SRG, vol. vi.

Annals of Fulda, The, ed. T. Reuter, Manchester, 1992

Annals of St-Bertin, The, ed. J.L. Nelson, Manchester, 1991

Carolingian Chronicles, trans. and ed. B.W. Scholz and B. Rogers

Charlemagne, Translated Sources, ed. P.D. King, Kendal, 1987

Chronique de St-Maixent, La, 751–1140, ed. J. Vernon, Paris, 1979

Delisle, L.V., *Catalogue des Actes de Philippe Auguste*, Paris, 1856

Dudo of St-Quentin, *History of the Normans*, trans. E. Christiansen, Woodbridge, 1998

Dutton, Paul Edward, ed., *Carolingian Civilization*, Ontario, 2004

Einhard, *The Life of Charlemagne*, trans. and ed. L. Thorpe, London, 1970

Fouracre, Paul & Richard A. Gerberding, eds., *Late Merovingian France*, Manchester, 1996

Fulbert of Chartres, *The Letters of Poems of*, ed. & trans. Frederick Behrends, Oxford, 1976

Fulcher of Chartres, *Chronicle of the First Crusade*, ed. Martha Evelyn McGinty, London, 1941

Gerald of Wales, *Opera*, ed. J.S. Brewer, J.F. Dimock and G.F. Warner, 8 vols., RS no. 21, London, 1861–91

Gervase of Canterbury, *Opera Historica*, ed. W.Stubbs, 2 vols., RS no. 73, London, 1879–80

Gesta Normannorum Ducum of William of Jumièges, Orderic Vitalis, &

Gesta Regis Henri Secundi (Benedict of Peterborough), ed. W. Stubbs, RS no. 49, 2 vols., London, 1867

Giselbert of Mons, *La Chronique*, ed. L. Vanderkindered, Brussels, 1904

Glaber, Rodulfus, *The Five Books of the Histories*, ed. and trans. J. France, Oxford, 1989

Grandes Chroniques de St-Denis, ed. J. Viard, 9 vols., Paris, 1920–37

Gregory of Tours, *The History of the Franks*, ed. L. Thorpe, Harmondsworth, 1974

Guibert of Nogent in *Self and Society in Medieval France: The Memoirs of Abbot Guibert of Nogent*, ed. and trans. John F. Benton, Toronto, 1984

Guizot, François, *Chroniques des premiers capétiens, 987–1108*, ed. and trans. F. Guizot & R. Fougères, Paléo, Clermont-Ferrand, 2003

Hariulf, *Chronique de l'Abbaye de St-Riquier*, ed. F. Lot, Paris, 1894

Life of King Edward who rests at Westminster, 1992

Joinville, Jean de, *Joinville and Villehardouin, Chronicles of the Crusades*, trans. M.R.B. Shaw, Harmondsworth, 1963

Joinville, Jean de, *The Life of St Louis*, trans. René Hague, ed. Natalis de Wailly, London, 1955

King, P.D., ed., *Charlemagne, translated sources*, Kendal, 1987

Luchaire, Achille, *Louis VI le Gros, Annales de Sa Vie et de Son Règne (1081–1137)*, reprint, Paris, 1964

Mouskes, Philip, *Chronique rime*, ed. Baron de Reiffenberg, 2 vols., Brussels, 1836–38

Odo of Deuil, *De profectione ludovici vii in orientem*, ed. and trans. Virginia Gingerick Berry, New York, 1948

Oevres de Rigord et de Guillaume le Breton, ed. H-F. Delaborde, SHF, vols. 210, 224, Paris, 1882–85

Orderic Vitalis, *The Ecclesiastical History*, 6 vols., ed. and trans. M.Chibnall, Oxford, 1968–80

Ralph of Diceto, *Opera Historica*, ed. W. Stubbs, RS no. 68, 2 vols, London, 1876

Receuil des Actes de Philippe Auguste, ed. H-F. Delaborde & others, 4 vols., Paris, 1916–79

Registres de Philippe Auguste, Les, ed. J.W. Baldwin and others, RHF, Documents financiers et administratifs, VII, Texte, Paris, 1992

Richer, *Histoire de France*, ed. & trans. R. Latouche, 2 vols., Paris, 1930, 1937

Richer, *Historia*, ed. H. Hoffman, Hanover, 2000

Robert of Torigni, 2 vols., ed. & trans. Elisabeth M.C. Van Houts, Oxford, 1992,1995

Robert of Torigny, *Chronicle*, in R. Howlett, ed., *Chronicles of the Reigns of Stephen, Henry II and Richard I*, RS no. 82, 4 vols., London, 1884–9

Roger of Howden, *Chronica*, ed. W. Stubbs, RS no. 51, 4 vols., London, 1868–71

Roger of Wendover, *Flores Historiarum*, ed. H.G. Hewlett, RS no.84, 3 vols., London, 1886–89

St-Bertin: *Life of King Edward who rests at Westminster, attributed to a monk of St-Bertin*, ed. and trans. F. Barlow, 2nd edn., Oxford, 1992

Suger, *The Deeds of Louis the Fat*, ed. Richard Cusimano and John Moorhead, Washington, 1992

Suger, *Vie de Louis VI le Gros*, ed. Henri Waquet, Paris, 1964

Thietmar of Mersenberg, *Chronicon, Ottonian Germany*, ed. and trans. D.A. Warner, Manchester, 2001

Villehardouin, Geoffrey de, *La Conquète de Constantinople*, ed. E. Faral, 2 vols., Paris, 1938–39

Walter Map, *De Nugis Curialum, Courtiers' Trifles*, ed. F. Tupper & M.B. Ogle, London, 1924

William of Poitiers, *Histoire de Guillaume le Conquérant*, ed. and trans. R. Foreville, Paris, 1952

William of Tyre, *A History of Deeds Done Beyond the Sea*, ed., E.A. Babcock and A.C. Krey, 2 vols., New York, 1943

William the Breton, *La Philippide, Poème*, ed. and trans. M. Guizot, Paris, 1825

SECONDARY SOURCES

Angold, Michael, *The Fourth Crusade*, Harlow, 2003

Bachrach, Bernard S., *Armies and Politics in the Early Medieval West*, Variorum, Aldershot, 1993

Bachrach, Bernard S., *Fulk Nerra, the Neo-Roman Consul, 987–1040, a political biography of the Angevin count*, London, 1983

Bachrach, Bernard S., *State-Building in Medieval France*, Variorum, Aldershot, 1995

Baldwin, John W., *Aristocratic Life in Medieval France*, Baltimore, 2000

Baldwin, John W., *Masters, Princes and Merchants*, 2 vols., Princeton, 1970

Baldwin, John W., *The Government of Philip Augustus*, Berkeley, 1986

Baratier, Édouard, ed., *Histoire de la Provence*, general ed., É. Privat, Toulouse, 1969

Barber, Malcolm, *The Trial of the Templars*, Cambridge, 1978

Barber, Malcolm, *The Two Cities, Medieval Europe 1050–1320*, 2nd edn., London, 2004

Barlow, Frank, *Edward the Confessor*, London, 1970

Barlow, Frank, *Thomas Becket*, London, 1986

Barlow, Frank, *William Rufus*, London, 1983

Barraclough, Geoffrey, *The Crucible of Europe, the Ninth and Tenth Centuries in European History*, London, 1976

Barton, R.E., 'Lordship in Maine: Transformation, Service and Anger', *ANS*, xvii, 1994, pp. 41–63

Bautier, Robert-Henri, ed., *La France de Philippe Auguste, le Temps des Mutations*, Actes du Colloque International organise par le CNRS, 1980, Paris, 1982

Bautier, Robert-Henri, *Recherches sur h'histoire de la France médiévale*, Variorum, Aldershot, 1991

Benton, J.F., 'The Revenue of Louis VII', in ed. Thomas N. Bisson, *Culture, Power and Personality in Medieval France*, London, 1991, pp. 183–90

Bloch, Marc, *La France sous les Derniers Capétiens, 1223–1328*, Paris, 1958

Bolton, B., 'Philip Augustus and John: two sons in Innocent III's vineyard', *The Church and Sovereignty c.590–1918, Essays in Honour of Michael Wiles*, ed., D. Wood, Oxford, 1991, pp. 113–34

Bordonove, Georges, *Les Rois qui ont fait la France, Hugues Capet, le* Bordonove, Georges, *Philippe Auguste, le Conquérant*, Paris, 1986

Fondateur, Paris, 1986 (includes two books of Richer)

Bottineau, Yves, *Notre-Dame de Paris & the Sainte-Chapelle*, trans. L.F. Edwards, London, 1967

Bournazel, G., *Le Gouvernement capétien au XIIe siècle, 1108–1180*, Limoges, 1975

Bradbury, Jim, 'Fulk le Réchin and the Origin of the Plantagenets', *Studies in Medieval History Presented to R. Allen Brown*, ed. C. Harper-Bill, C. Holdsworth & J.L. Nelson, Woodbridge, 1989, pp. 27–41

Bradbury, Jim, *Philip Augustus, King of France 1180–1223*, Harlow, 1998

Brooke, Christopher, *Europe in the Central Middle Ages, 962–1154*, London, 1964

Brown, Elizabeth A.R., *Politics and Institutions in Capetian France*, Aldershot, 1991

Brown, Elizabeth A.R., *The Monarchy of Capetian France and Royal Ceremonial*, Aldershot, 1991

Bull, Marcus, *France in the Central Middle Ages, 900–1200*, Oxford, 2002

Bur, Michel, *Suger, Abbé de Saint-Denis, Régent de France*, Paris, 1991

Cartellieri, A., *Phillip II, August, König von Frankreich*, 4 vols., Leipzig, 1899–1922

Castries, Duc de, *The Lives of the Kings and Queens of France*, trans. A. Dobell, London, 1979

Clanchy, M.T., *Abelard, A Medieval Life*, Oxford, 1997

Collins, Roger, *Charlemagne*, London, 1998

Collins, Roger, *Early Medieval Europe 300–1000*, 2nd edn., London, 1999

Coulson, C., 'Fortress-policy in Capetian tradition and Angevin practice: aspects of the Conquest of Normandy by Philip II', *ANS*, VI, 1983, pp. 13–38

Crosby, Sumner M., *L'Abbaye Royale de Saint-Denis*, Paris, 1953

Crouch, David, *The Normans, the History of a Dynasty*, London, 2002

Davidsohn, R., *Philipp II. August von Frankreich und Ingeborg*, Stuttgart, 1888

Delperrié de Bayac, Jacques, *Louis VI, la Naissance de la France*, Paris, 1983

Dhondt, J., *Études sur la Naissance des Principautés Territoriales en France (9e–10e siècles)*, Bruges, 1948

Dhondt, J., 'Henry Ie, l'Empire et Anjou (1043–56), pp. 87–109, *Revue Belge de Philologie et d'Histoire*, xxv, 1946–47

Douglas, David C., `Medieval Paris', in *Time and the Hour*, London, 1977, pp. 77–93, first published 1952

Douglas, D.C., *William the Conqueror*, London, 1964

Duby, Georges, *France in the Middle Ages, 987–1460*, trans. Juliet Vale, Oxford, 1991

Duby, Georges, *The Knight, the Lady and the Priest, the Making of Modern Marriage in Medieval France*, trans. B. Bray, London, 1984

Duby, Georges, *The Legend of Bouvines*, trans. C. Tihanyi, Cambridge, 1990

Duby, Georges and Robert Mandrou, *A History of French Civilization*, trans. J.B. Atkinson, London, 1965

Duggan, Anne J., ed., *Nobles and Nobility in Medieval Europe*, Woodbridge, 2000

Dunbabin, Jean, 'What's in a Name? Philip, King of France', *Speculum*, lviii, 1993, pp. 949–68

Dunlop, Ian, *The Cathedrals' Crusade, the Rise of Gothic Style in France*, London, 1982

Edbury, Peter, ed., *Crusade and Settlement*, Cardiff, 1985

Evans, Joan, *Life in Medieval France*, London, 1962

Favier, Jean, *Le Temps des Principautés*, Paris, 1984

Favier, Jean, *Philippe le Bel*, Paris, 1978

Fawtier, Robert, *Autour de la France capétienne*, London, 1987

Fawtier, Robert, *The Capetian Kings of France, Monarchy and Nation (987–1328)*, trans. Lionel Butler and R.J. Adam, London, 1960

Finó, J-F., 'Quelques aspects de l'art militaire sous Philippe Auguste', *Gladius*, VI, 1967, pp. 19–36

Fleury, Michel & Venceslas Kruta, *Le Château du Louvre*, Dijon, 2000

Fliche, Augustin, *Le Règne de Philippe Ier, Roi de France (1060–1108)*, Paris, 1912

Fliche, Augustin, *L'Europe Occidentale de 888 à 1125*, Paris, 1941

Fouracre, Paul, *The Age of Charles Martel*, Harlow, 2000

Fryde, Natalie, *The Tyranny and Fall of Edward II, 1311–1326*, Cambridge, 1979

Funck-Brentano, Fr., *The National History of France, the Middle Ages*, trans. E. O'Neill, London, 1922

Ganshof, François Louis, *The Carolingians and the Frankish Monarchy*, Studies in Carolingian History, trans. J. Sondheimer, London, 1971

Ganshof, François Louis, *Frankish Institutions under Charlemagne*, trans. B. & M. Lyon, New York, 1968

Gaposchkin, M.C., `Boniface VIII, Philip the Fair, and the sanctity of Louis IX', *JMH*, xxix, 2003, pp. 1–26

Gasparri, Françoise, 'La politique de l'abbé Suger de St-Denis à travers ses chartes', *Cahiers des Civilisation Médiévale*, xlvi, 2003, pp. 233–45

Gillingham, John, *Richard I*, London, 1999

Gillingham, John, *Richard Coeur de Lion, Kingship, Chivalry and War in the Twelfth Century*, London, 1994

Gillingham, John, *Richard the Lionheart*, 2nd edn., London, 1989

Gillingham, John, *The Angevin Empire*, London, 1984

Gobry, Ivan, *Louis VI, Père de Louis VII*, Paris, 2003

Gobry, Ivan, Louis VII, Père de Philippe II Auguste, Paris, 2002

Godfrey, J., *1204, The Unholy Crusade*, Oxford, 1980

Godman, P. & R. Collins, *Charlemagne's Heir, New Perspectives on the Reign of Louis the Pious, 814–40*, Oxford, 1990

Grant, Lindy, *Abbot Suger of St-Denis, Church and State in Early Twelfth-Century France*, Harlow, 1998

Guillot, Olivier, *Le Comte d'Anjou et son Entourage au XIe Siècle*, 2 vols., Paris, 1972

Haines, Roy Martin, *King Edward II, Edward of Caernarfon, His Life, His Reign, and its Aftermath, 1284–1330*, London, 2003

Hallam, Elizabeth M. & Judith Everard, *Capetian France, 987–1328*, 2nd edn., Harlow, 2001

Hardengue, Antoine, *Philippe Auguste et Bouvines: Bouvines, victorie créatrice*, Paris, 1935

Heer, Friedrich, *The Medieval World, Europe from 1100 to 1350*, trans. Janet Sondheimer, London, 1962

Hollister, C. Warren, *Henry I*, London, 2001

Hutton, W.H., *Philip Augustus*, London, 1896

Iogna-Prat, Dominique & Jean-Charles Picard, eds., *Religion et culture autour de l'An Mil*, Paris, 1990

James, Edward, *The Origins of France, from Clovis to the Capetians, 500–1000*, London, 1982

Jessee, W. Scott, 'Urban Violence and the *Coup d'État* of Fulk le Réchin in Angers, 1067', *Haskins Society Journal*, vii, 1995, pp. 75–82

Jones, Colin, *The Cambridge Illustrated History of France*, Cambridge, 1994

Jones, Michael, *The Creation of Brittany*, London, 1988

Jordan, William Chester, *Louis IX and the Challenge of the Crusade*, Princeton, 1979

Kerrebrouck, Patrick Van, *Les Capétiens, 987–1328, Nouvelle Histoire Génealogique de l'Ausguste Maison de France*, vol ii, Villeneuve d'Asq, 2000

Kibler, William W. & Grover A.Zinn, *Medieval France, an Encyclopedia*, London, 1995

Knecht, Robert J., *The Valois, Kings of France 1328–1589*, London, 2004

Labarge, Margaret Wade, *Saint Louis, The Life of Louis IX of France*, London, 1968

Langlois, Ch.-V., *Les Derniers Capétiens direct, 1226–1328*, Paris, 1911, vol. iii pt.2 of *Histoire de France*, ed. E. Lavisse.

Lasko, Peter, *The Kingdom of the Franks*, London, 1971

Le Goff, Jacques, *Medieval Civilization, 400–1500*, trans. Julia Barrow, Oxford, 1988

Le Goff, Jacques, *St Louis*, S-Amand (Cher), 1996

Lewis, Andrew W., *Royal Succession in Capetian France, Studies on Familial Order and the State*, London, 1981

Leyser, Karl, *Communication and Power in Medieval Europe, the Carolingian and Ottonian Centuries*, ed. T. Reuter, London, 1994

Luchaire, Achille, *Les Premiers Capétiens (987–1137)* from *Histoire de France*, ed. E. Lavisse, vol. ii, Paris, 1911

Luchaire, Achille, *Social France at the Time of Philip Augustus*, trans. E.B. Krehbiel, New York, 1912

McKitterick, Rosamond, *The Frankish Kingdoms under the Carolingians, 751–987*, Harlow, 1983

MacLean, Simon, *Kingship and Politics in the Late Ninth Century, Charles the Fat and the End of the Carolingian Empire*, Cambridge, 2003

Masson, Gustave, *Mediaeval France, from the Reign of Hugues Capet to the Beginning of the Sixteenth Century*, 5th edn., London

Mélanges d'Histoire du Moyen Age dédiés à la Mémoire de Louis Halphen, Preface Charles-Edmond Perrin, Paris, 1951

Mollat, Michel, ed., *Histoire de l'Île-de-France et de Paris*, Toulouse, 1971

Nelson, Janet L., *Charles the Bald*, Harlow, 1992

Nelson, Janet L., *The Frankish World, 750–900*, London, 1996

Nelson, Janet L., 'England & the Continent in the 9th century: IV, Bodies and Minds', *TRHS*, 6th series, xv, 2005

Nolan, Kathleen, ed., *Capetian Women*, Basingstoke, 2003

Norgate, Kate, *Richard the Lionheart*, London, 1924

Owen, D.D.R., *Eleanor of Aquitaine, Queen and Legend*, Oxford, 1993

Pacaut, Marcel, *Louis VII et les Élections Épiscopales dans le Royaume de France*, Paris, 1957

Pacaut, Marcel, *Louis VII et son Royaume*, Paris, 1964

Panofsky, Erwin, ed., *Abbot Suger on the Abbey Church of St-Denis and its Art Treasures*, Princeton, 1946

Pernoud, Régine, *Le Siècle de St Louis*, Paris, 1970

Phillips, Jonathan, *The Fourth Crusade and the Sack of Constantinople*, London, 2004

Phillips, Jonathan and Martin Hoch, eds., *The Second Crusade, Scope and Consequences*, Manchester, 2001

Pognon, Edmond, *Hugues Capet, Roi de France*, Paris, 1966

Reuter, Timothy, ed., *The New Cambridge Medieval History, vol. iii*, Cambridge, 1999

Richard, Jean, *St Louis, Crusader King of France*, ed. S. Lloyd, trans. J. Birrell, Cambridge, 1992

Riché, Pierre, *The Carolingians, a Family who Forged Europe*, trans. M.I. Allen, Penn, 1993

Saaler, Mary, *Edward II, 1307–1327*, London, 1997

Sayers, Jane, *Innocent III, Leader of Europe, 1198–1216*, Harlow, 1994

Slocum, Kay, *Medieval Civilisation*, London, 2005

Strayer, Joseph R., *The Reign of Philip the Fair*, Princeton, 1980

Tan, Elaine S., `An empty shell? Rethinking the usury laws in Medieval Europe', *Journal of Legal History*, xxiii, 2002, pp. 177–96

Taylor, Claire, *Heresy in Medieval France, Dualism in Aquitaine and the Agenais, 1000–1249*, Woodbridge, 2005

Thalamas, A., *La Société Seigneuriale Française, 1050–1270*, Paris, 1951

Theis, Laurent, *Robert le Pieux, le roi de l'an mil*, Paris, 1999

Tilley, Arthur, ed., *Medieval France, a Companion to French Studies*, Cambridge, 1922

Verbruggen, J.F., *The Art of Warfare in Western Europe during the Middle Ages*, trans. S. Willard and Mrs. R.W. Southern, 2nd edn., Woodbridge, 1997

Warren, W.L., *King John*, 2nd edn., London, 1978

Wood, Charles T., *The French Apanages and the Capetian Monarchy, 1224–1328*, Cambridge Massachusetts, 1966

Wood, Ian, *The Merovingian Kingdoms, 450–751*, Harlow, 1994

Index